A Visual Cruising Guide to the
MAINE COAST

A Visual Cruising Guide to the
Maine Coast

James L. Bildner

International Marine / McGraw-Hill

Camden, Maine ■ New York ■ Chicago ■ San Francisco ■ Lisbon ■ London

Madrid ■ Mexico City ■ Milan ■ New Delhi ■ San Juan ■ Seoul

Singapore ■ Sydney ■ Toronto

Fox Islands Thorofare, looking west (page 156)

The McGraw-Hill Companies

Published by International Marine

1 2 3 4 5 6 7 8 9 QPD QPD 0 9 8 7 6

Library of Congress Cataloging-in-Publication Data
Bildner, Jim.
A visual cruising guide to the Maine coast / James Bildner.
p. cm.
Includes index.
ISBN 0-07-145328-8 (hardcover : alk. paper)
1. Pilot guides–Maine. I. Title.
VK982.M35B55 2006
623.89'29741–dc22
2006000749

Questions regarding the content of this book should be addressed to:
International Marine
P.O. Box 220
Camden, ME 04843
www.internationalmarine.com

Questions regarding the ordering of this book should be addressed to:
The McGraw-Hill Companies
Customer Service Department
P.O. Box 547
Blacklick, OH 43004
Retail customers: 1-800-262-4729
Bookstores: 1-800-722-4726

Book design by Harrah Lord/Yellow House Design.

NOTICE: The information, charts, and illustrations contained in this book are not for navigational purposes. None of the material in this book is intended to replace any government-issued navigational charts or other government publications (including Notices to Mariners) for up-to-date information regarding changes, additions, and deletions to existing navigational materials. All material in this book is subject to change at any time. The author and publisher do not guarantee nor warrant that the information in this book is complete, correct, or current. The author and publisher shall not be liable to any user of the book for any loss or injury allegedly caused, in whole or in part, by relying on information contained in this book.

amden Harbor with Curtis Island in the foreground (page 134)

To Nancy and Lizzie, who, like the sun rising against the bluest of skies, always keep my eyes and my heart focused on the next horizon. I love you both.

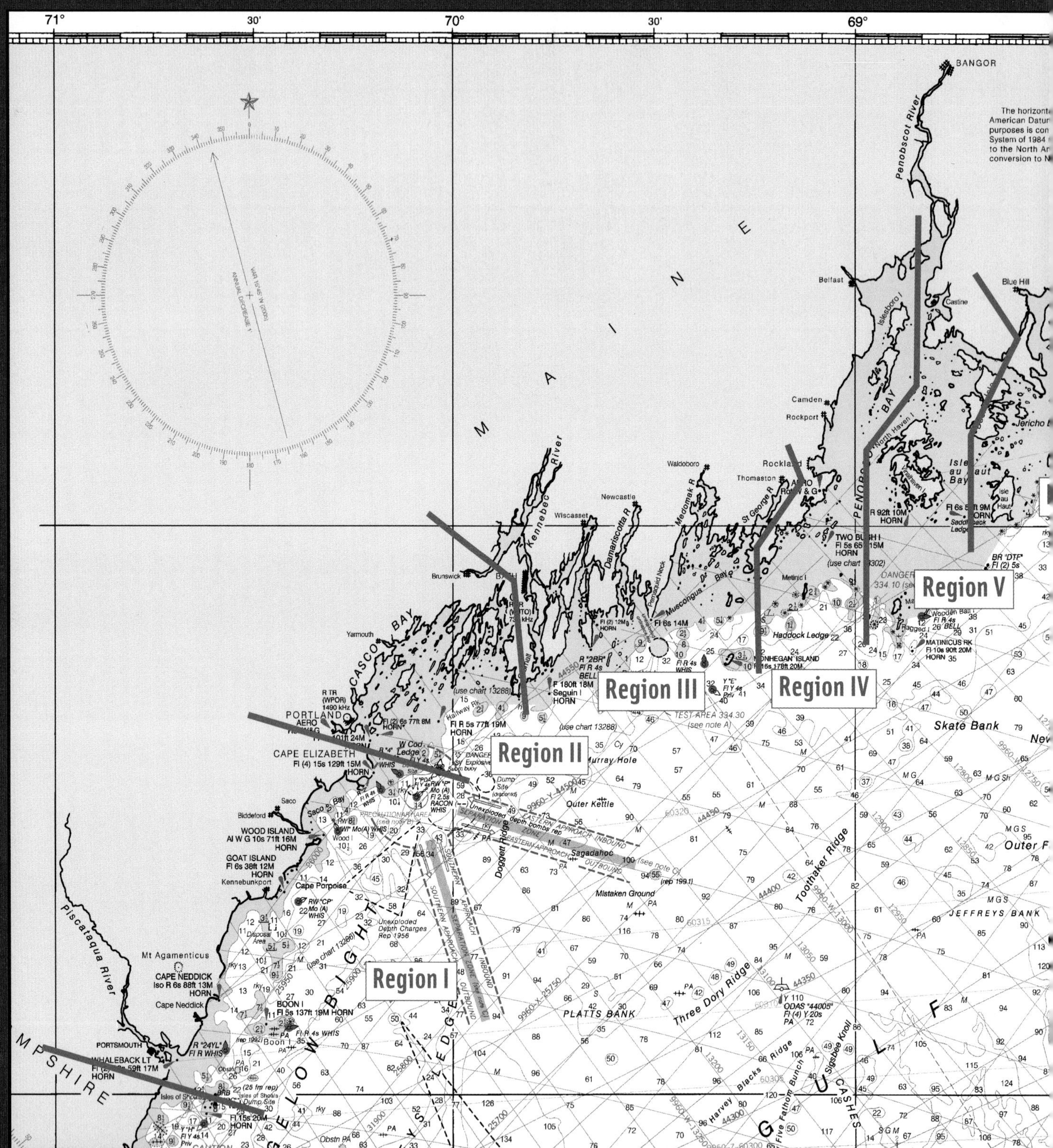

71°
30'
70°
30'
69°
BANGOR
Penobscot River
M
A
I
N
E
Belfast
Castine
Blue Hill
Camden
Rockport
Rockland
Thomaston
Waldoboro
Newcastle
Wiscasset
Kennebec River
Damariscotta R
Medomak R
St George R
Brunswick
Yarmouth
CASCO BAY
PORTLAND
CAPE ELIZABETH
Saco
Biddeford
WOOD ISLAND
GOAT ISLAND
Kennebunkport
Cape Porpoise
Mt Agamenticus
CAPE NEDDICK
Cape Neddick
PORTSMOUTH
WHALEBACK LT
Piscataqua River
MPSHIRE
Isles of Shoals
Muscongus Bay
Pemaquid Neck
Haddock Ledge
MONHEGAN ISLAND
TWO BUSH I
Isle au Haut Bay
Region I
Region II
Region III
Region IV
Region V
Skate Bank
Murray Hole
Outer Kettle
Doggett Ridge
Sagadahoc
Mistaken Ground
Toothaker Ridge
Three Dory Ridge
PLATTS BANK
Jeffreys Bank
Blacks Ridge
Sigsbee Knoll
Five Fathom Bunch
Harvey
CASHES
G U L F
BIGHT
JEFFREYS LEDGE

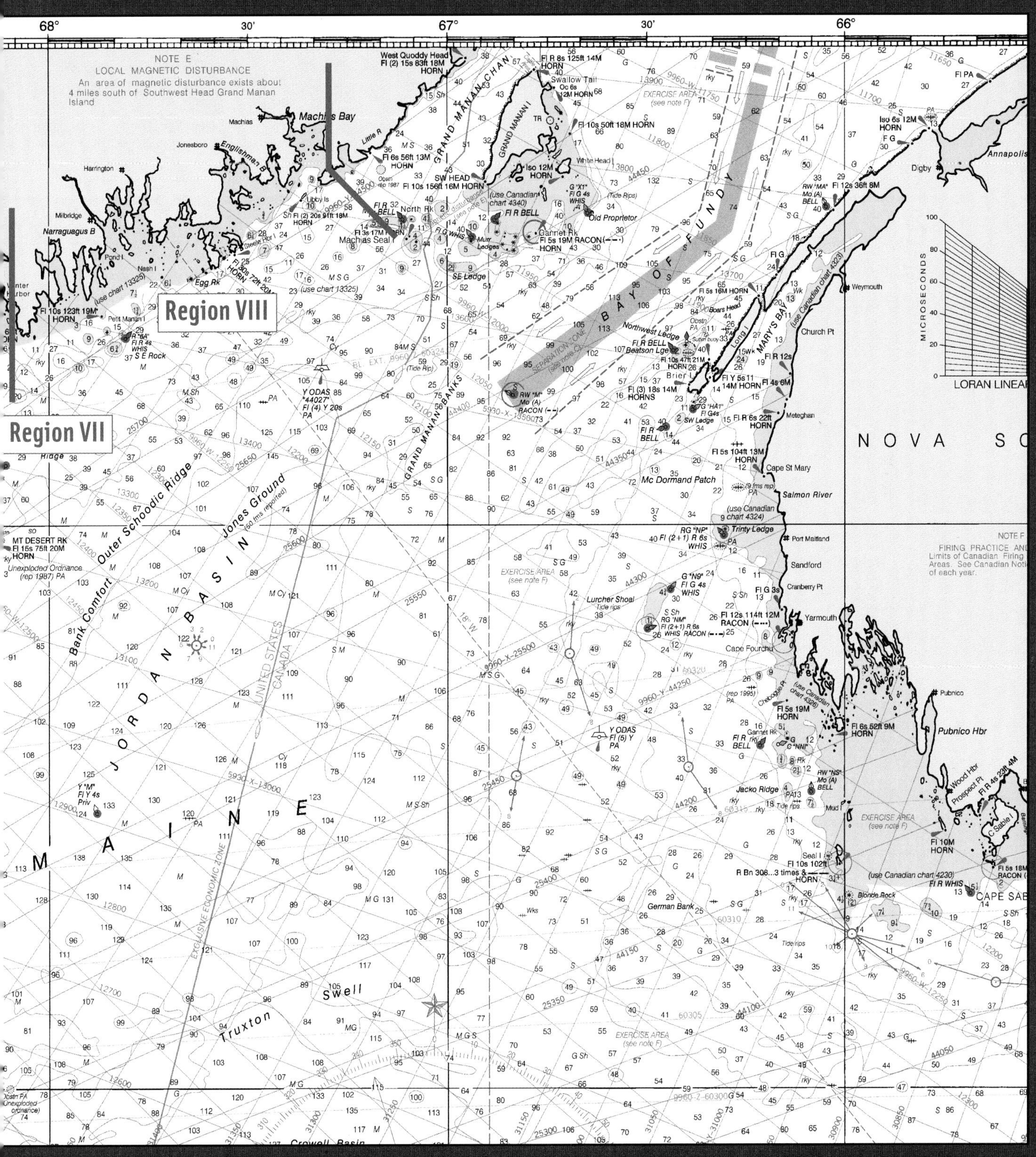

68°
30'
67°
30'
66°
NOTE E
LOCAL MAGNETIC DISTURBANCE
An area of magnetic disturbance exists about 4 miles south of Southwest Head Grand Manan Island
Region VIII
Region VII
West Quoddy Head
Machias Bay
Machias
Jonesboro
Englishman B
Harrington
Milbridge
Narraguagus B
Petit Manan I
Nash I
Egg Rk
Libby Is
Machias Seal I
North Rk
GRAND MANAN CHAN
Grand Manan I
Swallow Tail
SW HEAD
White Head I
Old Proprietor
Gannet Rk
Murr Ledges
SE Ledge
GRAND MANAN BANKS
BAY OF FUNDY
SEPARATION ZONE
EXERCISE AREA
Digby
Annapolis
Weymouth
Church Pt
MARY'S BAY
Long I
Brier I
Boars Head
Northwest Ledge
Meteghan
Cape St Mary
Salmon River
Mc Dormand Patch
Trinity Ledge
Port Maitland
Sandford
Cranberry Pt
Yarmouth
Cape Fourchu
Lurcher Shoal
Pubnico
Pubnico Hbr
Wood Hbr
Prospect Pt
Jacko Ridge
Seal I
Blonde Rock
German Bank
NOVA SC
MT DESERT RK
Outer Schoodic Ridge
Jones Ground
Bank Comfort
JORDAN BASIN
MAINE
Truxton
Swell
EXCLUSIVE ECONOMIC ZONE
UNITED STATES
CANADA
Crowell Basin
MICROSECONDS
LORAN LINEAR

Contents

REGION V

REGION VI

REGION VII

REGION VIII

Introduction

This book has been a labor of love.

But, truth be told, it was a project of necessity. Just ask my wife, Nancy. For over twenty-five years, we have been sailing these waters in every imaginable condition (despite her completely rational pleas to the contrary). On one of those trips, as Nancy looked at me with the "I told you so" look, it occurred to me that maybe there is a better way of doing this. There I was, spread out by the wheel, with the boat lurching side to side and up and down, staring through pea-soup fog, with charts on one side, books on the other, and the VHF and fog horn breaking the sound of howling wind. And every few minutes, I was making a 15-yard dash up and down the companionway to check the radar.

Though technological advances have brought us electronic aids such as GPS receivers, digital charts, integrated navigation software, and the like, there's nothing like battery failures or software and computer crashes to make all that expensive hardware useless in a second often just when you need it most.

Identifying the need for this book was one thing. Knowing what approach to take was quite another. But I was lucky; I'd already had the pure pleasure of flying up and down this Maine Coast of ours for several years. During that time, I realized that flying a few hundred above "mast height" provided a unique vantage point to see approaches and harbors with a perspective not available at deck height.

And so this book was born.

To get the photos you see between these covers, my co-pilot, Roger, and I flew many thousands of miles up and down and all around this craggy coast. We hovered over secluded, hard-to-reach hurricane holes, and we flew over larger, more easily accessed ports of call with their parades of boat traffic and panoplies of shoreside amenities. The coast of Maine has it all. From the air we could often see plenty of untouched berths for anchoring in even the most crowded anchorages. While flipping through this book, take a close look at the photos of your favorite destinations; you may get some new ideas for where to drop the hook on your next visit.

If my hopes are realized, this book will guide both your navigation and your daydreams. When you're cruising, it will guide you to safe harbor. When you're away from your boat, it will guide your planning and trigger daydreams of lighthouses that stand as sentinels to our hopes and dreams; of lone spruce and fir that seem to grow out of the granite bedrock itself and yet survive, even though bent and blasted by winter storms; of miles of undisturbed shorelines populated by herons, gulls, and ospreys; and of seals, porpoises, minke whales, and great schools of mackerel and herring in harmony with their surroundings. This is what the Maine coast is all about.

The book is organized in west-to-east sections that allow quick access to each selected harbor and passage. We do not cover every anchorage. Rather, we highlight those ports and passages that called the loudest for aerial pictorial treatment. We sought out the hidden entrances, the ledge-strewn approaches, the cluttered or winding channels, the confusing shorelines and the crowded anchorages for which a picture is worth a thousand words. In each such case, one or more pictures depict the harbor approach as well as the important navigation aids that will help you relate your own position to the photographic view. Next to the photograph is a segment of the corresponding navigation chart for convenient reference and orientation ast, we provide pilotage notes based on our own observations that may help your planning. You should note that this book is intended to augment—not replace—the excellent Maine cruising guides written by Taft, Duncan, and others.

A deep debt of gratitude is owed to the fantastic team at International Marine—Jonathan Eaton, Molly Mulhern, and Benjamin McCanna. Their efforts and their vision helped make this book a reality. You guys are the best!

I want to also acknowledge my two collaborators on this project, Roger Brul and Abby Crocker. Roger, my co-pilot and friend, lent his considerable piloting experience to every flight and his analytical perspective to every location, chart, and photograph we saw. Roger's knowledge of these waters is so exhaustive, he's a walking encyclopedia of the Maine coast, and his sense of direction is so infallible, he's a virtual compass. Roger and I shared nearly a hundred hours flying along this immense and wonderful shoreline. Abby—who was pregnant for much of this time—logged countless hours transcribing pilotage notes (that were often muffled by the drone of the helicopter's rotating blades), organizing chapters, locating reference charts, and attending to the never-ending details of a book project. Someday, when her twin girls are sailing this coast, they will appreciate the hard work their mom put in to this project.

We hope this book will help you enjoy the wonders of the Maine coast and provide a quick point of reference and an added navigation tool for those all-too frequent foggy days.

We'll see you out there.

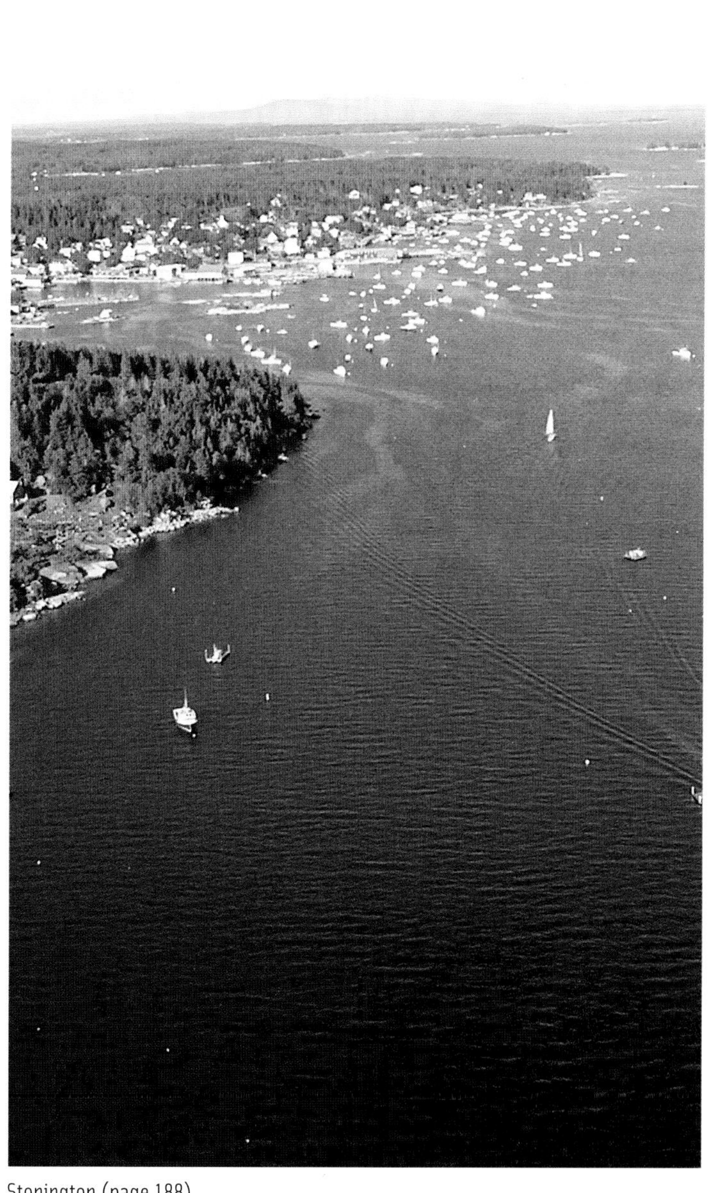

Stonington (page 188)

A Few Notes on Using This Guide

This book is intended to supplement a set of up-to-date charts, tide tables, and other navigation aids. It is by no means intended to replace them. This book is also intended to be used *in conjunction* with the any of the Maine cruising guides by Taft, Duncan, and others. The photos within this book do, however, provide a perspective of the Maine coast that is not available from any other printed resource or navigation tool.

Here's how the book works: One or more numbered arrowhead icons have been added to every chart within this book. Each icon number corresponds to a photo of the same number that was shot at that approximate location, looking in the direction of the arrowhead. The icons are intended to give the reader a quick understanding of how each photo relates to the chart, and how both the photos and charts relate to what you're seeing from the helm. Again, the placement of the icons is approximate.

For your further guidance, we've overprinted key buoys on the aerial photos, along with a recommended track to follow. (There are many buoys that we did not add to the photos; we chose only the most useful approach buoys.) These buoy and tract locations are likewise approximate. Be sure to use your own navigation tools and wits to determine your position, course, and intended destination. Nothing replaces good common sense.

The text provides further clues and instructions on how to enter each harbor and navigate the passageways. Please note that steering directions within the text are *general* directions—mostly cardinal and intercardinal compass points. They are not intended as actual courses to steer. They are expressed with reference to the *true* compass rose, and with no regard to magnetic variation.

It's also important to note that Maine has many thoroughfares, narrows, and passages. As such, it is possible for a navigator to enter a waterway from two direc tions, *both* of which seem to be coming from sea, or a least open water. Obviously the buoys cannot b arranged to follow the "red-right-returning" maxim fro both directions. The rule of thumb for intracoast passageways is that as you move clockwise around th continental United States, red is to starboard. But give the complexity of coastal Maine, even this doesn't cov all situations—especially in the greater Penobscot Ba region. The book proceeds from southwest to north east, as would a navigator approaching Maine from th south. From this approach, many of the thoroughfar will be entered with green to starboard. Pay close atte tion to your charts.

The waters of Maine are constantly changing an so are the navigational aids that mark them; be sure us the most up-to-date NOAA charts when underway. Re member, too, that tides and currents play a critical ro in navigating the waters of Maine. Tides are significan and weather and astronomical conditions can quickl make a seemingly easy daysail seem like the Sydney–Ho bart race. Know your tides and currents well.

This book doesn't pretend to cover every harbo or anchorage on the Maine coast. We have include most of the ones that are considered the core jewels o these waters, but there are many more within you reach. Take the time to explore the land and wate around you—they won't disappoint.

Finally, a note on the chart segments in the pages: We've labeled each one with chart number, ed tion, and scale to make it easier for you to select ap propriate charts. But in adapting the chart segments t these pages, we've often had to enlarge or reduce ther Thus, the scale shown is the scale of the original NOA chart but not necessarily the scale of the chart segme in this book.

ıs Head Harbor, looking north (page 128)

REGION I

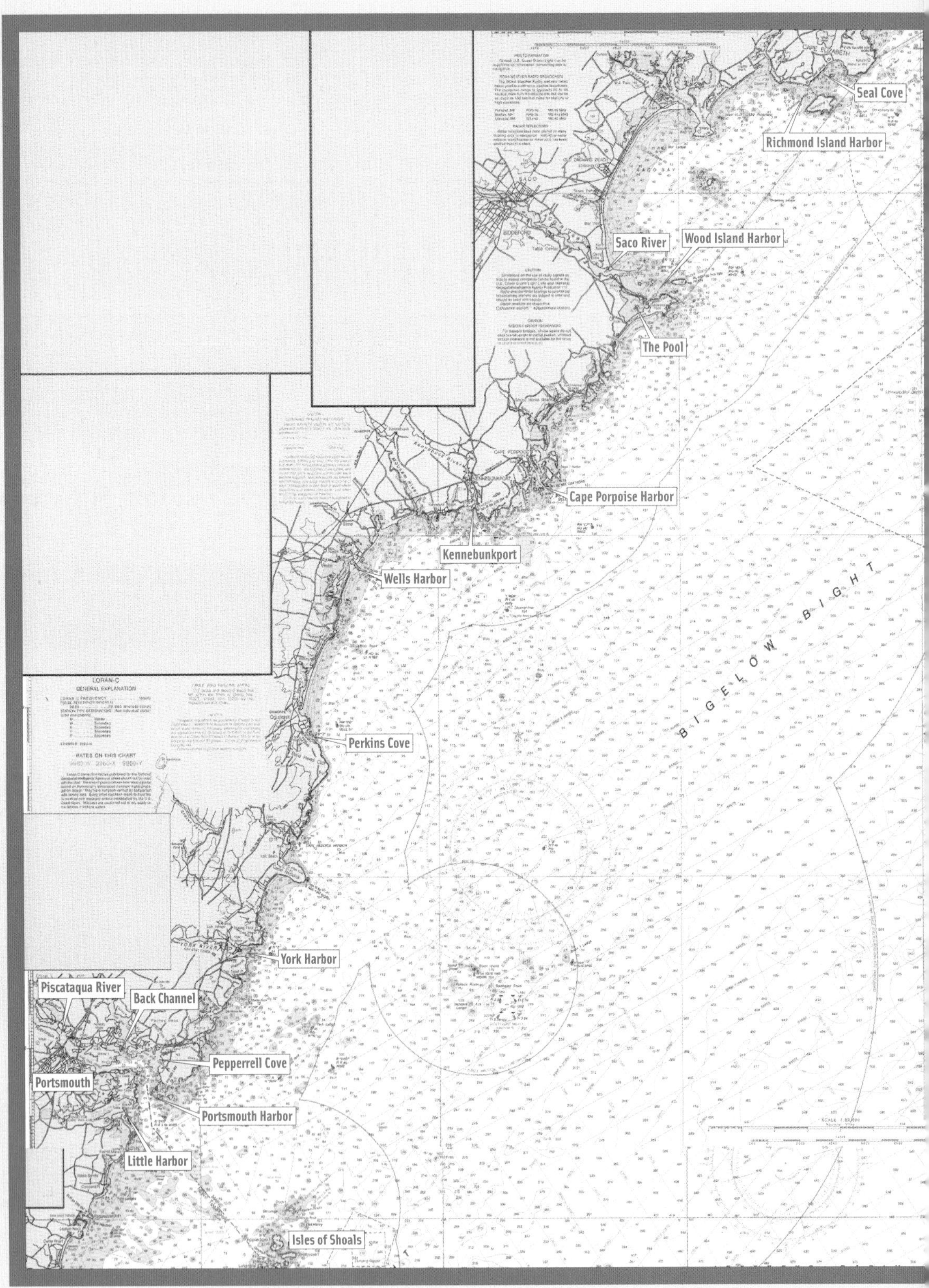

Seal Cove
Richmond Island Harbor
Saco River
Wood Island Harbor
The Pool
Cape Porpoise Harbor
Kennebunkport
Wells Harbor
BIGELOW BIGHT
Perkins Cove
York Harbor
Piscataqua River
Back Channel
Pepperrell Cove
Portsmouth
Portsmouth Harbor
Little Harbor
Isles of Shoals

SOUTHERN MAINE
—ISLES OF SHOALS TO RICHMOND ISLAND HARBOR—

ood Island Harbor (page 40)

From the unprotected waters off the Isles of Shoals to the gracious shorefront homes and andscapes of Cape Elizabeth, the southern Maine coast s, for cruisers approaching from the south, the shake- own phase of a summer adventure. The waters are a lit- le milder than those Down East, the tides smaller, the igh summer days just a bit balmier, the fog less fre- uent. When you're heading east, it's an opportunity to est your boat's rigging and hardware as your mind slips nto cruising mode.

This is also the most populous stretch of the Maine oast, and its miles of sand beaches and comparatively ncomplicated coastal geography, while simplifying avigation in some ways, also put a high premium on berths in widely separated anchorages. Easy highway access to beaches and harbors sometimes creates a frenetic layer of watercraft activity on hot July weekends, and with many of the prime anchorages in estuaries—especially in the Kittery-Portsmouth approaches—river and tidal currents pose their own challenges. But these occasional inconveniences are offset by the many amenities within walking distance of the dinghy docks along this part of the coast.

Many cruisers regard this stretch of the coast as miles to be transited en route to or from the islands and passageways east of Richmond Island. But look again. There are charms aplenty here for those who take the time to find them.

■ ISLES OF SHOALS ■

WHEN you approach from the south, the Isles of Shoals provide your first glimpse of Maine. This cluster of nine islands straddles the state line, with five in Maine and four in New Hampshire. As you round Cape Ann, the islands beckon from the distance, some twenty miles north. Below the horizon at first, they materialize as you draw closer in clear weather, their mysterious allure somehow in keeping with their bloody, legendary history. Though they lie just six miles off the entrance to Portsmouth Harbor, the islands impress you first with their stark remoteness. As you approach, the 82-foot lighthouse on White Island, the most southerly of the group, becomes ever more prominent guiding you in.

On a sunny day, light may reflect off the massive structure of the old hotel, the Oceanic House, on Star Island. As you get closer, the passageway into Gosport Harbor becomes more obvious, with the light house still providing your clearest marking to port. The islands' distant aura of brooding remoteness will be replaced by a vision of wild beauty as you leave Anderson's Ledge to starboard and see more

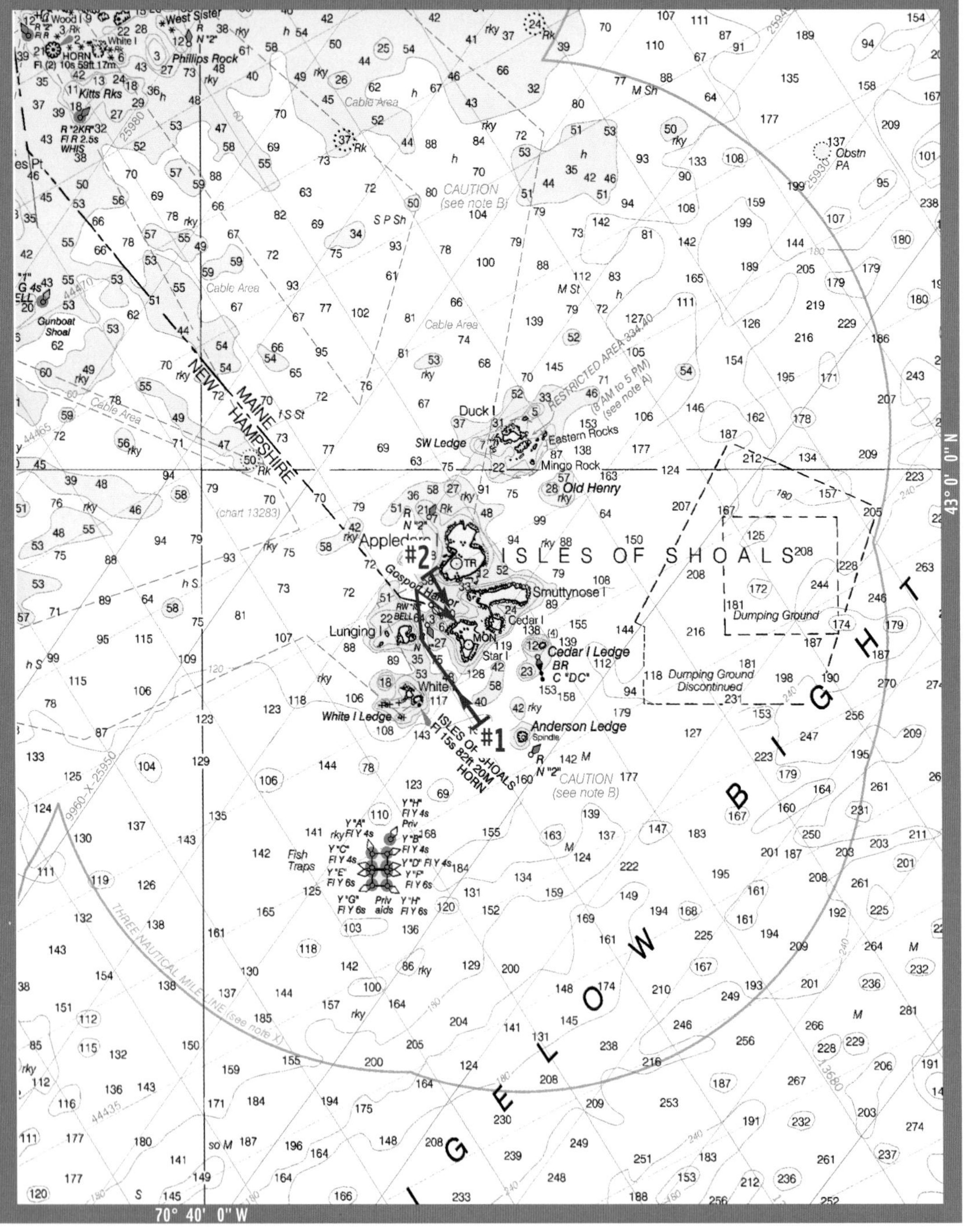

13278
26th ed., June 05
NAD 83
Soundings in feet
1:80,000

learly the outlines of the Oceanic Hotel. Leaving White Island to port, you shape your approach so as to leave Lunging Island immediately to port. You have plenty of deep water on this route. As you get closer to Halfway Rocks, nun "4" comes squarely into view.

Leaving the nun to starboard, you will see immediately in front of you the channel marker bell where you turn east into the centerline fairway for Gosport Harbor. Once in the harbor, Star, Cedar, and Smuttynose Islands surround you on the south, east, and north sides, respectively. Some moorings may be available depending on the time and day you arrive. The harbor is well protected from everything but a westerly blow. In a westerly you can make your way around Smuttynose to find shelter east of the bar between Smuttynose and Cedar. Star Island, where the hotel long ago stopped accommodating overnight guests but once again welcomes visitors to its gift shop and restrooms, is a functioning community—with restored buildings, tennis courts, gardens, recreational facilities, and an obelisk that is a dead ringer for the Washington Monument.

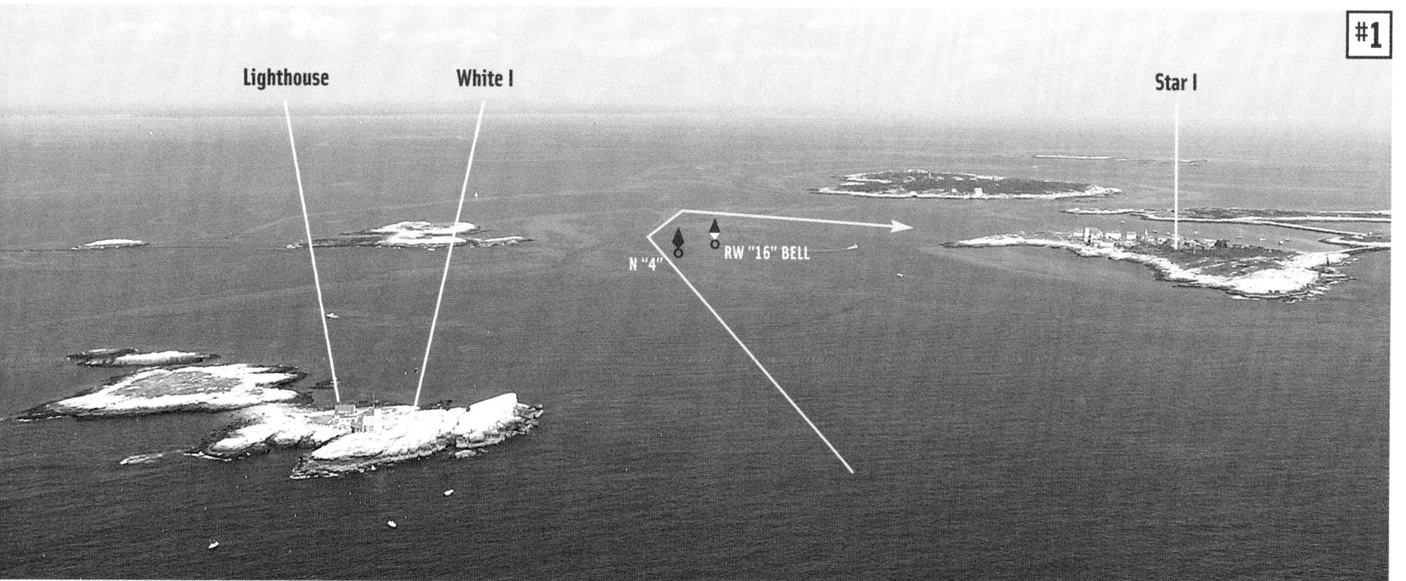

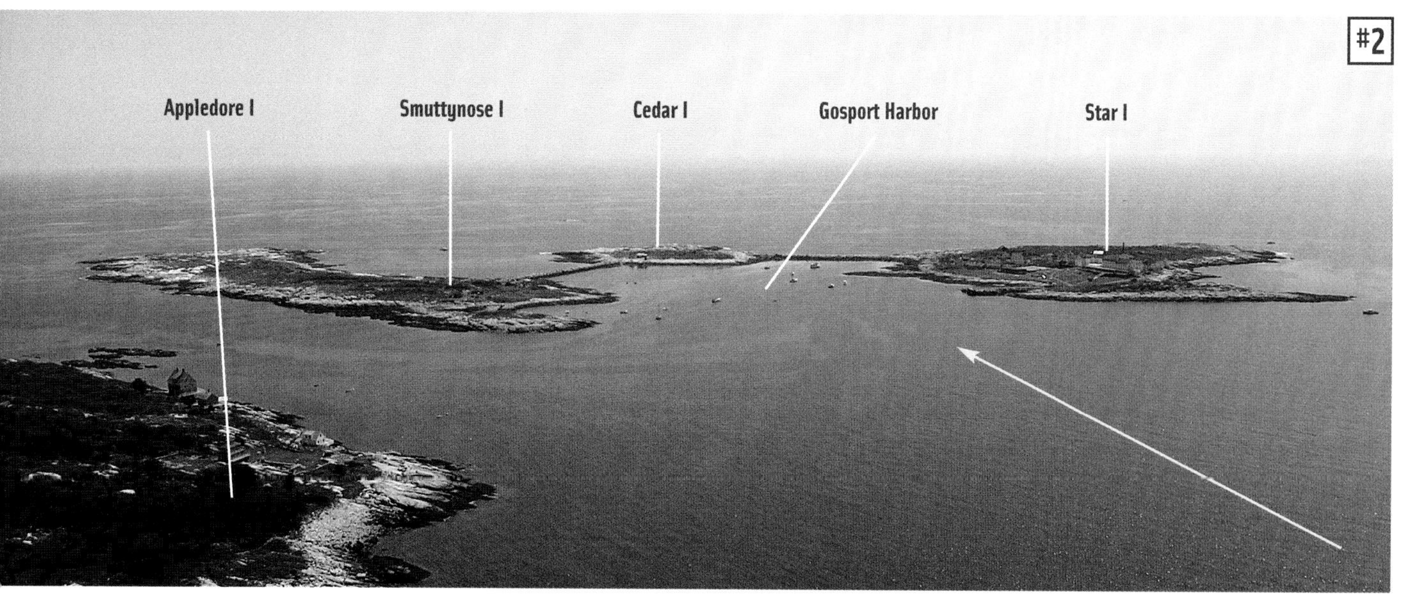

■ PISCATAQUA RIVER ■

(Approach to Portsmouth and Kittery)

AT the mouth of the Piscataqua River, which defines the boundary between New Hampshire and Maine, is a complex of inviting and well-protected anchorages. Channels and entrances are well marked; your chief navigational challenges will be the currents, which ca reach as high as six knots due to the influence of th river, and commercial shipping approaching and leavin Portsmouth.

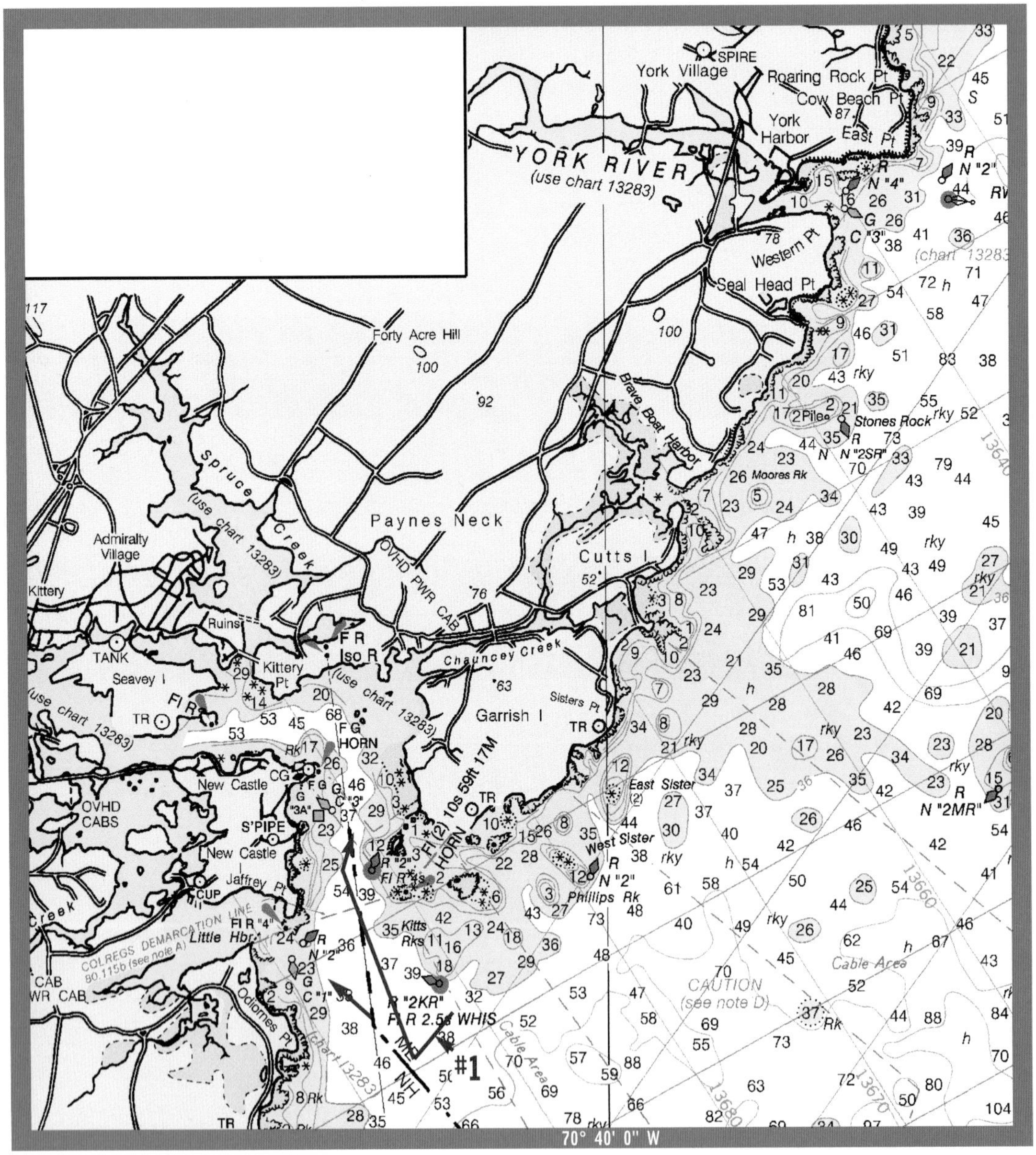

Little Harbor

Located immediately we of the Portsmouth Harbo entrance, Little Harbor the first significant mair land anchorage north o Newburyport. Green be "1," about one nautic mile southeast of the ha bor entrance, provides good approach path whe you're coming from th south or from the Isles o Shoals. The entranc channel is clearly marke with cans, nuns, and beacon on the breakwat that juts south from Ja frey Point. At high tic the entrance breakwate

13286
30th ed., March 04
NAD 83
Soundings in feet
1:80,000

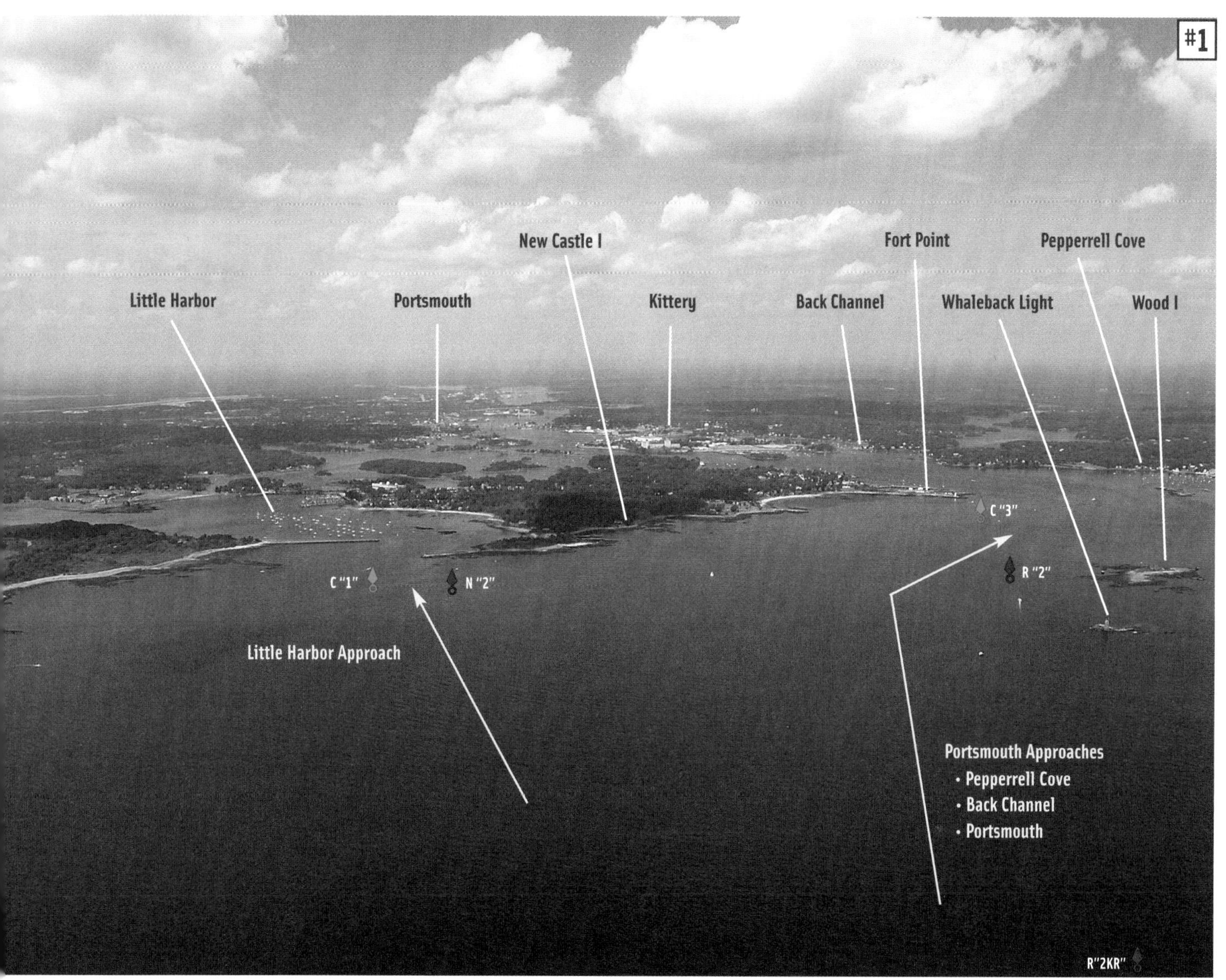

ıay not be readily apparent, but stay between the nav-ȝation aids and watch for currents and small-boat traf-c, and you'll be fine. Little Harbor is remarkably well rotected, and in rough conditions it makes a wonderful lace to spend the day or night. Once you leave the reakwater on Frost Point to port, turn west to follow ıe buoyed channel in. There is deep water on the orth side almost as far as the bascule bridge that gives road access to New Castle Island. The Wentworth Marina offers full facilities and 170 slips, and overlooking the harbor from New Castle Island is a new Marriott Hotel refurbished from the historic but long-defunct Wentworth-By-The-Sea hotel. In the summer, Little Harbor becomes very crowded with yachts and all manner of small craft, and there is no room to anchor and few if any rental moorings.

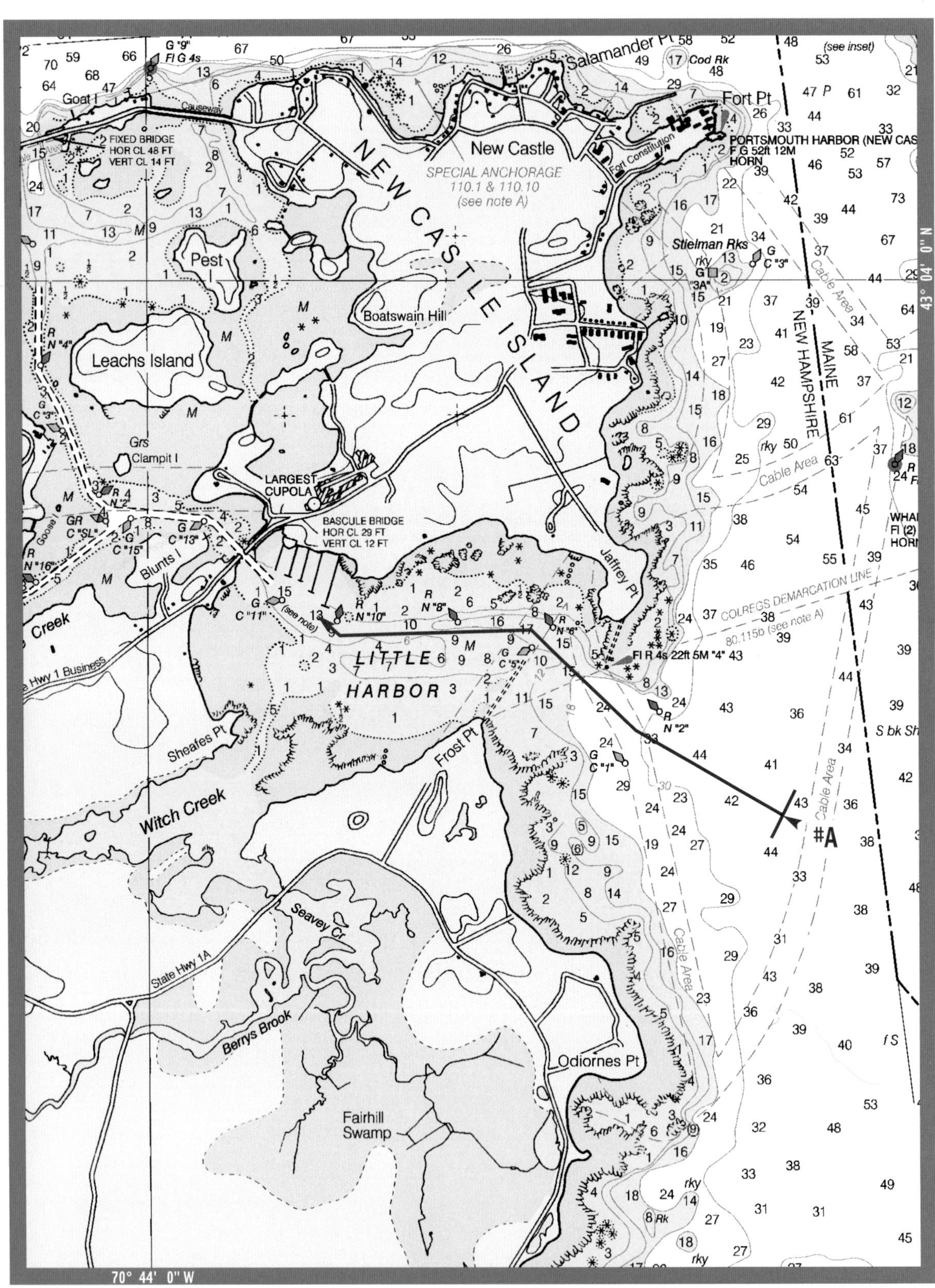

13283
19th ed., Feb 05
NAD 83
Soundings in feet
1:20,000

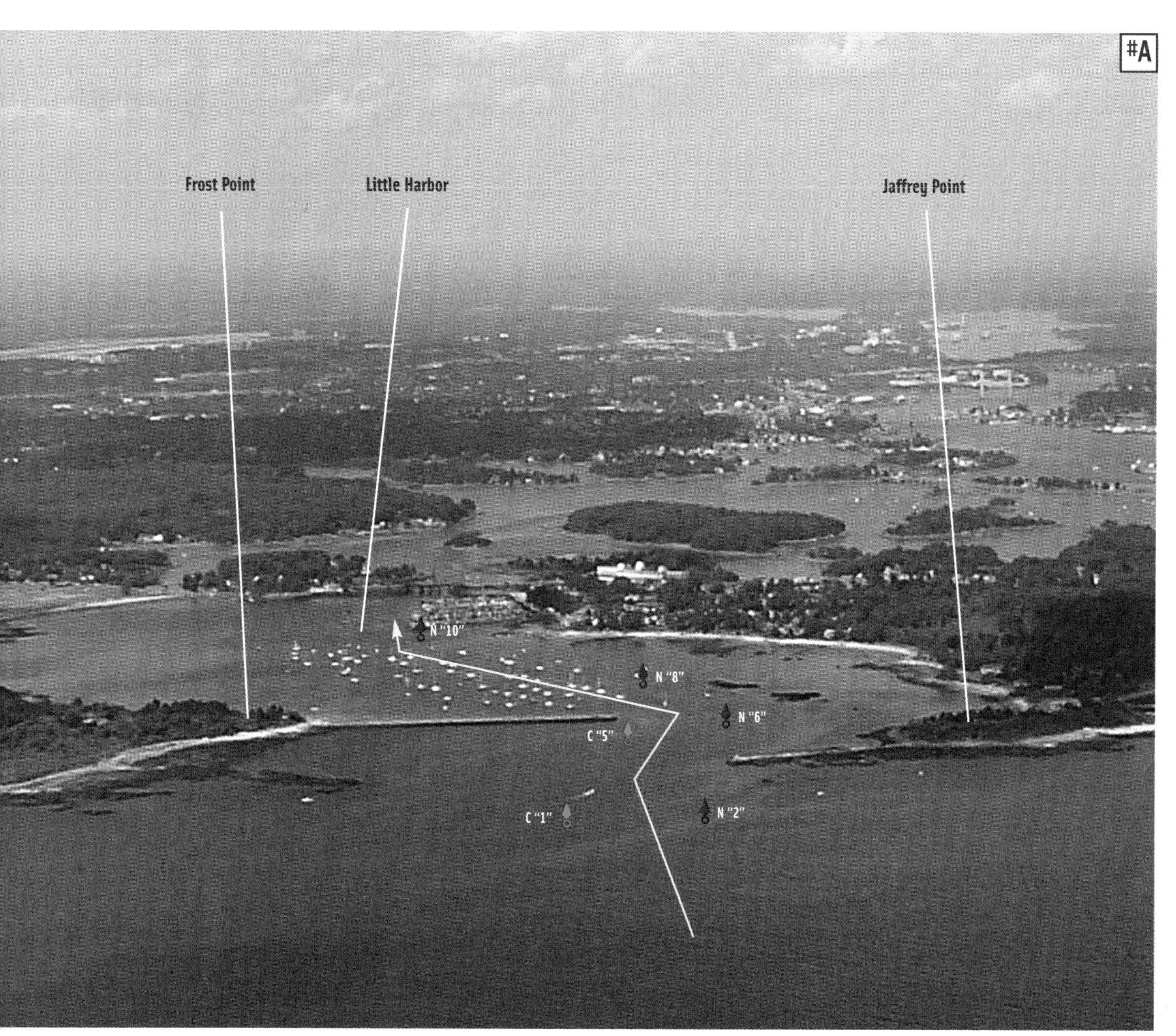
#A
Frost Point
Little Harbor
Jaffrey Point
N "10"
N "8"
N "6"
C "5"
C "1"
N "2"

Portsmouth Harbor

The entrance to multibranched Portsmouth Harbor and its offshoot anchorages is marked first by flashing red whistle buoy "2KR" and then by the 59-foot lighthouse on Whaleback Reef, both of which you should leave to starboard to bypass the rocks and shoal waters bounding the east side of the entrance. The buoyed channel runs north between Wood Island to starboard, with its abandoned lifesaving station, and New Castle Island to port. Shape your course to the right of Fort Point, which juts prominently from the northeast corner of New Castle Island. This is the site of Fort Constitution, a Revolutionary War-era fort, and the bright white Fort Point lighthouse should stand out in clear weather.

As you pass northward through the entrance, Garrish Island will be on your right. After leaving Fort Point to port, you'll glimpse to the west the highway bridges that span the Piscataqua River between Portsmouth and Kittery. You can either continue north into Pepperrell Cove, or turn west toward Portsmouth and Kittery on Back Channel. Along the way, you'll see many possible anchoring spots, but the swift currents make a mooring or slip preferable.

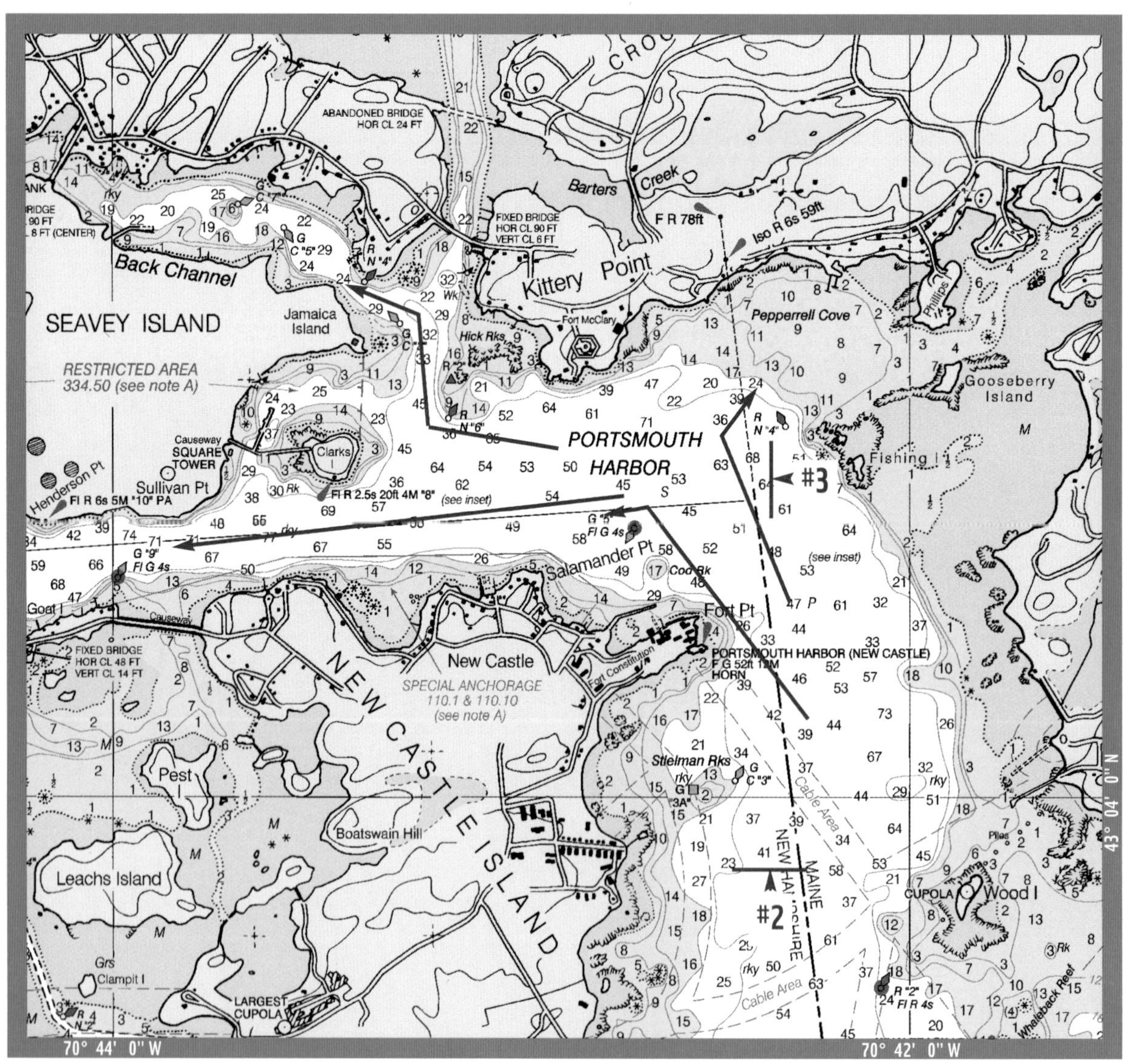

13283
19th ed., Feb. 05
NAD 83
Soundings in feet
1:20,000

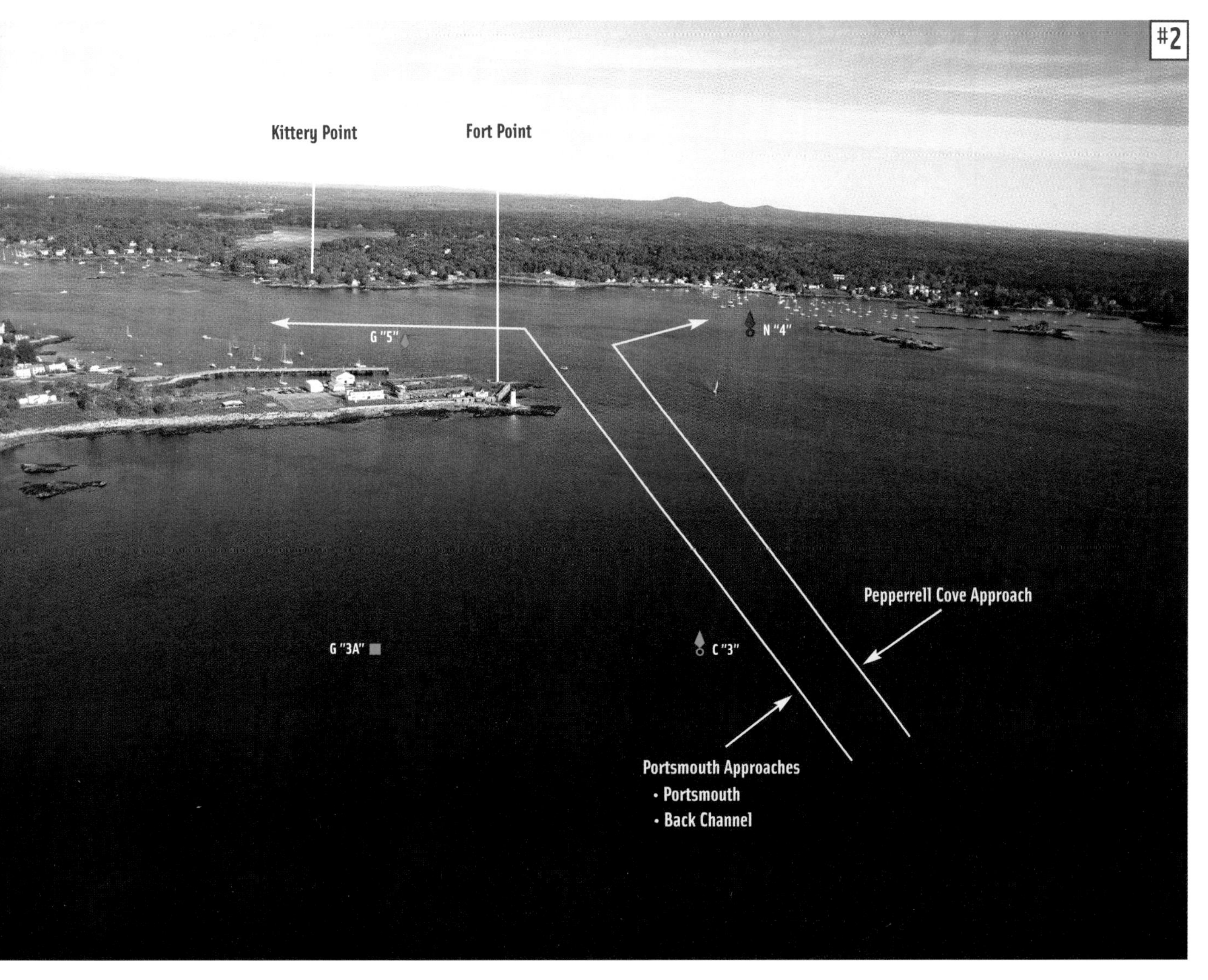
#2
Kittery Point
Fort Point
G "5"
N "4"
Pepperrell Cove Approach
G "3A"
C "3"
Portsmouth Approaches
• Portsmouth
• Back Channel

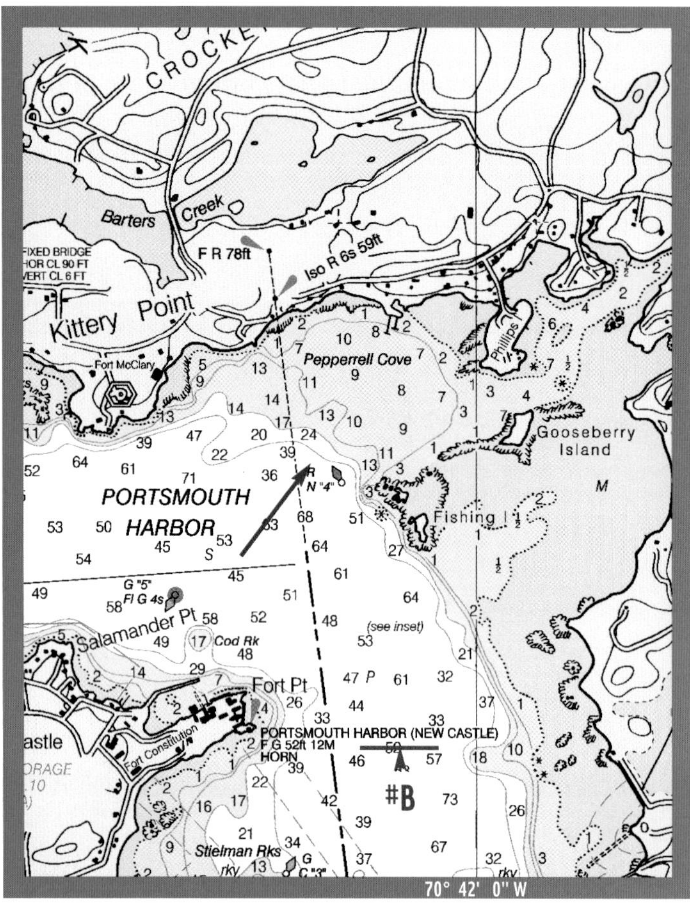

Pepperrell Cove (Kittery Point)

Continue north from Fort Point to approach Pepperre Cove. Leaving nun "4" off Fishing Island to starboarc swing slowly to starboard to enter the cove. The en trance is easy, but the cove is exposed to the south, sub ject to crosscurrents, and busy with commercial an recreational traffic. Moorings are available from th town of Kittery and the Portsmouth Yacht Club, an you may find room to anchor near Fort McClary.

13283
19th ed., Feb. 05
NAD 83
Soundings in feet
1:20,000

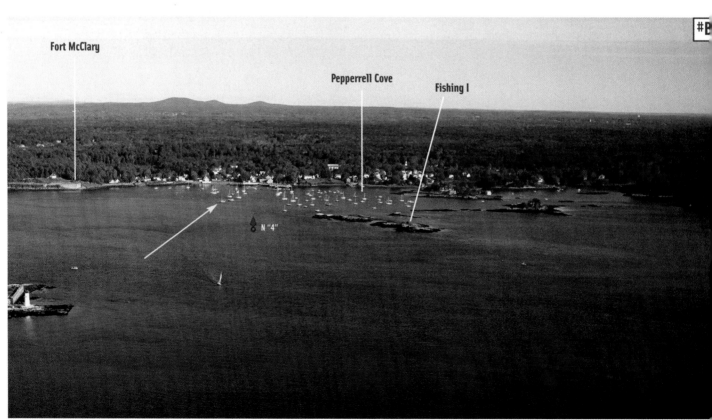

#B
Fort McClary
Pepperrell Cove
Fishing I
N "4"

Portsmouth and Kittery

If you elect to follow the main channel of the Piscataqua River toward Portsmouth and Kittery, you'll leave tiny Clarks Island and large Seavey Island to starboard and Kittery Point Yacht Club (which is not on Kittery Point but rather on the eastern end of Goat Island) to port. The Portsmouth Naval Shipyard occupies most of Seavey, and as you pass beyond that, the bridges across the Piscataqua River will dominate your view over the bow. The first two of these—the Route One Memorial Bridge and the Route One bypass bridge—are both lift bridges. See your cruising guide and coast pilot for instructions on communicating with the bridge tenders and coping with these bridges in the swift river currents. The fixed Interstate-95 bridge upriver provides 135 feet of vertical clearance, but navigation gets progressively trickier upriver. You may find a rental mooring or slip off Portsmouth, but the currents—equally strong on ebb and flood—complicate all maneuvers.

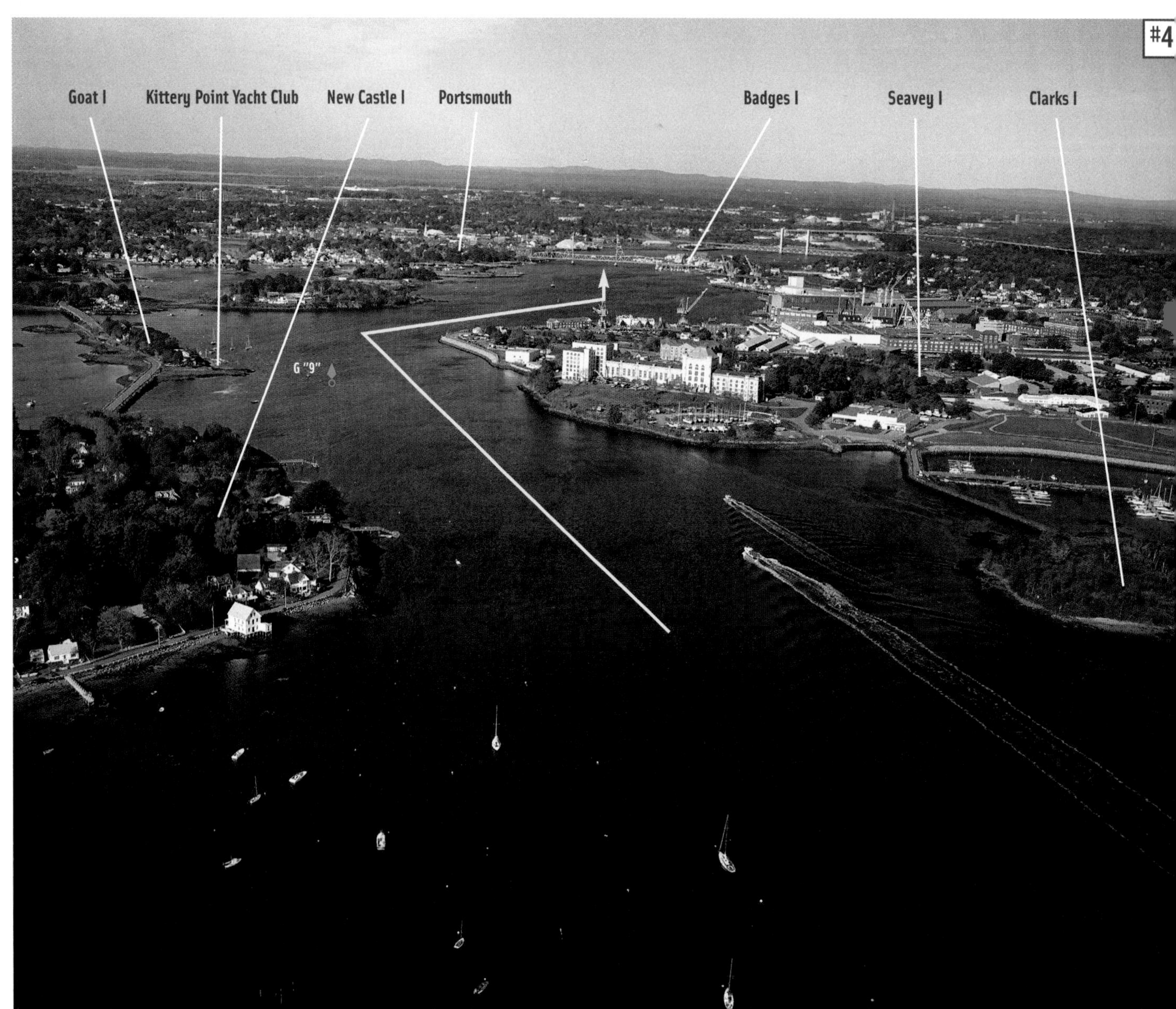
#4
Goat I
Kittery Point Yacht Club
New Castle I
Portsmouth
Badges I
Seavey I
Clarks I
G "9"

PISCATAQUA RIVER
KITTERY
SEAVEY ISLAND
Back Channel
Badgers Island
PORTSMOUTH
#5
#4
70° 44' 0" W
43° 04' 0" N

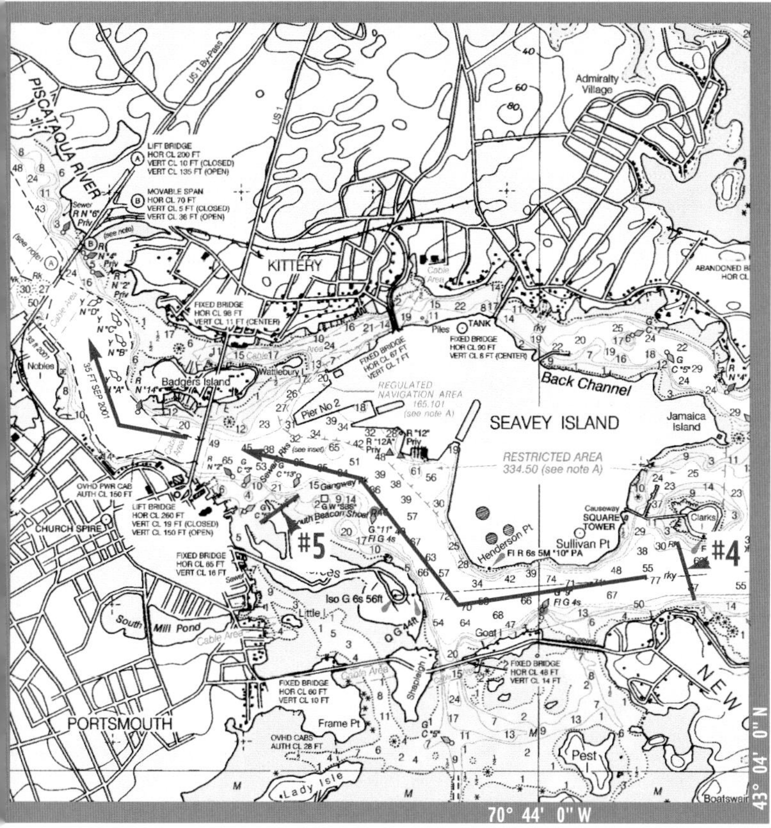

13283
19th ed., Feb. 05
NAD 83
Soundings in feet
1:20,000

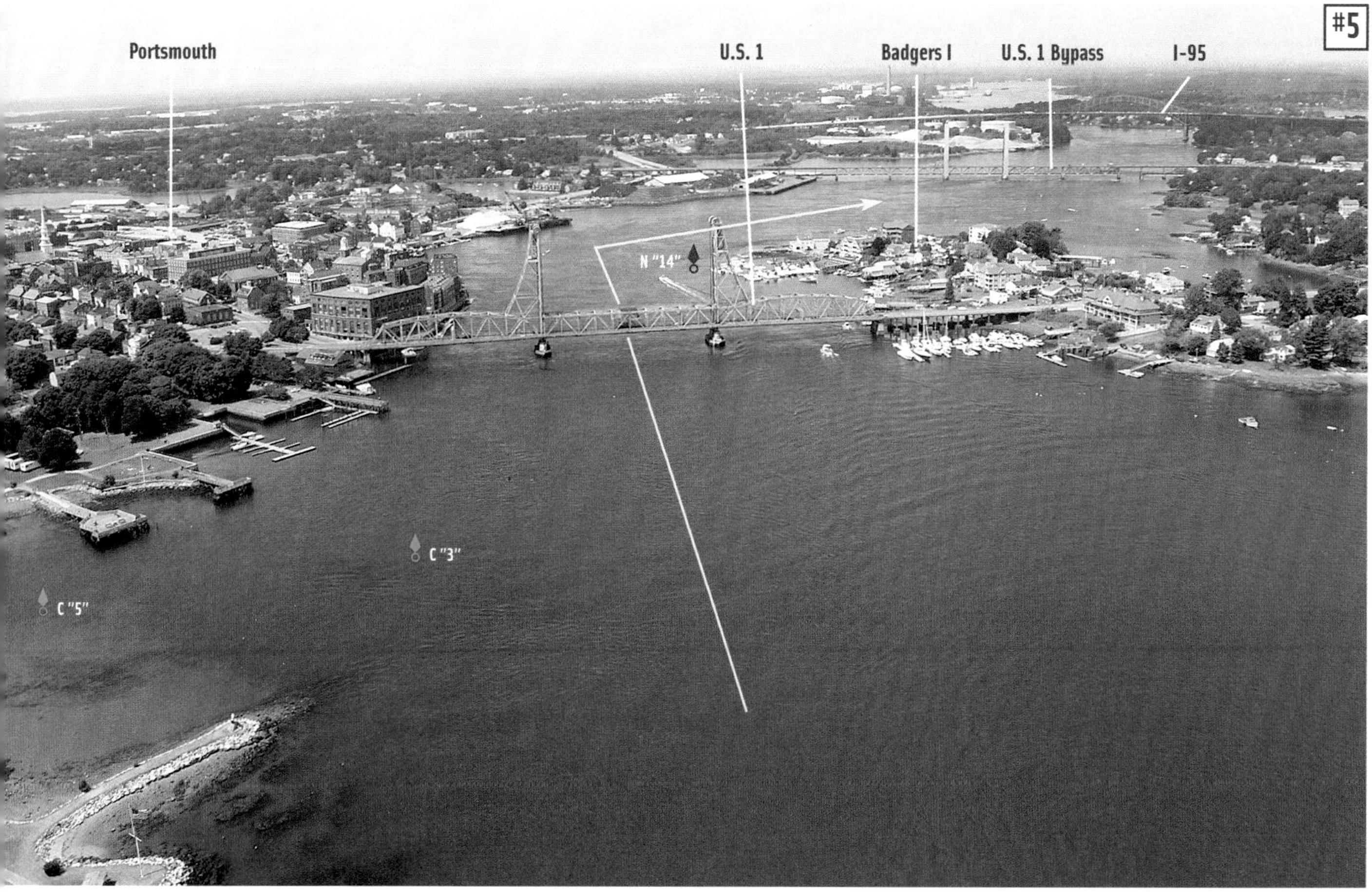

#5
Portsmouth
U.S. 1
Badgers I
U.S. 1 Bypass
I-95
N "14"
C "3"
C "5"

Back Channel

As an alternative to the navigational challenges upriver or the southern exposure of Pepperrell Cove, Back Channel has much to offer. Entered between Kittery Point and Seavey Island, it provides all-weather protection and a partial respite from the currents of the main channel. Average currents here are 1.5 knots (2.5 knots maximum). Leave the daybeacon and nun markin Hick Rocks, off Kittery Point, to starboard, then follo the green-red sequence through the narrow fairway be tween the town of Kittery and Seavey Island. There ar no places to anchor here, but moorings and slips ar available in season from Dion's Yacht Yard.

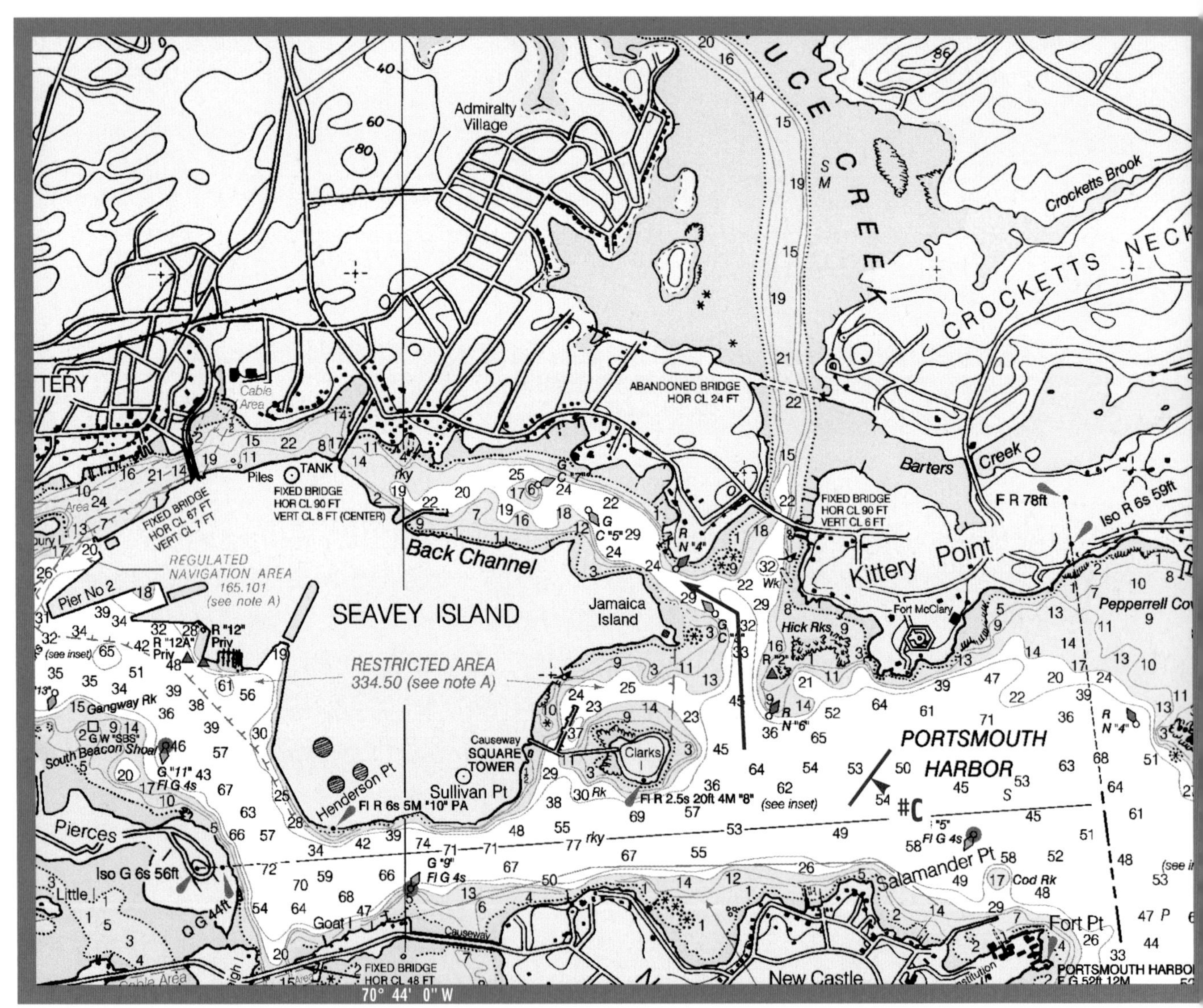

13283
19th ed., Feb. 05
NAD 83
Soundings in feet
1:20,000

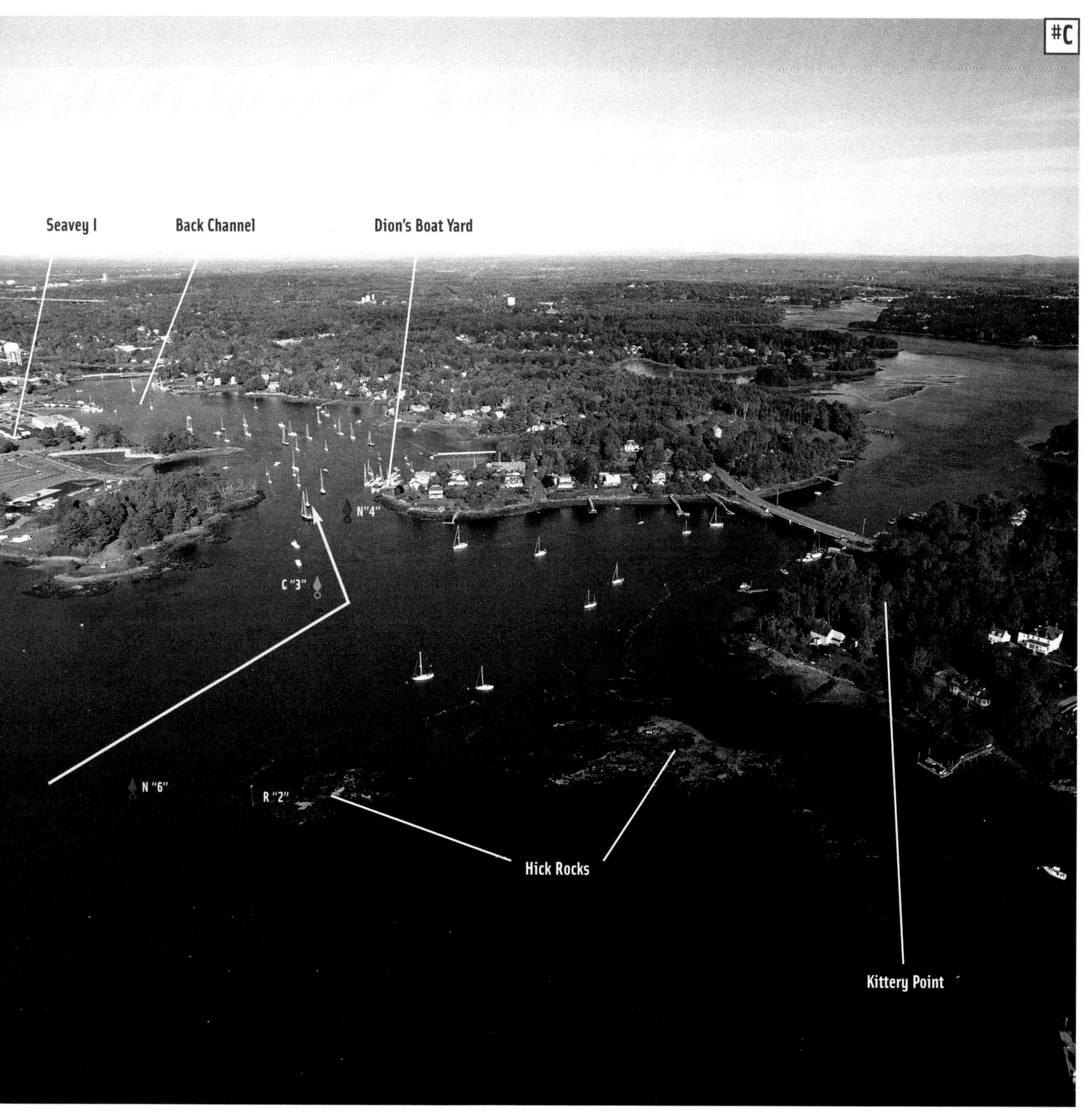
#C
Seavey I
Back Channel
Dion's Boat Yard
N"4"
C"3"
N "6"
R "2"
Hick Rocks
Kittery Point

■ YORK HARBOR ■

THE York Harbor entrance is hard to see from the southwest until you get within a quarter of a mile of it. Even when you begin to make out the York River entrance, this protected harbor is not in full view. Start your approach from the red-and-white "YH" bell buoy, heading west so as to pass between can "3" and nun "4" marking the river entrance. From this vantage you get your first full view of the long river mouth fairway into the harbor. Entering the river mouth, you begin to make out the boats at anchor inside Stage Neck, but at first

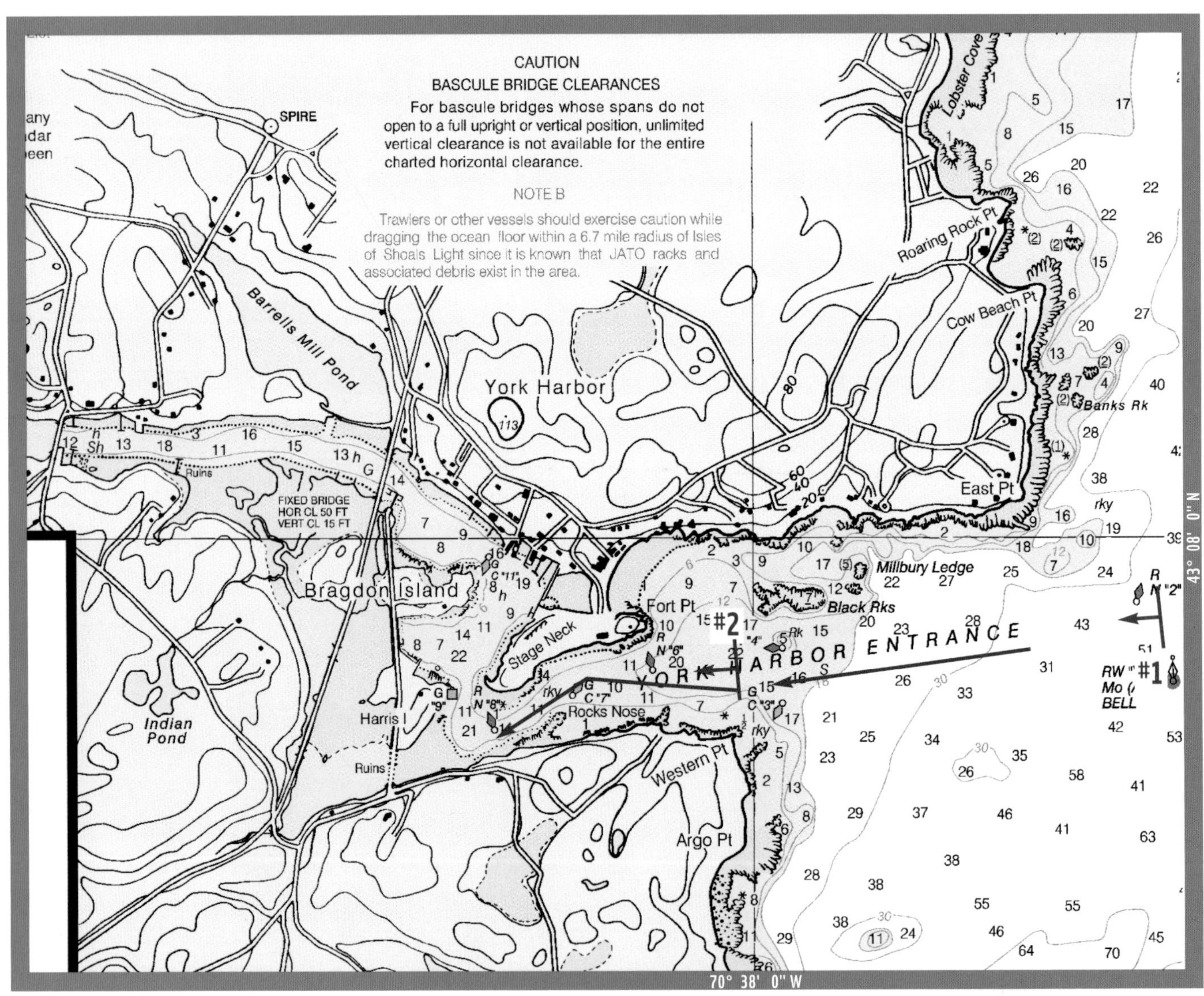

13283
19th ed., Feb. 05
NAD 83
Soundings in feet
1:20,000

'ou might be convinced there is no way of getting in here. Keep following the channel buoys, however, and .oon it becomes clear that a hard turn to starboard—ricky when the tide is running strong enough to pull ıun "8" underwater, as sometimes happens—gives ac-:ess to this majestic little New England harbor. On your starboard side, Stage Neck is lined with condominiums and hotels. The harbormaster monitors channels 9 and 16. This is a secure, all-weather harbor with full facilities. Anchoring is not permitted, but ten rental moorings are reported.

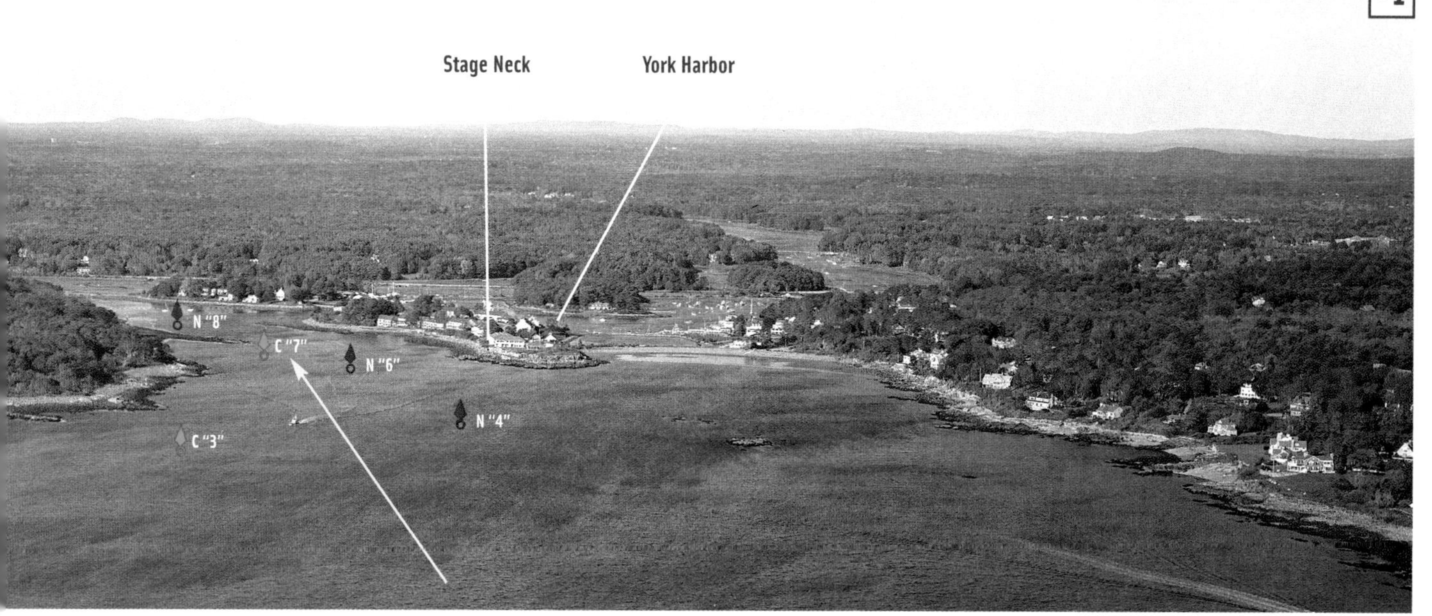

■ PERKINS COVE ■

APPROACHING Perkins Cove from the red-and-white "PC" bell buoy offshore, head between can "1" and nun "2," then shape your course toward the daybeacon (spindle) that marks the shoals on the north side of the entrance. Leave the spindle to starboard, then turn to starboard to proceed up the narrow slot. There is no room to anchor, and moorings are limited. You should find the harbormaster at the public floats to starboard immediately before the bascule bridge that gives access to the inner harbor. Do not pass through the bridg (which you must operate yourself) without the harbor master's permission. In any event, the chart indicates three-foot spot at the bridge, so you might want to wai for high tide or find a local pilot before attempting t reach the inner harbor. Though well protected an charming, this is a working harbor with few opportuni ties for transient boats.

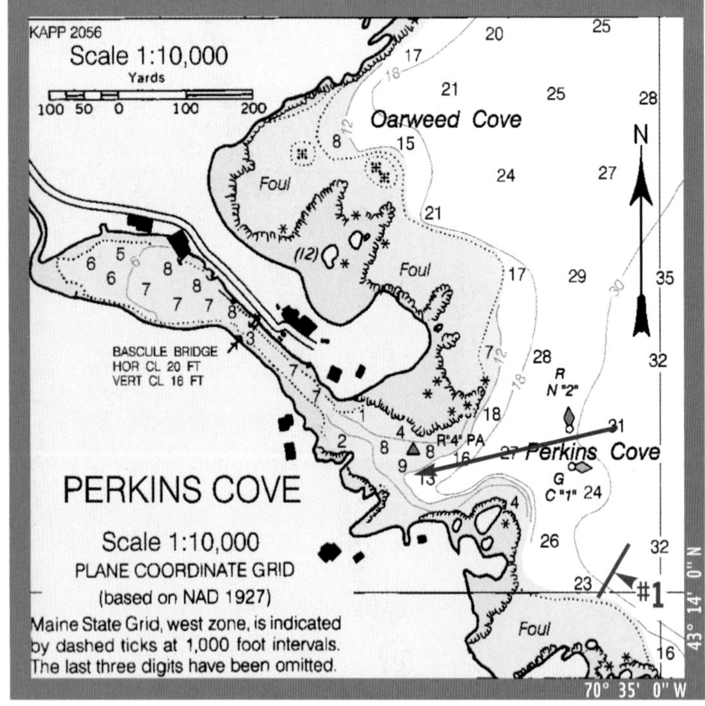

13286
30th ed., March 05
NAD 27
Soundings in feet
1:10,000

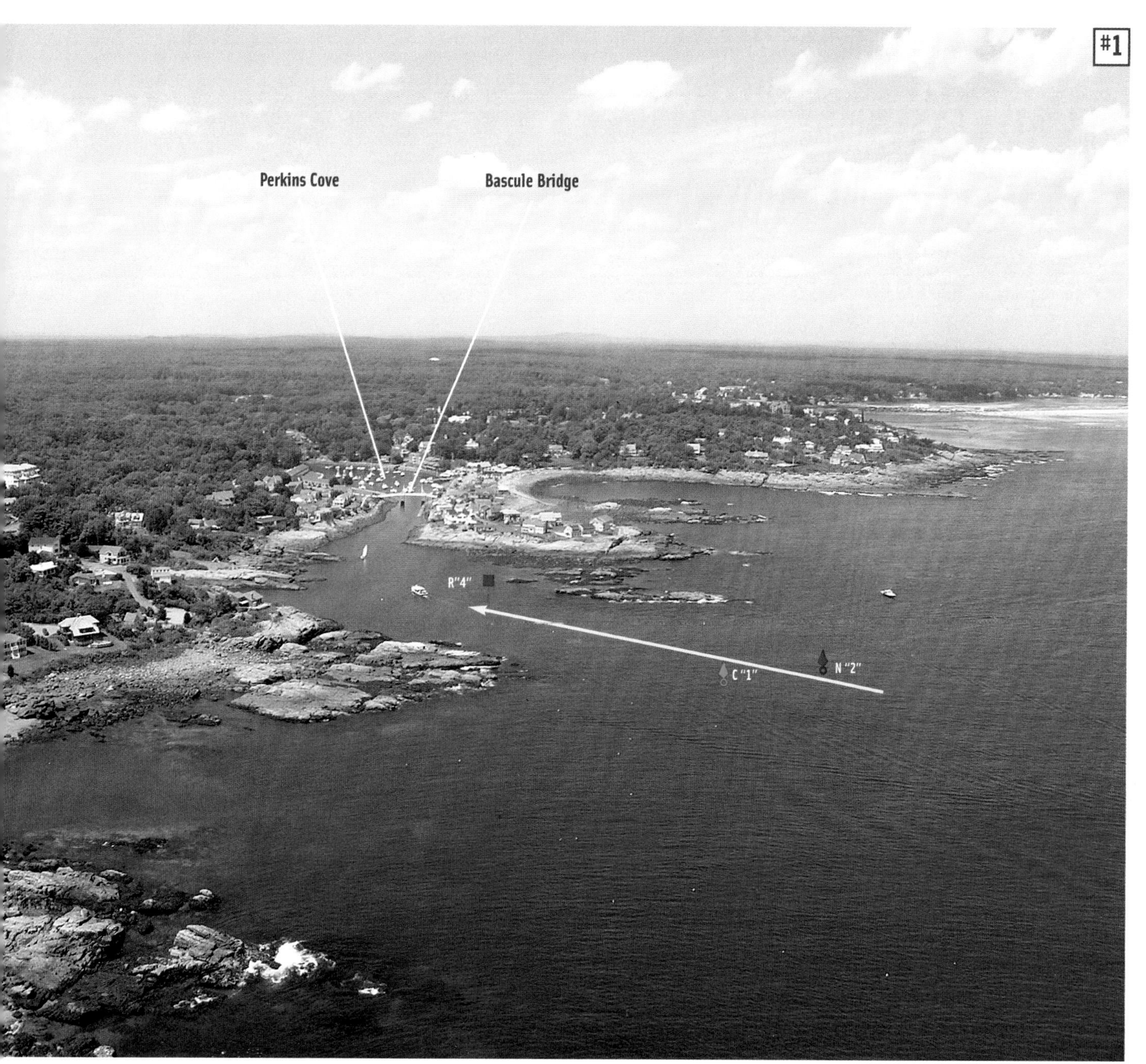
#1
Perkins Cove
Bascule Bridge
R"4"
C "1"
N "2"

■ WELLS HARBOR ■

AS you approach Wells Harbor from the south, it is easy to imagine that the beach in front of you extends without interruption all the way to Cape Elizabeth. But then you will see the paired breakwaters that extend almost a quarter mile seaward to provide a clear but narrow entrance into this protected harbor. Though easil visible and simple to approach from red-and-whit lighted bell buoy "WH," the dredged entrance—actu ally the mouth of the Webhannet River—should b treated warily for its tidal currents and shifting sands When an ebb curren meets ocean swells, yo may encounter breakin seas at the entrance, an the margin for error i small. Once inside, a har turn to port reveals small boat moorings and serv ices, but there is littl water depth because—de spite regular dredging to controlling depth of feet—the anchorage silt rapidly between dredg ings. You'll find little o no room to anchor. Mak your first visit to thi lovely spot a daytime sto timed around high tide.

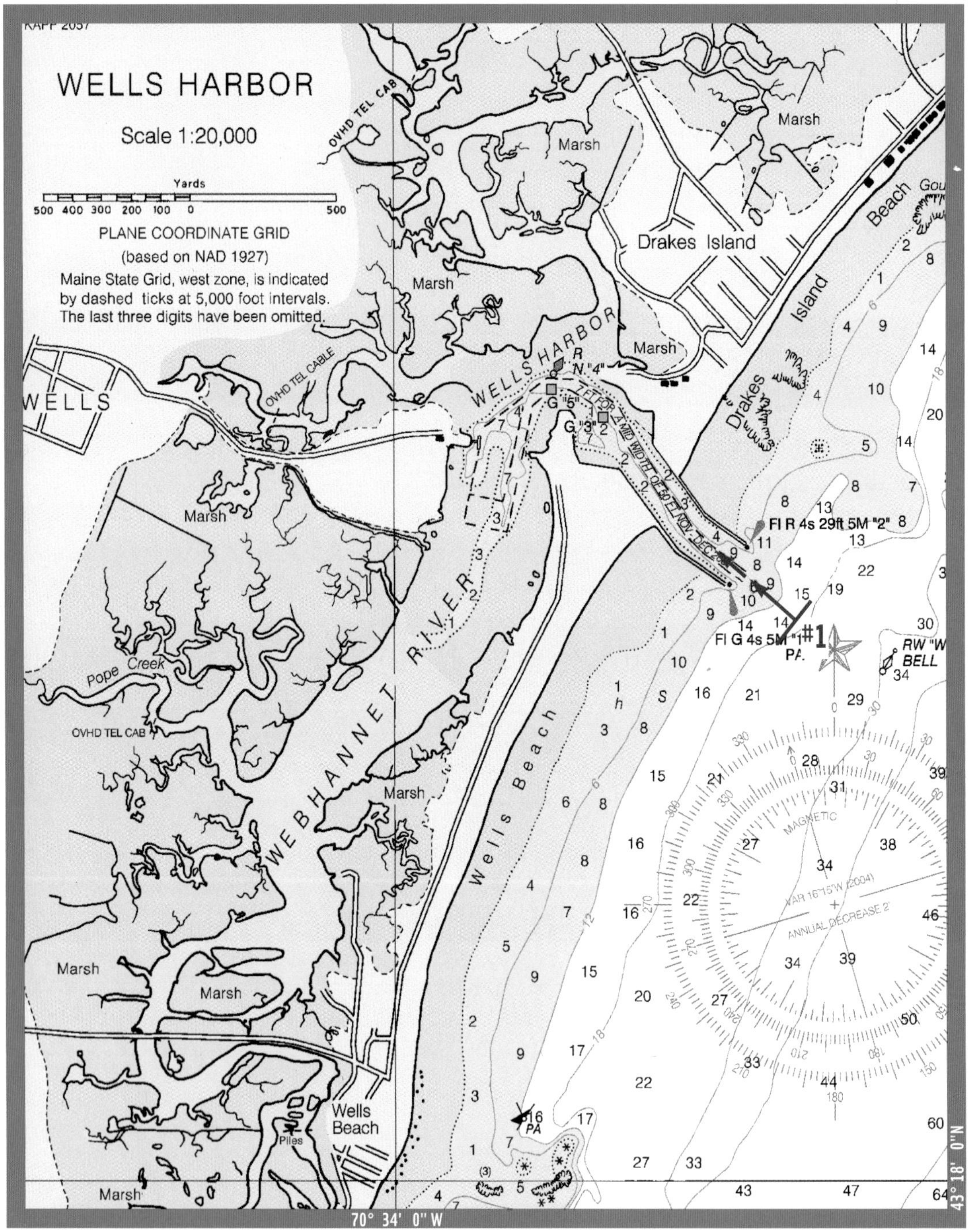

13286
30th ed., March 05
NAD 27
Soundings in feet
1:20,000

#1
Wells Harbor
G "5"
G "3"
N "4"

■ KENNEBUNKPORT ■

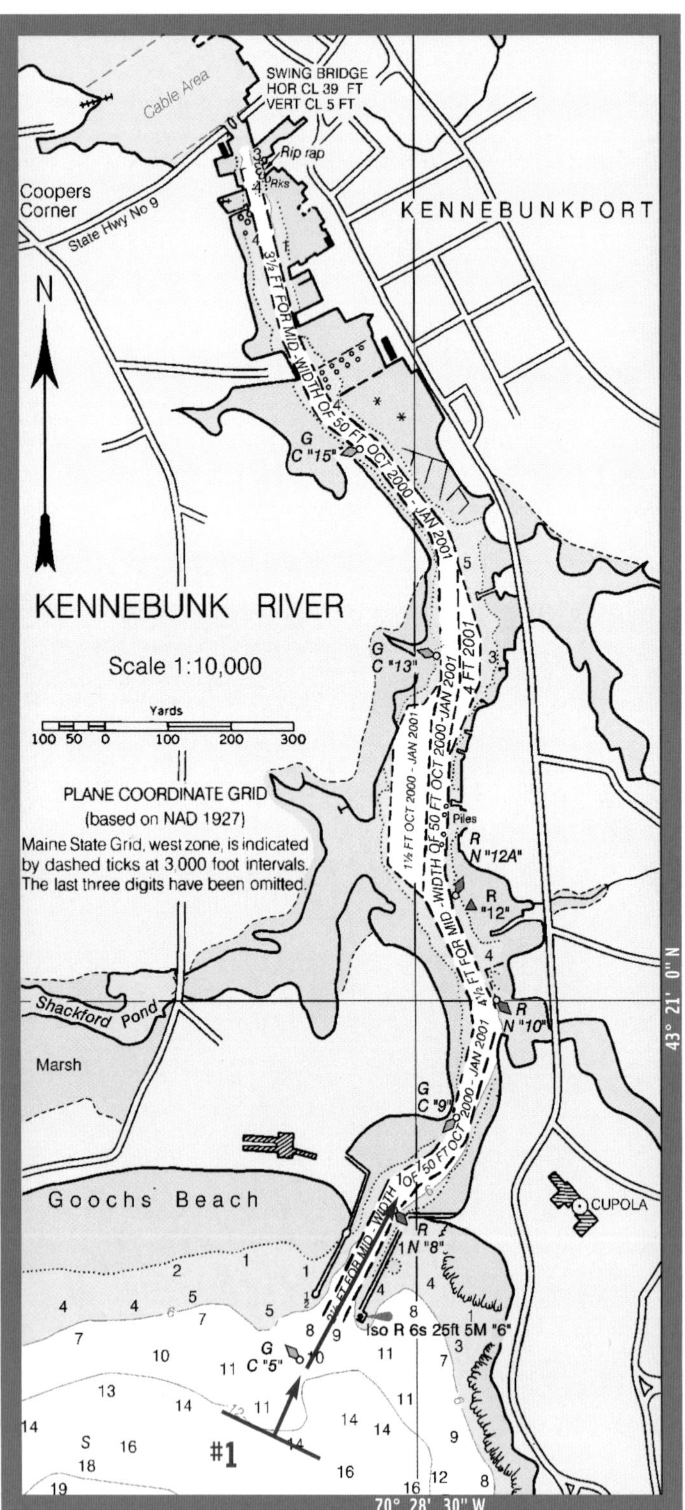

13286
30th ed., March 05
NAD 27
Soundings in feet
1:10,000

IT'S hard to miss the mouth of the Kennebunk Rive with its prominent, parallel breakwaters extending mor than a tenth of a mile seaward. On a clear day, the ap proach is also marked by the white sand at Gooch Beach, just west of the river mouth, and the cupola o the Colony Hotel, on the eastern shore about one eighth of a mile from the eastern breakwater. Also vis ble on the approach is Fishing Rock, the rocks approx mately one-eighth mile south of the breakwate entrance. Give these rocks a good berth one side or th other, either by leaving can "3" to port or red daybeaco "2" to starboard, then aim for the center of the breakwa ter entrance, leaving can "5" immediately to port. If yo approach from the south and elect to leave Fishing Roc to starboard, give a good berth to the rock betwee daybeacon "2" and can "5."

Once through the breakwater, follow the buoye channel along the river's circuitous route. Pay attention— the current is usually less than two knots, but the dredge channel is narrow, and the boats moored along the po side make it narrower still. The Kennebunk River known for its shoaling. Nominal dredged low wate depth is said to be 6 feet, but treat that number with cau tion. Depending on your boat's draft and the stage c ide, you can make your way more than half a nautical mile upriver to the town center—Kennebunkport on the east bank, the Lower Village of Kennebunk on the west bank—passing several marinas and the Arundel Yacht Club to starboard en route. It's a safe harbor, and it's busy in the summer. Anchoring is not permitted, and you may have trouble finding an open mooring. Your best bet is probably a marina slip.

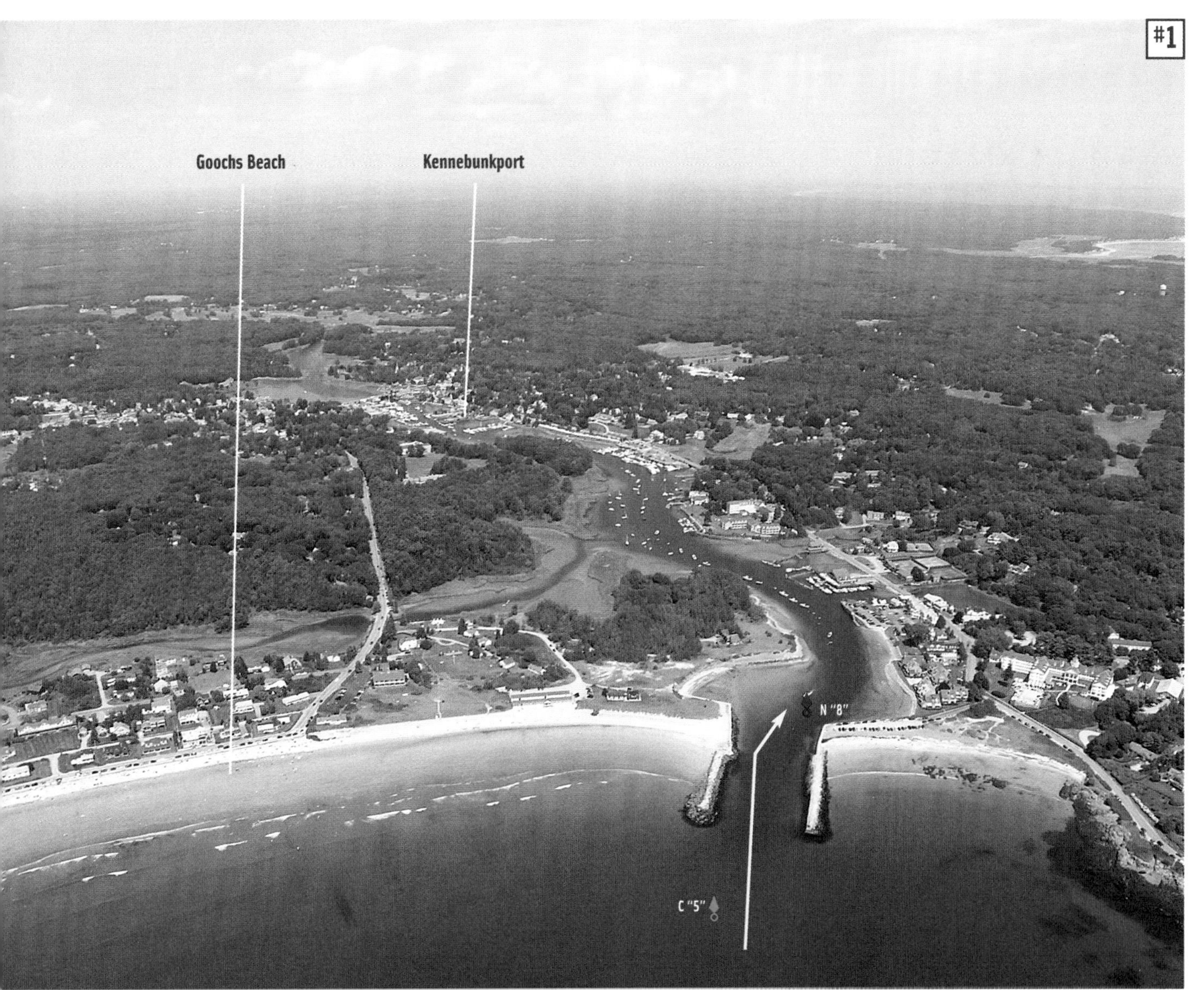

CAPE PORPOISE HARBOR

THE approach to Cape Porpoise Harbor is well marked. From any direction, red bell buoy "2," marking the approach channel, is visible in all but the densest fog. From the bell, a heading of approximately 300 degrees magnetic will leave nun "4," marking Old Prince Ledge, and nun "6," marking a 10-foot spot, to star board. You should then discern Goat Island, with its ol coast guard station and lighthouse, on the starboar bow. Extensive shoals make out from both the Goat Is land and Folly Island sides of the entrance, so keep i midchannel between th two daybeacons, givin both a fair berth, the head midway betwee can "9" and nun "10." An choring room in the sum mer is scarce but possible with good holdin ground, and moorin availability is spotty a best. The dredged chan nel is crowded with th lobster boats of a workin community. Nevertheless in an emergency, it's a saf and reasonably well-pro tected harbor.

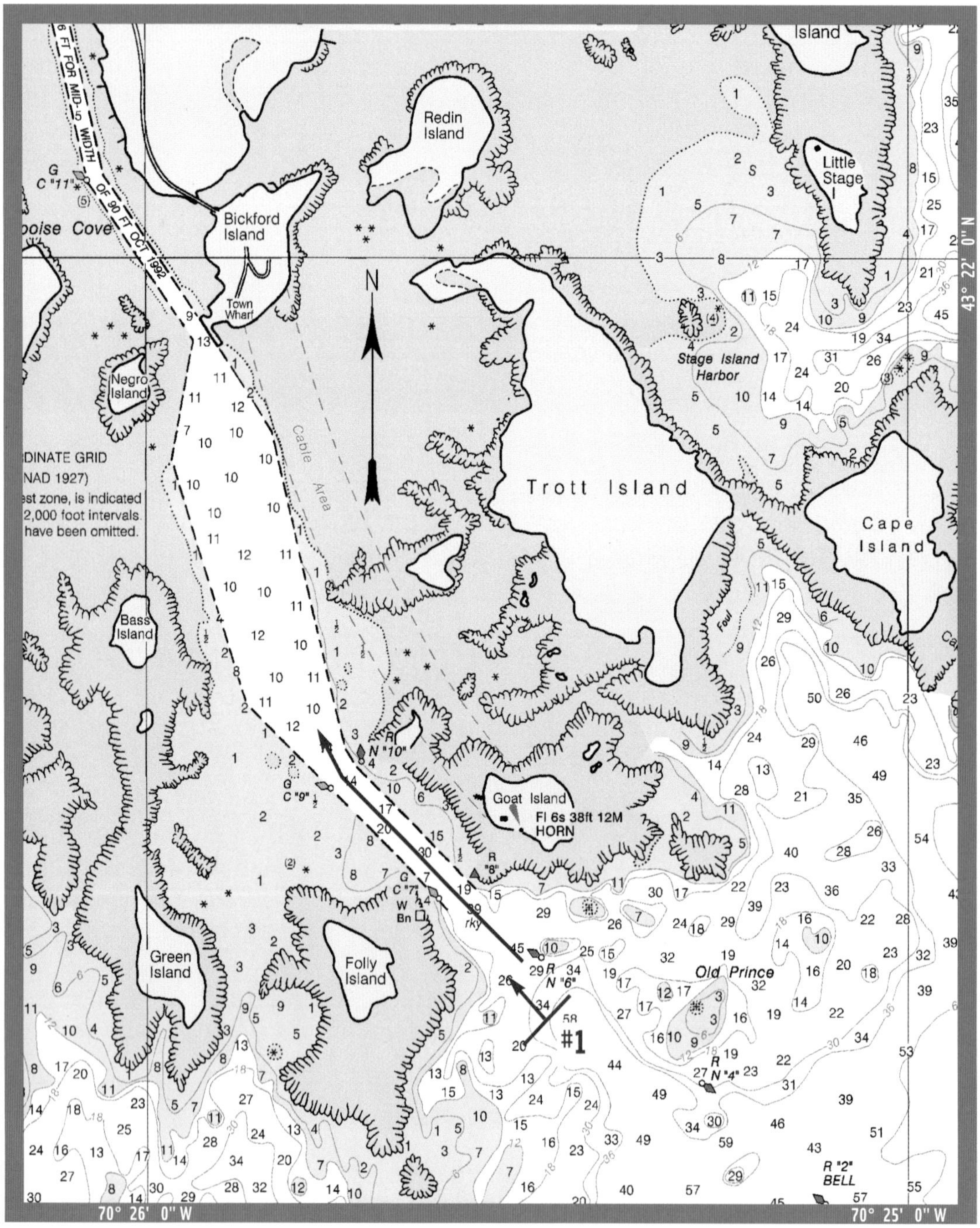

13286
30th ed., March 05
NAD 27
Soundings in feet
1:10,000

#1
Folly I
Cape Porpoise Harbor
Goat I
C "9"
N "10"
W BN
C "7"
R "8"
N "6"

WOOD ISLAND HARBOR AND THE POOL

WOOD Island Harbor and its inner sanctum, The Pool, can be entered north or south of Wood Island. Approaching from the north, head southwesterly from red-and-white bell buoy "SA," aiming midway between Stage and Negro Island so as to give a respectful berth to their off-lying shoals. (Note the Saco River mouth off to starboard.) Leave can "7" to port, and you're entering Wood Island Harbor. Alternatively, when approaching from the northeast, you can pass between can "1," marking Negro Ledge, and Wood Island before merging with the approach just mentioned. Approaching from the south or east, pass either side of Dansbury Reef a

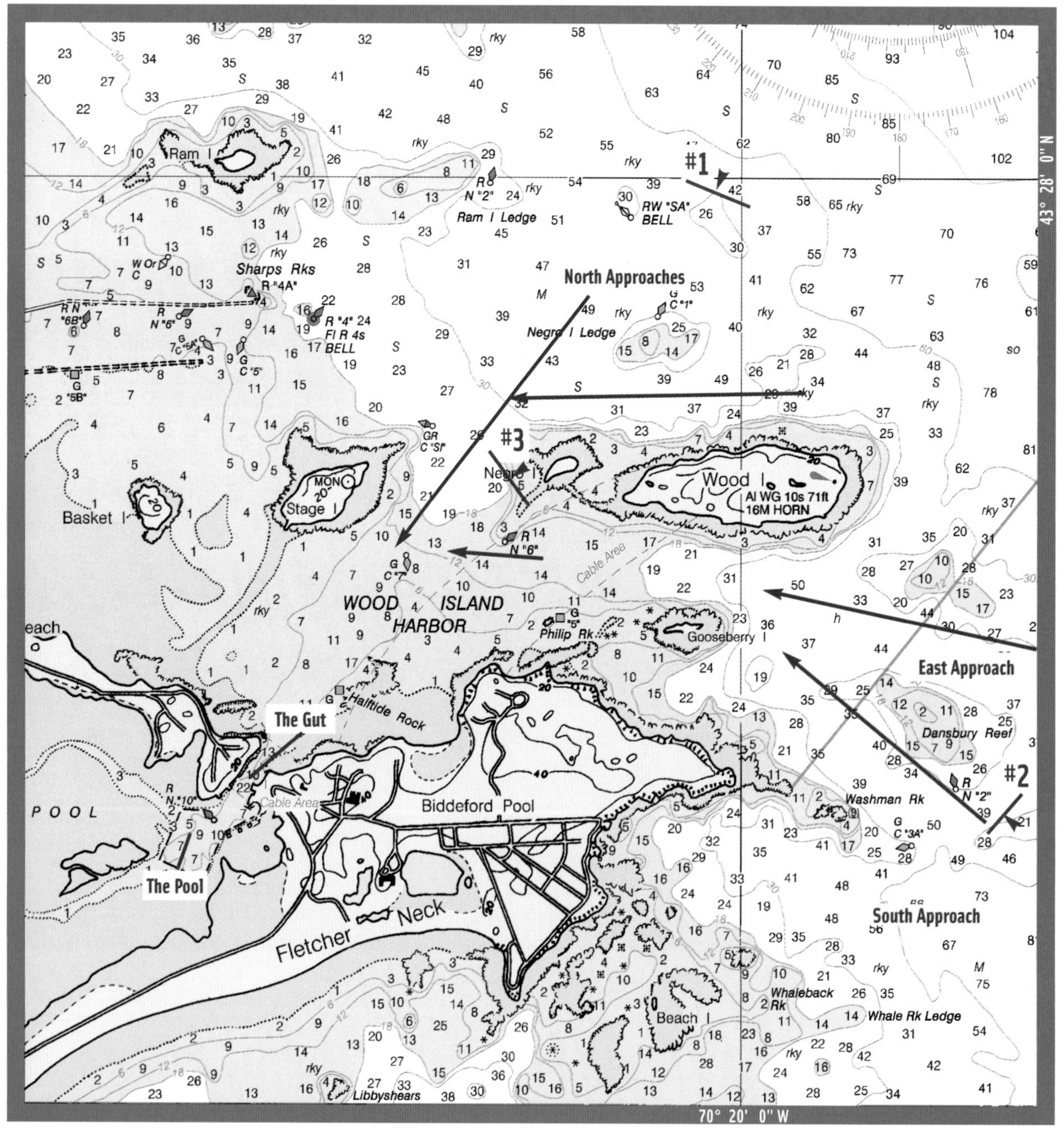

13287
12th ed., Sept. 04
NAD 83
Soundings in feet
1:20,000

hown on the chart, then turn west midway between ooseberry and Wood islands and leave nun "6" to star-oard before making the turn southwest around can "7." ou'll see The Gut, giving access to The Pool, across the arbor to the southwest. Wood Island Harbor is less rotected than The Pool but offers room for anchoring s well as mooring rentals from the Biddeford Pool acht Club. To proceed into The Pool, you must negotiate the strong ebb and flood through The Gut, keeping to the middle or slightly favoring the right side. Once inside, you'll find a lovely sheltered embayment that looks large at high tide but drains to almost nothing at all at low tide. Moorings crowd the navigable portion; do not venture beyond the mooring field. The yacht club may be able to find a mooring for you in The Pool, but don't count on it. There is no room to anchor.

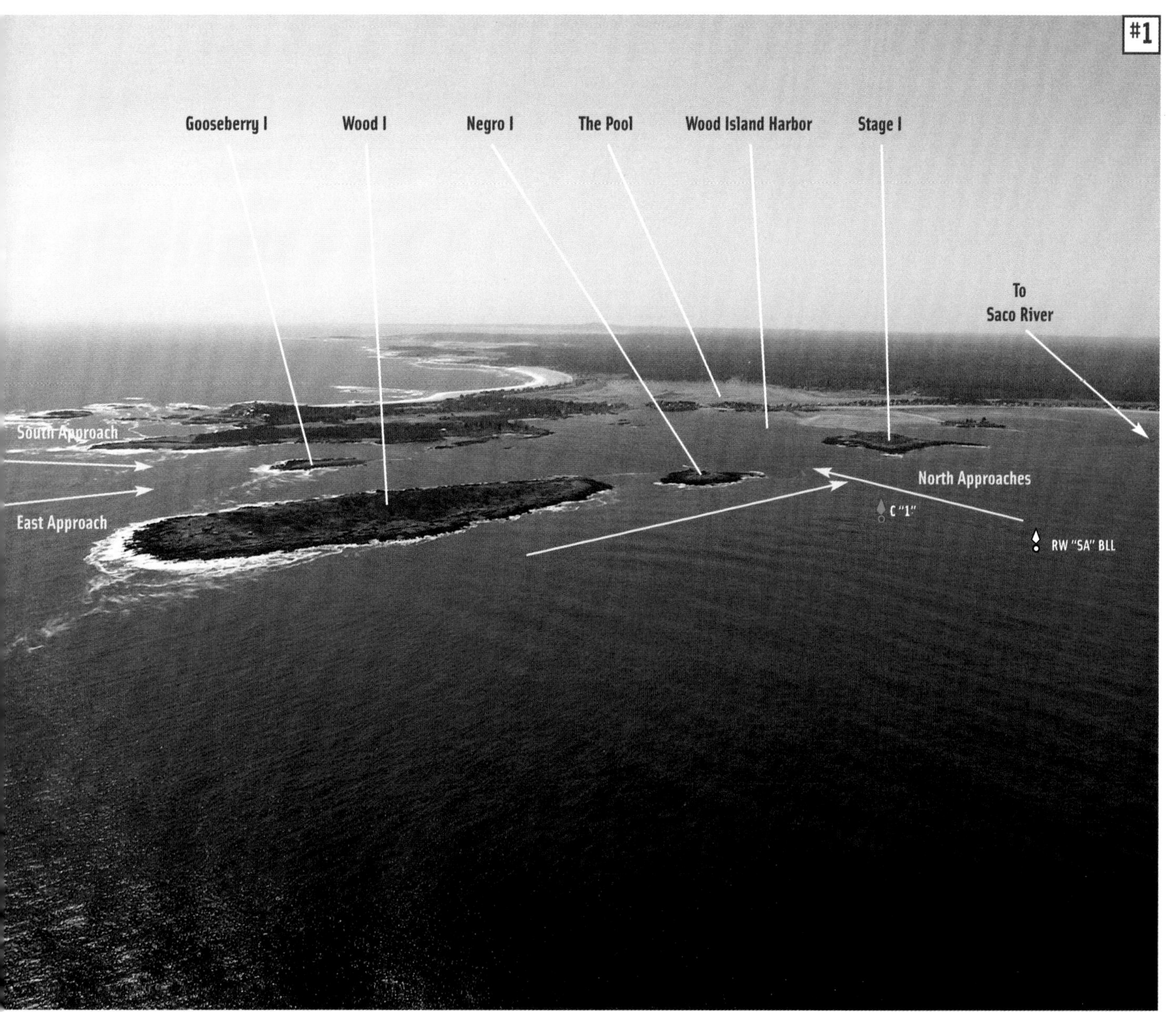

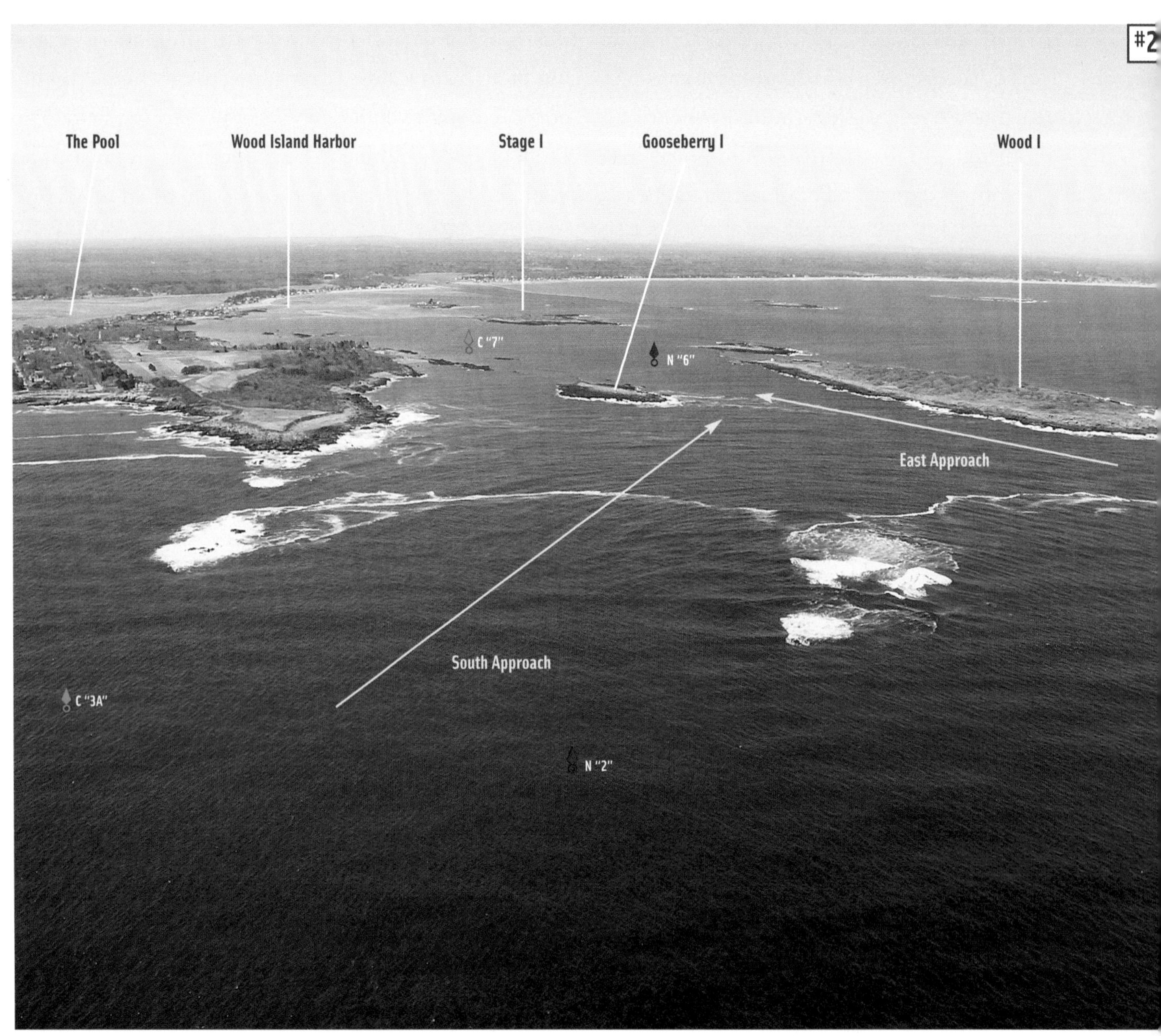
#2
The Pool
Wood Island Harbor
Stage I
Gooseberry I
Wood I
C "7"
N "6"
East Approach
South Approach
C "3A"
N "2"

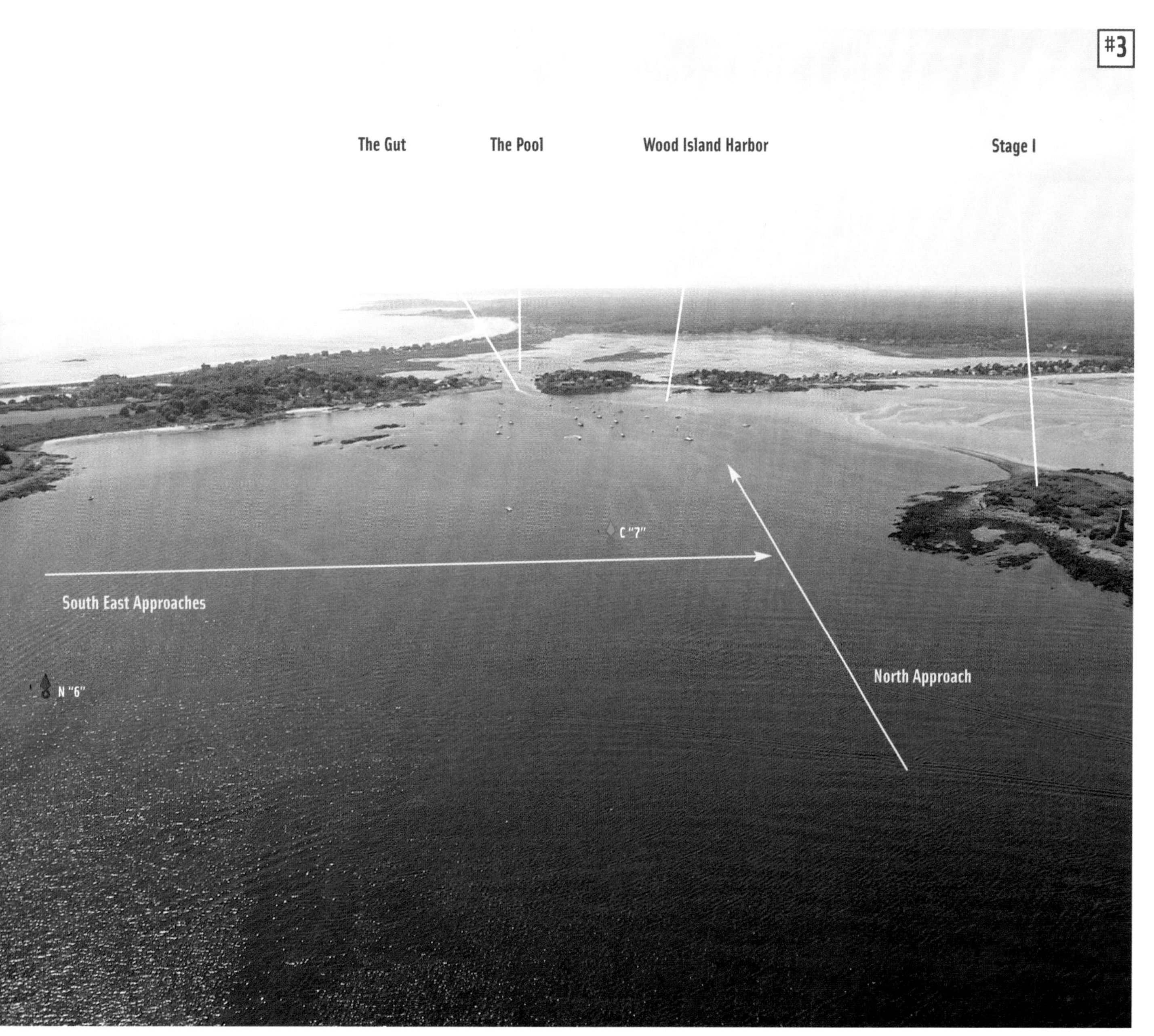
#3
The Gut
The Pool
Wood Island Harbor
Stage I
C "7"
South East Approaches
North Approach
N "6"

■ SACO RIVER ■

AS mentioned, the entrance to the Saco River can be seen from the northern approach to Wood Island Harbor. Leave nun "2" and flashing red bell buoy "4" to starboard, then continue west to pass between can "5" and red daybeacon "4A," which mark the submerged outer ends of the river entrance breakwaters. Continue down the centerline of these parallel breakwaters, respecting the cans and nuns on either side, to enter the Sacc River. The river is navigable for five miles, to head o tide at the twin mill towns of Biddeford and Saco. Th currents are moderate—no more than 2 or 3 knots— and the controlling depth is said to be 7 feet at low tide There are opportunities to anchor on either side, bu mooring rentals are spotty.

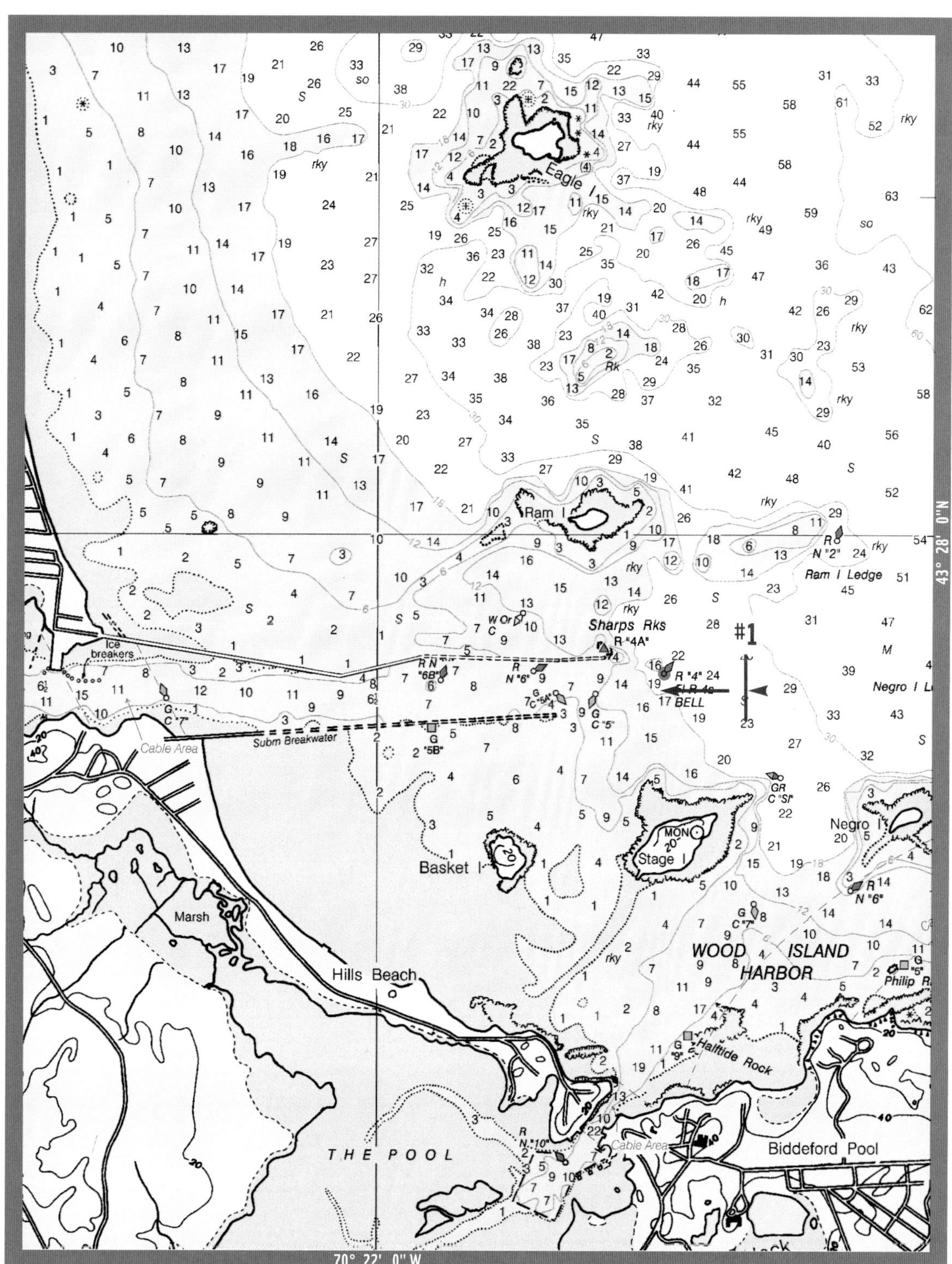

13287
12th ed., Sept. 04
NAD 83
Soundings in feet
1:20,000

■ SEAL COVE AND RICHMOND ISLAND HARBOR ■

SEAL Cove, off Cape Elizabeth, provides the visiting mariner with easy access from north or south. The protected bay forms a nearly perfect horseshoe, with ample opportunity for anchoring near the northern shore of Richmond Island, where the chart shows 9 or 10 feet of water at low tide. Depending on the sea conditions, you might also anchor just east of the sandbar and causeway between Cape Elizabeth and Richmond Island, though the sandy bottom there is not as secure. The northern shore of the cove is Crescent Beach, a state park, and picnicking on the shores of Richmond Island is also permitted. In an easterly wind you can make your way around the island to find shelter in Richmond Island Harbor.

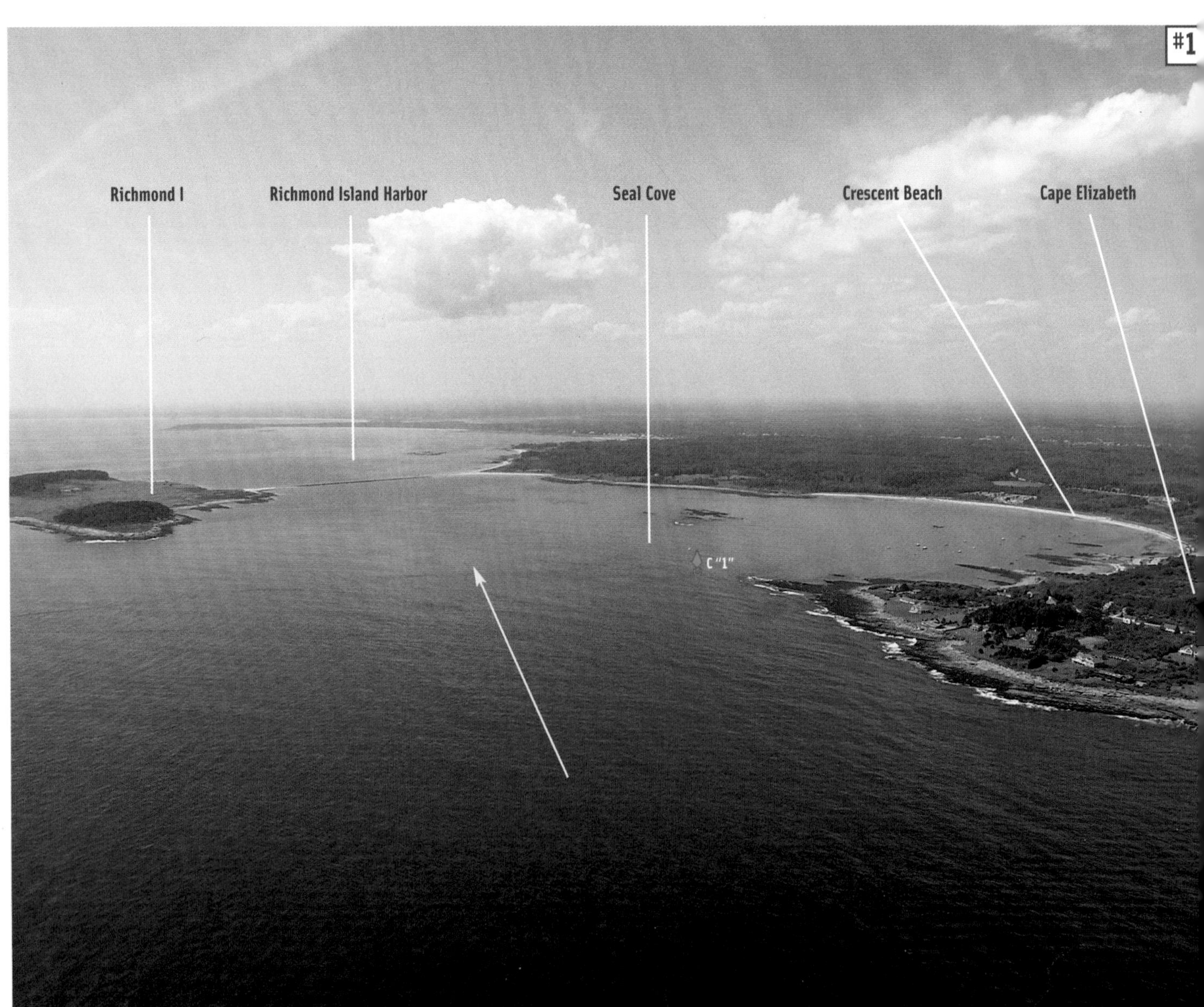

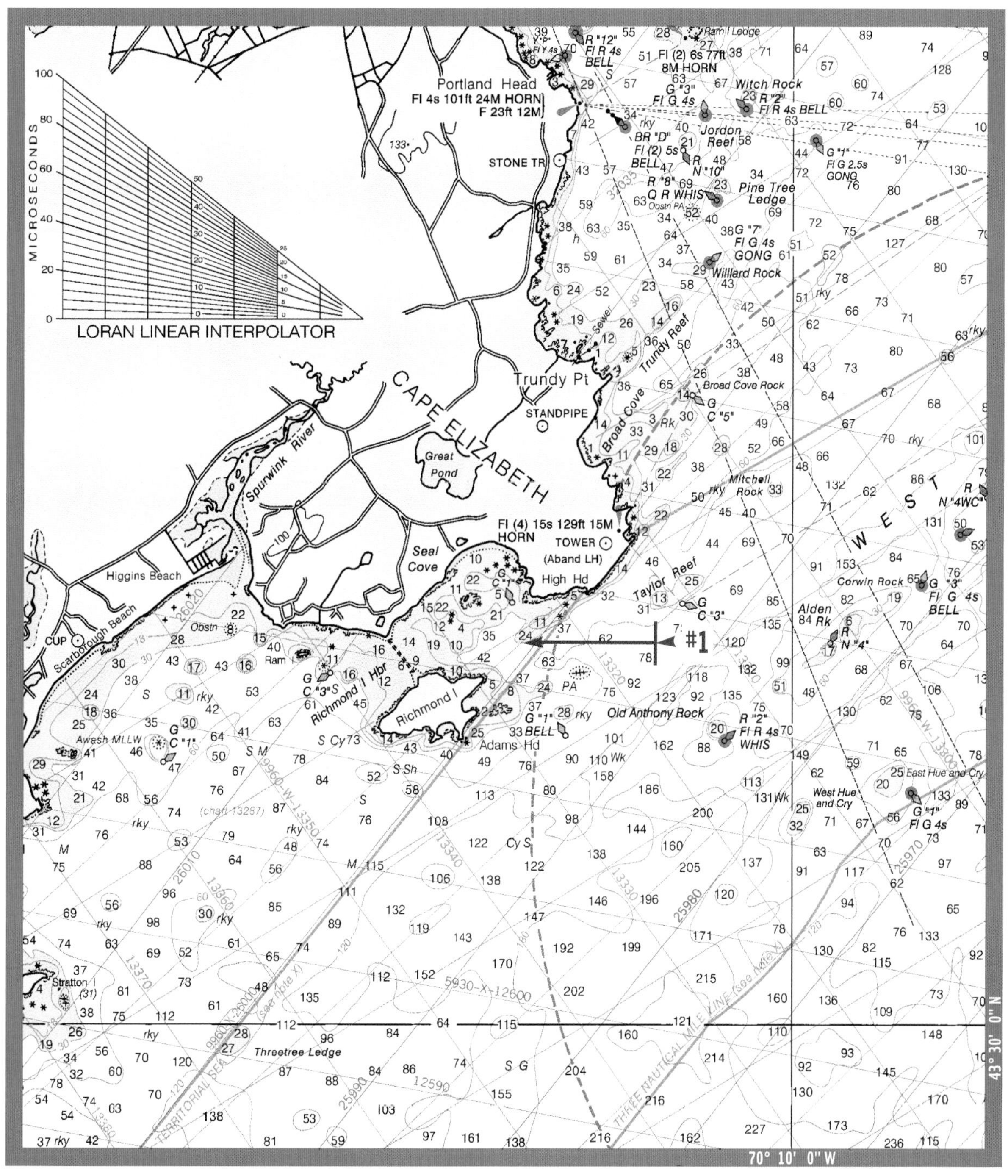

13288
41st ed., Sept. 04
NAD 83
Soundings in feet
1:80,000

REGION II

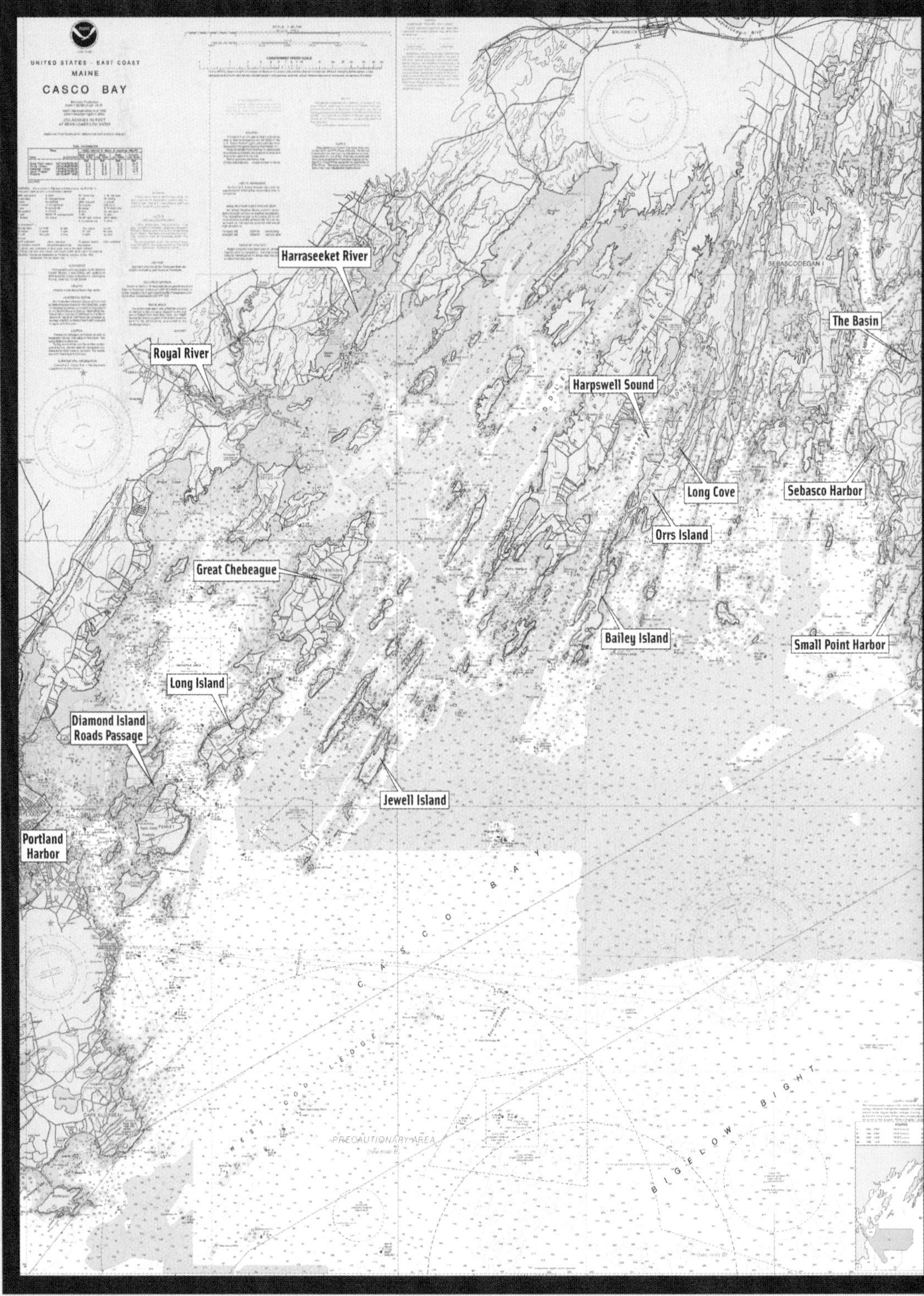

UNITED STATES - EAST COAST
MAINE
CASCO BAY
Harraseeket River
Royal River
The Basin
Harpswell Sound
Long Cove
Sebasco Harbor
Orrs Island
Great Chebeague
Bailey Island
Small Point Harbor
Long Island
Diamond Island Roads Passage
Jewell Island
Portland Harbor
PRECAUTIONARY AREA

CASCO BAY
—PORTLAND TO THE BASIN—

ooking north toward Long Island and Great Chebeague Island (page 56)

When Portland Head Light comes into view, the many advantages of Casco Bay come quickly o mind. Inside this stretch of water is every conceivable ruising pleasure. Hundreds of islands dot these vaters—so many, indeed, that they have been called ollectively the Calendar Islands, because it seems that here is an island for every day of the year. From this rofusion of island passages, to the city life just steps way from Portland's busy harbor, to the pristine solitude and hurricane-hole security of The Basin, tucked up the New Meadows River, there are enough wonderful places to explore to easily occupy a two-week cruise.

A sailor can think of Casco Bay as a transition between the hustle and bustle to the west and the wilder, more remote coastline and offshore islands to the east. When you're headed eastward, it's a place to test the anchor and become comfortable with the pace of things to come. Cooler winds and colder waters are just a day ahead.

■ PORTLAND HARBOR AND APPROACH ■

THE entrance to Portland Harbor can be readily seen as one approaches the centerline between Portland Head Light and the Ram Island Ledge Light. In front of you, depending on visibility, you'll see a large breakwater, with a short, white lighthouse (Spring Point Ledge Light) on the northeast end. More often than not, an oil tanker in the "parking lot" just beyond the breakwater will be visible. As you proceed into the Portland main channel, commercial activity will be apparent in every direction, day and night. As you make your way in, on your starboard side will be Cushing Island and to your port side ahead will be the neck of South Portland protruding out into the open bay. Northeast of Cushing Island, you'll see the historic homes on Peaks Island and to the northwest of Peaks Island, Fort Gorges sits, surrounded by water on all sides. Once you reach red nu "4" just southwest of the Civil War-era fort, a turn to th west and then southwest will take you directly to Portland's newly revitalized Old Port area. To the northeas of Fort Gorges lies an almost endless area of exploration. Great Diamond Island, Peaks Island, Long Island, and numerous coves provide endless opportunities. There is a wonderful passageway to the east sid of Fort Gorges, leading to a channel that runs up th east side of Little Diamond and Great Diamond islands All of these vibrant island communities are served b numerous ferries from Portland on a daily basis.

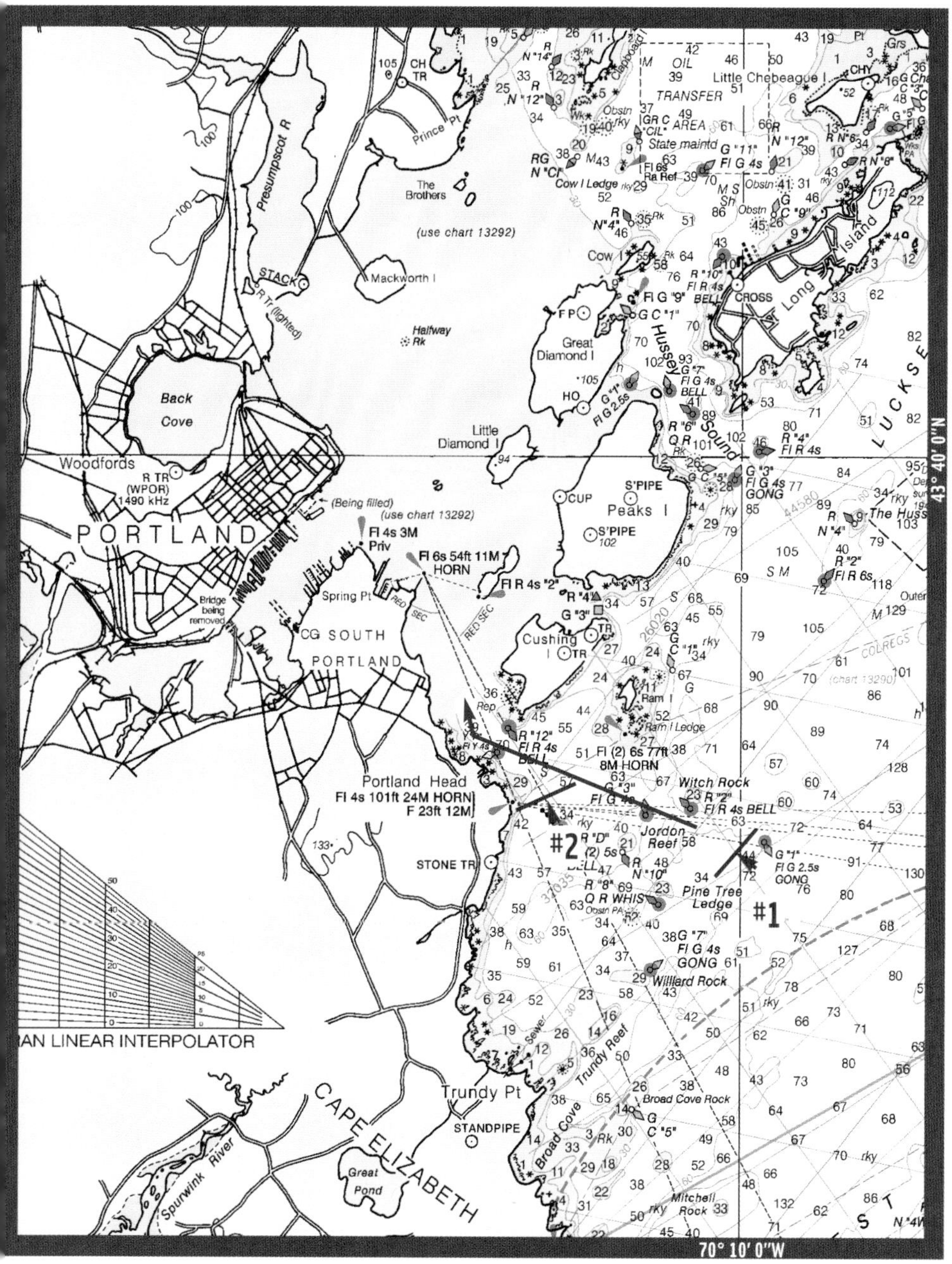

13288
41st ed., Sept. 04
NAD 83
Soundings in feet
1:80,000

#3
South Portland
Portland
Fish Point
G "5"
G "3"
G "1"
R "4"
Fort Gorges

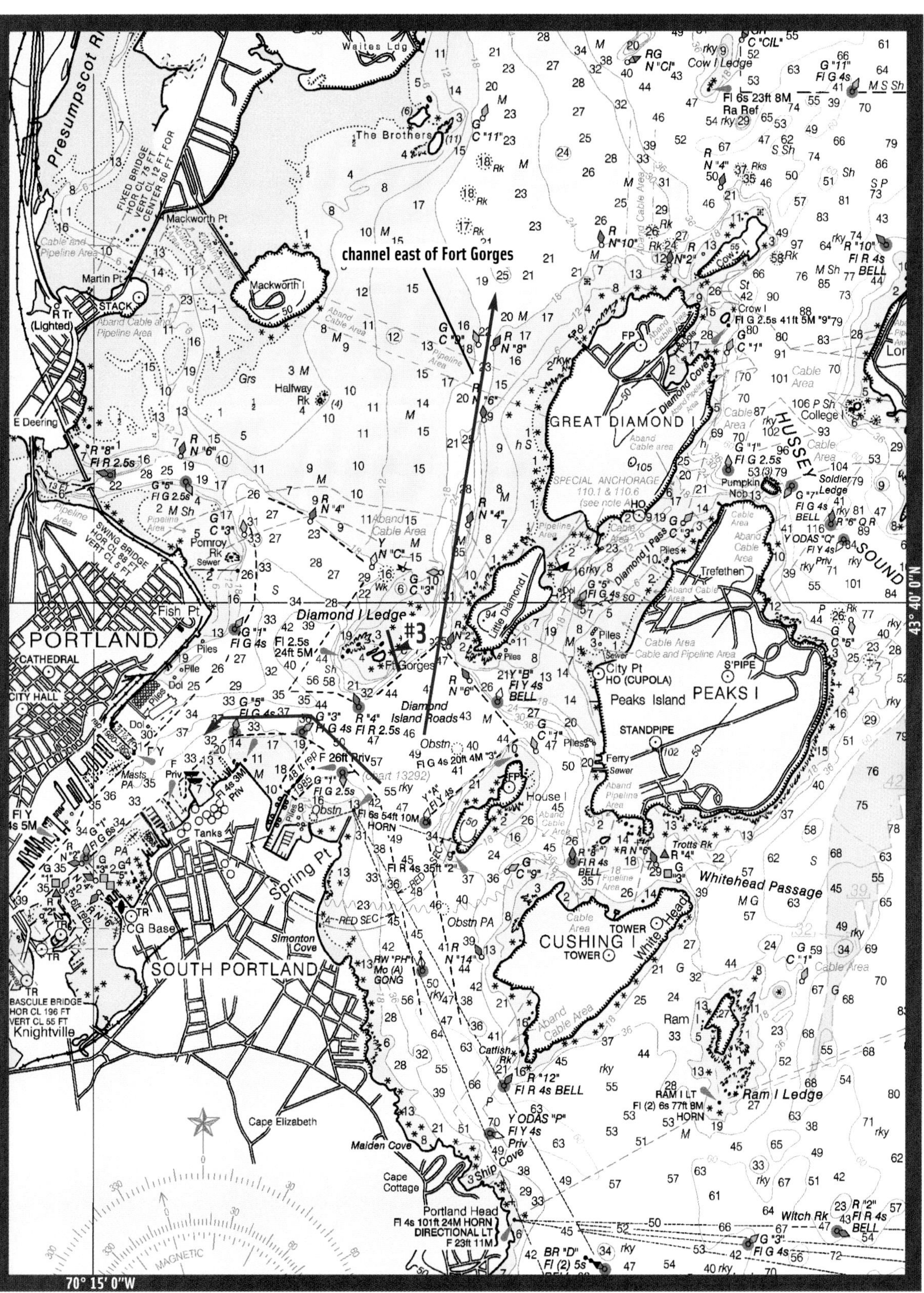

13290
36th ed., July 05
NAD 83
Soundings in feet
1:40,000

■ DIAMOND ISLAND ROADS PASSAGE ■

THE approach to Diamond Island Roads and Diamond Island Passage begins off Portland Head Light. From here proceed on a northerly heading keeping red bell buoy "12" southwest of Cushing Island to starboard. Once past Cushing Island, you can either use the passage between Cushing Island and House Island or continue northwest of House to Diamond Island Roads. Either way, you'll end up at the flashing yellow bell buoy "B" midway between House Island and Little Diamond Island. From the bell, you'll head northeast through Diamond Island Passage. Once through Diamond Island Passage, you'll enter Hussey Sound and can choose any number of passageways in and around Great Diamond Island, Long Island, and Great Chebeague Island.

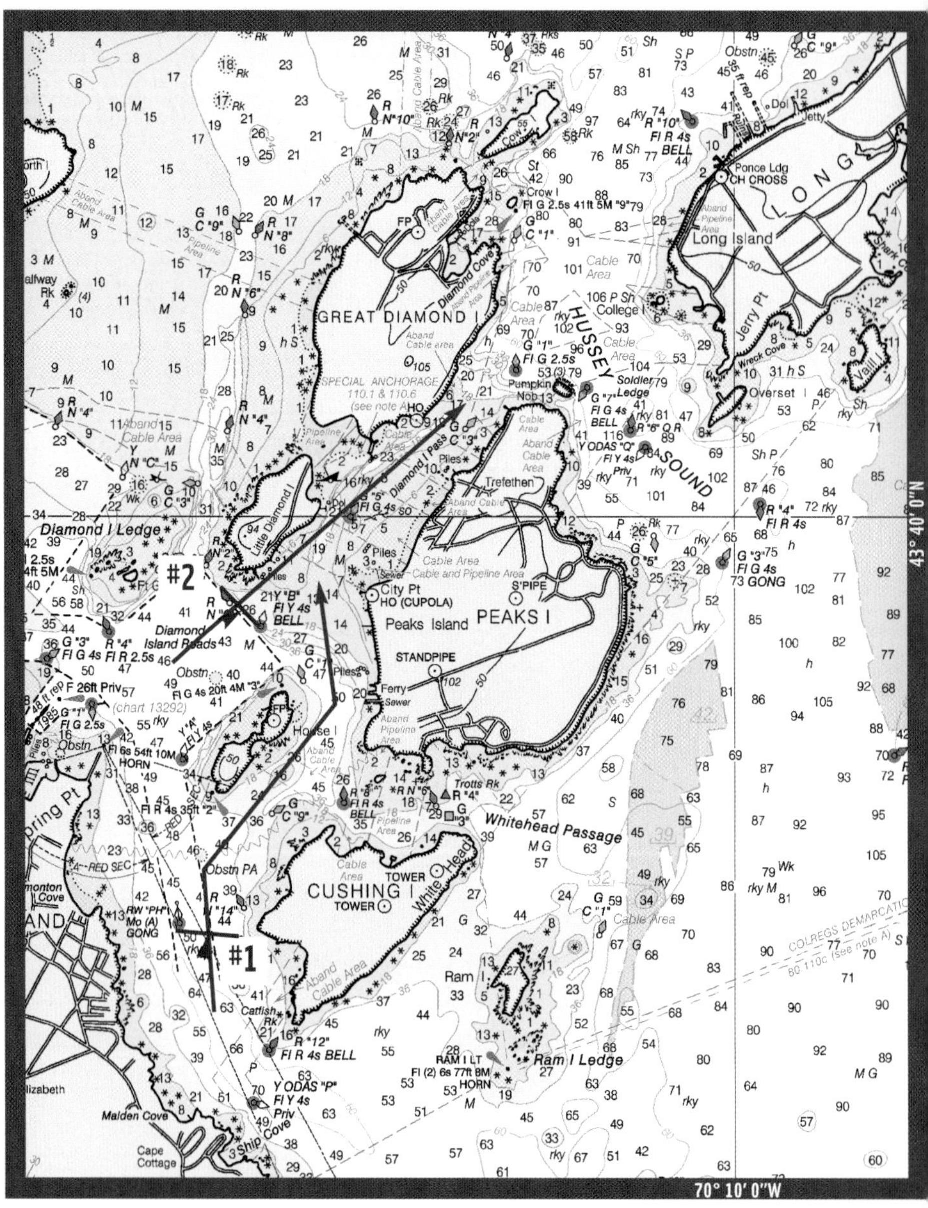

13290
36th ed., July 05
NAD 83
Soundings in feet
1:40,000

#1

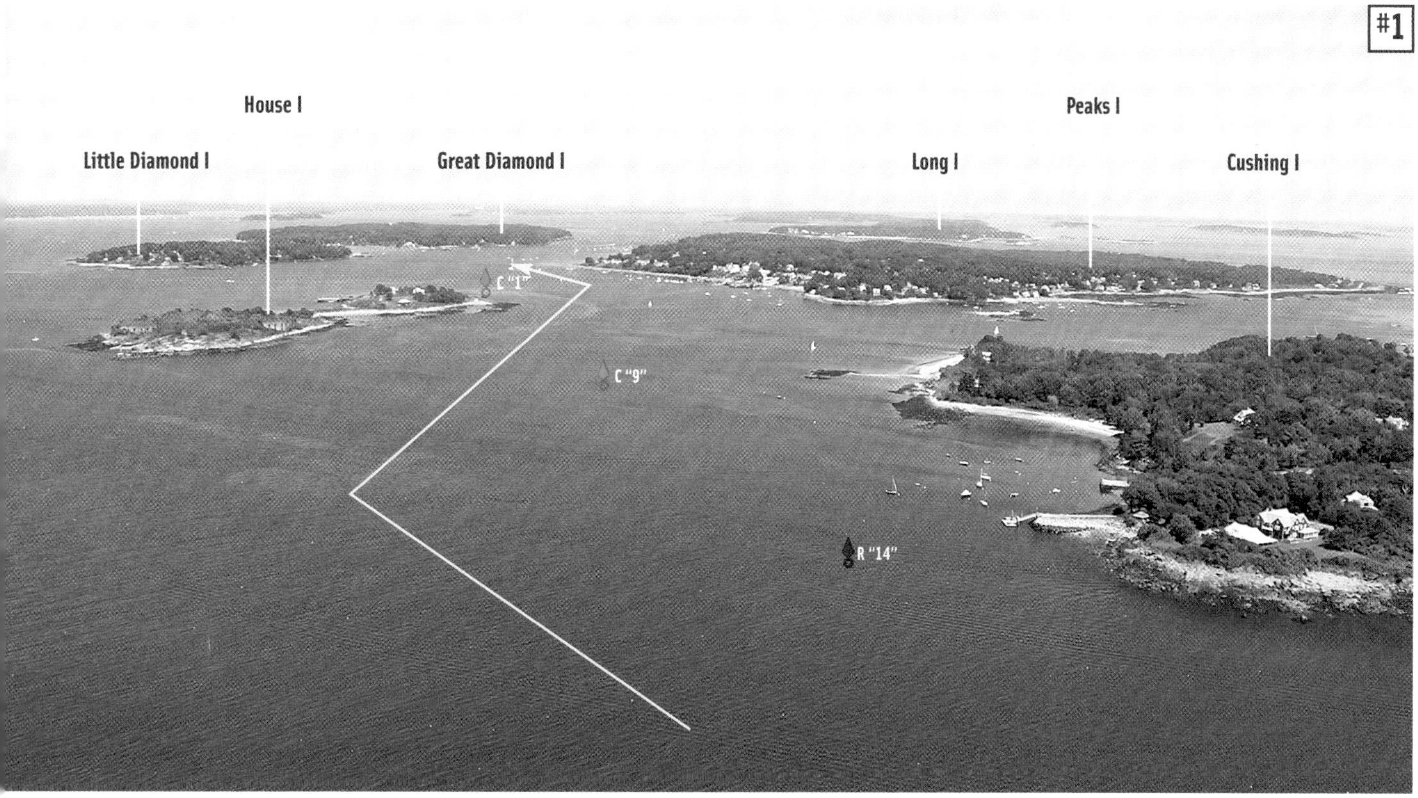

House I
Peaks I
Little Diamond I
Great Diamond I
Long I
Cushing I
C "1"
C "9"
R "14"

#2

Long I
Great Diamond I
Little Diamond I
Peaks I
C "3"
G "5"
Y "B"
N "6"

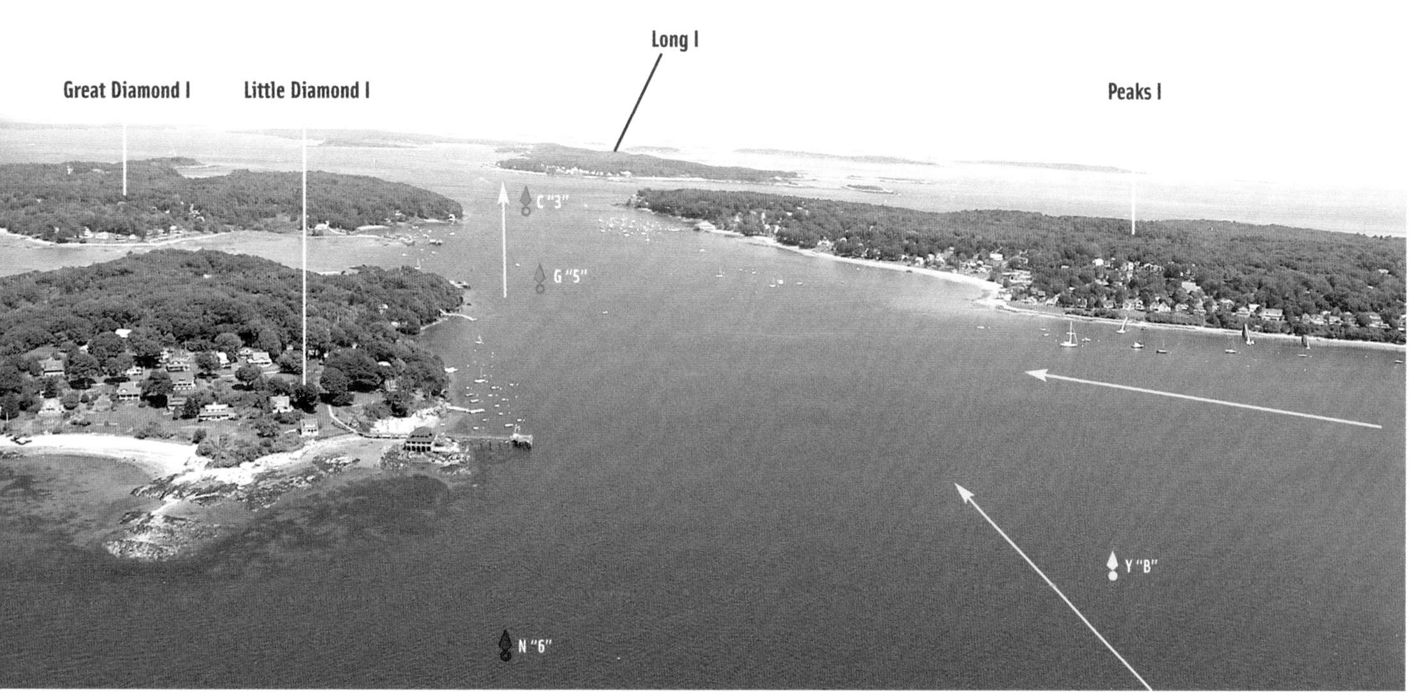

■ LONG ISLAND AND GREAT CHEBEAGUE ■

FROM Luckse Sound, which is southeast of Long Island, a pretty little passageway exists between Long and Great Chebeague islands. The entrance is denoted by the flashing red bell buoy "2" off Hope Island. From the bell, head north to red nun "2" off Deer Point and continue in to Chandler Cove, on the southwestern side of Great Chebeague Island. The western exit of the horseshoe shaped passageway is between Little Chebeague and Long Island.

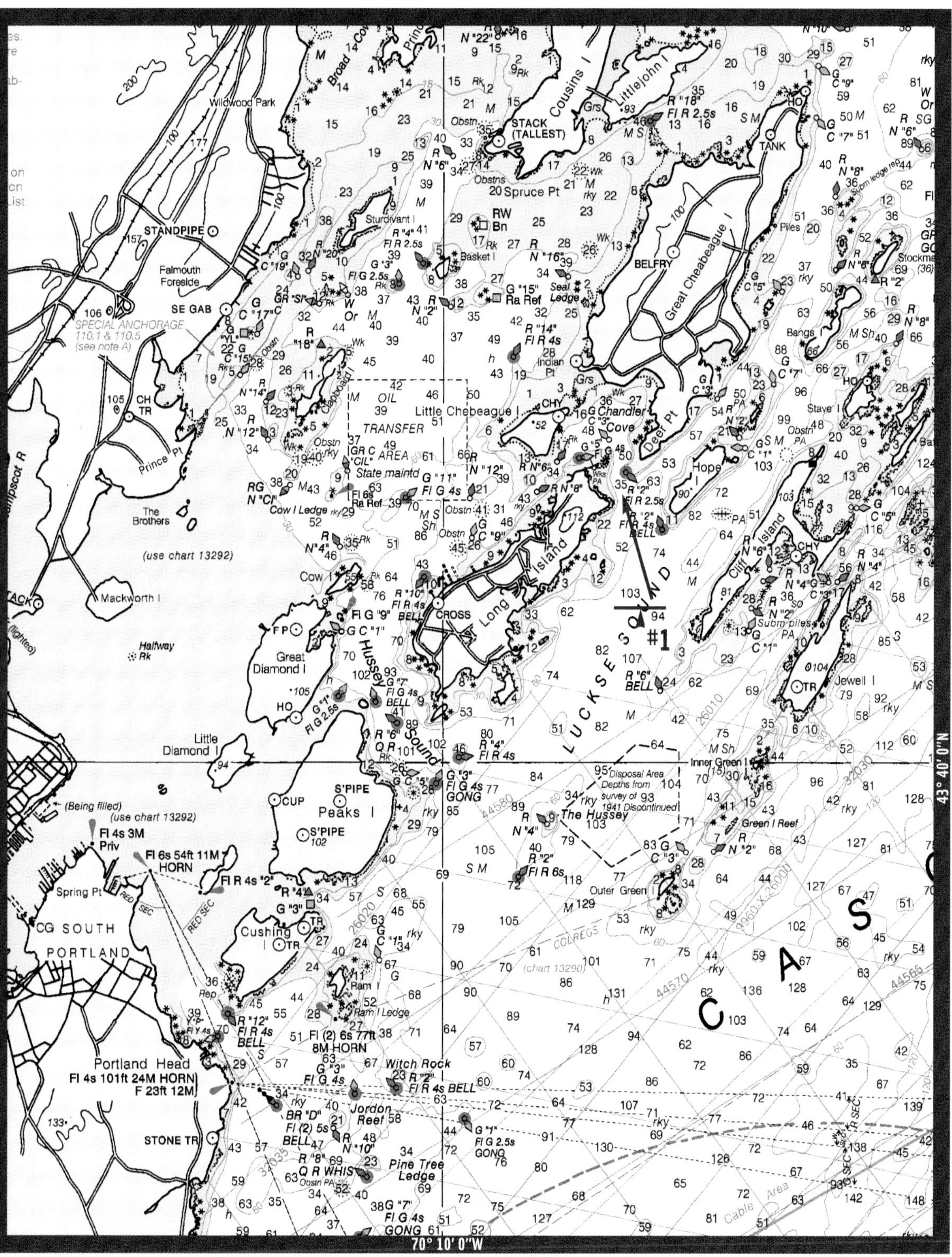

13288
41st ed., Sep. 04
NAD 83
Soundings in feet
1:80,000

▪ JEWELL ISLAND ▪

BECAUSE Jewell Island is a state park and one of the most accessible islands in Casco Bay, it also shares the distinction of being one of the most visited overnight anchorages for boats of all kinds, shapes, and descriptions. Approach from the open ocean well to the east-southeast. On a foggy day, pay particular attention to your navigation, as many experienced boaters will attest to missing the entrance to Jewell Island altogether and landing at Cliff Island by mistake. From the open water, you will see Halfway Rock with its 77-foot tower, horn, and flashing with red lights. Heading north and a bit west from Halfway Rock will place you in close proximity to Jewell Island's northeast tip. Northeast of Jewel Island, there are numerous rocks, ledges and low islets. You can avoid them by first finding Jewell's high northeast point, with Cliff Island's higher bold shore clearly visible just beyond to the northwest. Beyond Jewell's northeast end, turn immediately to port hugging the shore to the southwest and proceeding into the anchorage. In the summer, you'll know you've arrived because there will be numerous boats anchored well in advance of your arrival. Luckily, ample anchorage is available in the outer areas of this cove. The island is maintained with a caretaker courtesy of the Maine Island Trail Association. Touring the island will reveal many of its secrets including the remnants of an old hotel and concrete towers that were used to watch for enemy submarines during World War II.

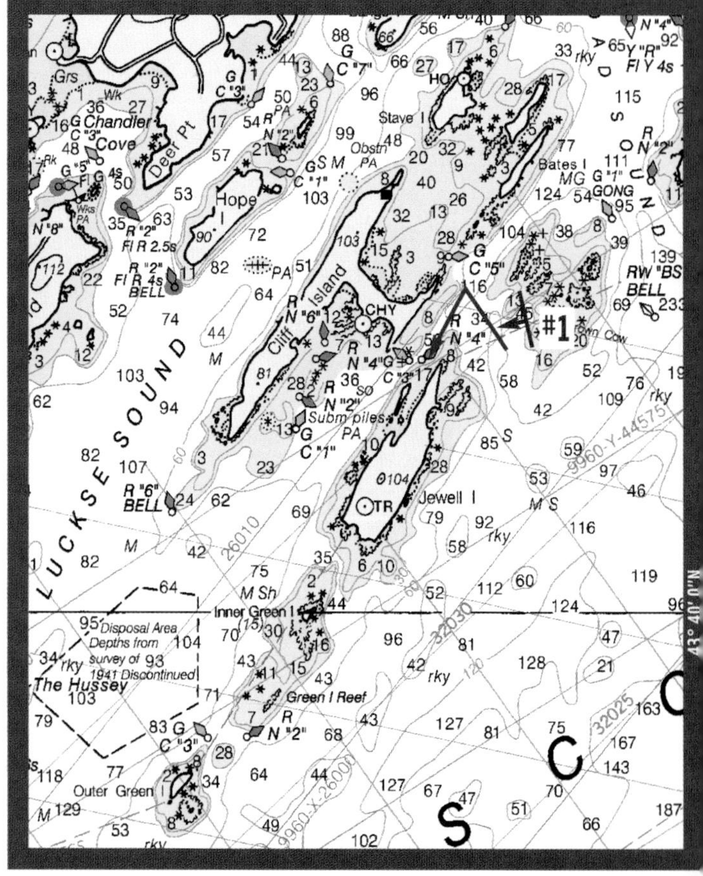

13288
41st ed., Sep. 04
NAD 83
Soundings in feet
1:80,000

#1
Jewell I
Cliff I
N "4"
C "3"

■ ROYAL RIVER ■

THE Royal River is best entered from the east side of Great Chebeague Island. As you proceed up the channel to the Royal River, you'll be keeping Littlejohn Island and its sister, Cousins Island, well to your port side. Visible from the northeastern point of Great Chebeague wi be the very prominent power plant stack on Cousins Islan to your west. To the north in front of you will be Littl Moshier Island, which, at low tide, is connected to Moshie

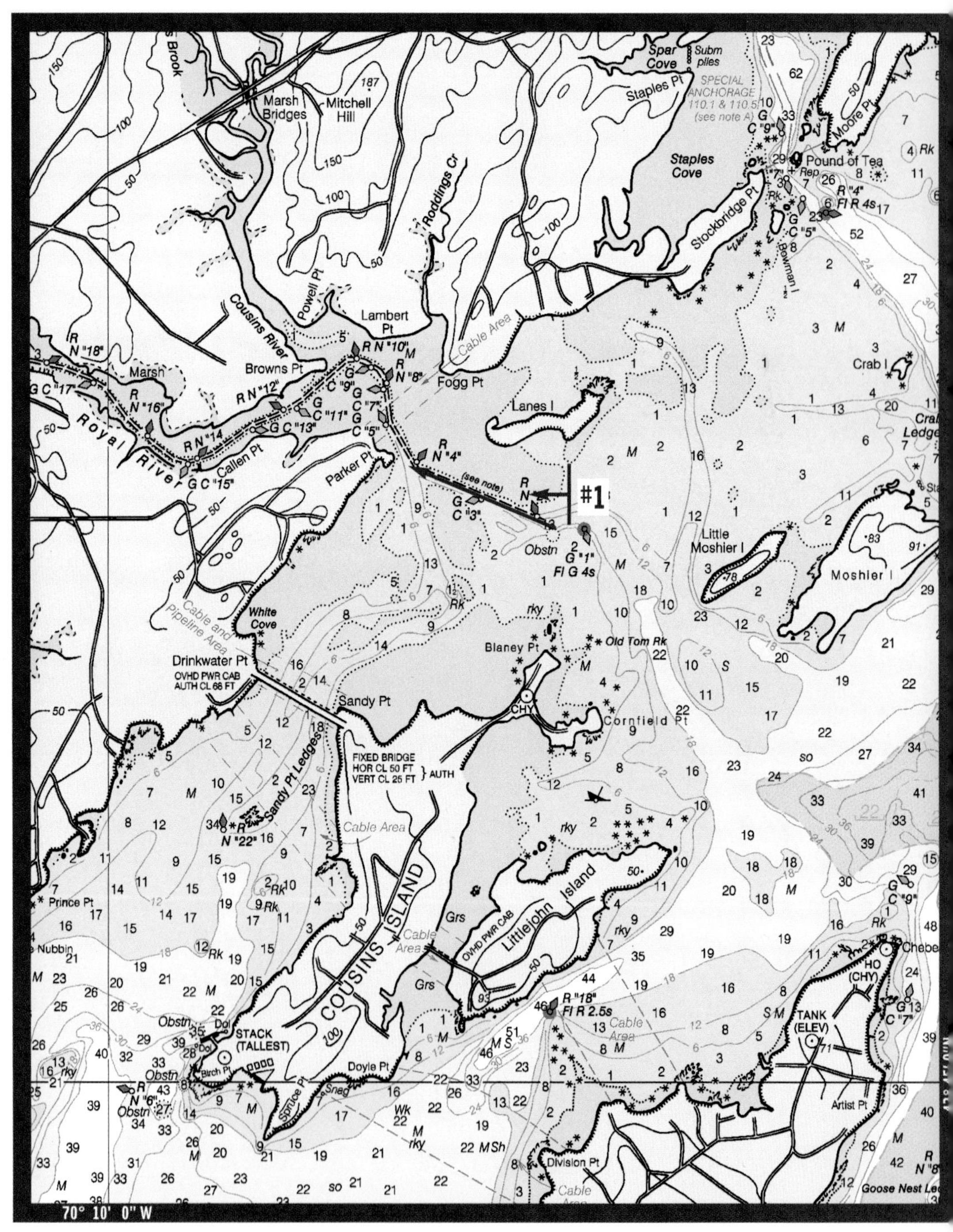

13290
36th ed., July 05
NAD 83
Soundings in feet
1:40,000

sland. Maintain a heading up the centerline between ittle Moshier and Cousins islands. Look for lighted reen can "1" which marks the entrance to the well-uoyed river. As you approach the mouth of the Royal River, begin looking for numerous, small red and green uoys, in addition to the Coast Guard buoys. The smaller, seasonal buoys are maintained by the town of Yarmouth. They will help you stay in the proper channel which at the beginning of the Royal River includes a sharp turn to port (the west-southwest). The Royal River entrance should be approached in clear conditions because of its many false turns.

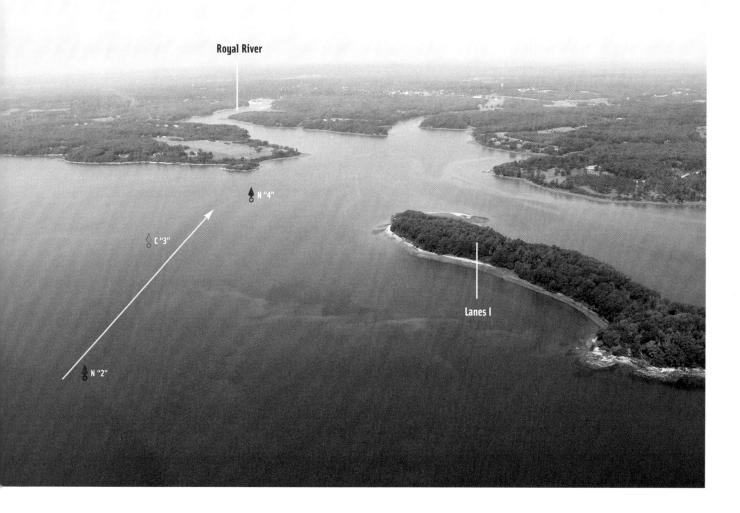

■ HARRASEEKET RIVER ■

TO enter the Harraseeket River from the south and anchor off the community of South Freeport, approach from the east side of Great Chebeague, keeping Moshier Island on your port side, and follow the channel markers into the main entrance. Be careful to stay west of Pound of Tea even though you may see boat taking a well-known but unmarked shortcut east of i Beyond Stockbridge Point, turn north and a bit east int the Harraseeket River. South Freeport offers numerou services and ample protection.

13290
36th ed., July 05
NAD 83
Soundings in feet
1:40,000

■ HARPSWELL SOUND APPROACH ■

HARPSWELL Sound is approached from the south by leaving the Little Mark Island Monument Light to the port side and the red gong "8" southwest of Turnip Island Ledge to starboard. From here, head northeast to proceed up Merriconeag Sound and to Harpswel Sound beyond. Obstructions in both sounds are wel marked by buoys.

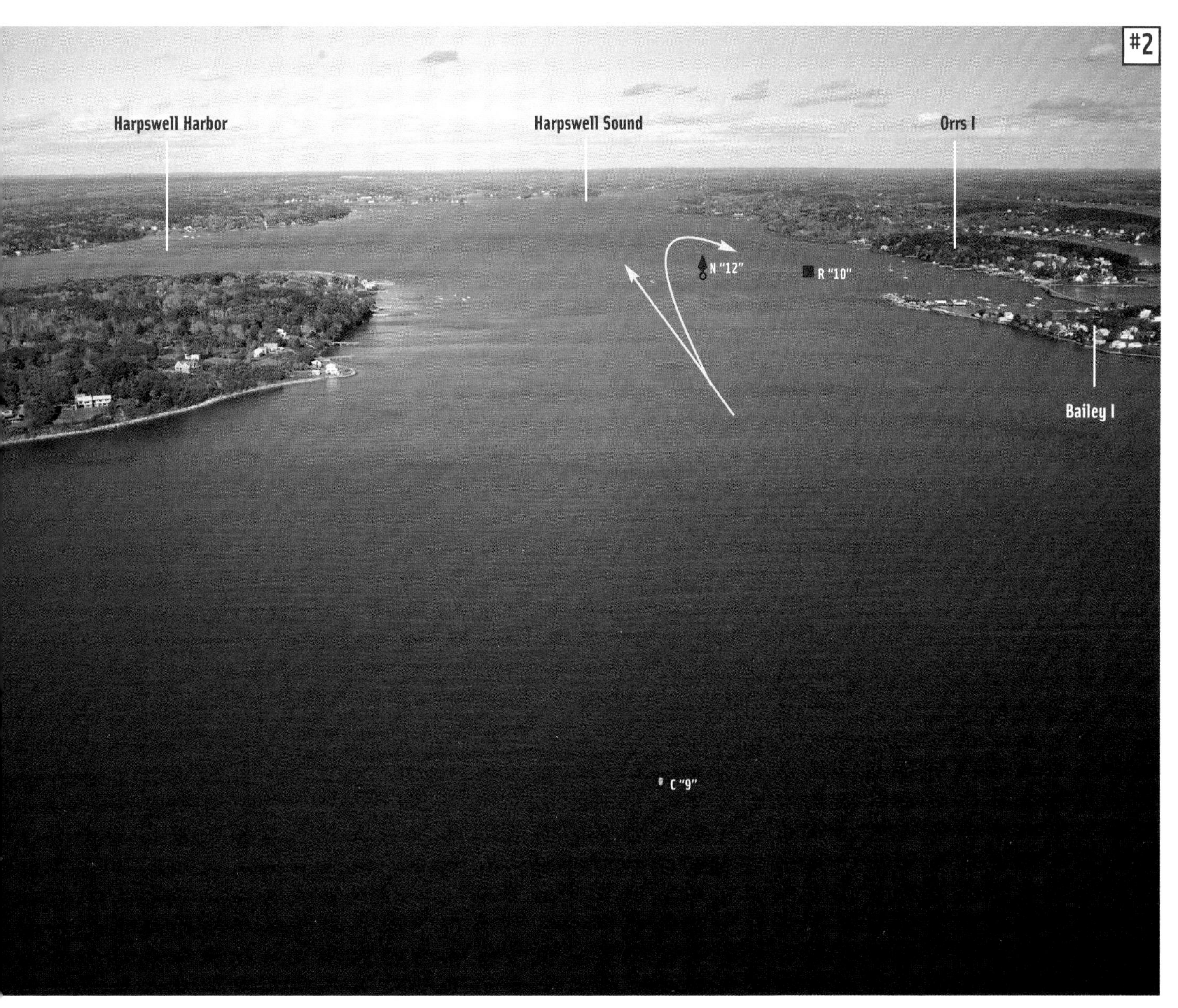
#2
Harpswell Harbor
Harpswell Sound
Orrs I
N "12"
R "10"
Bailey I
C "9"

■ Bailey Island and Orrs Island

Merriconeag and Harpswell sounds have a number of wonderful coves for the mariner. As you enter Merriconeag Sound, you'll see two submarine observation towers, which are on the southern tip of Bailey Island. A lighted green buoy "1" marks the entrance to Mackerel Cove. Inside you'll find a working harbor with limited services for the mariner. For the yachtsman in transit, the better alternative is a bit farther northeast in a little cove tucked near the causeway connecting Baile Island to Orrs Island. To enter the anchorage, procee northeast to just beyond a red spindle "10" and red nu buoy "12" northeast of Cox Ledge, and go around an to the east of them. Then proceed southwest up th cove. There are moorings, some limited services and restaurant specializing in lobster dinners.

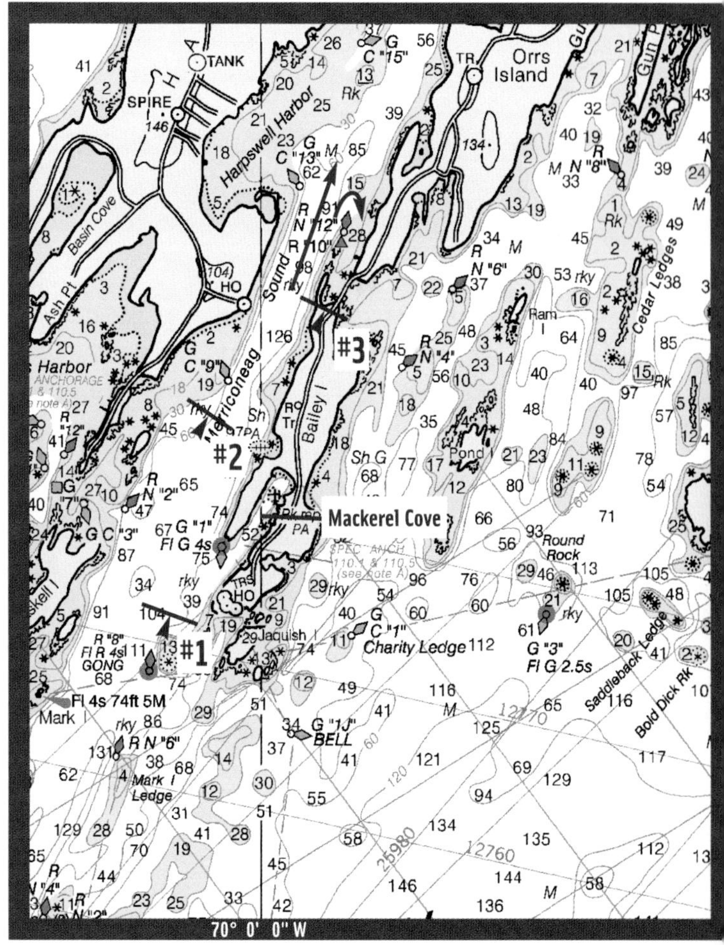

13288
41st ed., Sep. 04
NAD 83
Soundings in feet
1:80,000

#3

■ LONG COVE

For a secluded gunkhole, try Long Cove. Continue northeast up Harpswell Sound toward the northern end of Orrs Island. Long Cove is remote and beautiful with tall evergreens, but its entrance demands respect and careful attention as you enter. On a northeasterly course, stick to the centerline of Harpswell Sound until the steep shore of High Head appears dead ahead. As you continue up Harpswell Sound, keep Wyer Island well to starboard. Just beyond High Head to port, you'll see Dogs Head to starboard. It represents the northern end of Orrs Island. Once you've identified the island o Dogs Head, steer to just north of it and, with it abeam turn to starboard, making a gentle arc 180 degrees int the cove, giving a good berth to outcroppings of rock on each side. Keep to the centerline at first as you pro ceed up the cove, but once inside, favor the eastern side The water at the entrance is 10–14 feet deep, but as you go further it drops to 8–9 feet. Once inside, you'll fee you're in your own world surrounded by pure beauty.

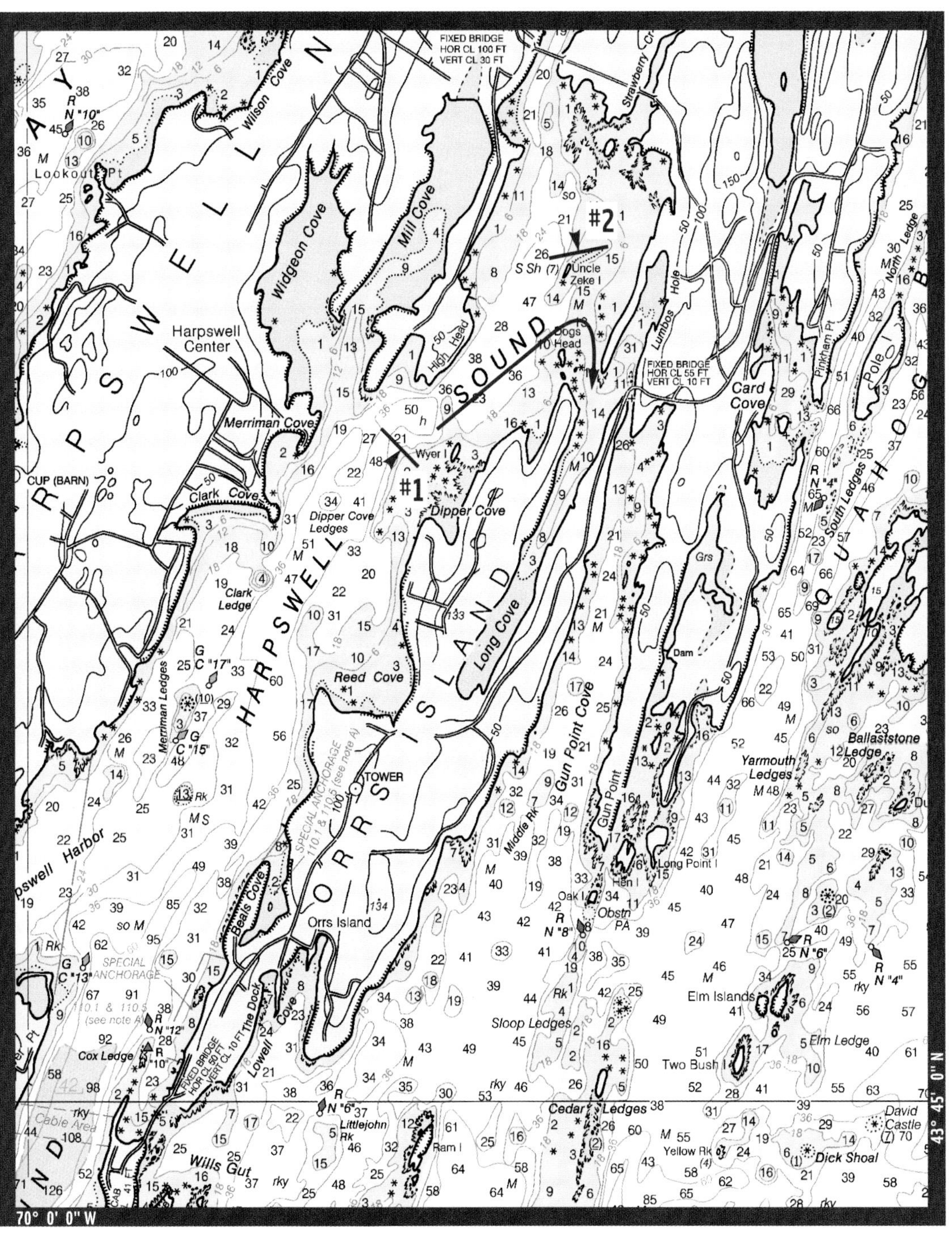

13290
36th ed., July 05
NAD 83
Soundings in feet
1:40,000

■ EASTERN CASCO BAY ■

EAST of Orrs and Bailey Island, Casco Bay becomes a bit more free of boat traffic and somewhat more difficult to navigate. But the harbors and gunkholes are worth the effort. Sebasco Harbor, The Basin and others are just some of what careful mariners will be happy to find inshore of high, uninhabited Mark Island.

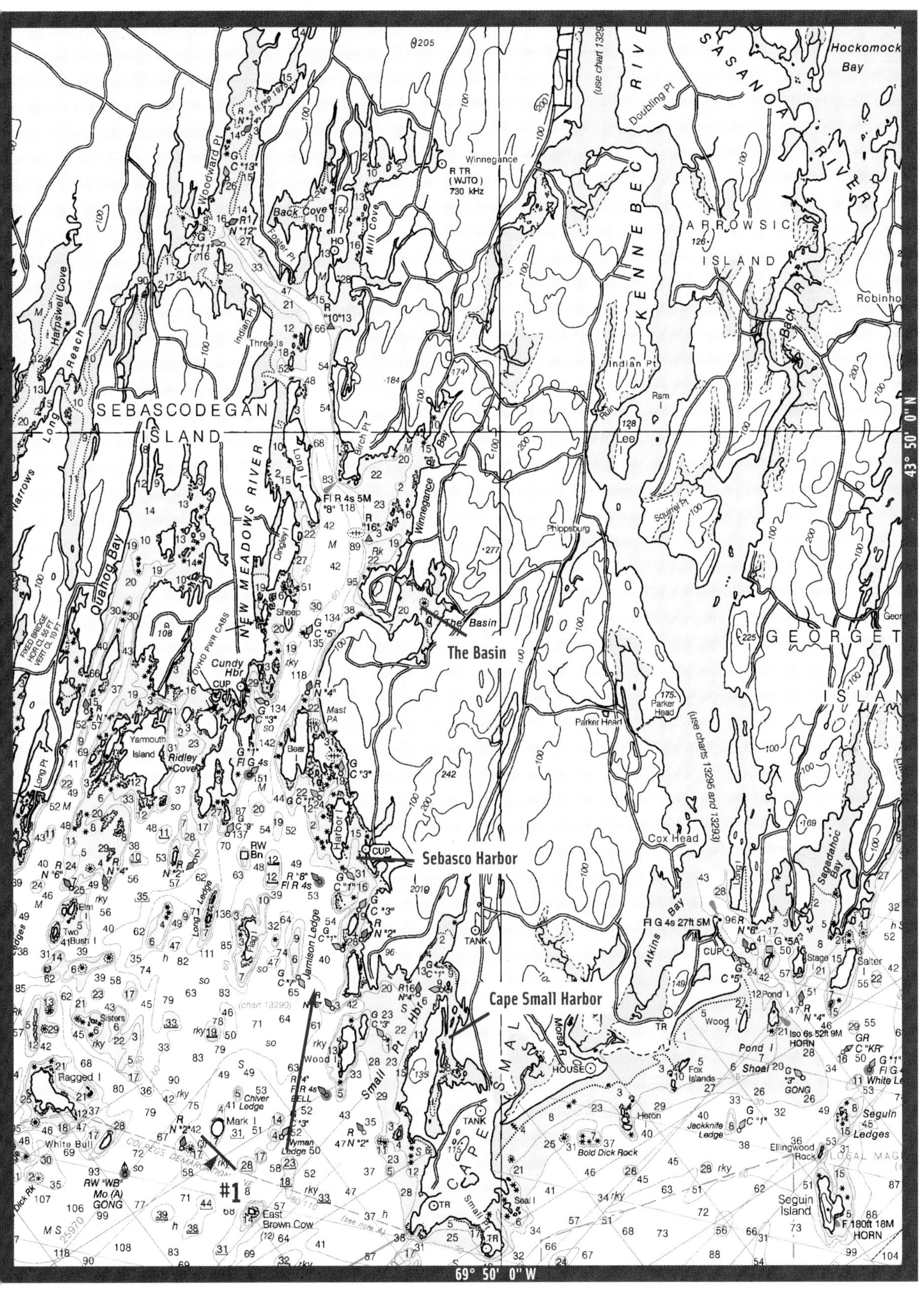

13288
41st ed., Sep. 04
NAD 83
Soundings in feet
1:80,000

■ Small Point Harbor and Cape Small Harbor

The entrance of Small Point Harbor is marked by red nun "2" off Gooseberry Island Ledge and the large red bell buoy "4" south of Wood Island. Splitting the distance between the two provides a midpoint for the entrance. Proceed along the harbor's centerline until you see the green can "3" about two thirds of the way up Small Point Harbor. Be careful to keep can "3" on your port side as it marks a shoal that will be visible only at the lowest tide. Continue up the centerline and you'll see red nun "4" which must be maintained on your starboard side. Once clearing it, begin adjusting the cours to aim at the center of the white sandy beach east of Fla Point. Approach slowly and during high tide, staying north of Goose Rock. Make a gentle turn up the centerline east of Goose Rock to Cape Small Harbor. Onc inside, the lobster boats and their moorings will mar the deep water. Continue up this wonderful but ver challenging harbor. Be careful of the shoals when yo anchor.

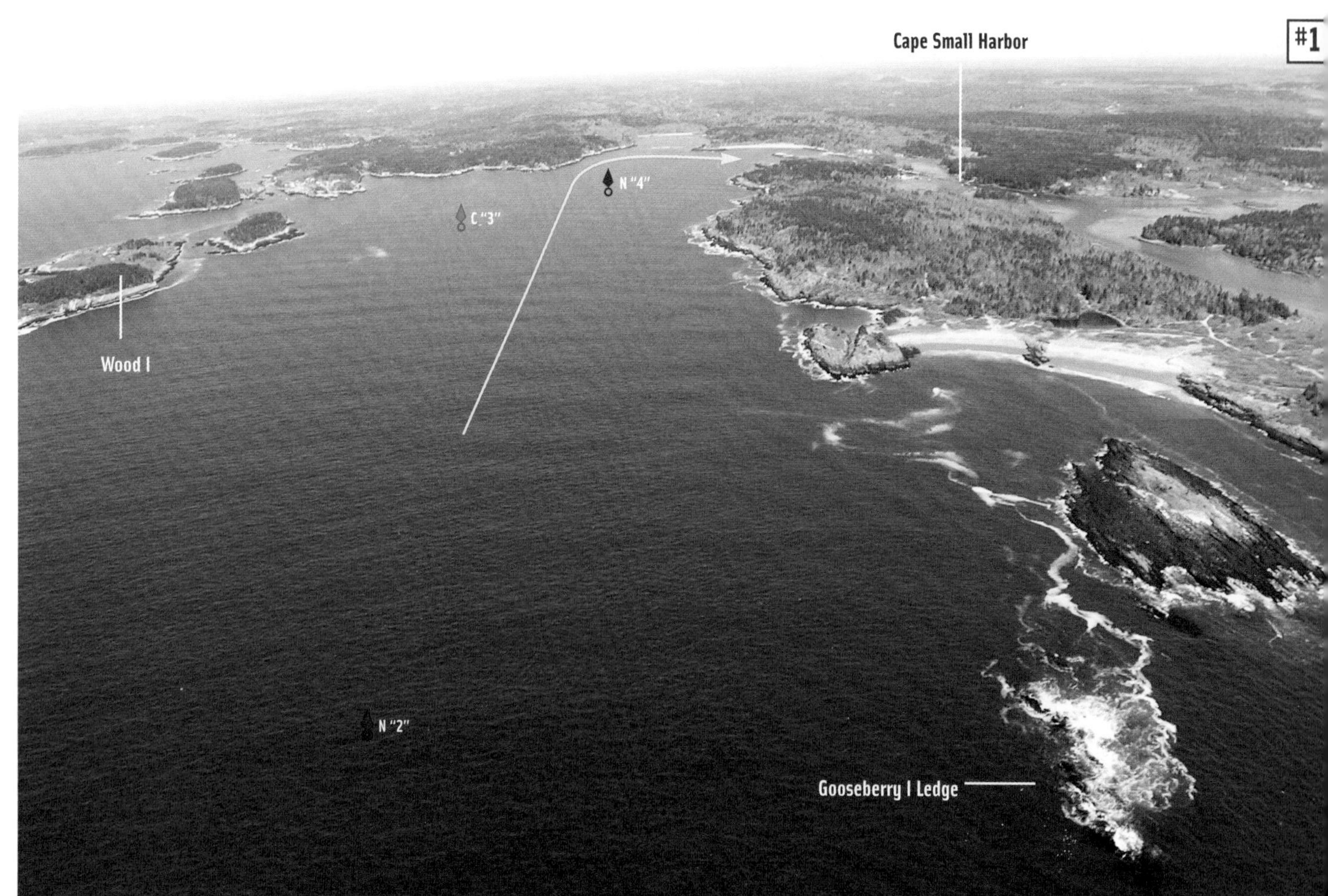

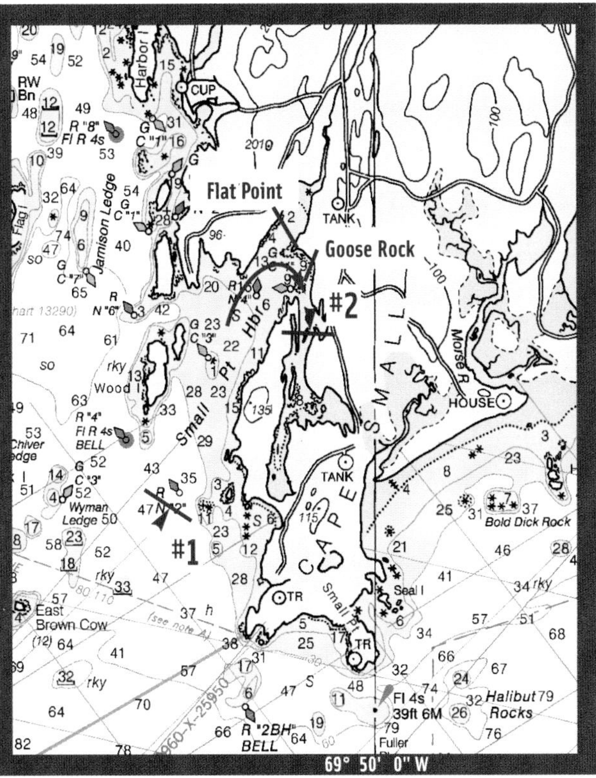

13288
41st ed., Sep. 04
NAD 83
Soundings in feet
1:80,000

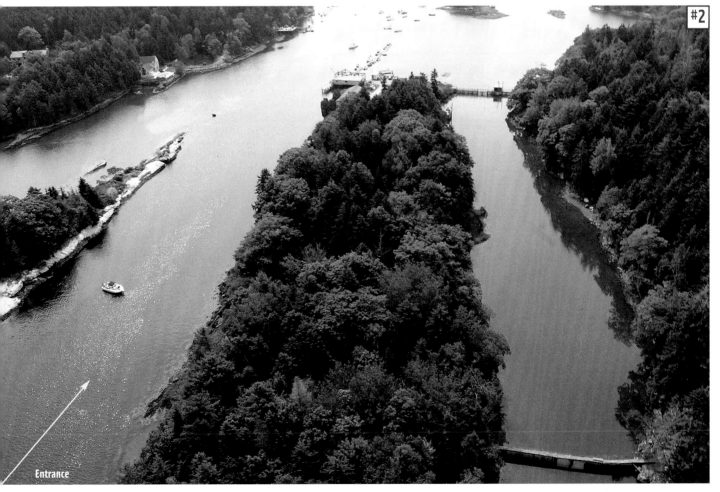

■ Sebasco Harbor

Sebasco Harbor is one of Casco Bay's most convenient harbors; it has a wide-open entrance, lots of moorings available, and numerous shoreside amenities at Sebasco Harbor Resort. In the event that no moorings are available, there is anchorage in mid-harbor. Sebasco harbor is located east of Harbor Island in the New Meadows River and easily recognized by the resort facilities and its lighthouse that resembles a tiered birthday cake.

#1

#2

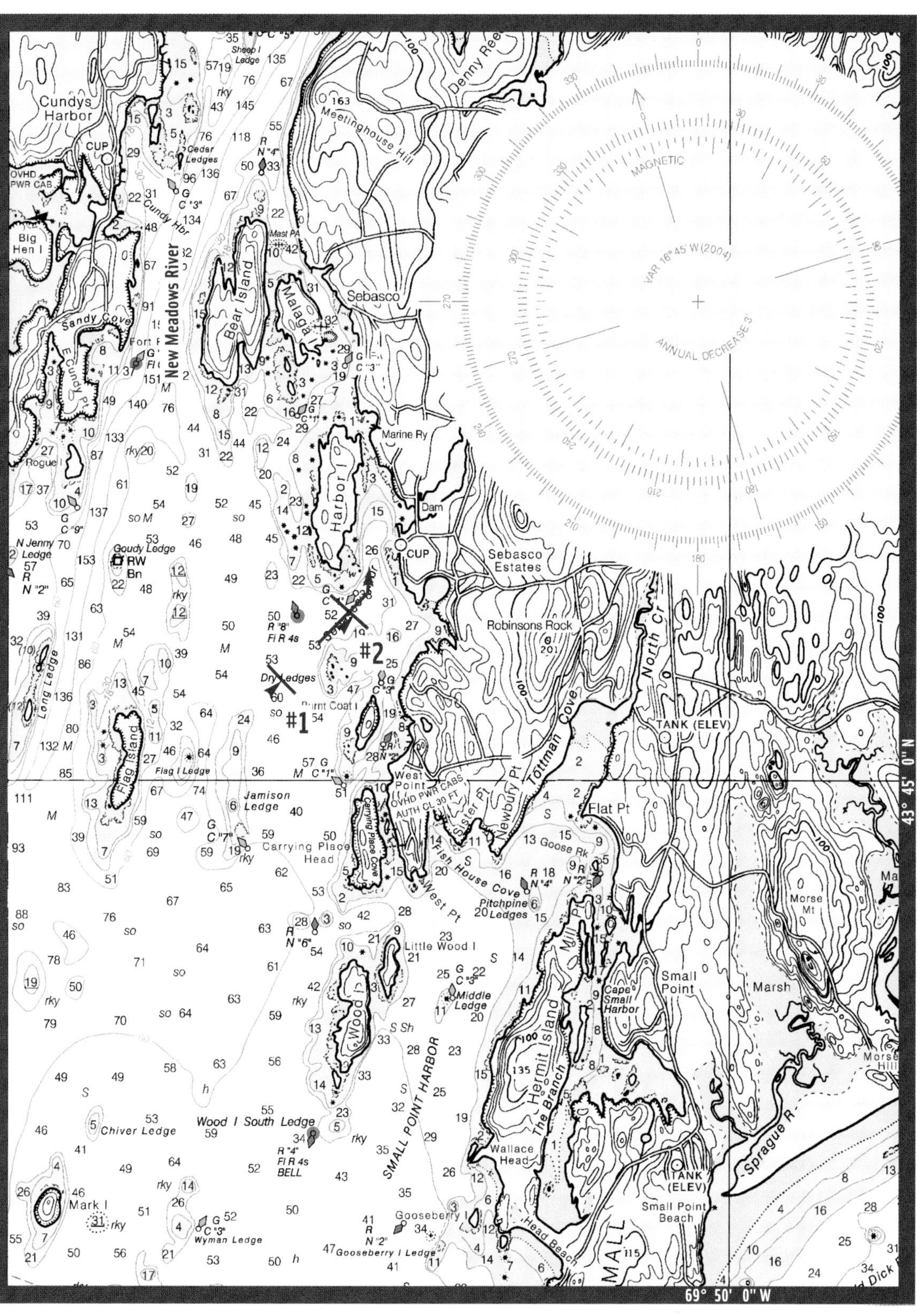

13293
34th ed., Dec. 04
NAD 83
Soundings in feet
1:40,000

■ The Basin

The Basin is approached via the New Meadows River from the south between Sandy Cove and Bear Island just off the flashing green buoy "1." Proceed up the middle of the New Meadows River, leaving green can "5" on your port side just off Sheep Ledge, and proceed until you reach the "V" notch formed between Elwell Point and Meetinghouse Hill. This is the entrance to The Basin. Enter the narrow channel and first head south-east, and then slowly round to the north, keeping about mid-channel for the best depths. Anchor in the 14- to 17-foot deep water at the northern end of The Basin. The anchorage is wonderfully protected and on a summer weekend it is usually jammed with dozens of pleasure boats.

13290
36th ed., Jul. 05
NAD 83
Soundings in feet
1:40,000

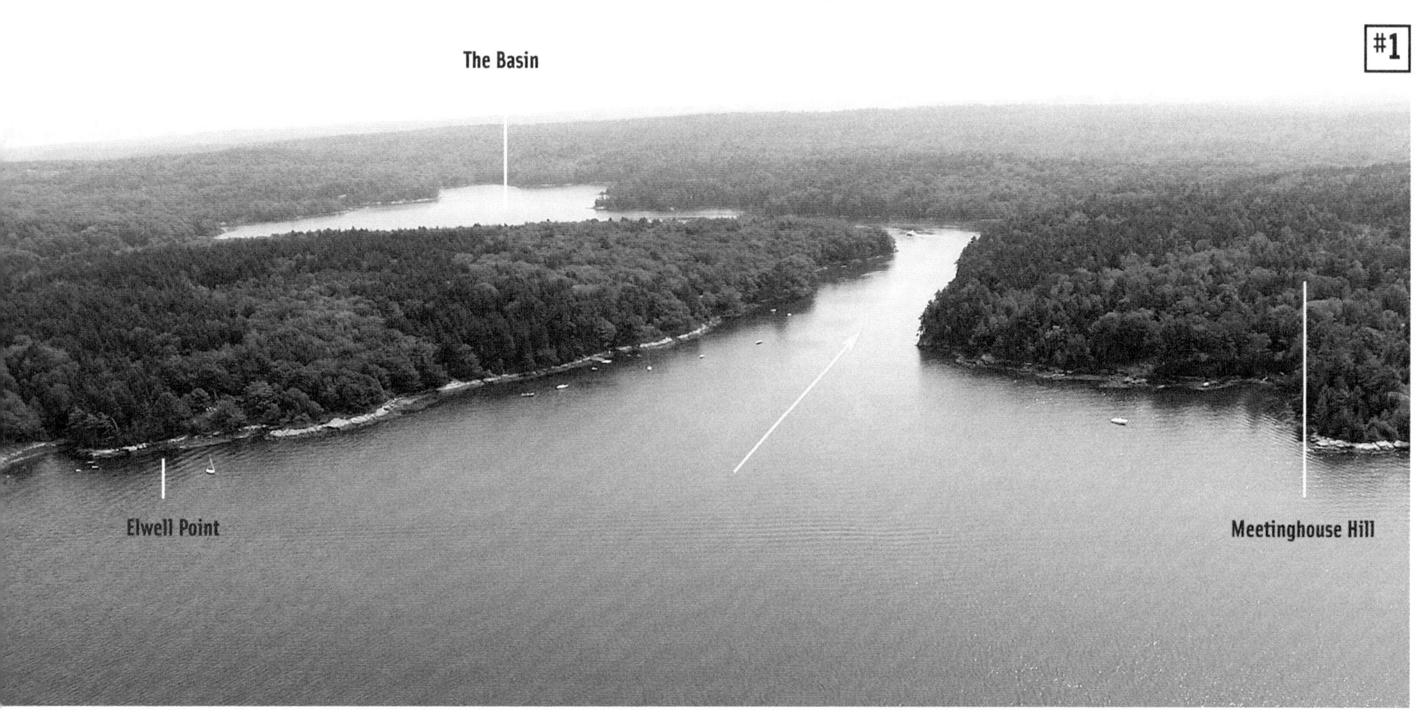

#2

New Meadows River

The Basin

REGION III

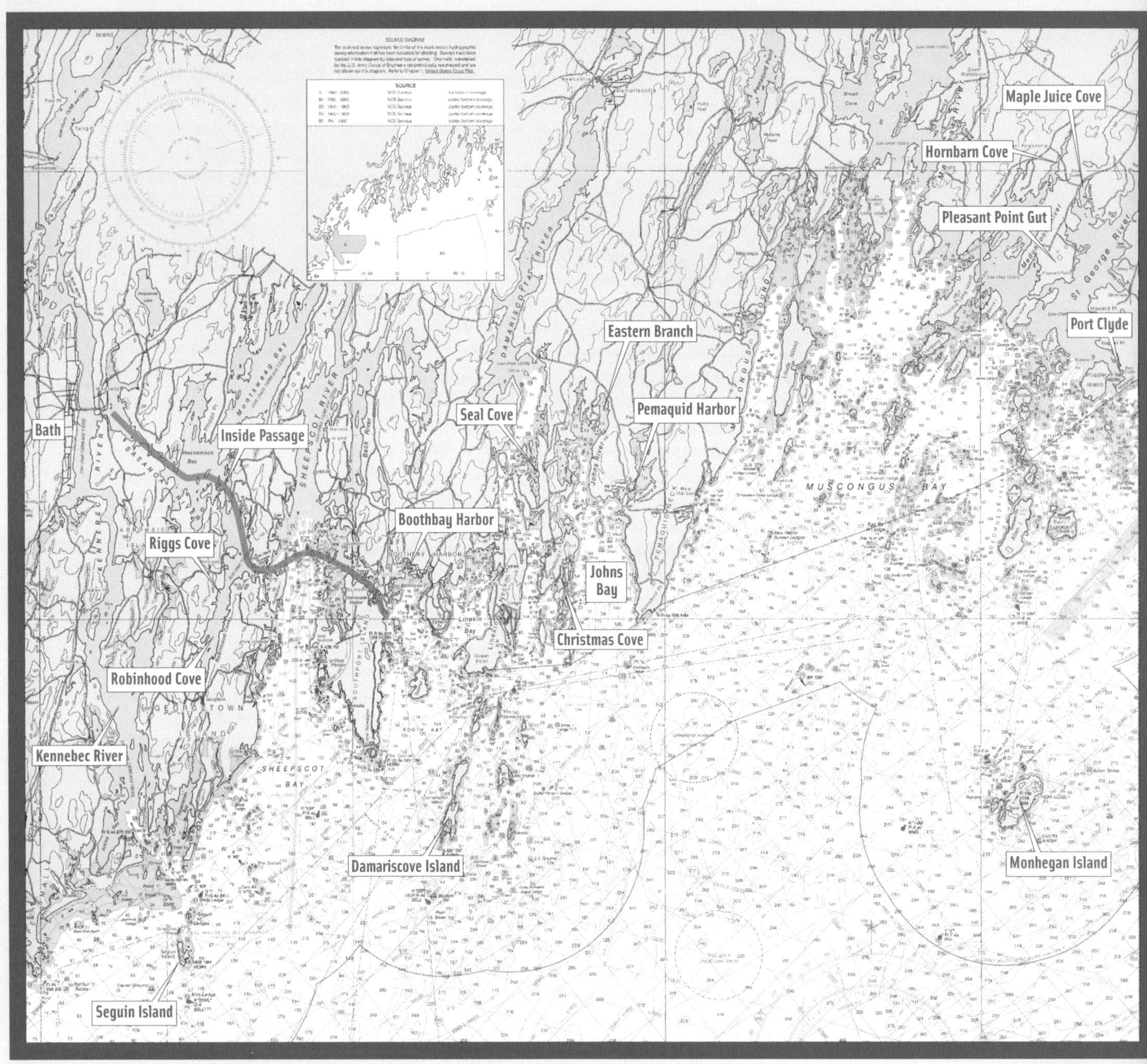

Maple Juice Cove
Hornbarn Cove
Pleasant Point Gut
Port Clyde
Eastern Branch
Pemaquid Harbor
Seal Cove
Inside Passage
Bath
Boothbay Harbor
Riggs Cove
Johns Bay
Christmas Cove
Robinhood Cove
Kennebec River
Damariscove Island
Monhegan Island
Seguin Island
MUSCONGUS BAY
SHEEPSCOT BAY
GEORGETOWN

Midcoast
—Seguin Island to Port Clyde—

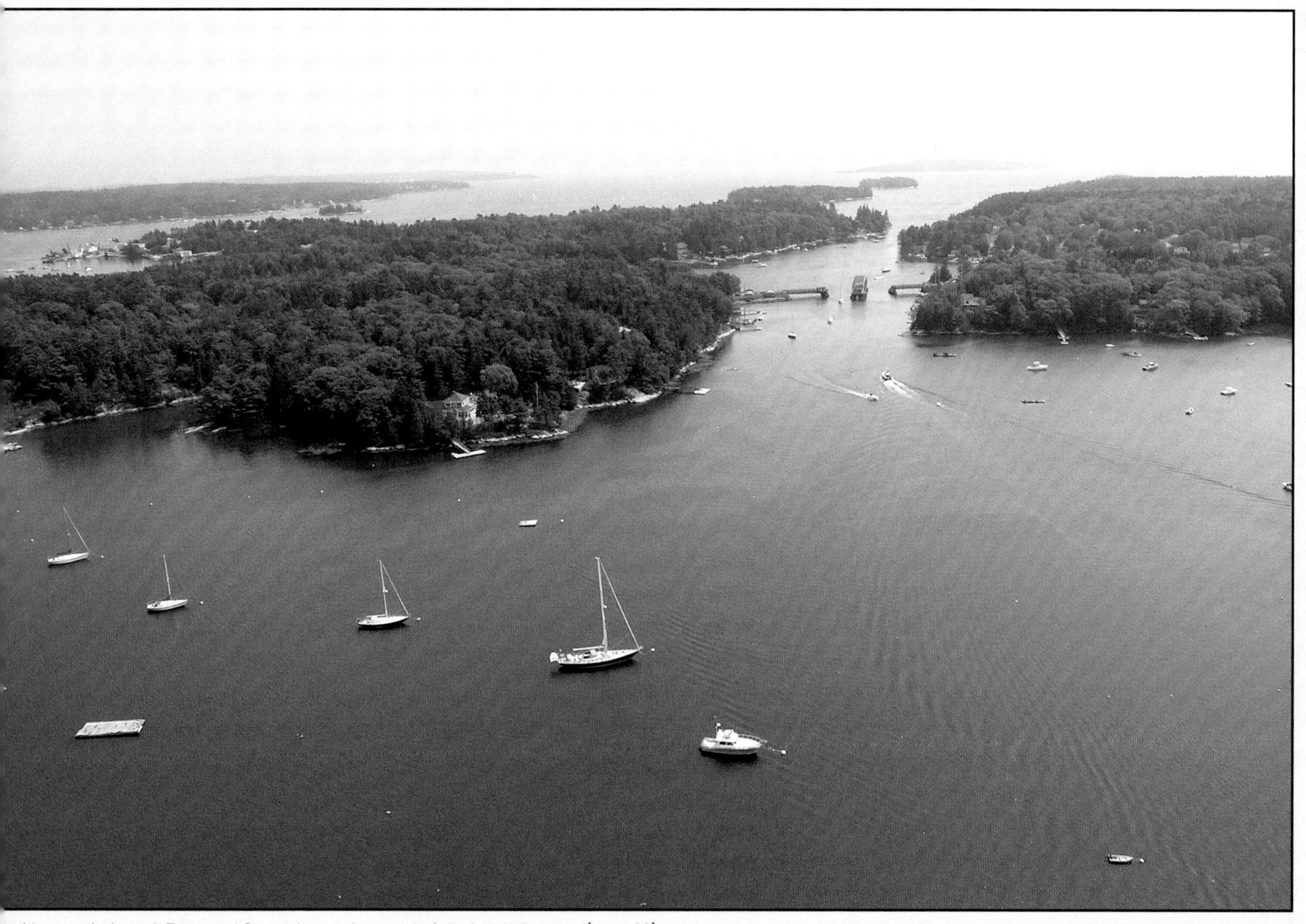

ooking south through Townsend Gut at the southern end of the Inside Passage (page 86)

East of Casco Bay, Seguin, Damariscove, and Monhegan Islands beckon us onward. Much of he rugged Maine coast lies ahead of the eastbound navigator, but this section of coast continues the transition hat began with Casco Bay. In this region, legendary gunkholes, secluded coves, and isolated islands share chart space with bustling tourist destinations.

Here too, for the adventurous mariner, is one of the rue wonders of the Maine coast—the "Inside Passage" rom Bath to Boothbay Harbor. Complete with tidal vhite water, historic swinging bridges, narrow passages spilling into tranquil millpond waters, and charming towns at either end, there is nothing else in the world quite like it.

Cruisers who bypass Muscongus Bay don't know what they're missing, and the lower St. George River offers Maple Juice Cove. If you're there, you owe it to yourself to at least poke into Pleasant Point Gut for a look around. And no trip through this area would be complete without a night spent in the anchorage at Damariscove Island. The sunsets and absolute serenity are sure to quiet even the most restless soul.

■ SEGUIN ISLAND ■

STANDING solitary watch near the mouth of the Kennebec River, Seguin Island is an impressive sight. It's sheer size and beauty overshadows anything else around you. A small cove on the northeast side provides some protection and courtesy moorings. The cove also marks the beginning of the trail to the lighthouse station on the hill. The volunteer civilian lighthouse keepers maintain a small museum and souvenir shop near the lighthouse during the summer months. Be mindful that there is local magnetic disturbance in this area and it will affect your compass.

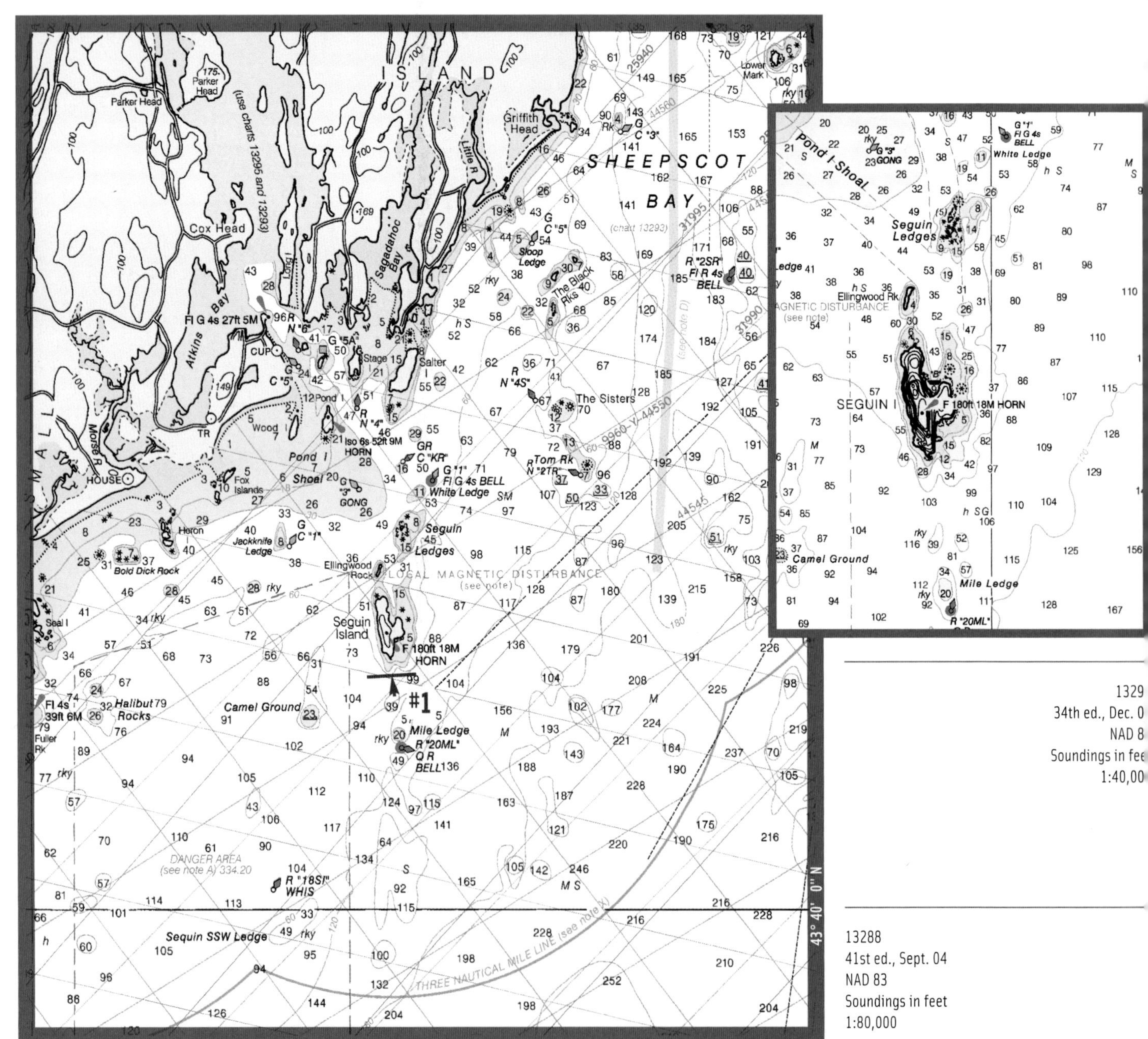

#1

■ KENNEBEC RIVER ■

THE Kennebec River is best approached from the green bell buoy "1," off White Ledge and just outside the mouth of the river. From it, head northwest up the channel toward Pond Island with its lighthouse and fog horn. At Pond Island, head for the unmistakable Fort Popham, a large, granite Civil War fort marked with navigation light. The mouth of the Kennebec als boasts the remarkable white sandy expanse of Popha and Hunnewell beaches. It's a beautiful and wonderfu spot. Anchoring in the river just off the beach and sout of the Fort is common during daylight hours. Beyon Fort Popham, the Kennebec is navigable up t Augusta and gives th cruising yachtsman an opportunity to travel 40 mile inland, a rare treat on th Maine coast.

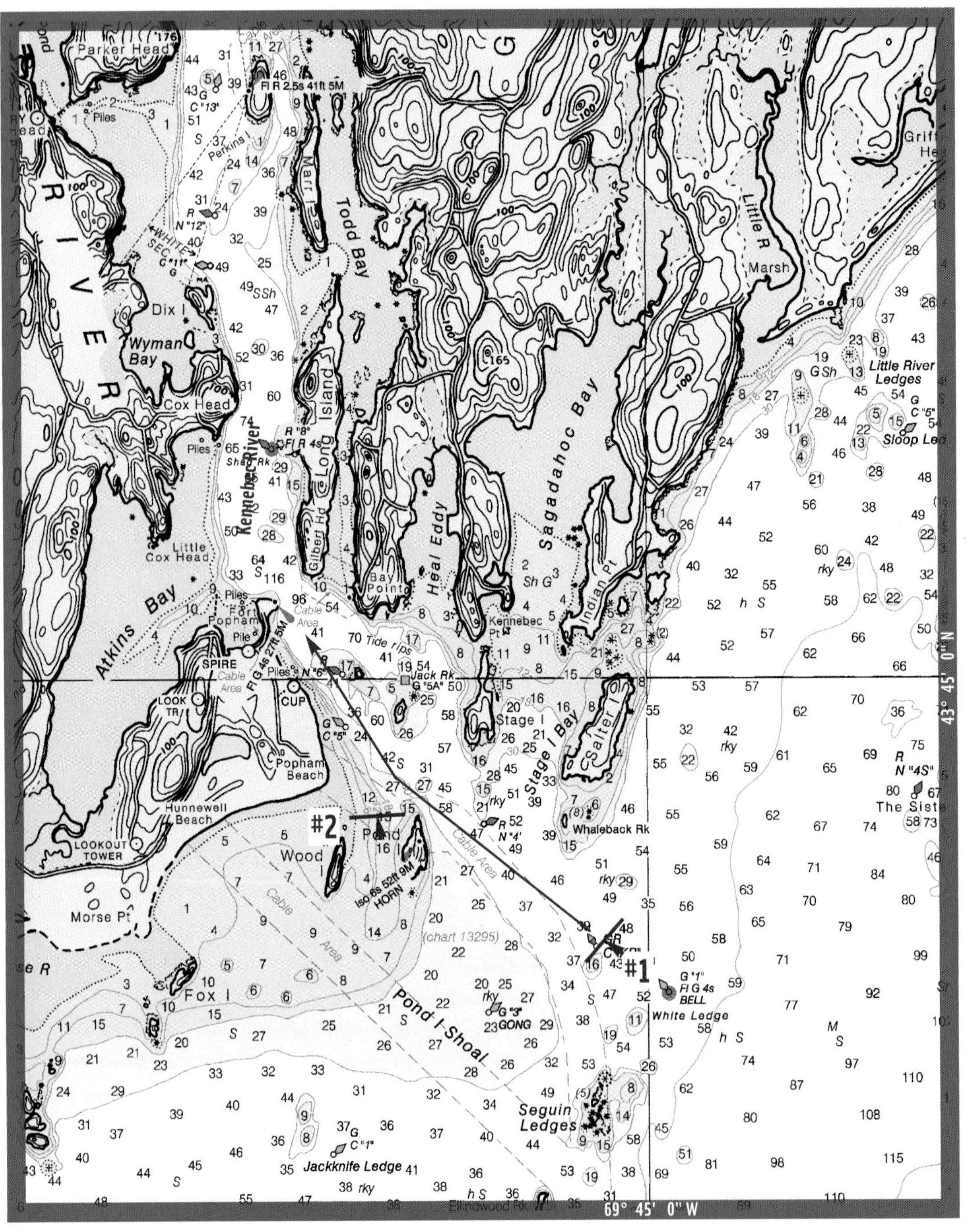

13293
34th ed., Dec. 04
NAD 83
Soundings in feet
1:40,000

#1

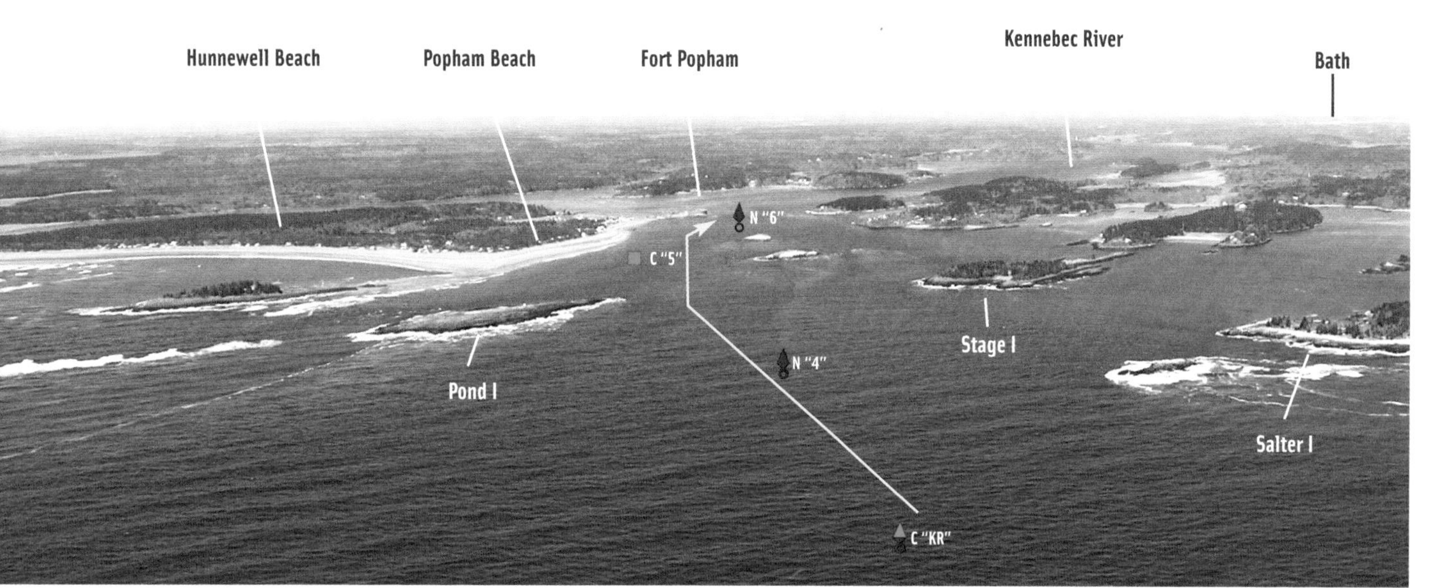

#2

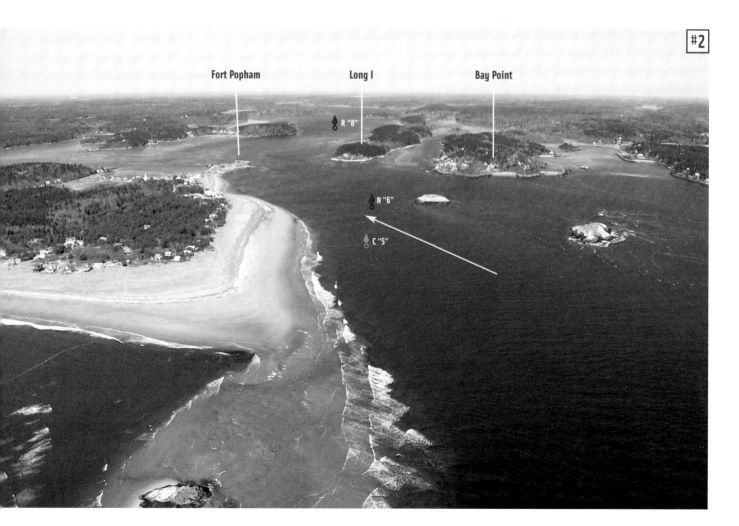

Fort Popham
Long I
Bay Point
R "8"
N "6"
C "5"

■ BATH ■

EIGHT miles up the Kennebec stands the city of Bath and Bath Iron Works, a shipbuilder producing U.S. Navy vessels. Having worked your way with the flood tide up the bucolic Kennebec, the shipyard—with its unmistakable tall cranes, huge dry dock, and formidable Navy ships—will seem as if you just entered another world. Beyond the two bridges spanning the river at Bath are restaurants, public and commercial docks, and numerous amenities for the traveler.

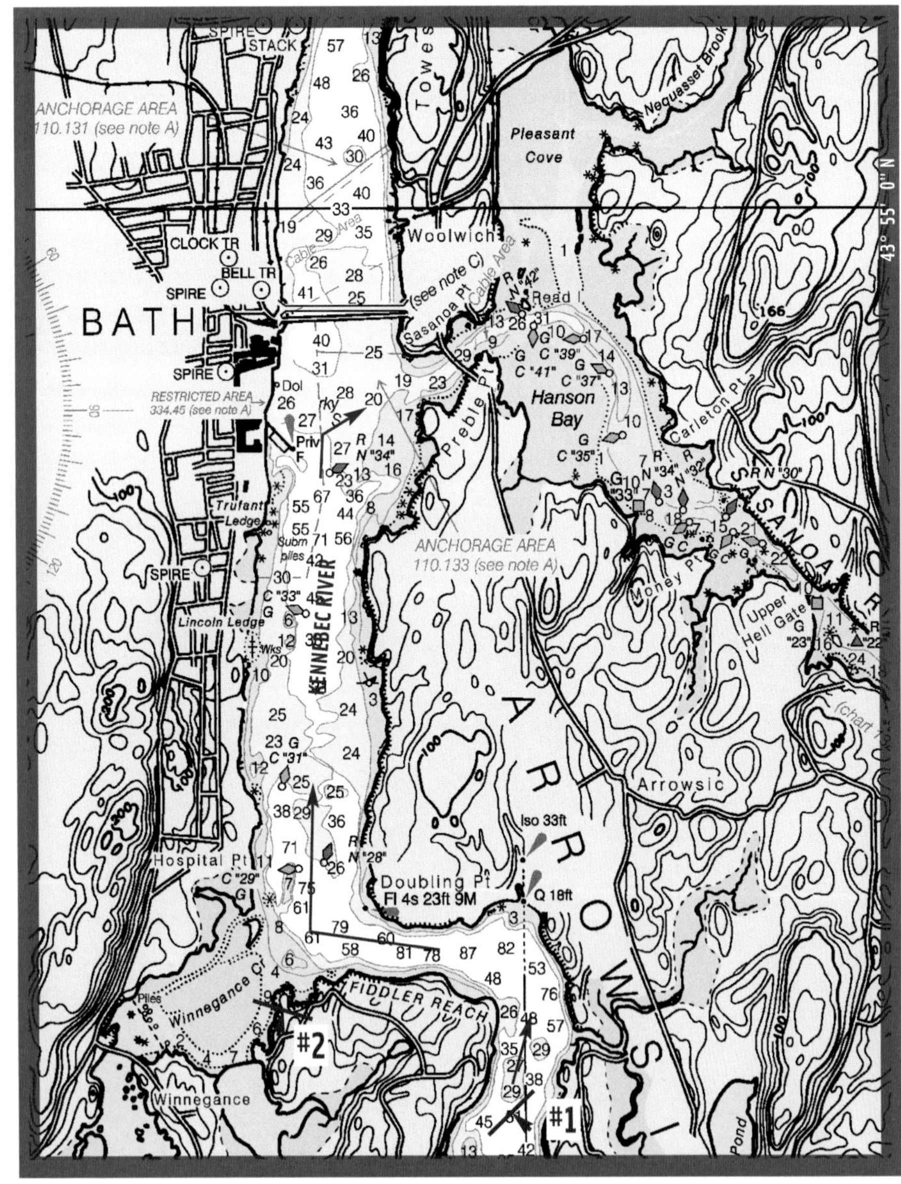

13293
34th ed., Dec. 04
NAD 83
Soundings in feet
1:40,000

#1

#2

Bath

Inside Passage

C "31"

C "29"

N "28"

■ INSIDE PASSAGE ■

(Bath to Boothbay Harbor)

ONE of the most intriguing features of the Maine coast actually lies well inland. Called the "Inside Passage," it is a circuitous water route from Bath to Boothbay Harbor. From Bath, mariners will navigate Upper Hell Gate and Lower Hell Gate, two of the most challenging stretches of this passage. Strong erratic currents, small whirlpools and heavy boat traffic frequently characterize both Gates. Success therefore depends on consulting tide charts and having a clear understanding of the height of your mast.

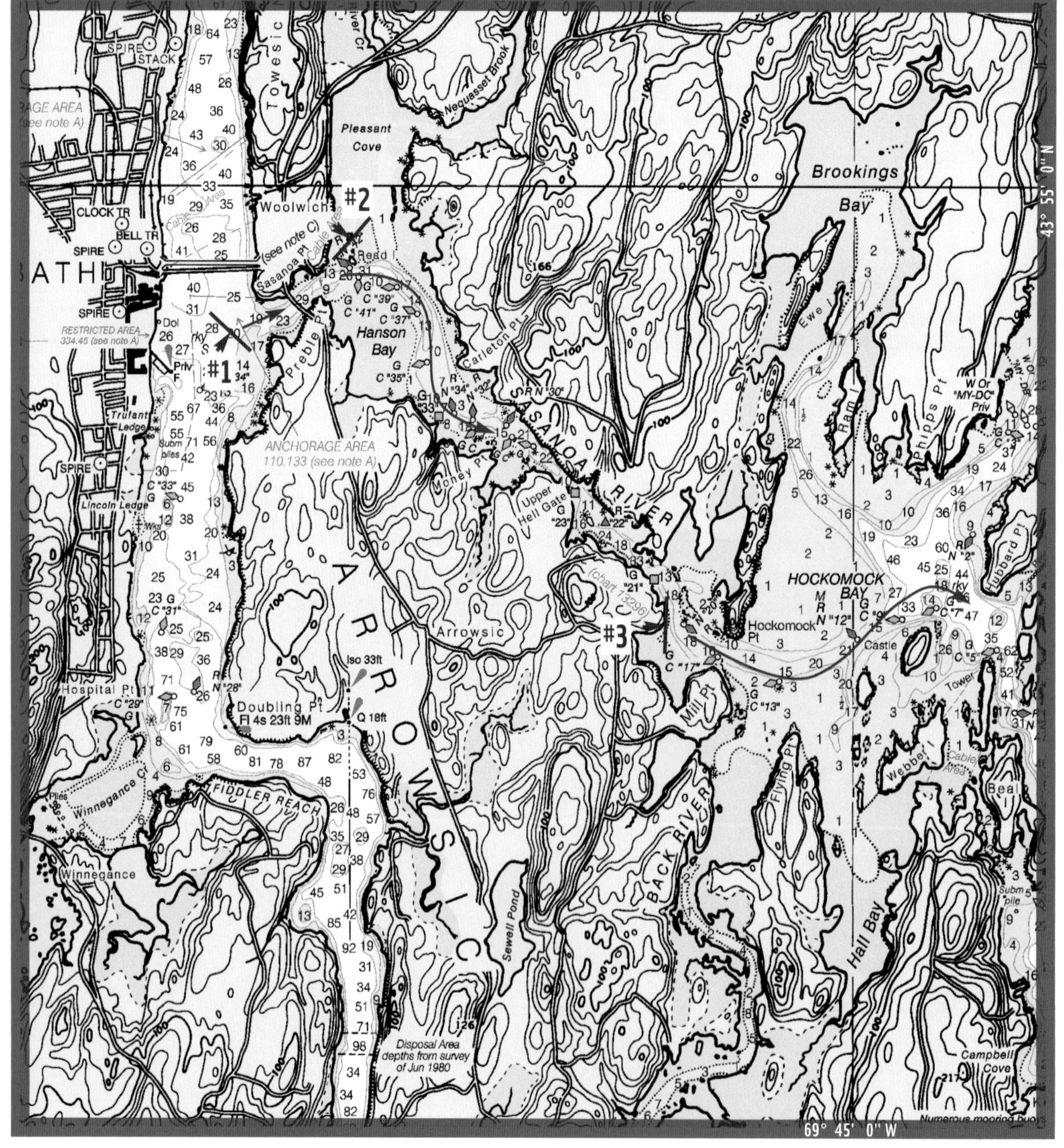

13293
34th ed., Dec. 04
NAD 83
Soundings in feet
1:40,000

UPPER HELL GATE

·OR those attempting the Inside Passage, first be sure he height of your vessel is under 51 feet, which is the :learance for the fixed bridge crossing the Sasanoa River ιt the western entrance of the Inside Passage. The ;asanoa River is a narrow passage, requiring careful attention to the numerous navigation aids that mark the critical turns. At some areas, less than 20 feet of water separates your boat from the rocky shores of this river. It is here where the currents rule and pose the most challenges.

#1

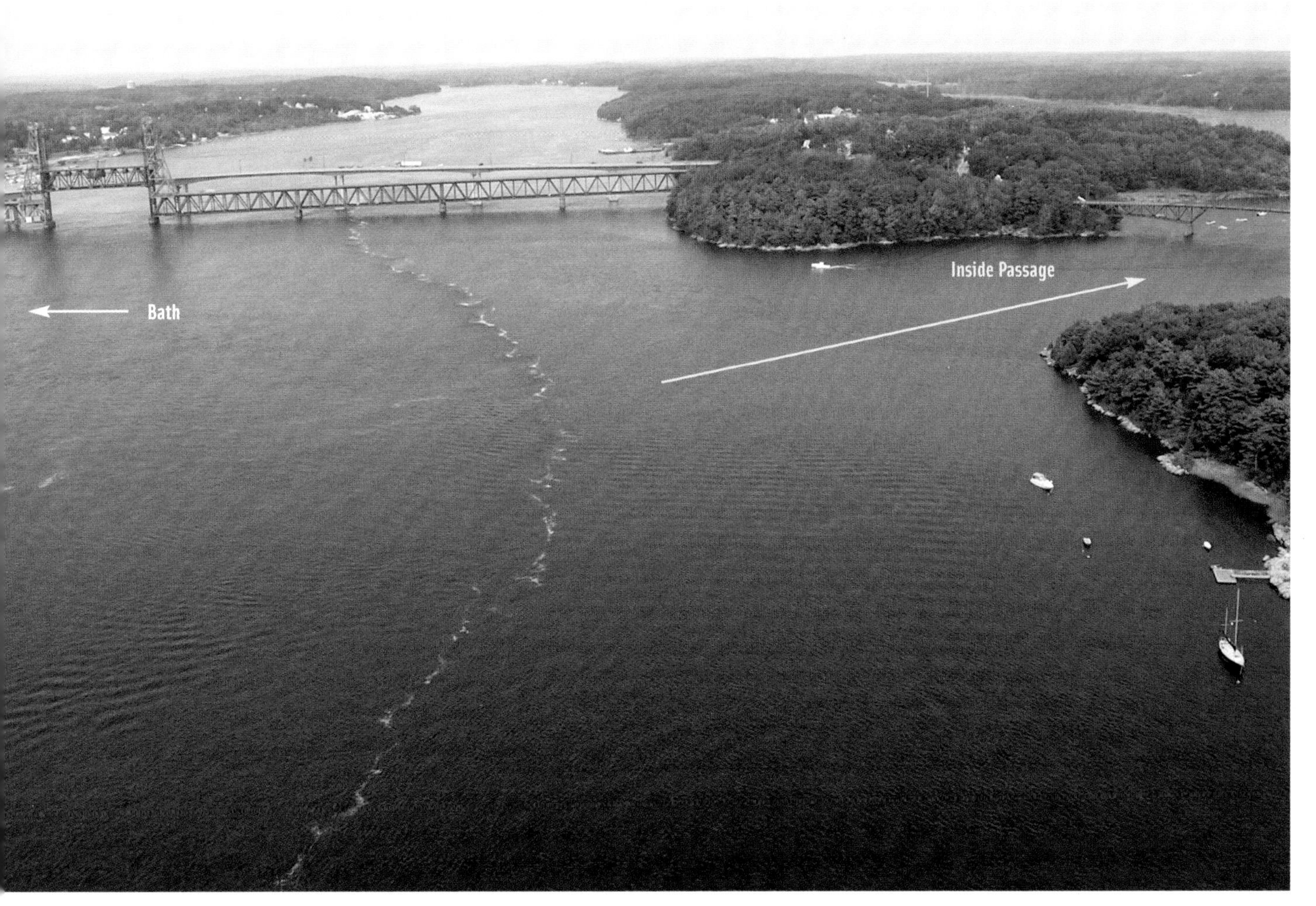

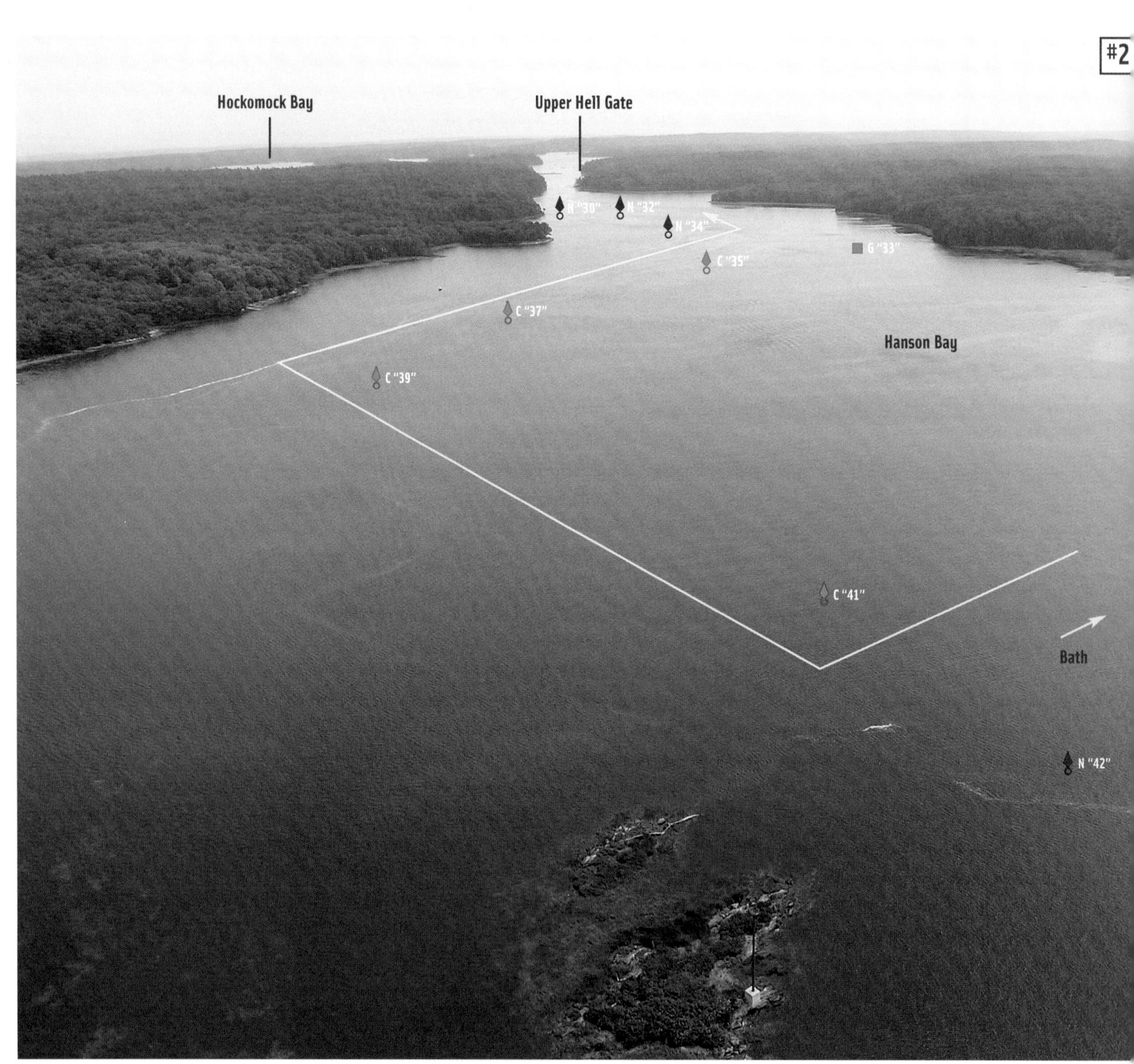
#2
Hockomock Bay
Upper Hell Gate
N "30"
N "32"
N "34"
C "35"
G "33"
C "37"
Hanson Bay
C "39"
C "41"
Bath
N "42"

#3

Hockomock Bay
Castle I
Hall Bay
Mill Point
C "17"
Hockomock Point
N "20"
Upper Hell Gate

■ Lower Hell Gate

CURRENTS slacken somewhat when crossing Hockomock Bay, but pick up again in Lower Hell Gate, which is the entrance to Knubble Bay. Whirlpools, lobster pots, and crosscurrents are most likely near red nun "2," but careful piloting should get you through without incident. Continue down Knubble Bay until you make a turn to port in Goose Rock Passage and reach the Sheepscot River. From there, you can either go the northern route around the Isle of Springs (as pictured) or the southern route past Dogfish Head and into Ebencook Harbor to reach Townsend Gut. Then it's onward to Boothbay Harbor.

When you have successfully traveled the Inside Passage through all its twists and turns from Bath to Boothbay Harbor, you might feel like you've just navigated the Grand Canyon!

13293
34th ed., Dec. 04
NAD 83
Soundings in feet
1:40,000

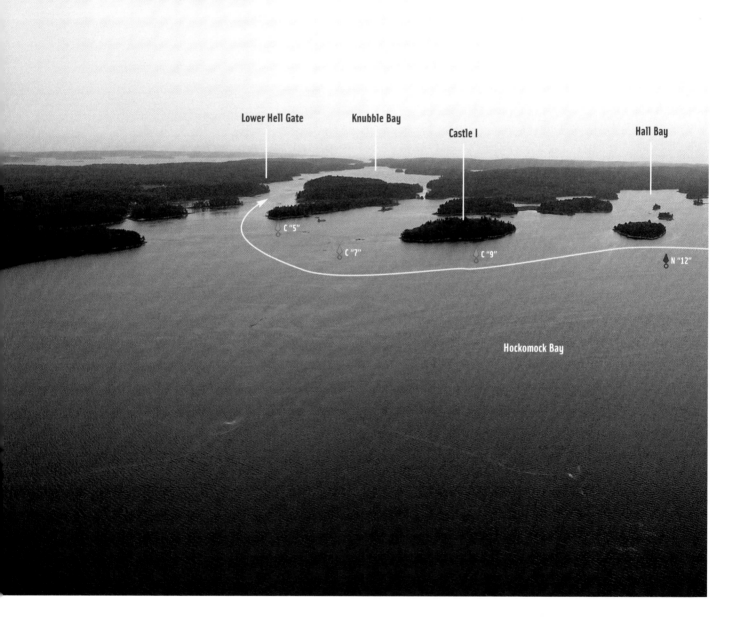

Lower Hell Gate
Knubble Bay
Castle I
Hall Bay
C "5"
C "7"
C "9"
N "12"
Hockomock Bay

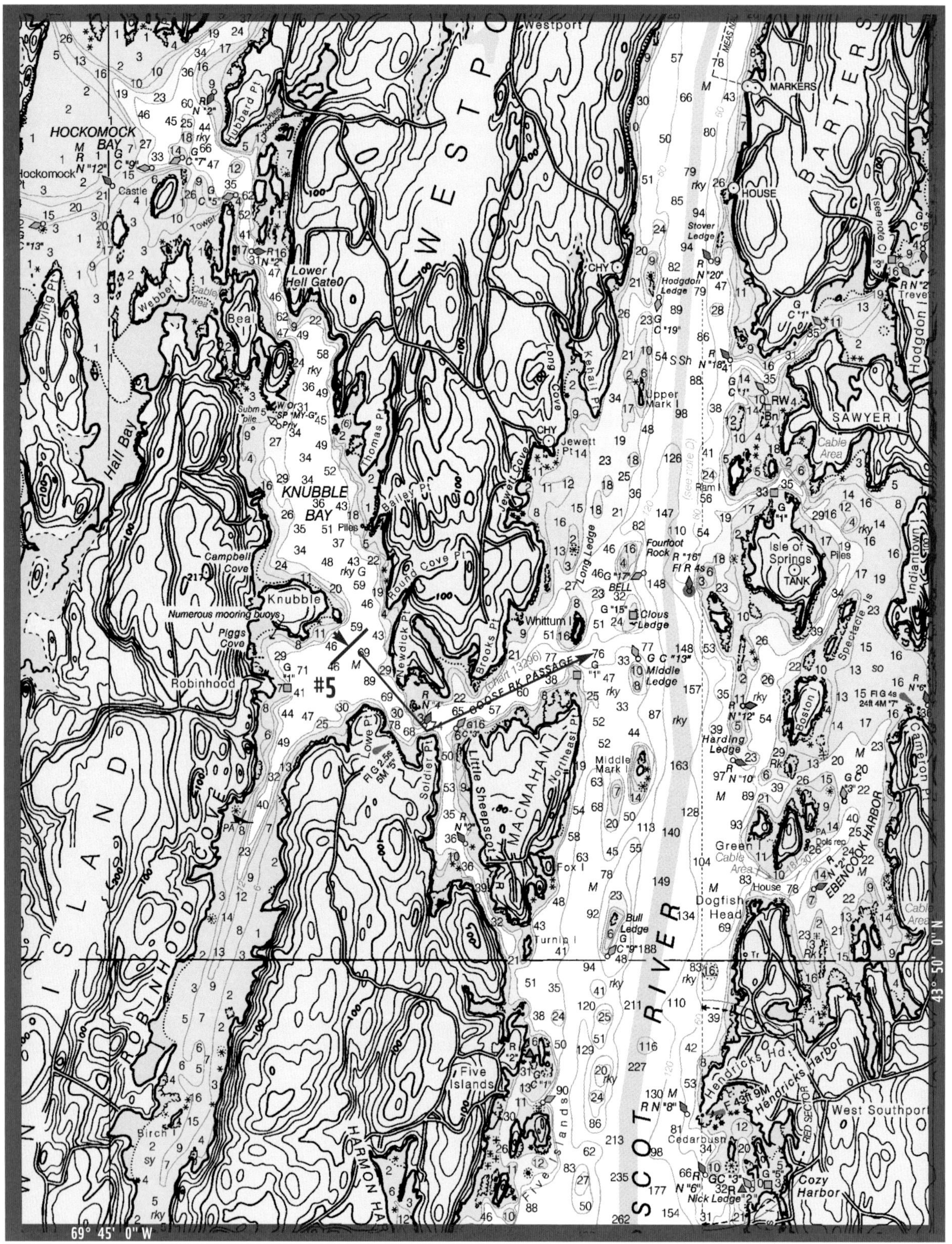

13293
34th ed., Dec. 04
NAD 83
Soundings in feet
1:40,000

#5

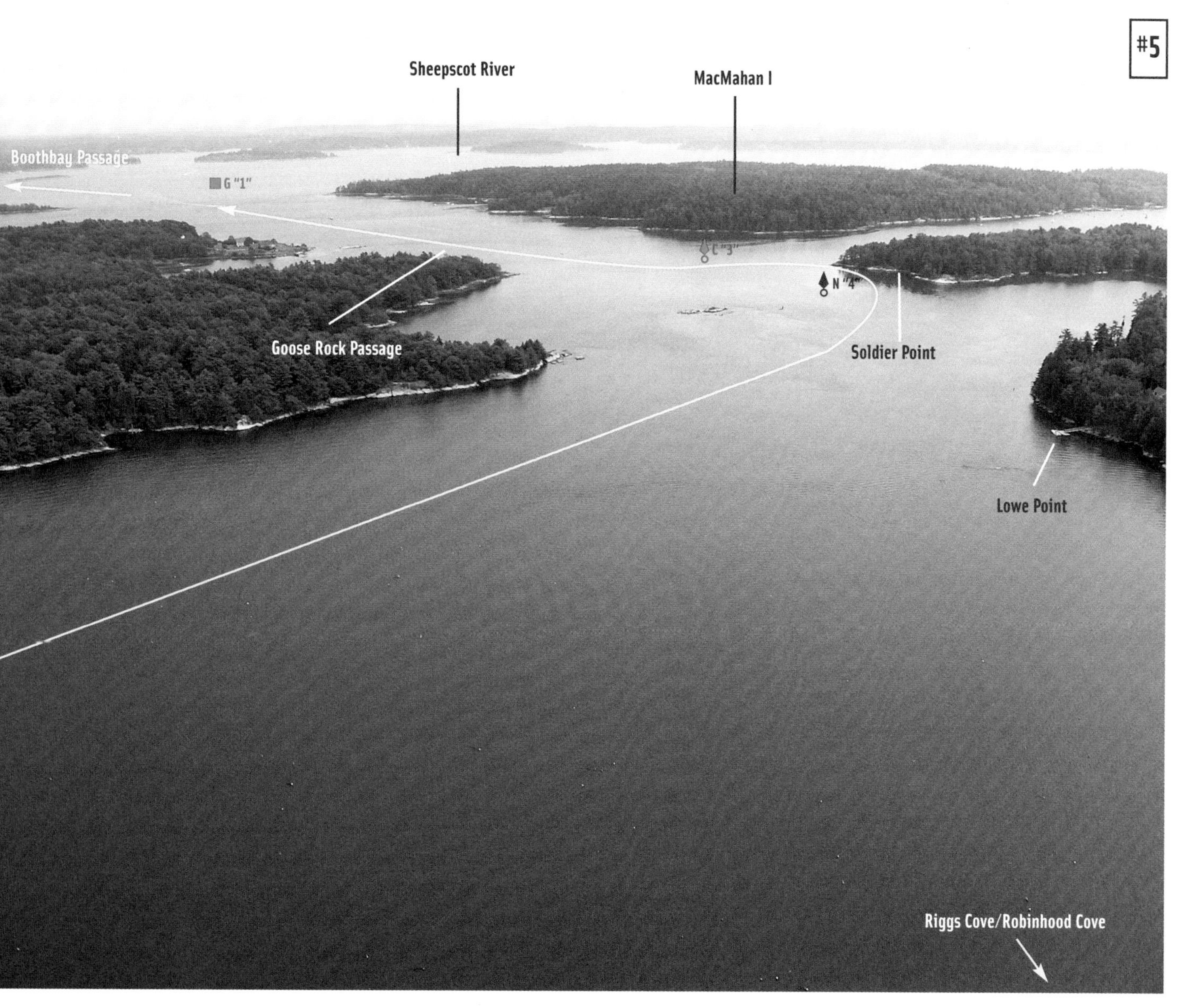
Sheepscot River
MacMahan I
Boothbay Passage
G "1"
C "3"
N "4"
Goose Rock Passage
Soldier Point
Lowe Point
Riggs Cove/Robinhood Cove

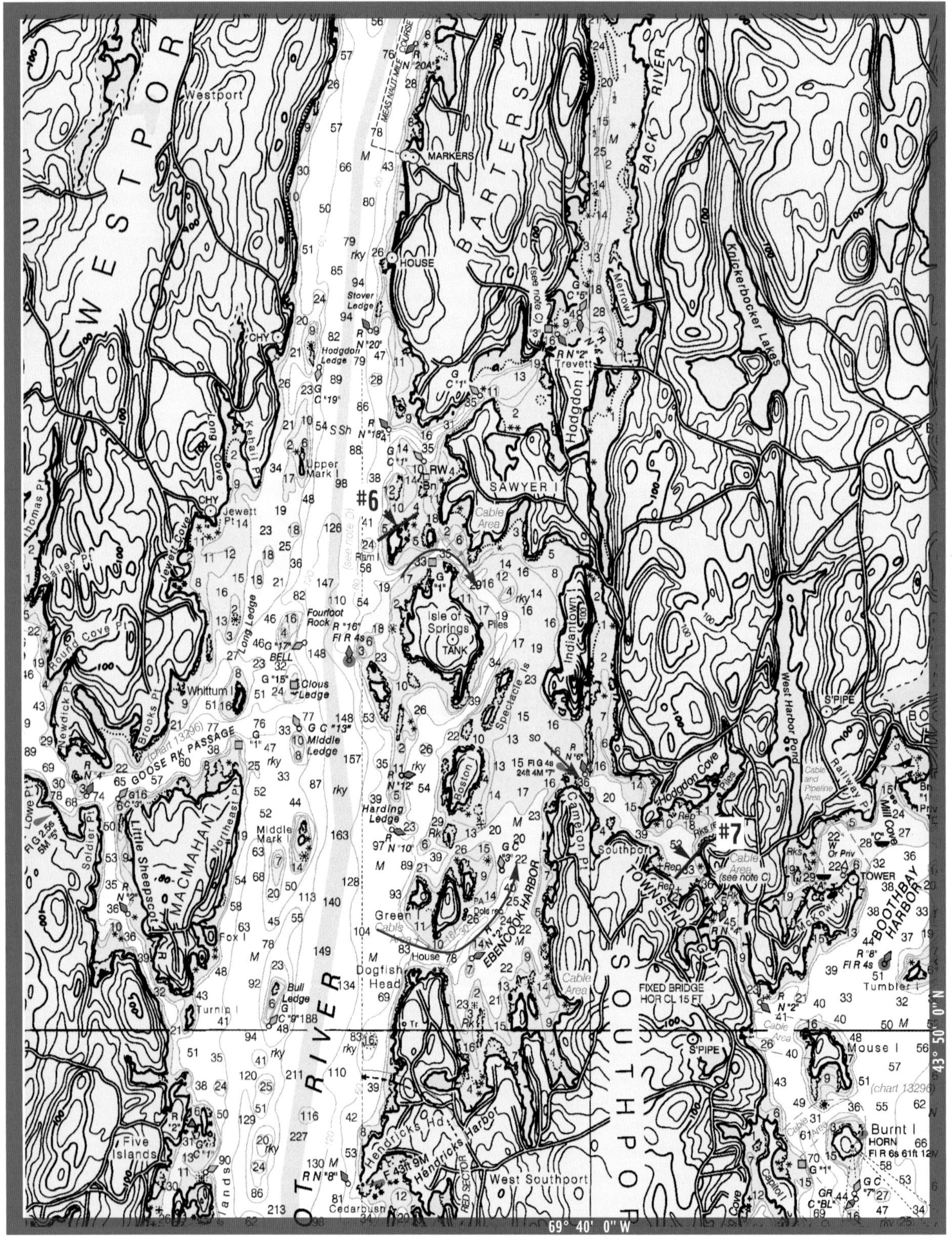

13293
34th ed., Dec. 04
NAD 83
Soundings in feet
1:40,000

#6

Boothbay
Townsend Gut
Boston I
N "6"
G "1"
Isle of Springs

#7

Boothbay
N "4"
Townsend Gut

■ ROBINHOOD COVE AND RIGGS COVE ■

MIDWAY through the Inside Passage at the southern end of Knubble Bay are Robinhood Cove and a nearby marina at Riggs Cove. Both coves are quiet and protected in most conditions. The marina at Riggs Cove has complete services and plenty of moorings—a good thing because the deep water, strong currents, and rocky bottom make anchoring nearly impossible. Robinhood Cove is a better bet for swinging on the hook. To get to these coves from the Sheepscot River, you'll enter Goose Rock Passage near green day beacon "1" off the northeast end north of MacMahan Island. Continue in Goose Rock Passage until you reach red nun "4" north of Soldier Point. Proceed around Lowe Point and head northwesterly for Riggs Cove or southwesterly for Robinhood Cove.

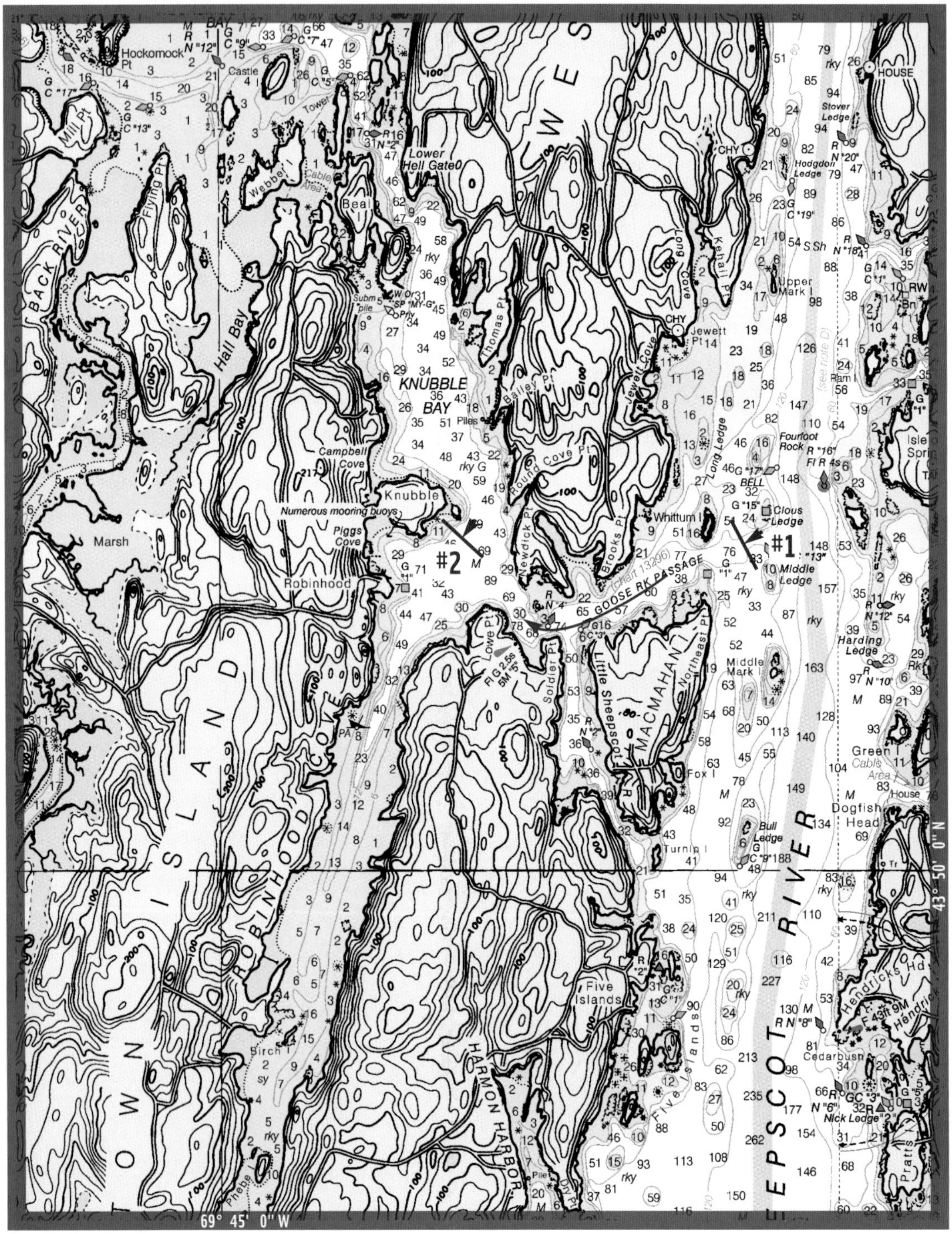

13293
34th ed., Dec. 04
NAD 27
Soundings in feet
1:40,000

#1

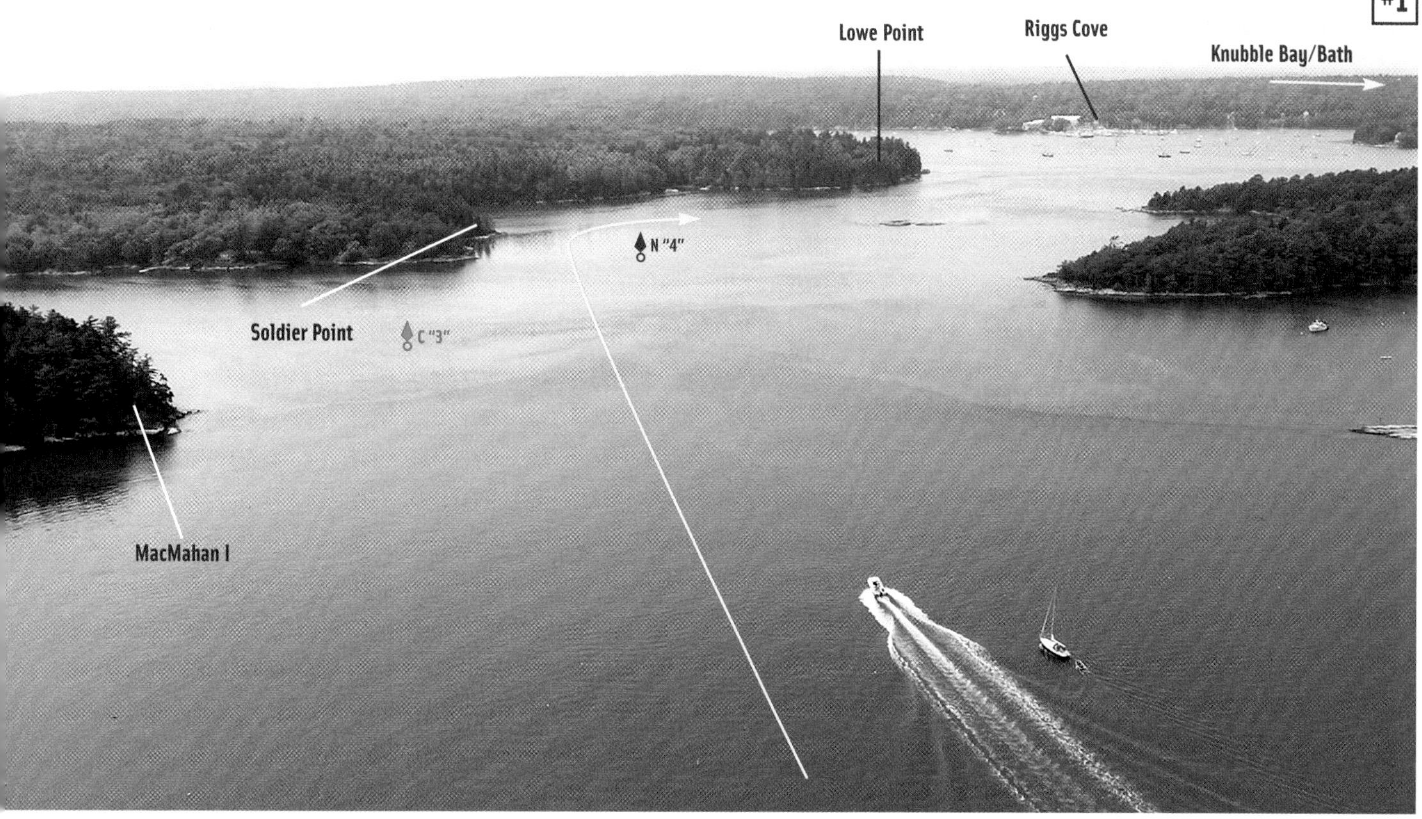

Lowe Point
Riggs Cove
Knubble Bay/Bath
N "4"
Soldier Point
C "3"
MacMahan I

#2

Robinhood Cove
Riggs Cove

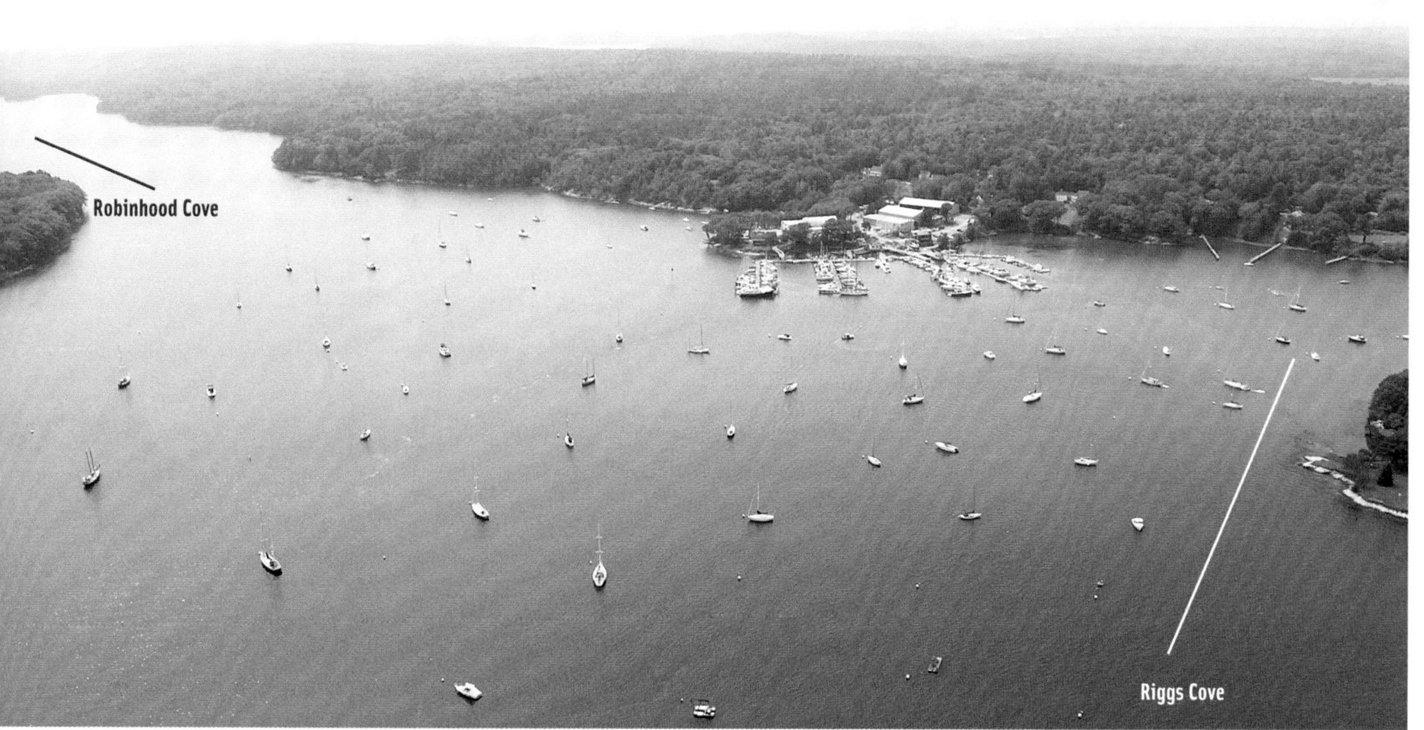

■ BOOTHBAY HARBOR ■

AS you enter the Boothbay Harbor area from the south, it will be impossible to miss large Squirrel Island, northeast of the Cuckolds Lighthouse off the southern tip of Southport Island. Boothbay can actually be approached from either the west side or east side of Squirrel. Continue onward keeping Tumbler Island to your starboard side. Civilization will soon be upon you. The outer harbor is large and wide open to the south. The two most popular anchorages include the cove at West Boothbay, or the inner harbor. If bound for the cove at West Boothbay, look for the prominent tower on McKown Point. Take a 90-degree turn to port and Boothbay Yacht Club will be directly in front of you. The yacht club maintains a number of moorings and offers a launch service. For more commercial services, the inner harbor will be obvious beyond green bell buoy "9" and McFarland Island's beautiful circular cupola and home.

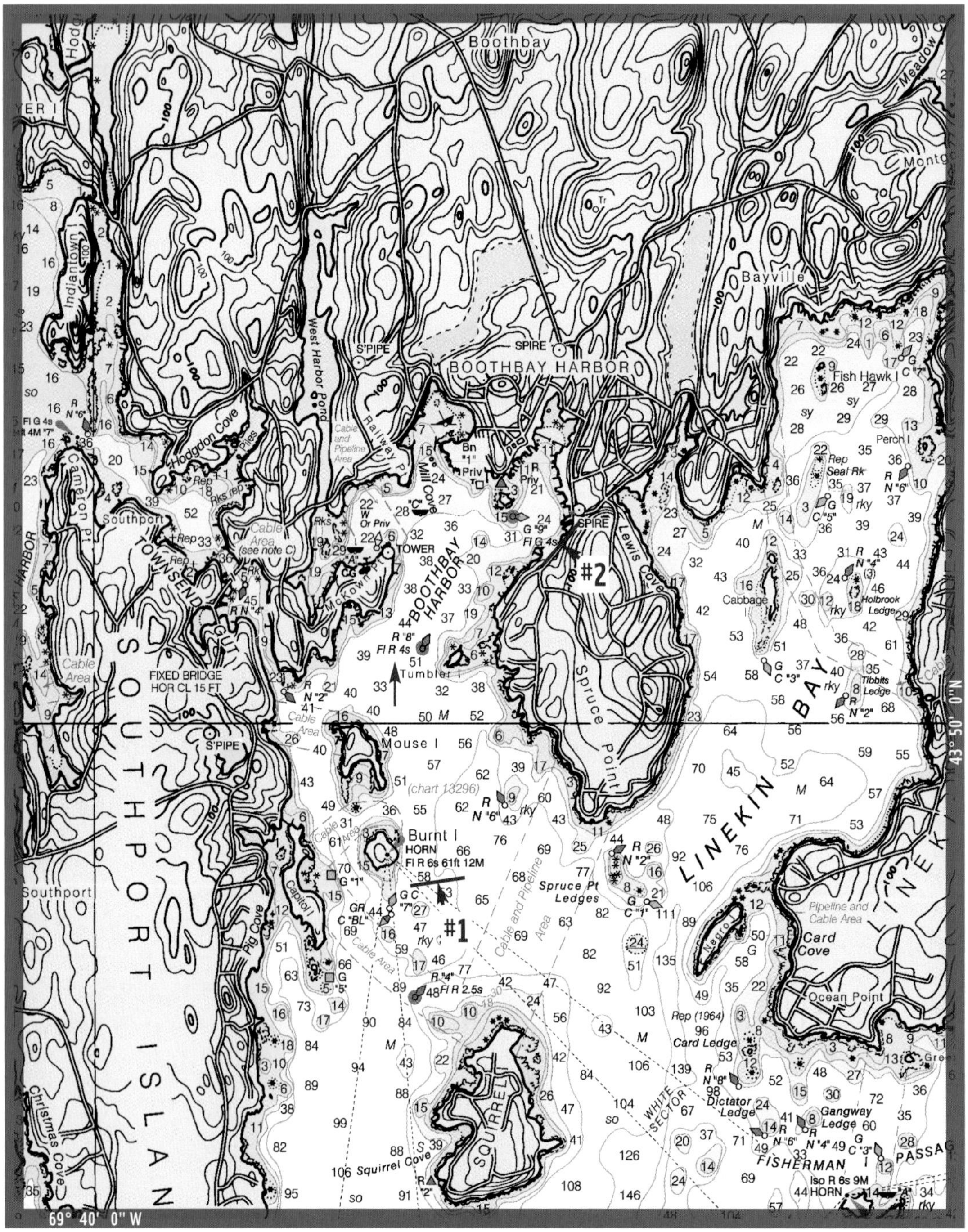

13293
34th ed., Dec. 04
NAD 83
Soundings in feet
1:40,000

#1

West Boothbay Yacht Club

Boothbay

McKown Point

R "8"

Inside Passage to Bath

Tumbler I

Mouse I

Burnt I

#2

McFarland I

G "9"

■ DAMARISCOVE ISLAND ■

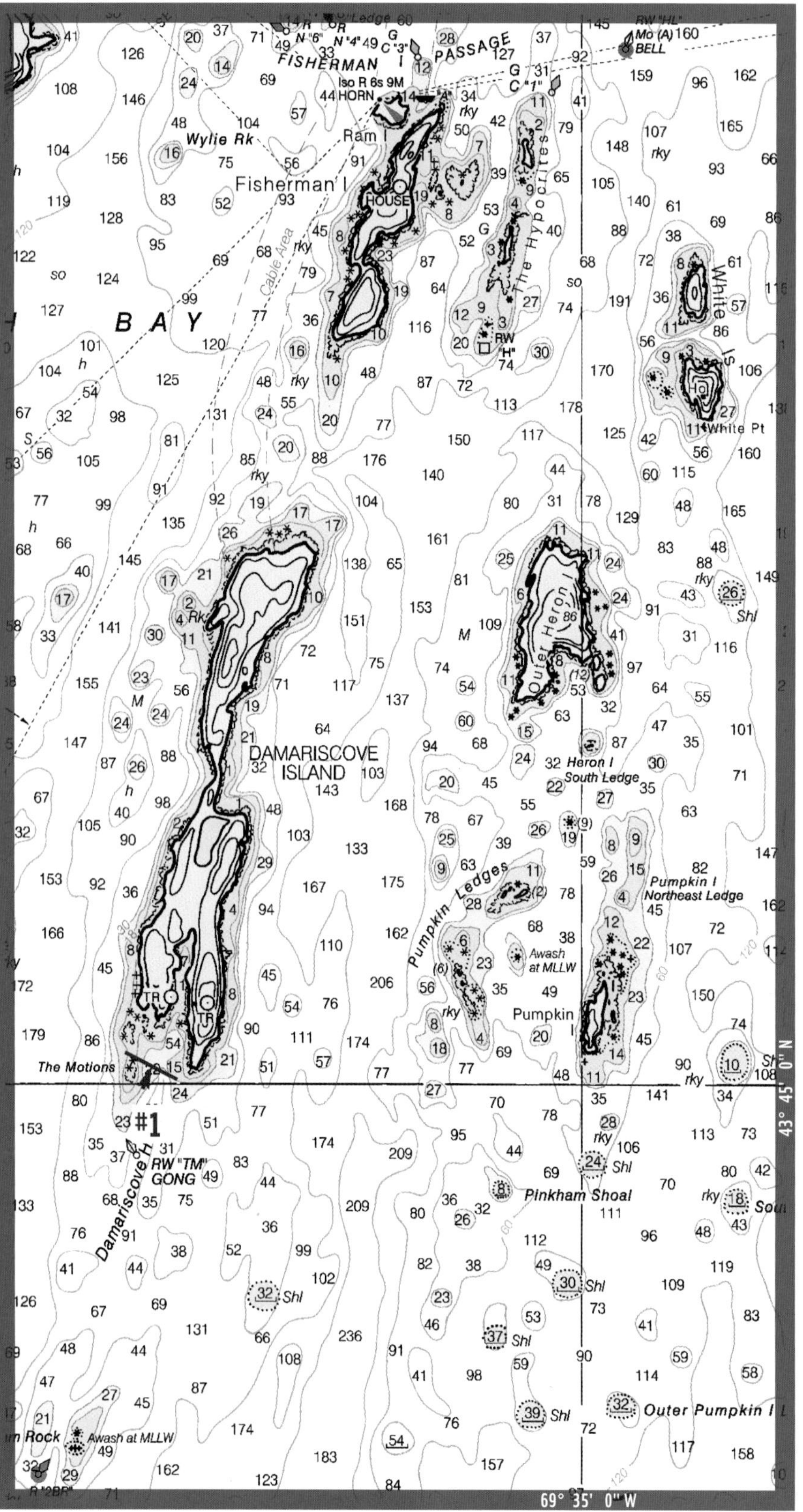

ONE of my favorite overnight spots in al of Maine is Damariscove Island. The is land's narrow but protected inner harbor i a classic—but in the summer, be certain tc get to Damariscove early in the day, as the harbor is likely to be crowded anytime af ter 5 p.m. Damariscove was once home to a U.S. Life Saving Station but now the islanc is privately owned. As you approach the harbor at the southern end of the island the former Life Saving Station is prominen on the west side of the harbor entrance with a separate observation tower on the east side. After being sure you've clearec the ledges known as The Motions, keep yourself equidistant between these promi nent landmarks, and enter the outer harbor which has the greatest depth. Be careful a you enter to give proper respect to the nu merous lobster trap buoys. The inner har bor is much shallower, with a depth of 6 feet. Once there, be sure to take you dinghy ashore as you'll find trails stewardec by The Nature Conservancy. This is a visi not to be missed.

13293
34th ed., Dec. 04
NAD 83
Soundings in feet
1:40,000

#1

■ CHRISTMAS COVE ■

ANOTHER popular harbor in the Midcoast region is Christmas Cove. The approach involves navigating the Damariscotta River on a northerly course and keeping Inner Heron Island and red nuns "2" and "4" to your starboard. Once clear of nun "4," continue northeasterly to Christmas Cove. At low tide, the many hazards tha protect the harbor will be apparent, including the rec day mark "2" on a ledge at the mouth. As you get closer the green day mark "3" opposite "2" clearly marks the channel into the harbor.

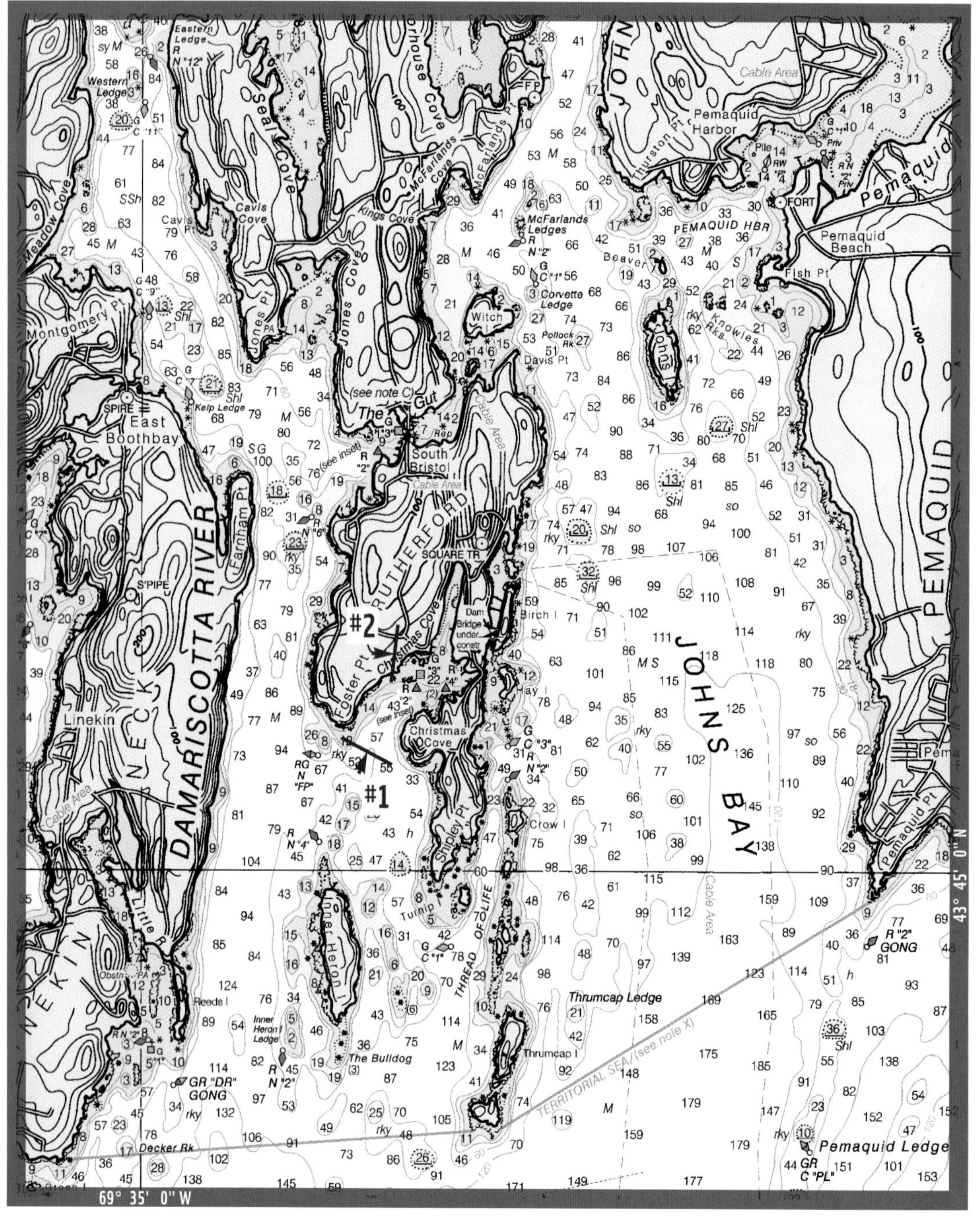

13293
34th ed., Dec. 04
NAD 83
Soundings in feet
1:40,000

#1

#2

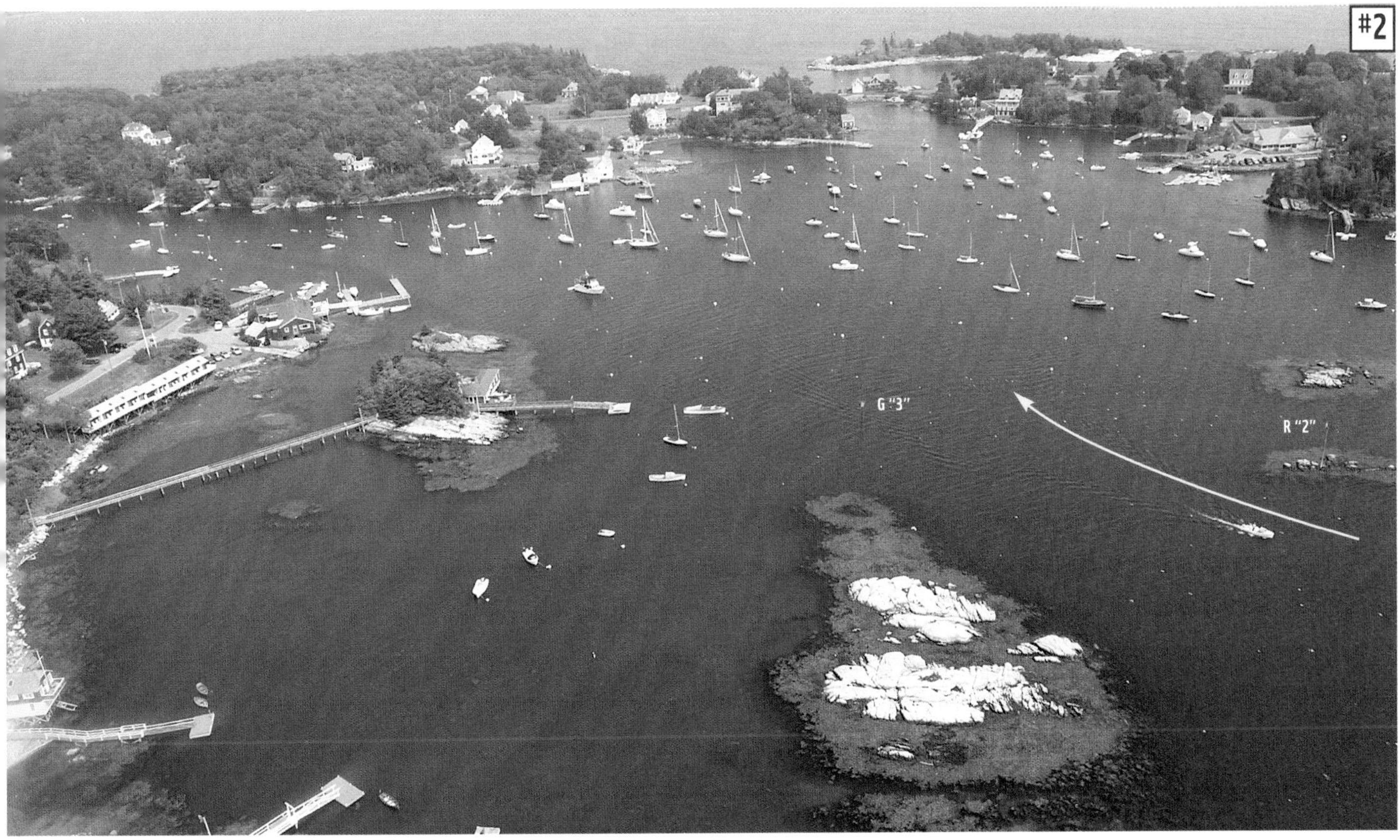

G "3"

R "2"

■ SEAL COVE ■

A NICELY protected harbor farther up the Damariscotta River is Seal Cove. To reach it, continue on a northerly course well past Christmas Cove. There is plenty of water if you favor the eastern side along Jones Point. Make your way carefully through the narrow passage between Fort Point to port and Eastern Ledge to starboard; give ample respect to red nun "12" off of Eastern Ledge, and be wary of the strong, turbulent currents near Fort Point. Continue in mid-river until you're abeam of Hodgsons Island's northern tip. Make a nice, clean turn around the island and head south into the protected waters of Seal Cove. Once inside, beauty and serenity await you in this wonderfully protected, long harbor.

13293
34th ed., Dec. 04
NAD 83
Soundings in feet
1:40,000

#1

■ PEMAQUID HARBOR/JOHNS BAY ■

ENTER Pemaquid Harbor from the south via Johns Bay which is defined by the landmasses of Pemaquid Neck to the east and Rutherford Island to the west. Look for prominent Johns Island in the upper bay. Keep Johns Island to your port and continue up the channel toward Beaver Island giving plenty of birth to Knowles Rocks on the starboard side. Then begin a slow turn to the east, toward the stone fort near the harbor entrance. Navigation buoys and moored boats will help keep you in deep water until you reach the Pemaquid River, which is the inner anchorage north of the remains of Fort William Henry. In the summer, this will be a busy harbor with plenty of activity.

13293
34th ed., Dec. 04
NAD 83
Soundings in feet
1:40,000

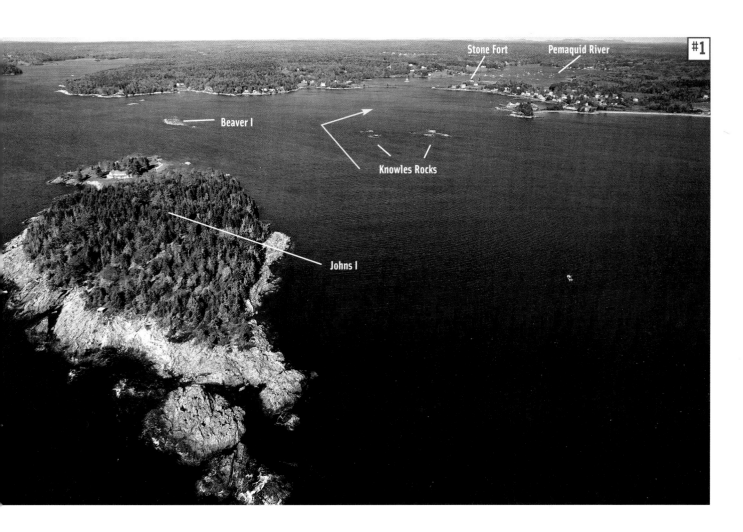

#1
Stone Fort
Pemaquid River
Beaver I
Knowles Rocks
Johns I

#2
Inner Harbor
Stone Fort
Fish Point
Knowles Rocks

■ EASTERN BRANCH ■

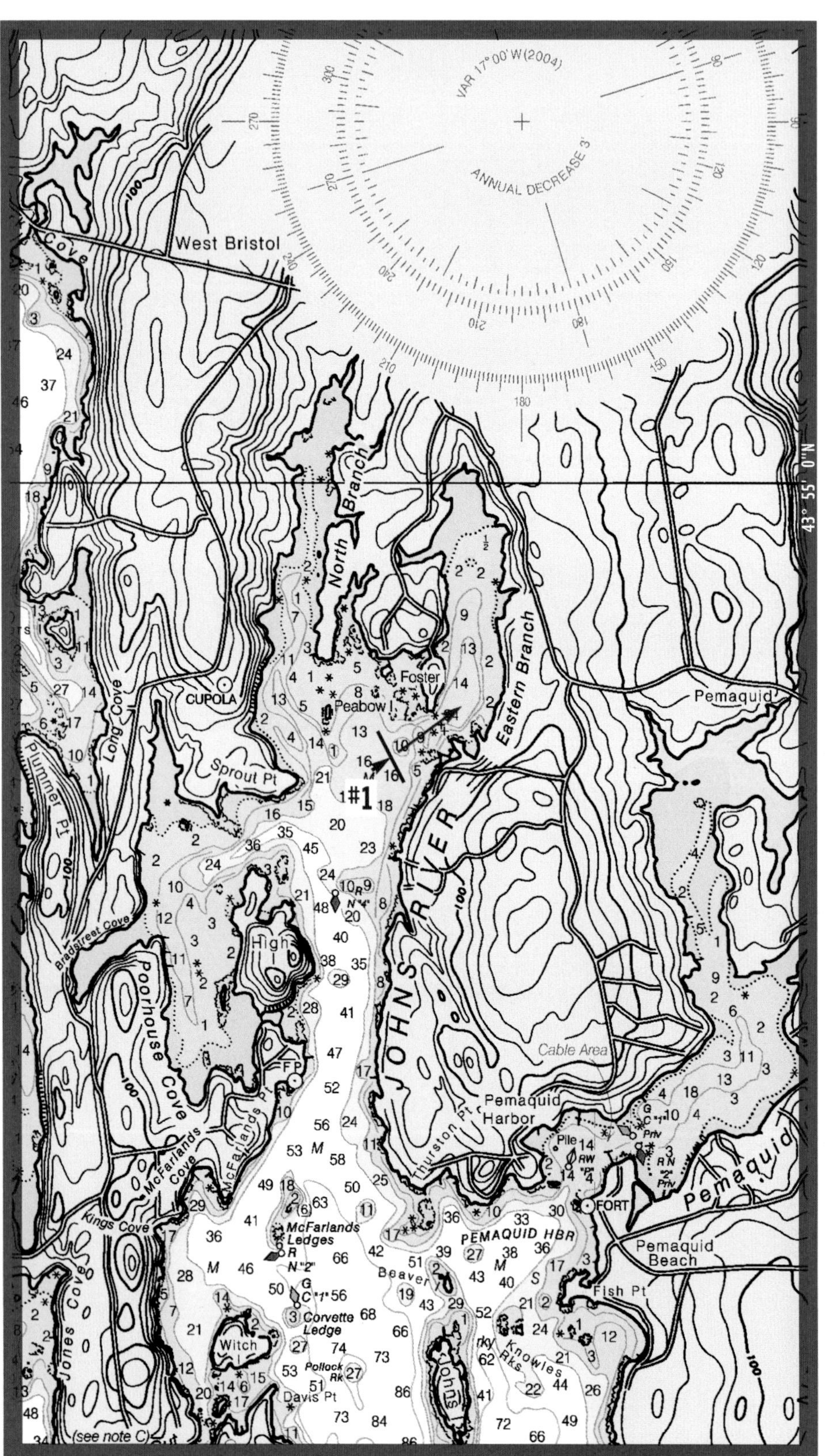

FOR the approach to the well-protected Eastern Branch of Johns River, keep Johns Island to starboard and stay in the middle of Johns Bay thereafter. As you continue up the bay into Johns River, the entrance into the Eastern Branch may seem like it will never come. Navigating into this hurricane hole, however, requires careful attention. The mariner will continue up Johns River, favoring the eastern shore after leaving red nun "4" to starboard. Then look for prominent Foster Island and use it to guide you to the harbor entrance. Beware of the so called Pinnacle Rocks, which are south of Foster Island. This entrance is best attempted at low tide, when the rocks are apparent. Leave the Pinnacle Rocks to starboard and head for the anchorage, which is about midway between Foster Island and the mainland to the east.

13293
34th ed., Dec. 04
NAD 83
Soundings in feet
1:40,000

#1

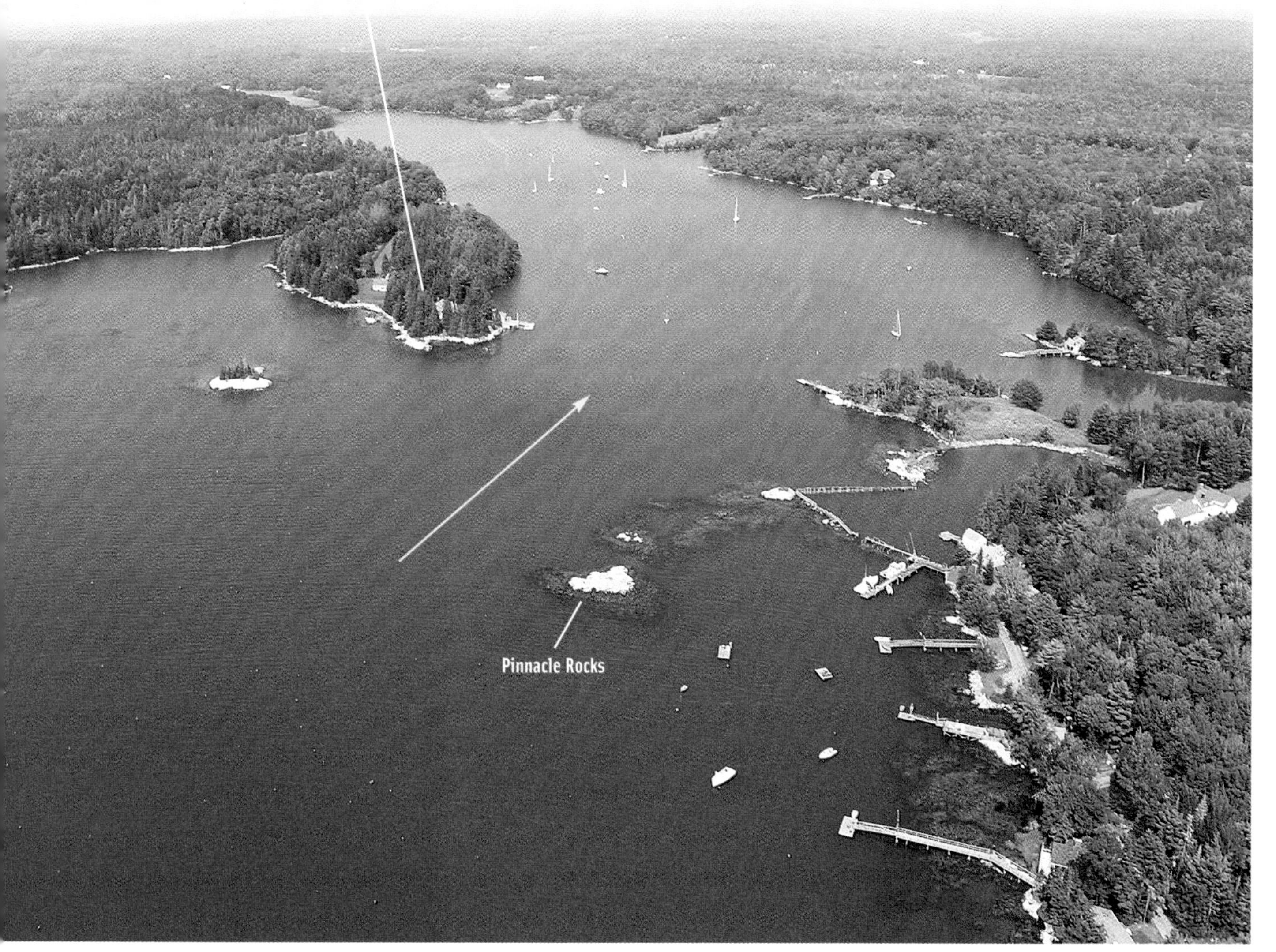

■ MONHEGAN ISLAND ■

IN all but the foggiest of conditions, Monhegan Island is difficult to miss. Approaching from the west, the red whistle buoy "14M" is located 2 miles off Monhegan's main anchorage. From the buoy, continue on an easterly heading, looking for the abandoned lighthouse on Manana Island to the west of Monhegan. Once inside the harbor, proceed up the middle. In addition to ocear swell, strong currents, and disturbing ferry traffic, the holding ground is notoriously bad. But occasionally you'll be able to pick up a mooring. Monhegan Harbo can be beautiful in calm conditions; choose the day and time to visit accordingly.

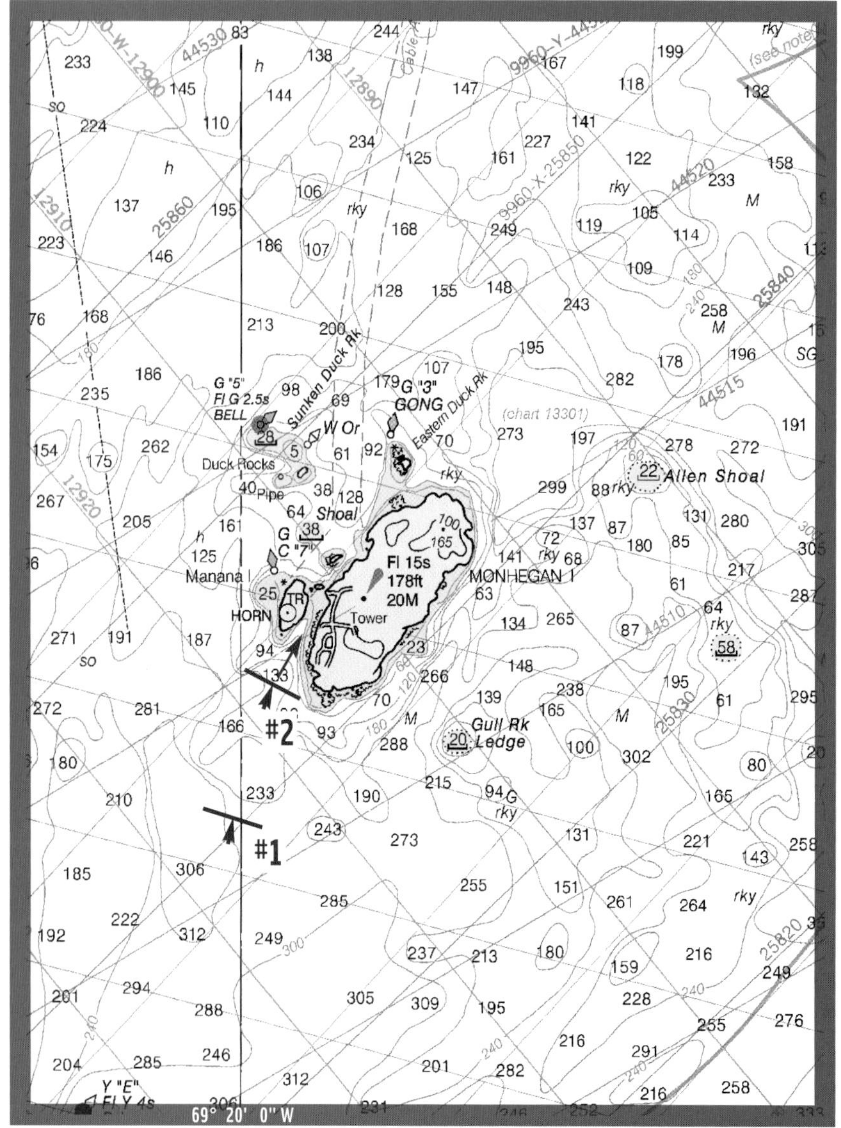

13288
41st ed., Sept. 04
NAD 83
Soundings in feet
1:80,000

#2

■ HORNBARN COVE ■

HORNBARN Cove is one of the most protected anchorages on the entire Maine coast. Lying up the Meduncook River, Hornbarn is approached from seaward between Morse Island and Gay Island, or from Friendship Harbor around the north end of Friendship Long Island. Approaching from seaward, favor the Morse Island shore, but be sure to keep green can "3" on your port side. From the buoy, head directly to the southern tip of Crotch Island. Proceed up the narrow inlet between Crotch Island and the ledges of the mainland on the starboard side. Hornbarn Cove will be directly ahead of you once you pass Crotch Island. Be sure to anchor out of the current.

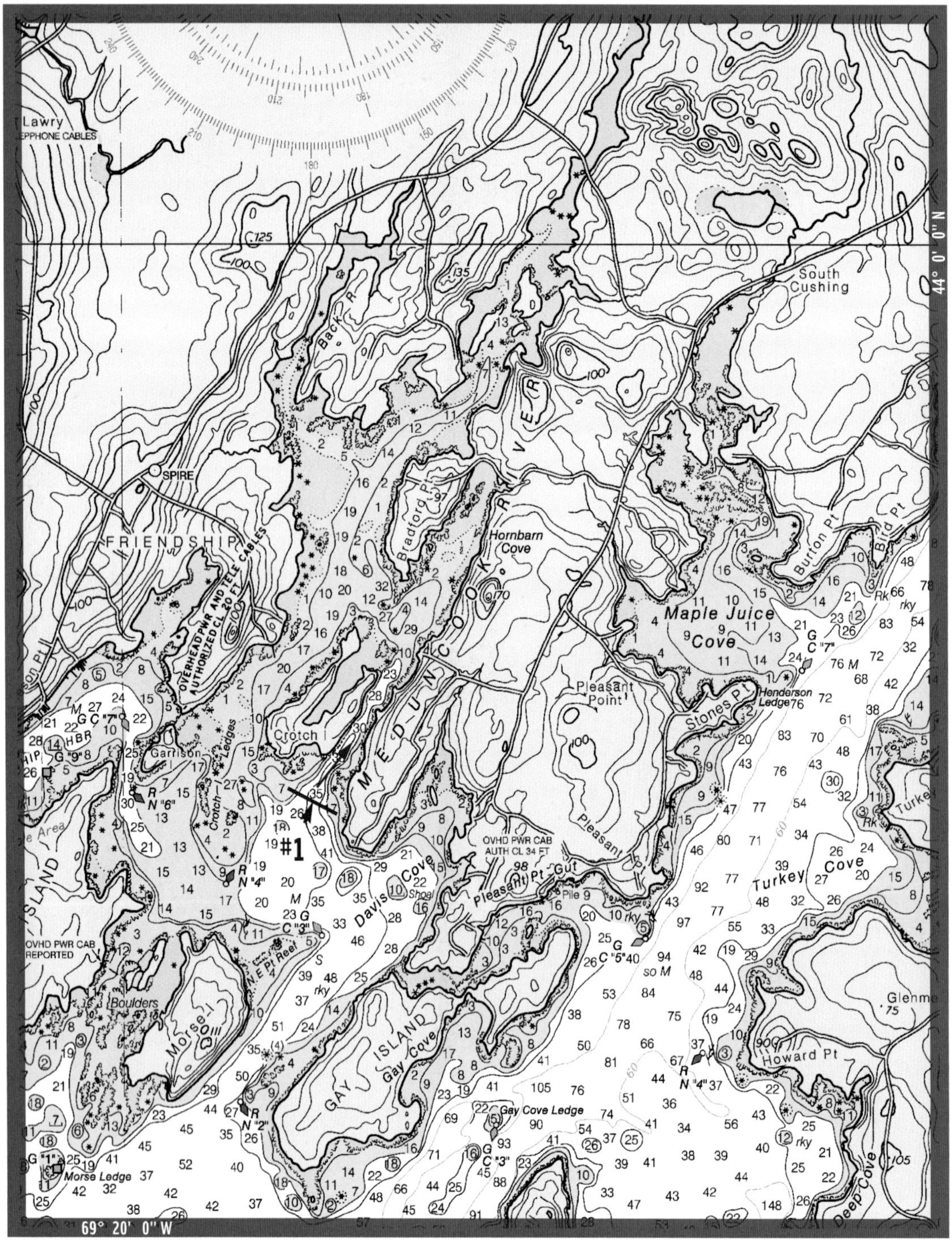

13301
20th ed., Mar. 97
NAD 83
Soundings in feet
1:40,000

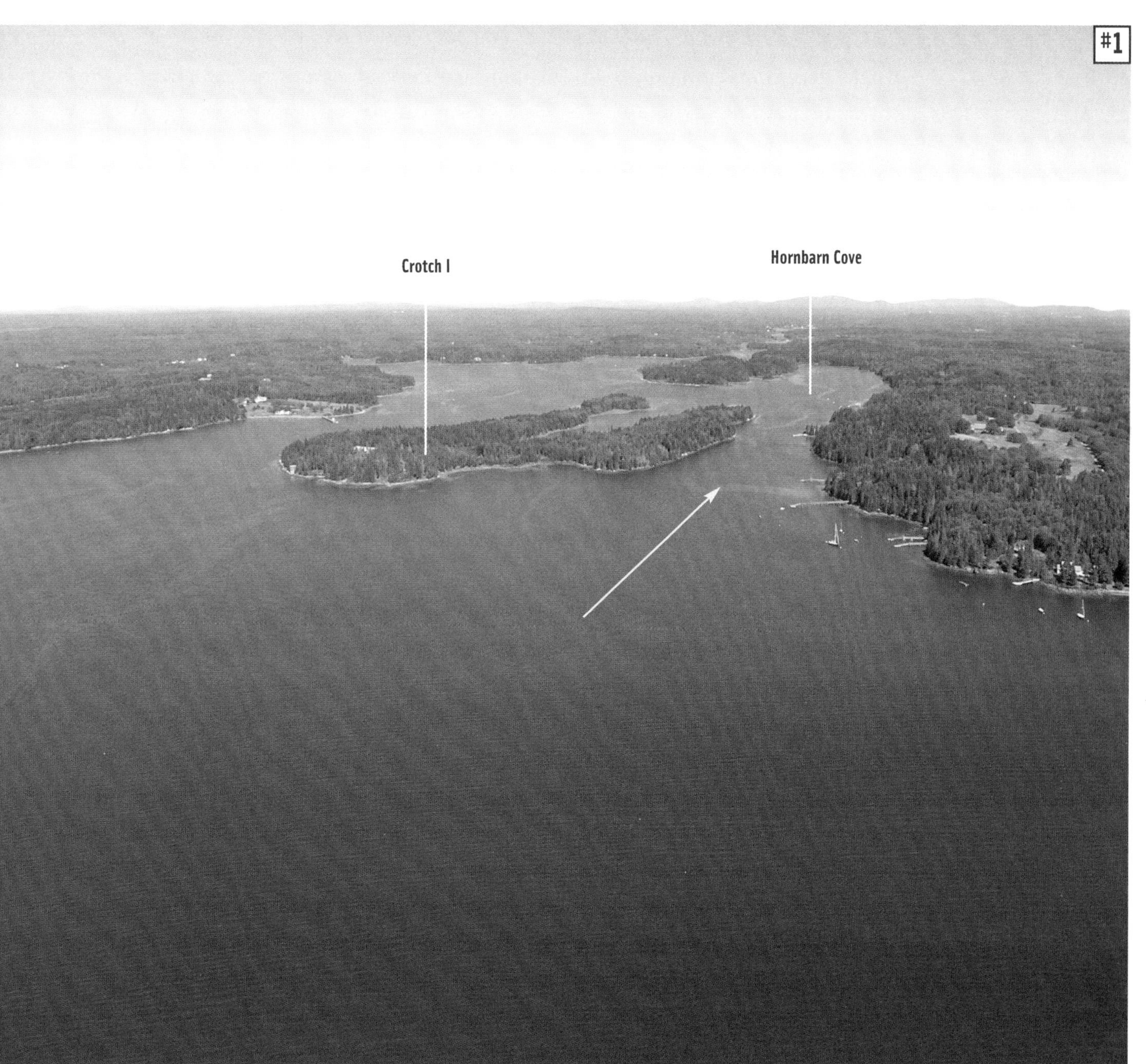
#1
Crotch I
Hornbarn Cove

PLEASANT POINT GUT

PLEASANT Point Gut is a popular and well-protected harbor in central Muscongus Bay. From Franklin Island Light in outer Muscongus Bay, pick up green can "1" marking Goose Rock Ledge. Proceed to green can "3" marking Gay Cove Ledge, leaving Caldwell Islanc to starboard. Head directly to green can "5." From there make a turn to the northwest and favor the northerr shoreline into Pleasant Point Gut. Continue on a south westerly course into th Gut and anchor wher room is available.

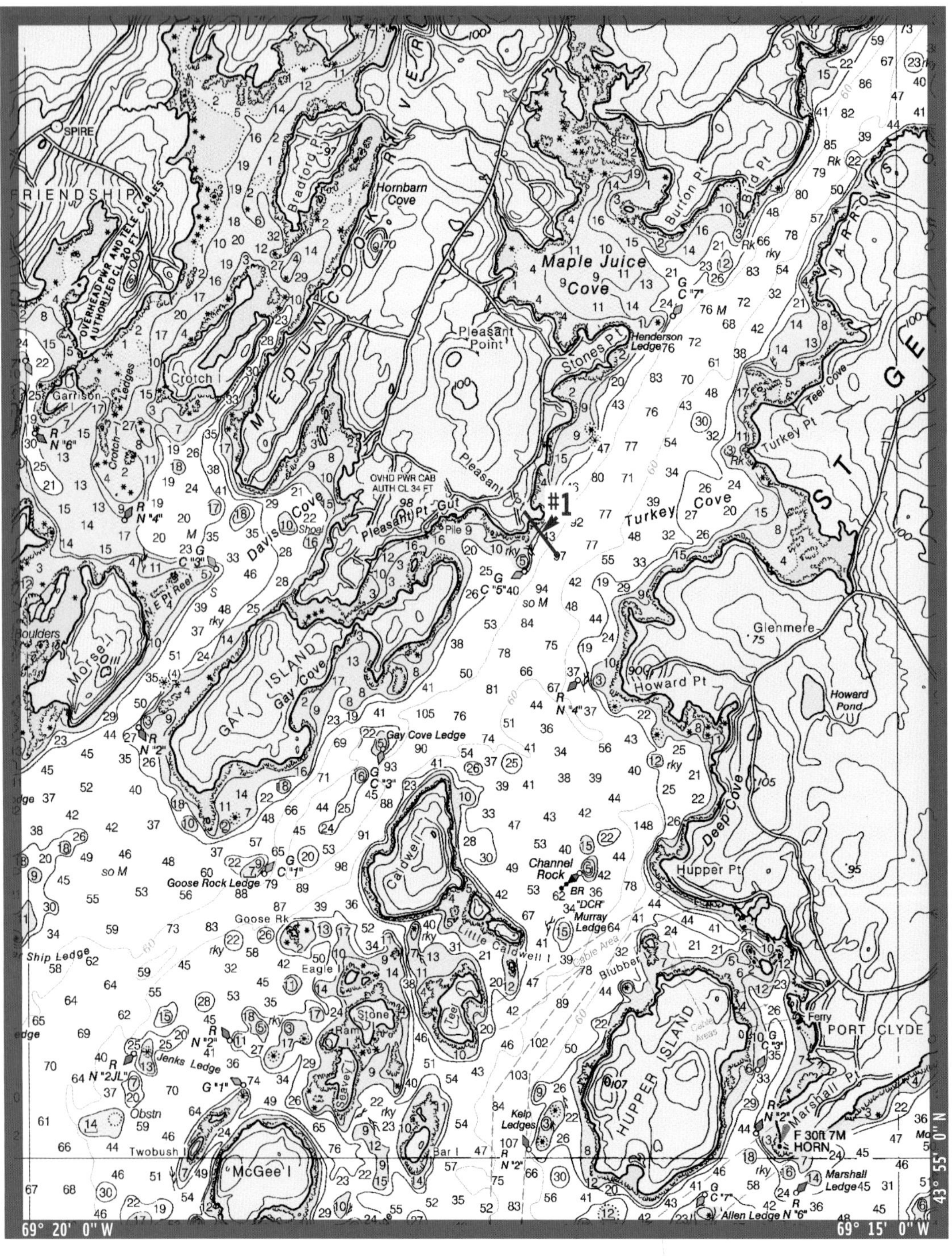

13301
20th ed., Mar. 97
NAD 83
Soundings in feet
1:40,000

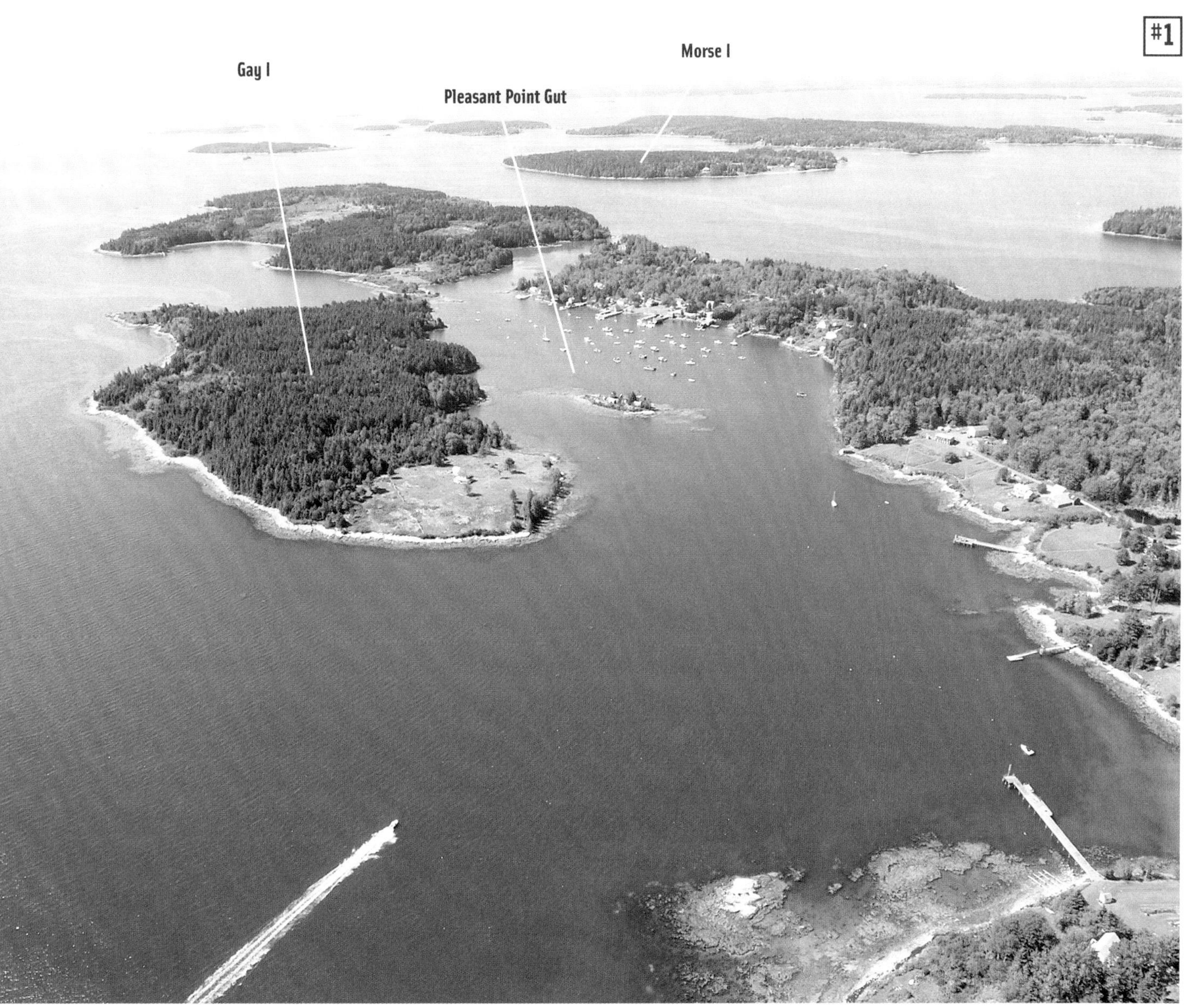
#1
Morse I
Gay I
Pleasant Point Gut

■ MAPLE JUICE COVE ■

A WONDERFUL respite on the St. George River is beautiful Maple Juice Cove. Easily accessible and relatively unobstructed, it can be approached from the south via the route to Pleasant Point Gut or via the channel east of Caldwell Island, with Hupper Island and Port Clyde on your starboard side. If using the easterly channel, proceed on a northerly course, passing either side of Channel Rock off Hupper Point. Continue north, leaving red nun "4" off Howard Point to starboard. Proceed until you reach green can "7" at Henderson Ledge. The can marks the mouth of Maple Juice Cove; keep it to port as you turn and head northwest. The holding ground is reported to be good in the center of the cove (at depth soundings of 9 to 11 feet). Anchoring in the south end of the cove will keep you out of the roll and currents, which are both mild in any event.

13301
20th ed., Mar. 97
NAD 83
Soundings in feet
1:40,000

#1
Stones Point
C "7"

■ PORT CLYDE ■

BUSY little Port Clyde is perhaps best known for its easy access and ferry terminal for Monhegan Island. The approach is straightforward. From any direction, proceed toward Marshall Point Lighthouse. Approaching from the east, leave red nun "6" marking Marshall Ledge to starboard, and leave nun "2" to starboard as well. Continue in the middle of the channel between Hupper Island and Marshall Point and you'll see green can "3" and the ferry terminal beyond. Rental moorings are available and anchoring is best well up the harbor, off the northeast end of Hupper Island.

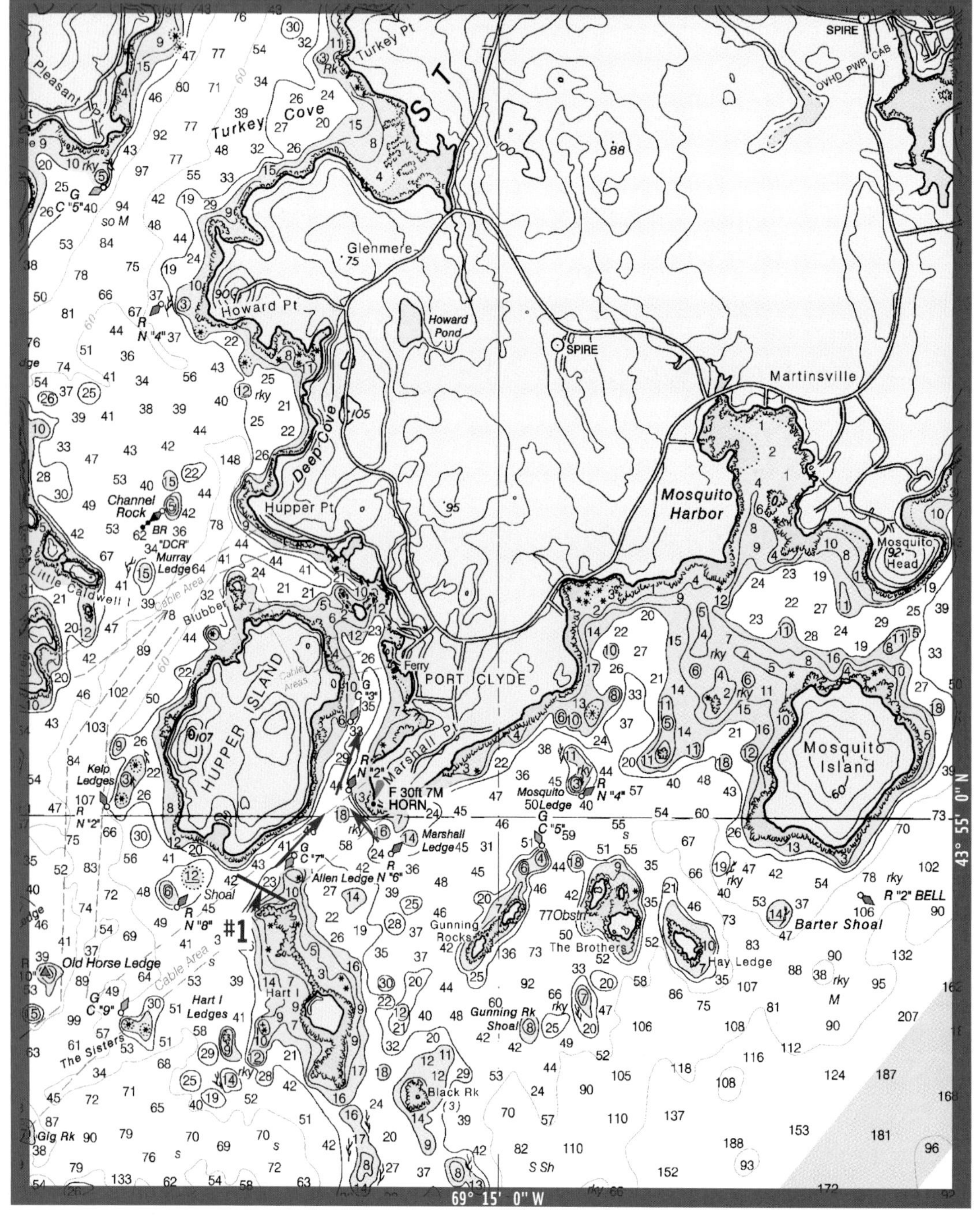

13301
20th ed., Mar. 97
NAD 83
Soundings in feet
1:40,000

#1
Port Clyde
Marshall Point
Hupper I
C "3"
N "2"
C "7"

REGION IV

ED STATES - EAST COAST
MAINE
BAY AND APPROACHES
Searsport
Belfast
Camden
Rockport
Gilkey Harbor
Rockland
Owls Head Harbor
Muscle Ridge Channel
Dix Island
Long Cove
Tenants Harbor

WEST PENOBSCOT BAY

—TENANTS HARBOR TO SEARSPORT—

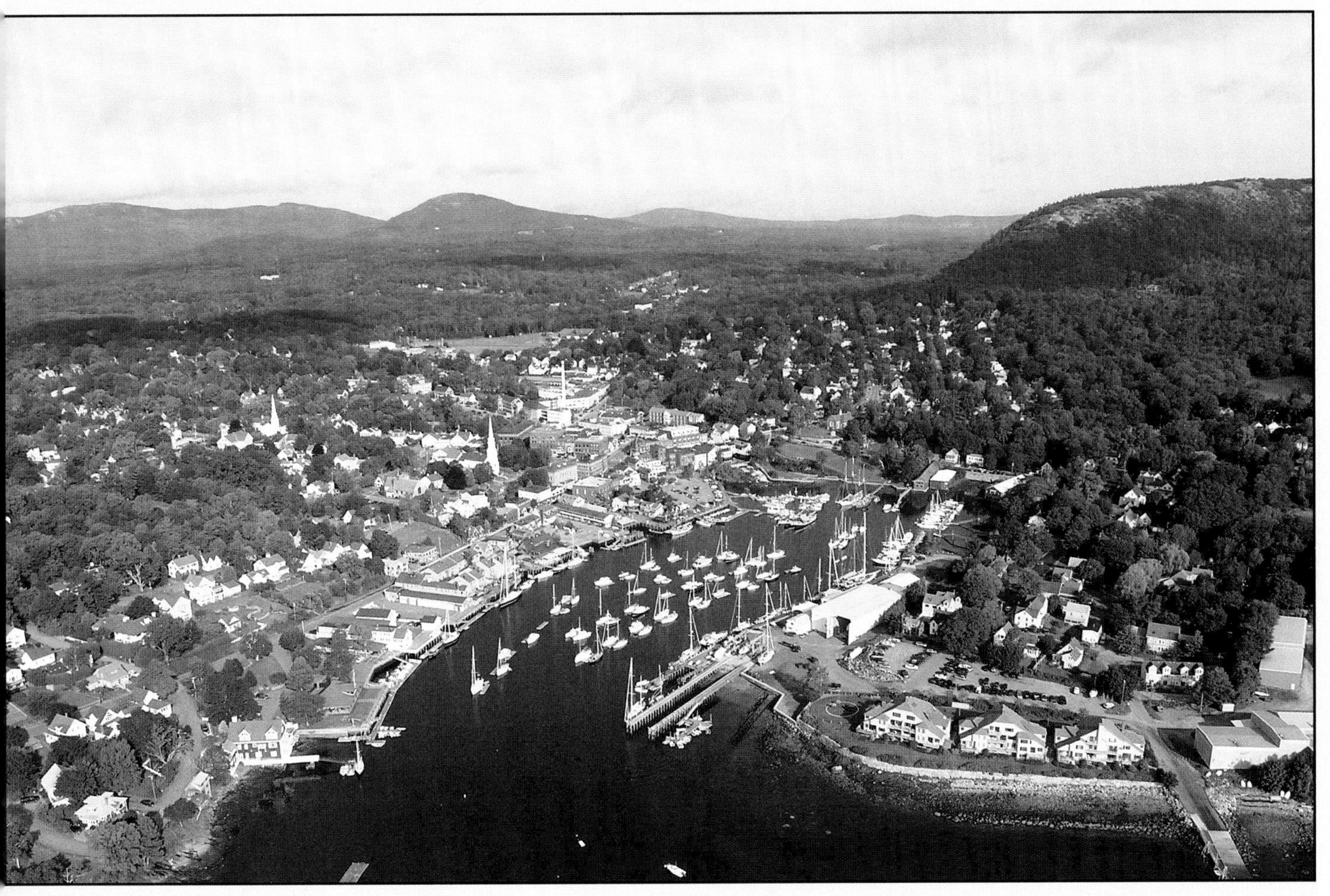

Camden Harbor (page 134)

East of Pemaquid Point's seaward thrust, east of Monhegan Island, east of Muscongus Bay with its hidden treasures, and east of the picturesque fishing villages of Friendship and Port Clyde, the eastbound navigator enters the approaches to Penobscot Bay—a cruising ground seemingly without end. The chief problem here is choosing a destination from so many offerings. Rounding Mosquito Island from the west, you could swing north for lovely, tucked-in Tenants Harbor, or cover the open-water miles to Whitehead Island (which you'll see ahead on a clear day), marking the entrance to Muscle Ridge Channel. Once there you might decide to spend a summer's night in the lovely remote anchorage at Dix Island, or you might push ahead to the port of Rockland, with its sprawling, commodious harbor and downtown bustle, or the picture-perfect villages of Rockport and Camden. Beyond them lie Belfast, Searsport, the Gatsby-esque summer mansions of Islesboro, and a host of other places to enjoy for themselves or to use as launching points for exploring East Penobscot Bay. The Camden Hills dominate the horizon in this region, and in clear weather you can always orient yourself by them.

Perhaps this region's greatest offering is the ability to combine "shore time" with island time, and all within convenient reach of cruising services.

■ TENANTS HARBOR AND LONG COVE ■

THE approach to Tenants Harbor is straightforward. Enter from the east leaving both green bell "1" and Southern Island to port. Steer a westerly heading directly into the harbor. The town, marine services and moorings are at the head of the harbor on the north side.

Long Cove is well protected, and a wonderfully serene alternative to busy Tenants Harbor. The approach to Long Cove begins as if you are going to Tenants Harbor but you'll turn sharply north after passing Northern Island on your starboard side. Be sure to keep red "2" close to starboard to avoid the ledges and shoal water to port. Moorings and anchorage can be found on the eastern side of the cove alongside Northern and High islands. The cove can be crowded at times so pick your way through with care. According to the chart, water depth is not less than nine feet at low tide, but it also shows isolated rocks and shoals toward the middle of the cove.

13301
20th ed., March 97
NAD 83
Soundings in feet
1:40,000

#1
Tenants Harbor
Long Cove
N "2"
Northern I
Southern I

#2
Long Cove
High I
Northern I
N "2"
Tenants Harbor
Southern I

■ MUSCLE RIDGE CHANNEL ■

FOR cruisers who have been tracing Maine's rocky Midcoast eastward, Muscle Ridge Channel offers a well marked and sheltered shortcut north into West Penobscot Bay. The southern entrance to Muscle Ridge Channel is marked by red bell "2SB" southwest of South Breaker. Leave the bell to starboard and the 75-foot lighthouse on Whitehead Island to port. Once past Whitehead Island, leave red daymarker "2" on Yellow Ledge to starboard, and continue northeast, honoring all navigation aids. The green-and-red can south of Burnt Island must be kept to port. As you approach the northern end of the channel, pick out green daymarker "11" on Otter Island Ledge, (see chart on p. 126), then find can "13" south of Ash Island and the red-and-green nun "RG" marking the Upper Gangway; pass between them. Continue toward Rockland by way of Owls Head Bay.

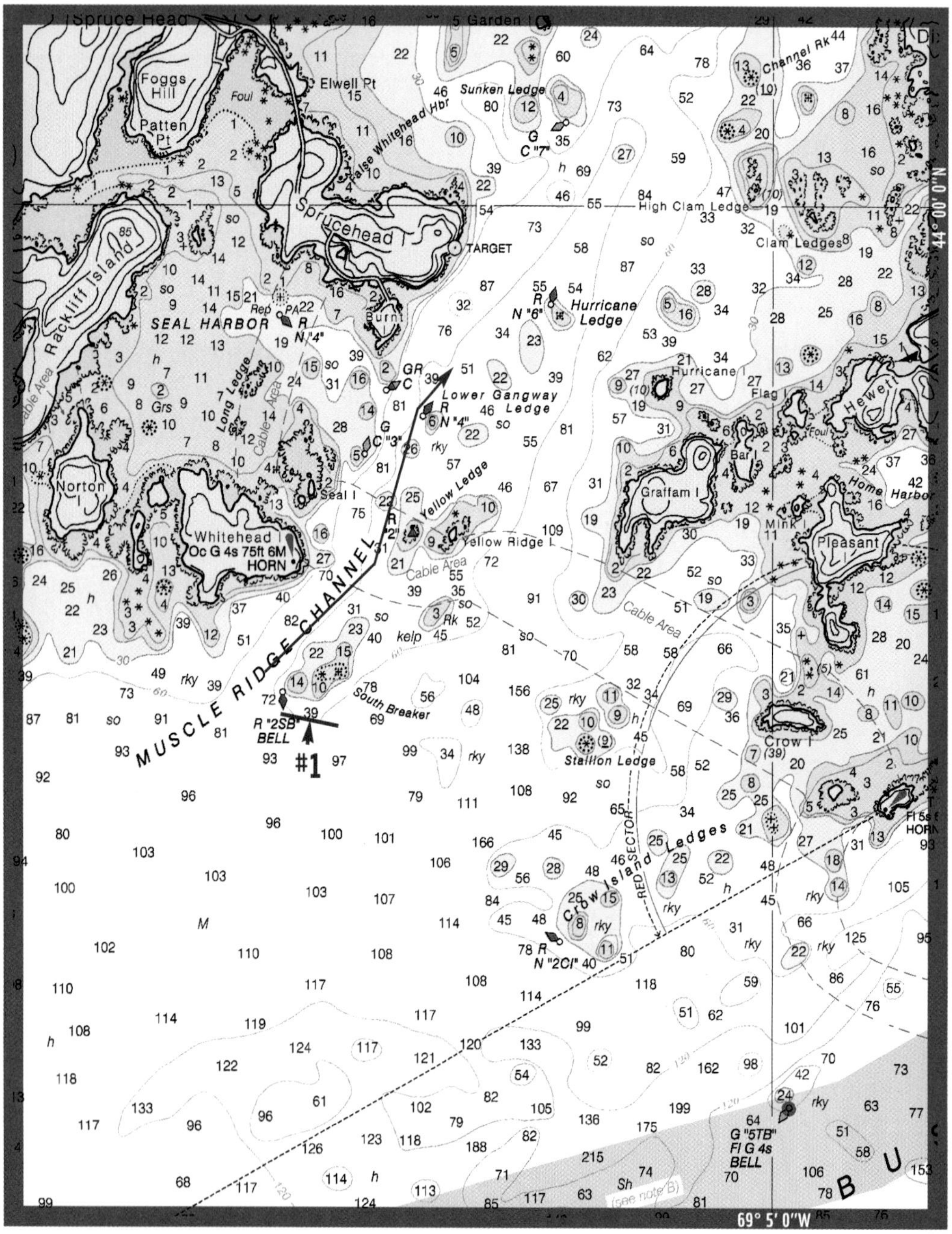

13303
12th ed., Sept. 02
NAD 83
Soundings in feet
1:40,000

#1

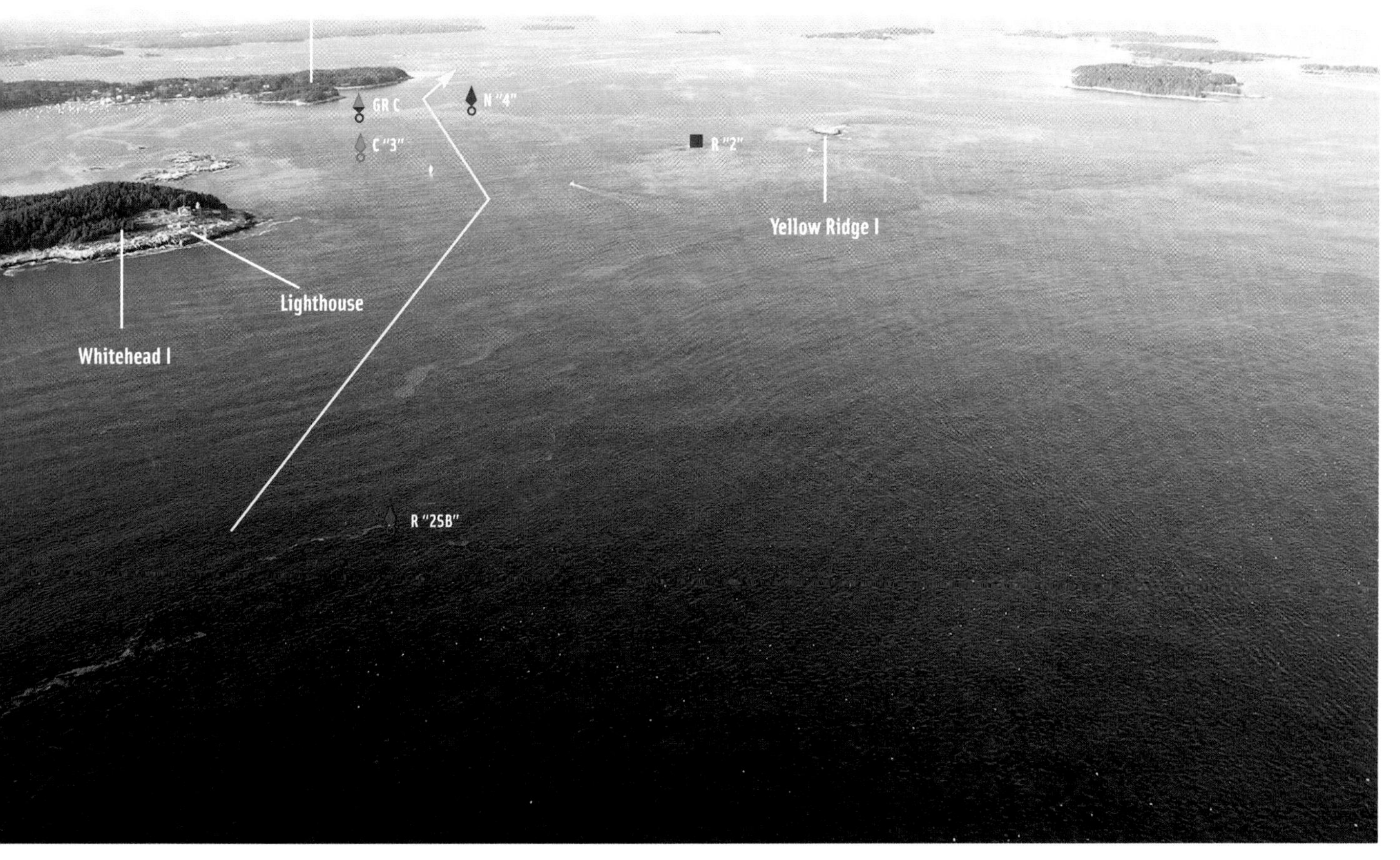
Burnt I
GR C
N "4"
C "3"
R "2"
Yellow Ridge I
Lighthouse
Whitehead I
R "25B"

DIX ISLAND HARBOR

THOUGH not accorded the same respect as other tricky entrances, the approach to Dix Island Harbor can be plenty challenging. To get there from Muscle Ridge Channel, find red nun "6" marking Hurricane Ledge, then turn east, keeping Clam Ledges to port. (Be sure to stay north of the 5-foot spot along the way.) After you pass the southern end of Clam Ledges, turn northeast and enter the deepwater channel that runs west of Nettle Island. Keep Nettle Island and its associated rocks to starboard, while keeping the string of islets and ledges off Dix Island to port. While isolated dangers do extend from the neighboring islands, good anchorage can be found in 19 to 28 feet of water in the shelter of Dix, Birch, Andrews islands, and The Neck. Alternatively, boats can tuck into the anchorage north of Dix Island formed by Birch, High and Little Green islands. For this latter anchorage the approach is made from Muscle Ridge Channel near red nun "10." Beware of the 3-foot spot west of High Island.

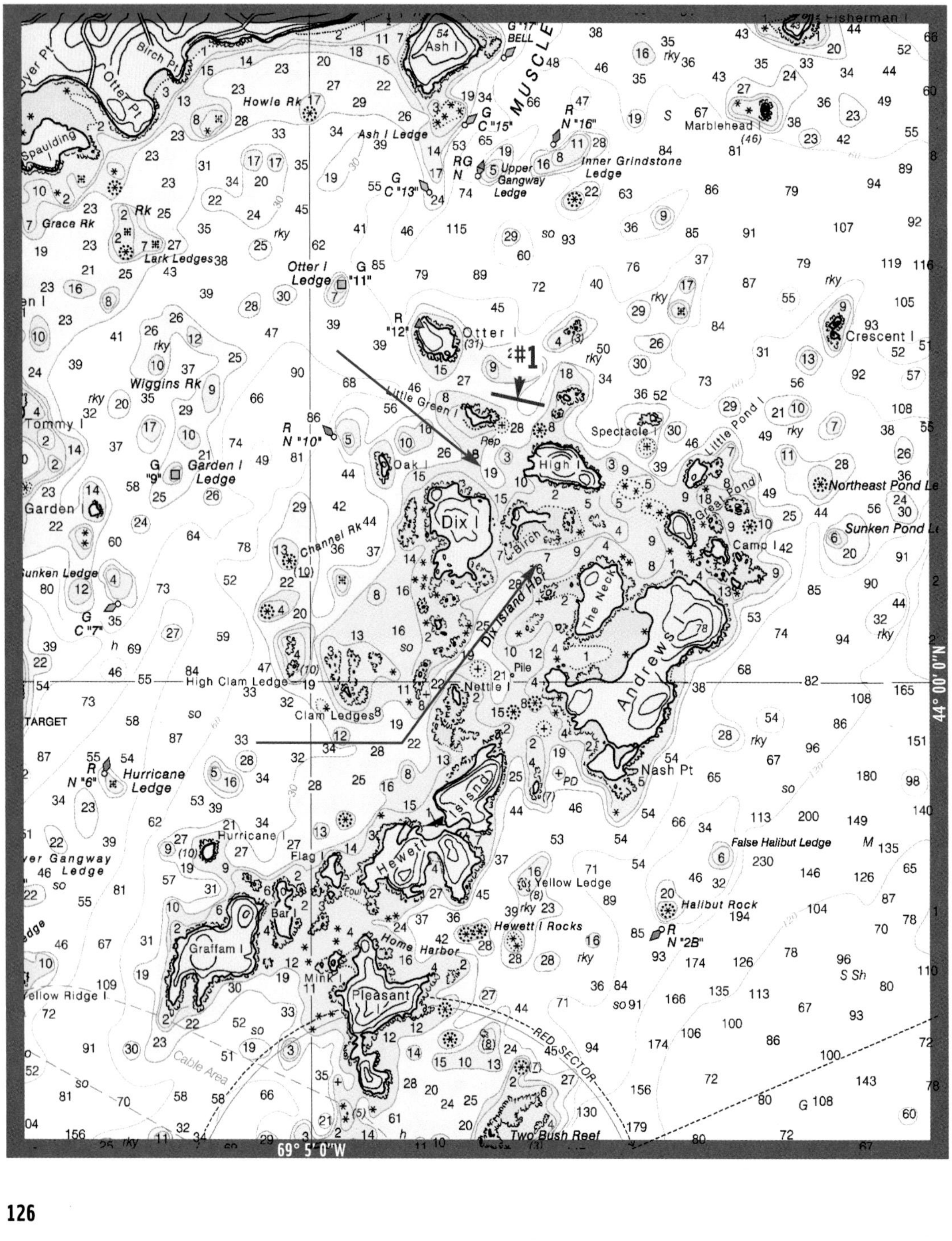

13303
12th ed., Sept. 02
NAD 83
Soundings in feet
1:40,000

#1

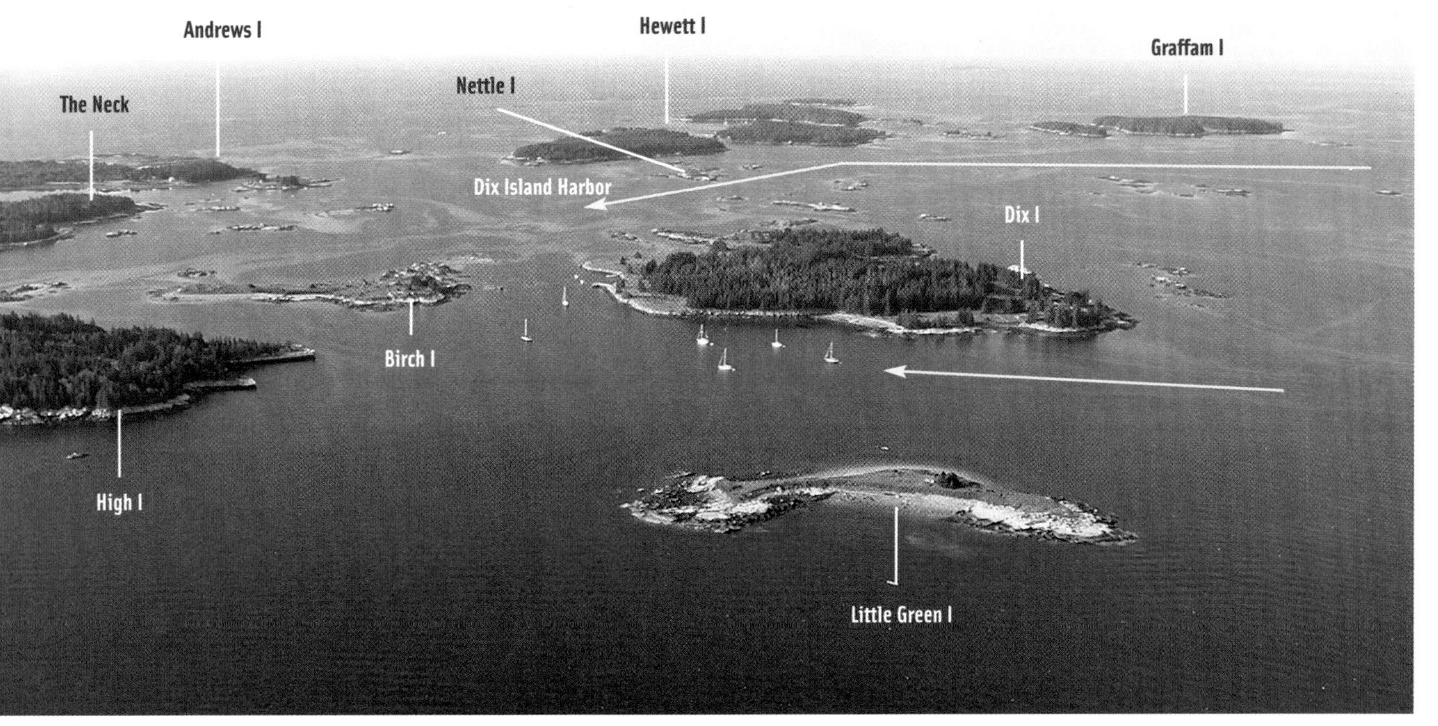
Andrews I
Hewett I
Graffam I
Nettle I
The Neck
Dix Island Harbor
Dix I
Birch I
High I
Little Green I

■ OWLS HEAD HARBOR ■

OWLS Head Harbor is a shallow indentation west of Dodge Point. The approach to Owls Head Harbor can be made two ways. If northbound in Muscle Ridge Channel, transit the narrows formed by nun "4" off Sheep Island and can "3" off Hendrickson Point. Continue up toward Dodge Point, where anchorage can be found in less than 30 feet of water. If coming from the north, pass scenic Owls Head light to starboard, keeping Monroe Island to port. Once abeam of green daymark "5" marking Dodge Point Ledge, a gradual turn to the west will bring you into the anchorage. Owls Head Bay is a thoroughfare for yachts and commercial traffic, therefore it is important to anchor inside the 30-foot contour, west of the main channel, especially if fog is expected.

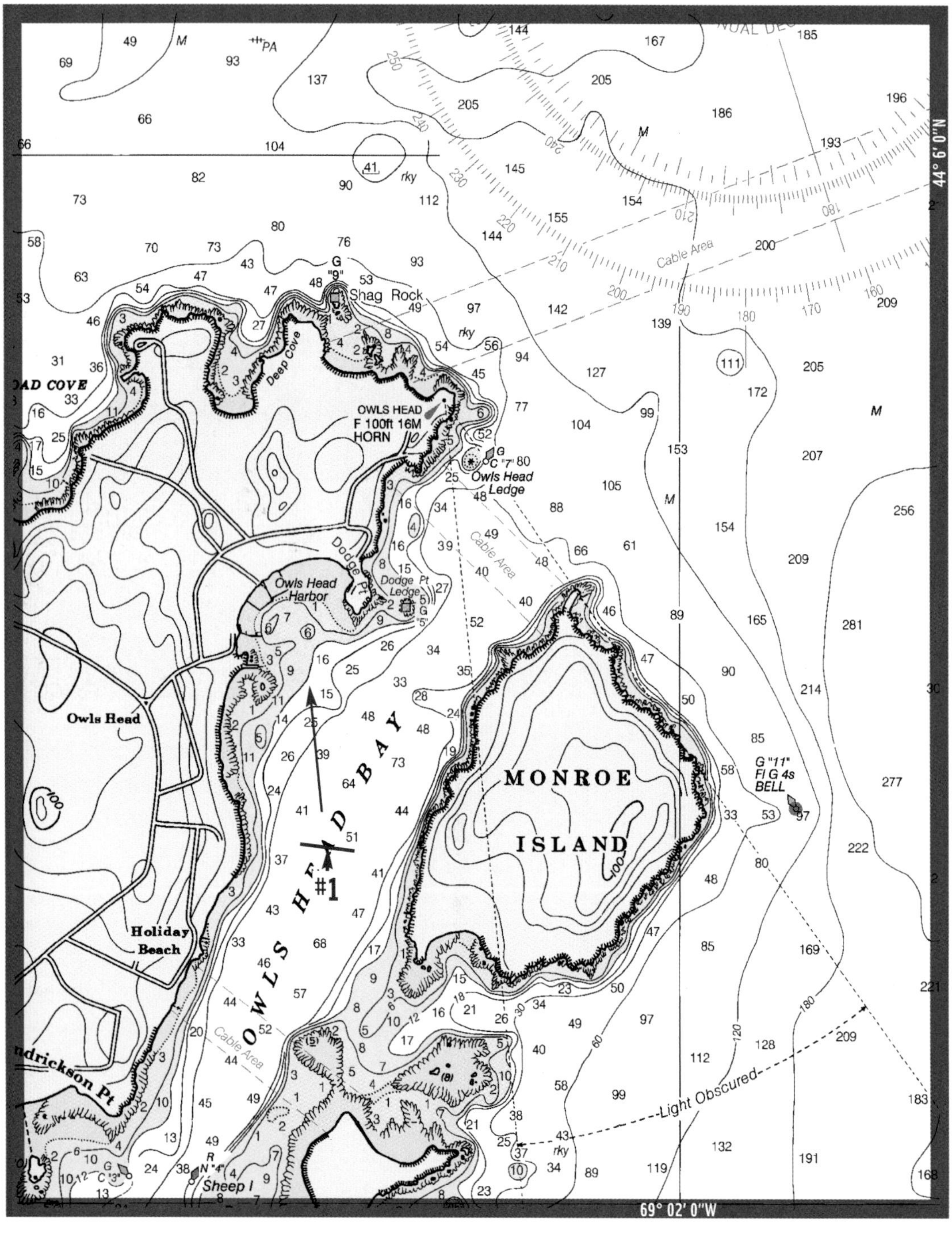

13307
10th ed., Oct. 01
NAD 83
Soundings in feet
1:20,000

#1

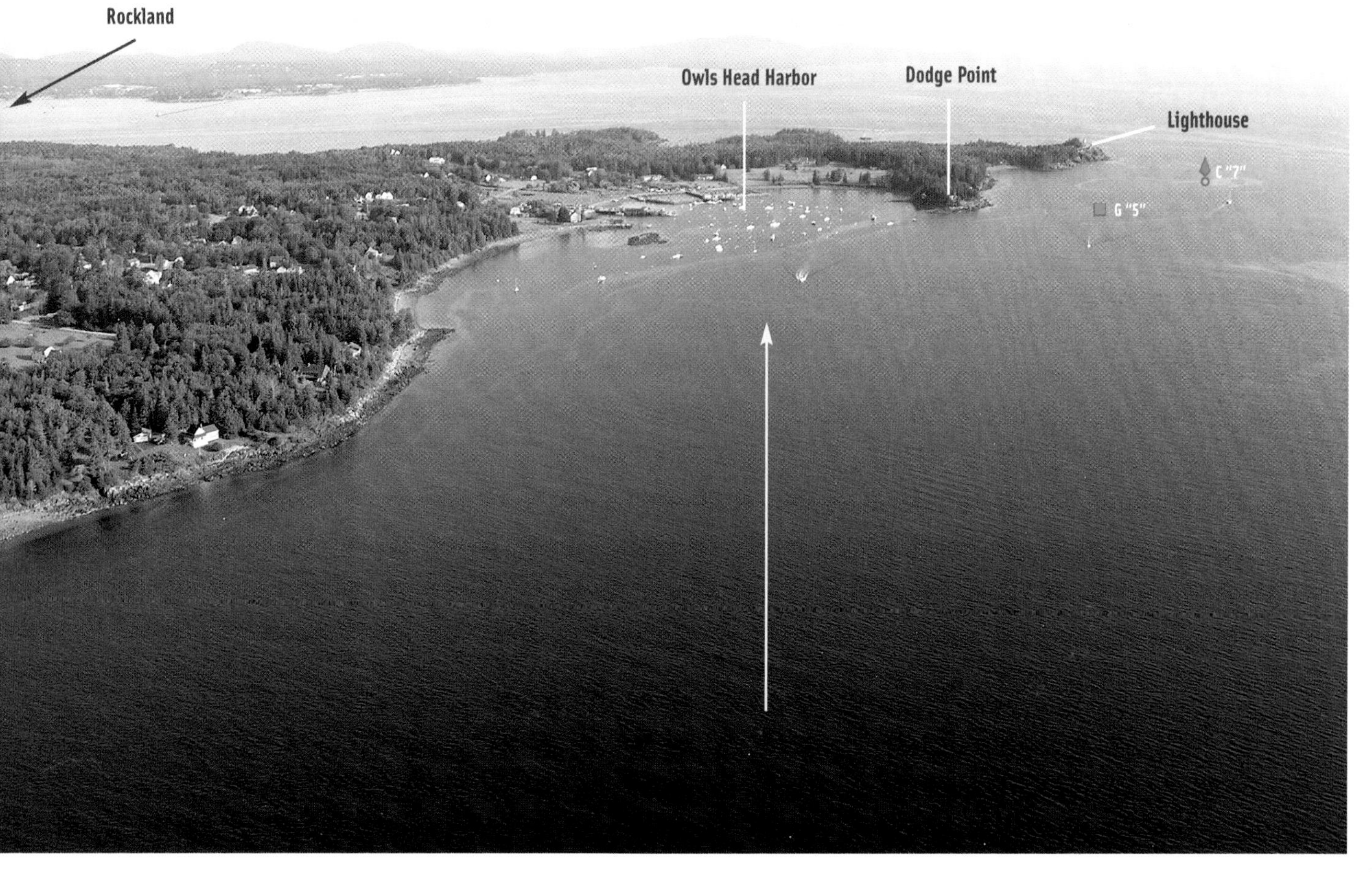

■ ROCKLAND HARBOR ■

ROCKLAND Harbor is one of the largest and busiest harbors in the Penobscot region. Its wide and forgiving entrance is easily navigable in all weather. There is plenty of deep water in this expansive port and a full range of marine services on the shore. The southern part of the harbor is exposed to the east. A mile-long breakwater originates at Jameson Point and terminates at a large brick lighthouse halfway across the mouth of the harbor. Keep the lighthouse to starboard as you enter the harbor, and maintain a sharp lookout for the Vinalhaven and North Haven ferries that run to and from the terminal at Rockland's north end.

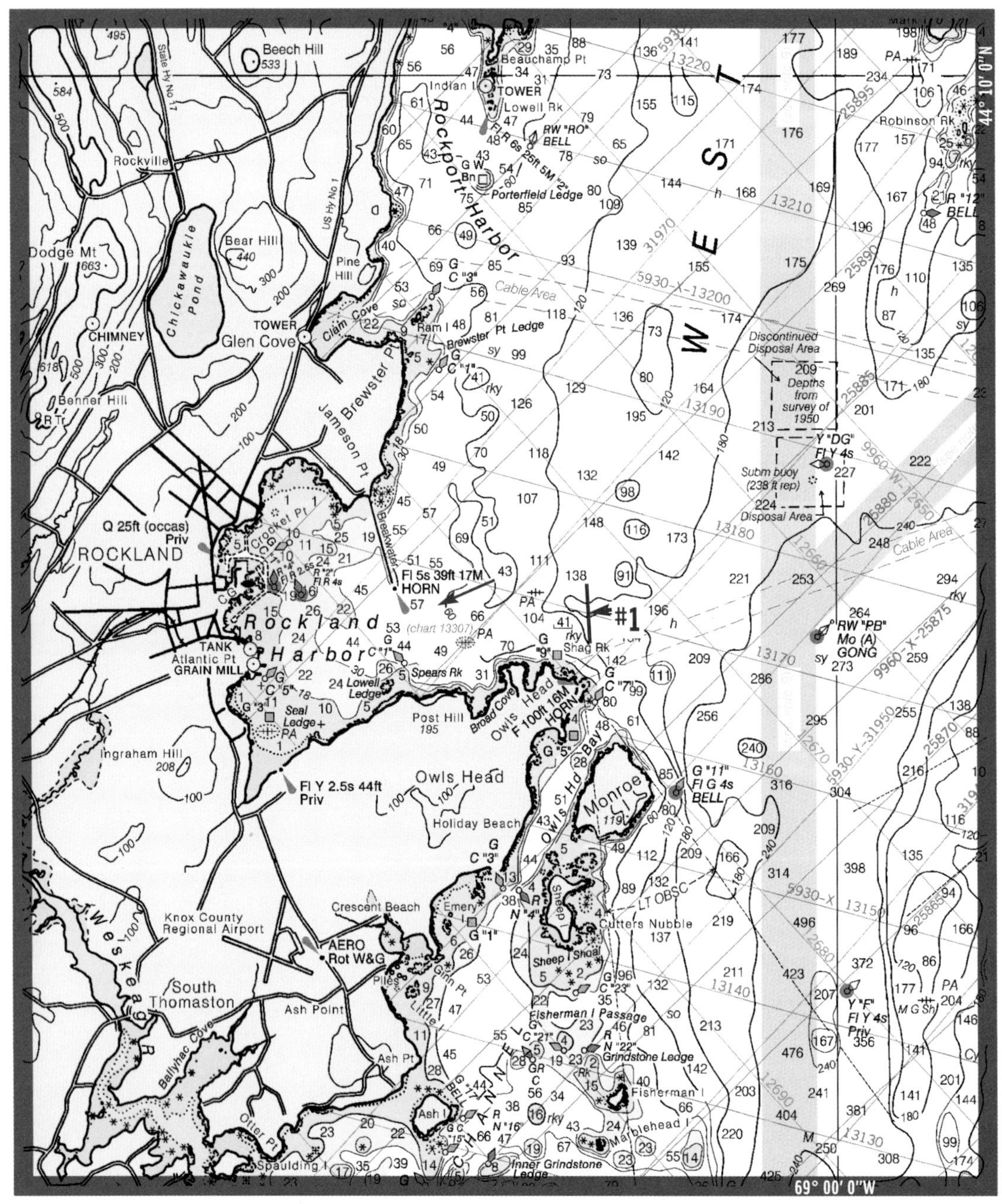

13302
21st ed., Nov. 01
NAD 83
Soundings in feet
1:80,000

#1

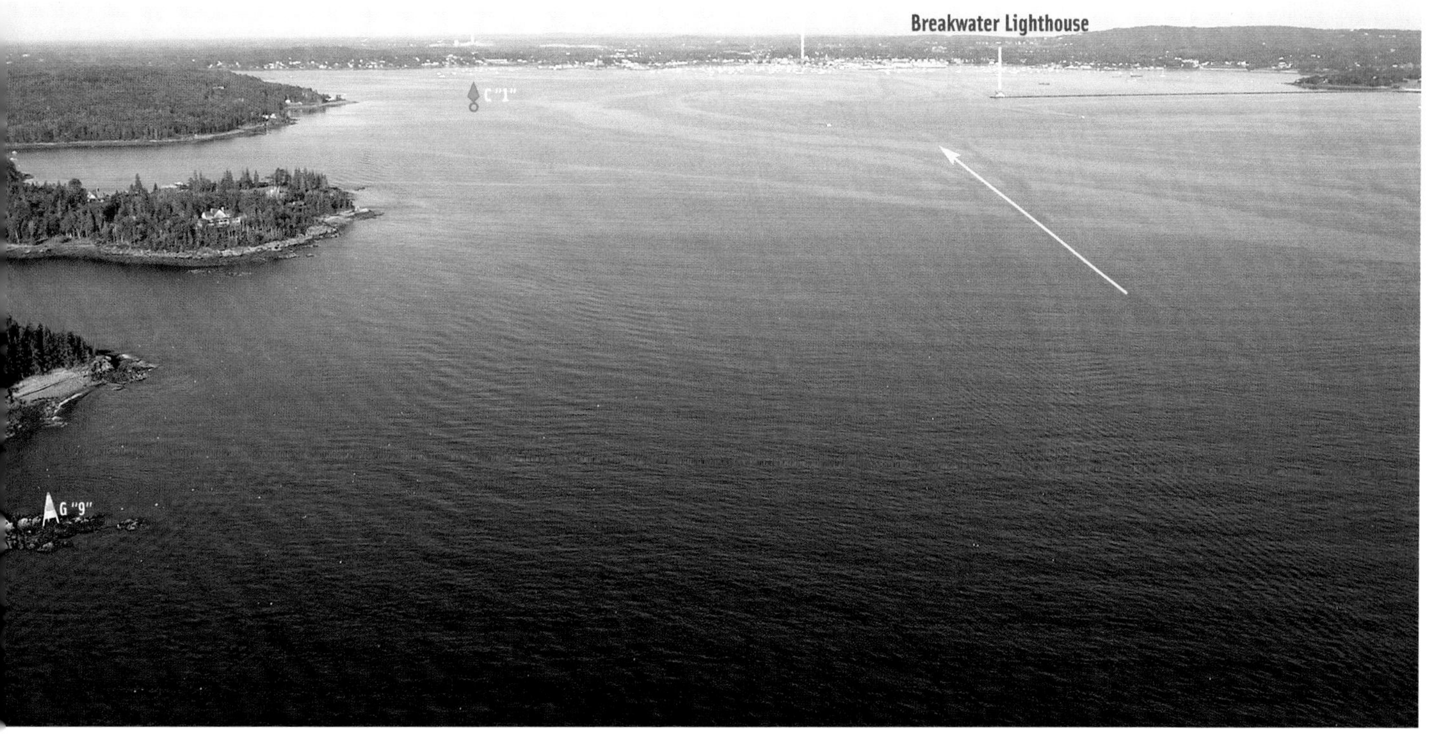

■ ROCKPORT HARBOR ■

PICTURESQUE Rockport Harbor is easy to enter and clearly visible from the south. If approaching from Owls Head or Rockland, keep the monument on Porterfield Ledge (GW Bn) to starboard. The same goes for the lighthouse on Indian Island. Continue on a northerly heading into the harbor. If coming from the north or east, pass close to the unlit red-and-white bell "RO," passing between Porterfield Ledge and Lowell Rock. Once you pass west of these two navigation aids, you can turn north toward Rockport Harbor. The harbor is exposed to southerly wind and swell. Limited services are available, but Rockport's quaint village is well worth the visit. Rockport Marine is located at the head of the harbor and is a premier yard for wooden boat construction and repair.

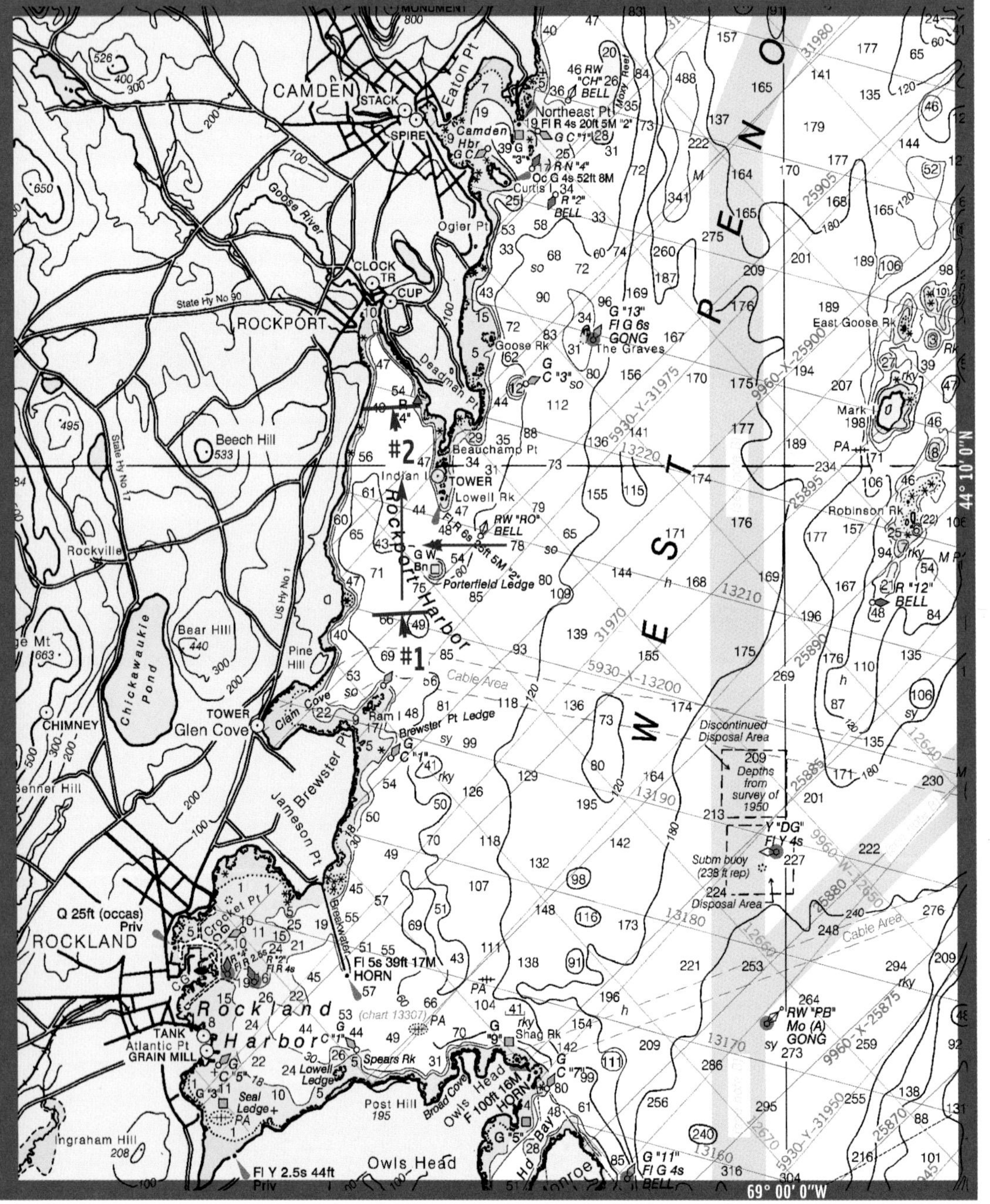

13302
21st ed., Nov. 01
NAD 83
Soundings in feet
1:80,000

#1

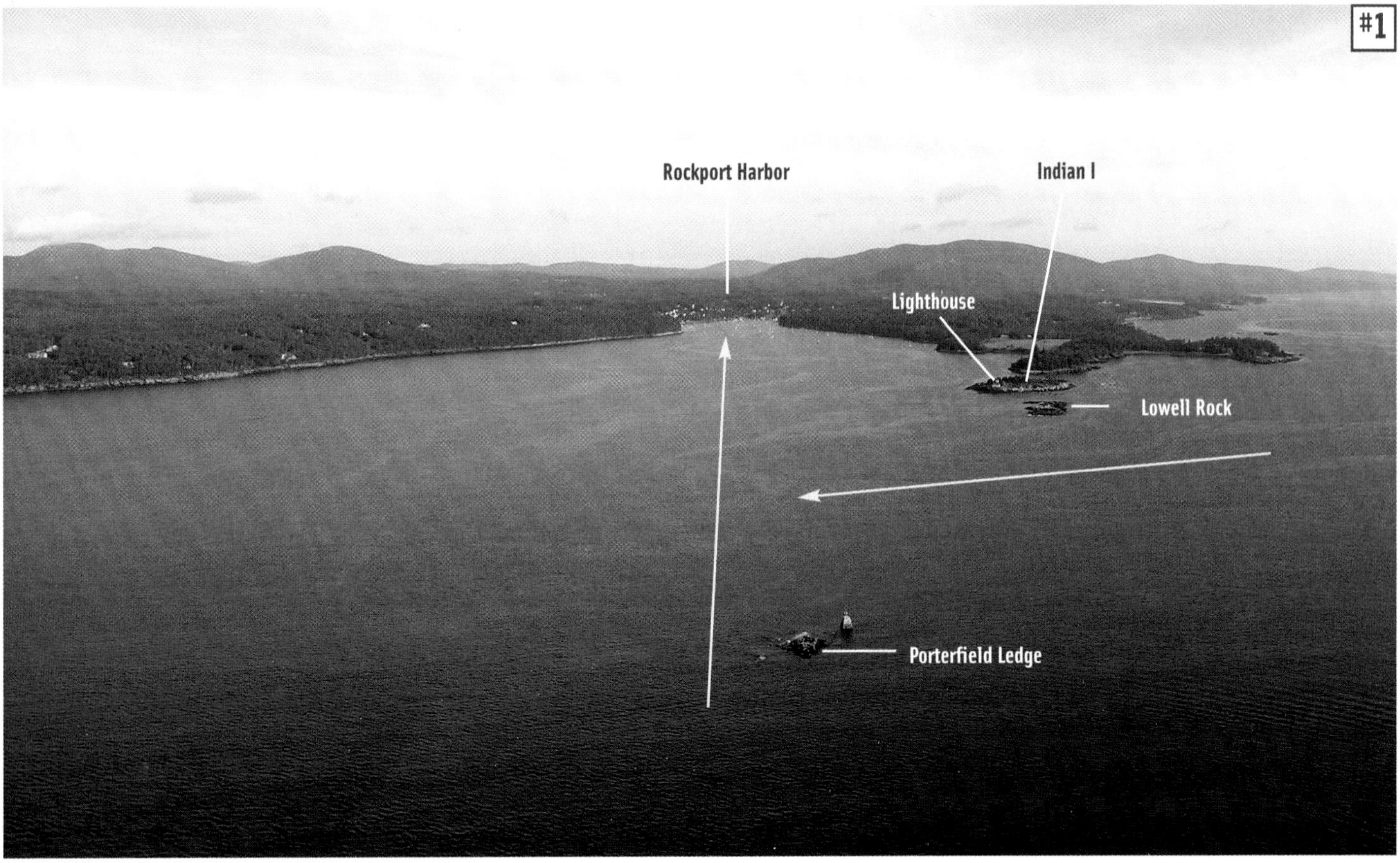

Rockport Harbor

Indian I

Lighthouse

Lowell Rock

Porterfield Ledge

■ CAMDEN HARBOR ■

CAMDEN is a major cruising destination and is home to about half the Maine Windjammer fleet. The approach to Camden can be deceptive. The critical element is to differentiate Curtis Island—with its lighthouse—from the mainland at Dillingham Point. Once identified, keep Curtis Island to port and follow the string of buoys that mark the channel. In the summer, the outer mooring field is easily recognized, as hundreds of boats call here every week. The Camden Harbormaster does a wonderful job maintaining a visible channel through this maze of boats. Large red and green balls demark the passageway through the mooring field into the inner harbor. Camden is known for its excellent marine services, restaurants, bed and breakfasts, and summer activities, as well as the hospitable Camden Yacht Club. It is a great spot for the visiting yachtsman.

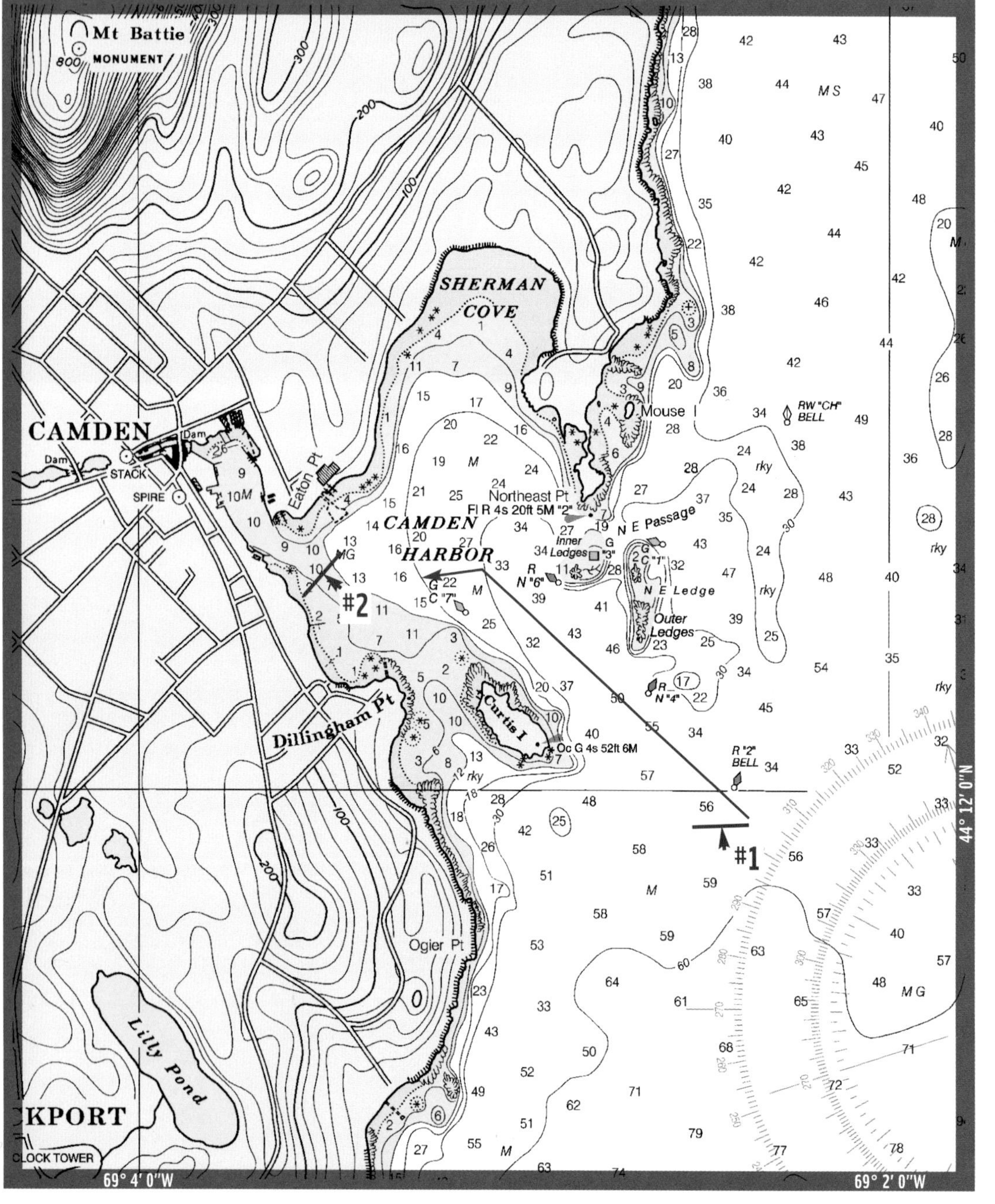

13307
10th ed., Oct. 01
NAD 83
Soundings in feet
1:20,000

#1

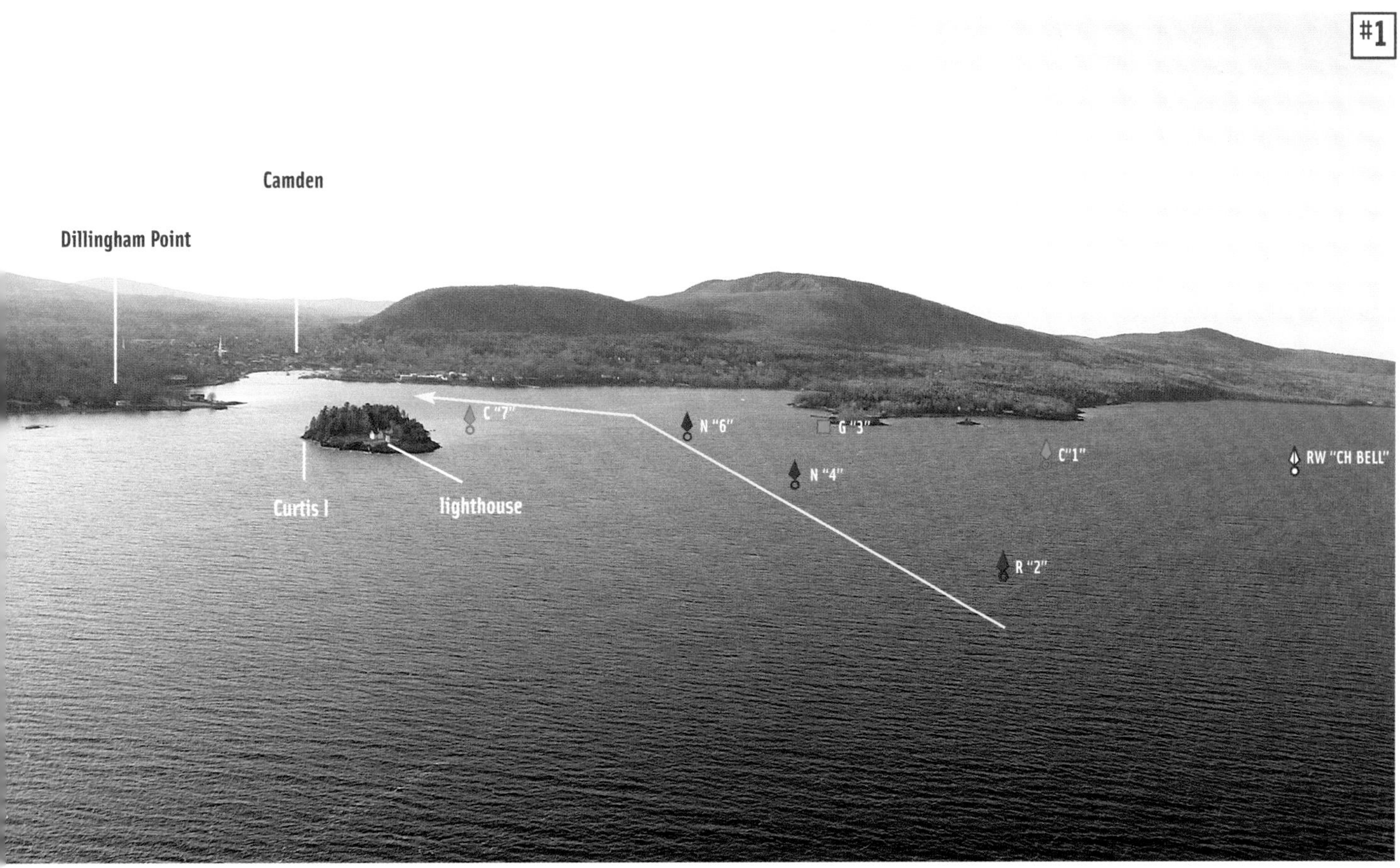

Camden

Dillingham Point

C "7"

N "6"

G "3"

C "1"

RW "CH BELL"

N "4"

Curtis I

lighthouse

R "2"

#2

■ GILKEY HARBOR ■

GILKEY Harbor is formed by Islesboro Island to the east and Seven Hundred Acre Island to the west. It can be approached from either the south or the north. Coming from the south, keep Lasell and Job islands to starboard and look for flashing green bell "1" south of Ensign Island. Leave the bell to port and run up to red nun "2" marking Minot Ledge. The anchorage at Ames Cove opens up to starboard, and, a little farther on, Cradle Cove opens up to port. If coming from the north or west, enter between flashing red bell "2" off Warren Island and the flashing white light by the ferry terminal at Grindel Point. Leave green can "7" off Spruce Island to starboard and nun "6" off Lobster Rock to port. Begin a slow turn south toward Thrumcap when you reach the eastern edge of Spruce Island and enter Gilkey Harbor. Gilkey Harbor is essentially a thoroughfare, so it's best to duck into one of the coves when choosing an anchorage.

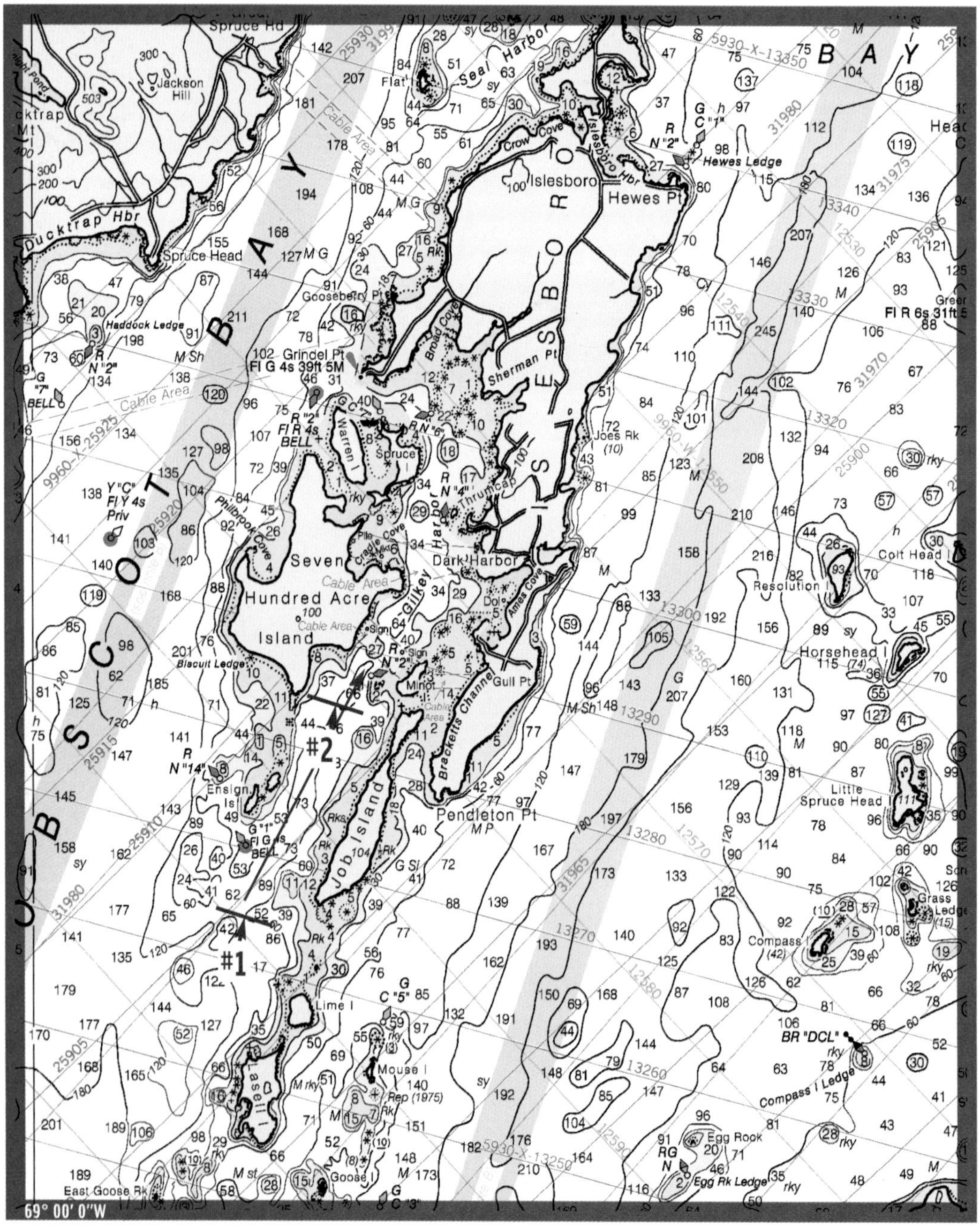

13302
21st ed., Nov. 01
NAD 83
Soundings in feet
1:80,000

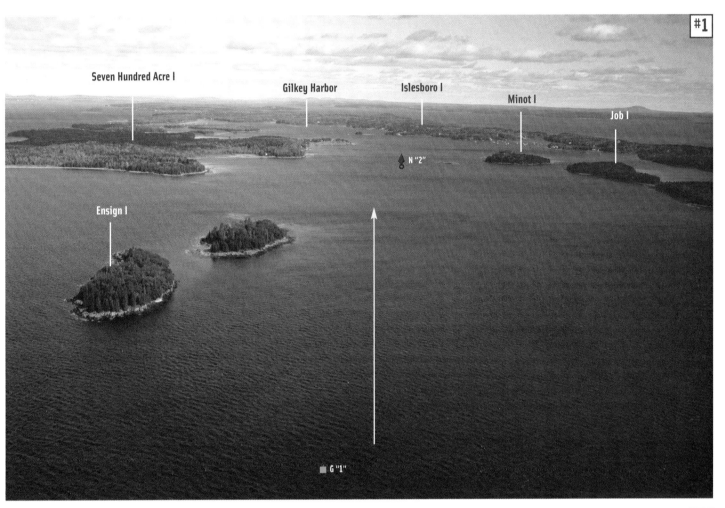

#1
Seven Hundred Acre I
Gilkey Harbor
Islesboro I
Minot I
Job I
N "2"
Ensign I
G "1"

#2

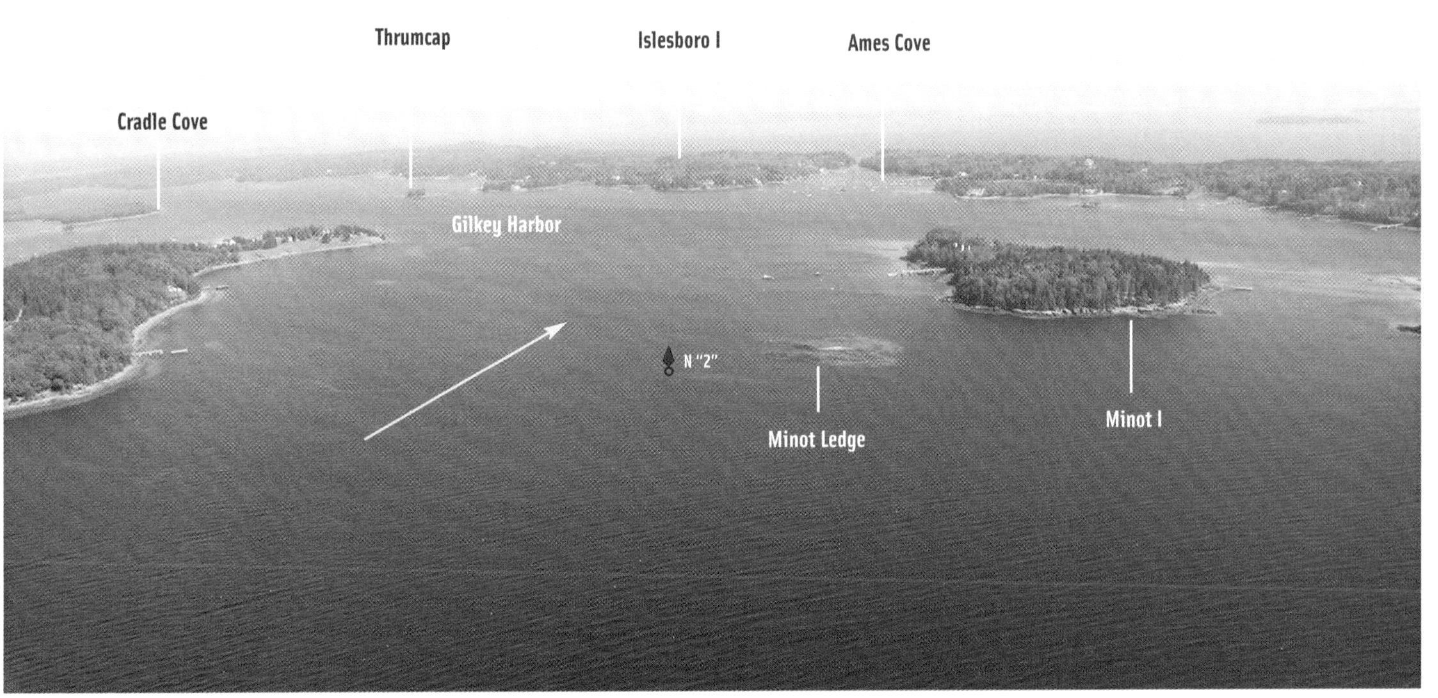
Thrumcap
Islesboro I
Ames Cove
Cradle Cove
Gilkey Harbor
N "2"
Minot Ledge
Minot I

■ BELFAST ■

BELFAST has a busy commercial harbor and a very attractive downtown. The easy, wide-open approach is made from Belfast Bay. Leave red bell "2" off Steets Ledge to starboard and proceed up the Passagassawakeag River past red nuns "4" and "6." The commercial district and town dock are on your port side. In theory, the river is navigable by small boat above the bridges, but large parts of the river bed completely dry out at low water, making it a bad place to get caught. Belfast is exposed to the east and southeast.

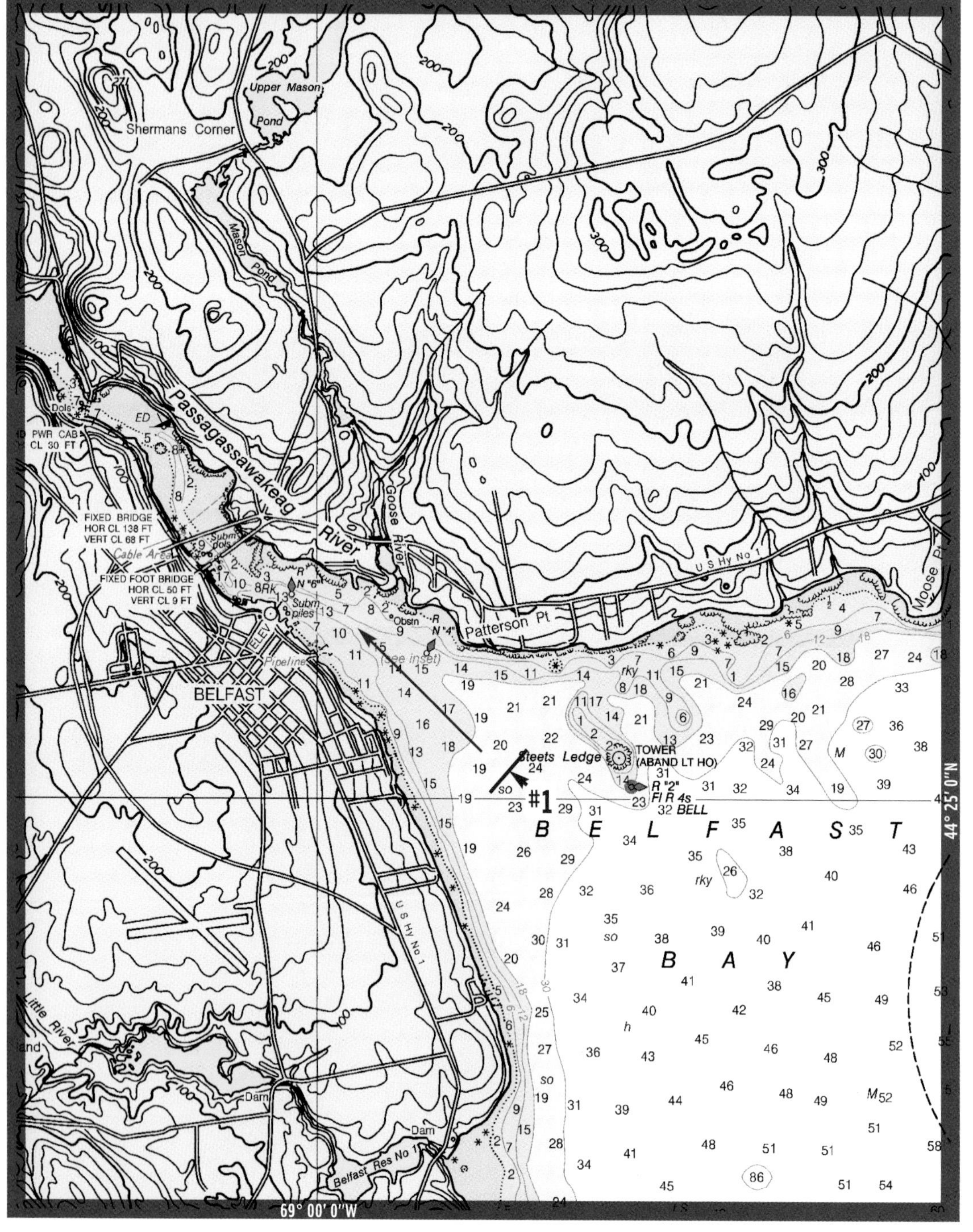

13309
28th ed., Sept. 02
NAD 83
Soundings in feet
1:40,000

#1

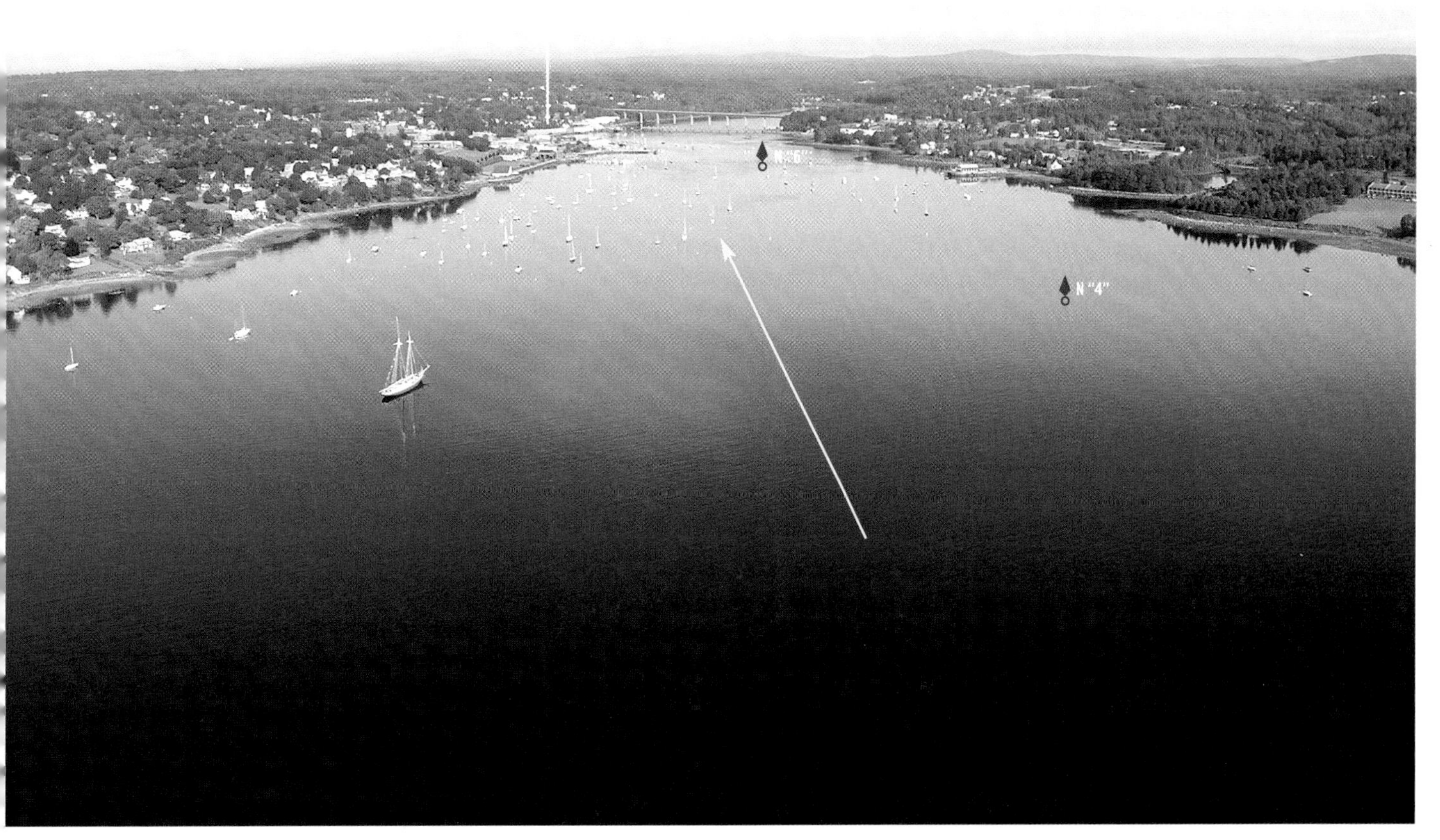

■ SEARSPORT ■

BEYOND its famed history of shipbuilding, another attribute of Searsport is its accessibility. From red-and-white bell "II" Mo (A) off Marshall Point on Islesboro Island, proceed north in the direction of the flashing green "5" bell south of Long Cove Ledge. Searsport Harbor, with its industrial infrastructure, will be immediately visible. Keep both green bell "5" and black-and-red "DLC" to starboard, and proceed directly into the harbor. Stay clear of the commercial traffic that operates in the vicinity of the Mack Point Terminal. Searsport is exposed to the south and east.

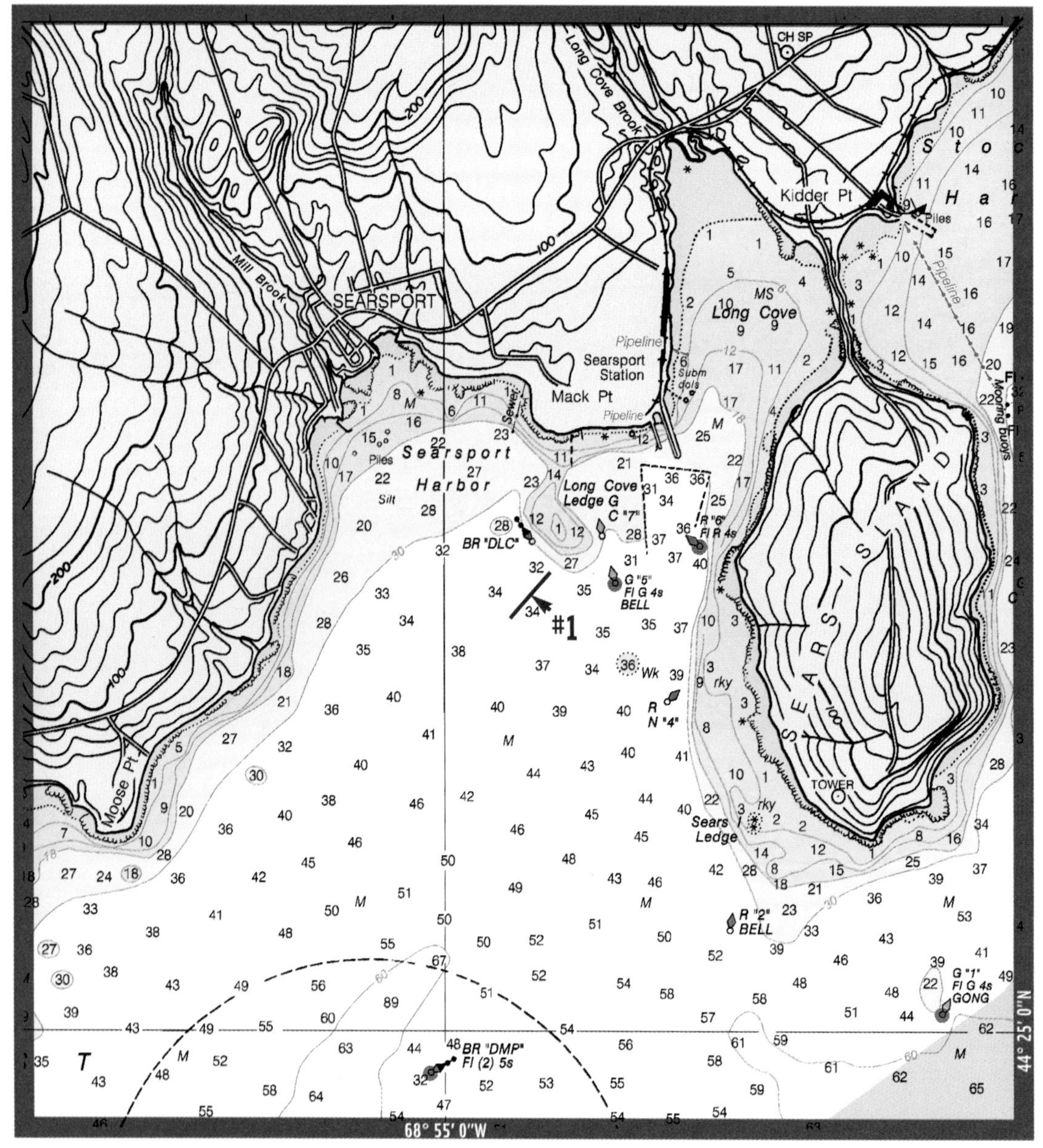

13309
28th ed., Sept. 02
NAD 83
Soundings in feet
1:40,000

#1

REGION V

Castine Harbor
Horseshoe Cove
Bucks Harbor
Eggemoggin Reach
Northwest Harbor
Marsh Cove
Pulpit Harbor
North Haven
Fox Islands Thorofare
Burnt Cove
Winter Harbor
Seal Bay
Perry Creek
Long Cove
The Basin
Vinalhaven
Hurricane Island
Matinicus Island
Ragged Island

EAST PENOBSCOT BAY
—MATINICUS ISLAND TO CASTINE HARBOR—

Fox Islands Thorofare looking west (page 156)

Clearly visible from Camden, Rockland, and the Muscle Ridge Islands on a clear day, the islands of Vinalhaven and North Haven stand like gatekeepers to the waters "Down East." But many a cruiser, whether eastbound or westbound, gets sidetracked here as inescapably as Odysseus on Circe's island. With fabled, protected passages like Fox Islands Thorofare and Eggemoggin Reach; remote offshore destinations like Matinicus and Ragged Island; tranquil all-weather anchorages like Pulpit Harbor, Long Cove, Perry Creek, and Winter Harbor; yachting centers like gem-perfect Bucks Harbor and Castine; and bustling fishing villages like Carver's Harbor, you could wander a lifetime here without getting your fill, and many cruisers do. Pick your way out of Carver's Harbor in a thick morning fog and turn north into Hurricane Sound as the fog rolls away and yields to a sparkling summer afternoon. Ease your sheets to a spritely sea breeze and wend your way from buoy to buoy, watching the shoreline unfold, dodging lobsterboats and other yachts, and giving a wide berth to the ferry from Rockland while you savor a sandwich and wonder where you'll anchor tonight. At some point you'll realize that the only thing you really want is to rewind the clock and keep on sailing through this summer afternoon forever. Then you will know with certainty that no matter what happens in that world you left behind, you will be back here next year.

■ MATINICUS ISLAND ■

DUE south of the entrance to Penobscot Bay and miles from anything, Matinicus and Ragged islands sit in quiet solitude, relatively unmarked by the passage of time. Matinicus Island is a unique and charming destination, and getting there presents a challenge. Surrounded by numerous ledges and isolated rocks, Matinicus should be approached with great care and only in fair weather. And, even in calm conditions, ocean swells often roll through here and tamper with otherwise reliable chart soundings; be sure to account for this when figuring keel clearances. The harbor at Matinicus is on the eastern side of the island. If approaching from the north, shoot for the water immediately north of flashing green "5" marking Zephyr Rock. It is critical to positively identify this buoy and not get inside it, as the water between it and Matinicus Island is littered with obstructions. From here proceed south toward green can "5," leaving it to port. Next, follow a rhumb line straight to the red-and-green bell marking the entrance to Matinicus Harbor; keep it to starboard. This approach should keep you clear of The Barrel, but in the event of a strong northerly set, a little extra clearance may be desirable.

If coming from the south, leave Ragged Island and associated ledges well to port. Once abeam of The Hogshead, it is possible to steer straight for Matinicus

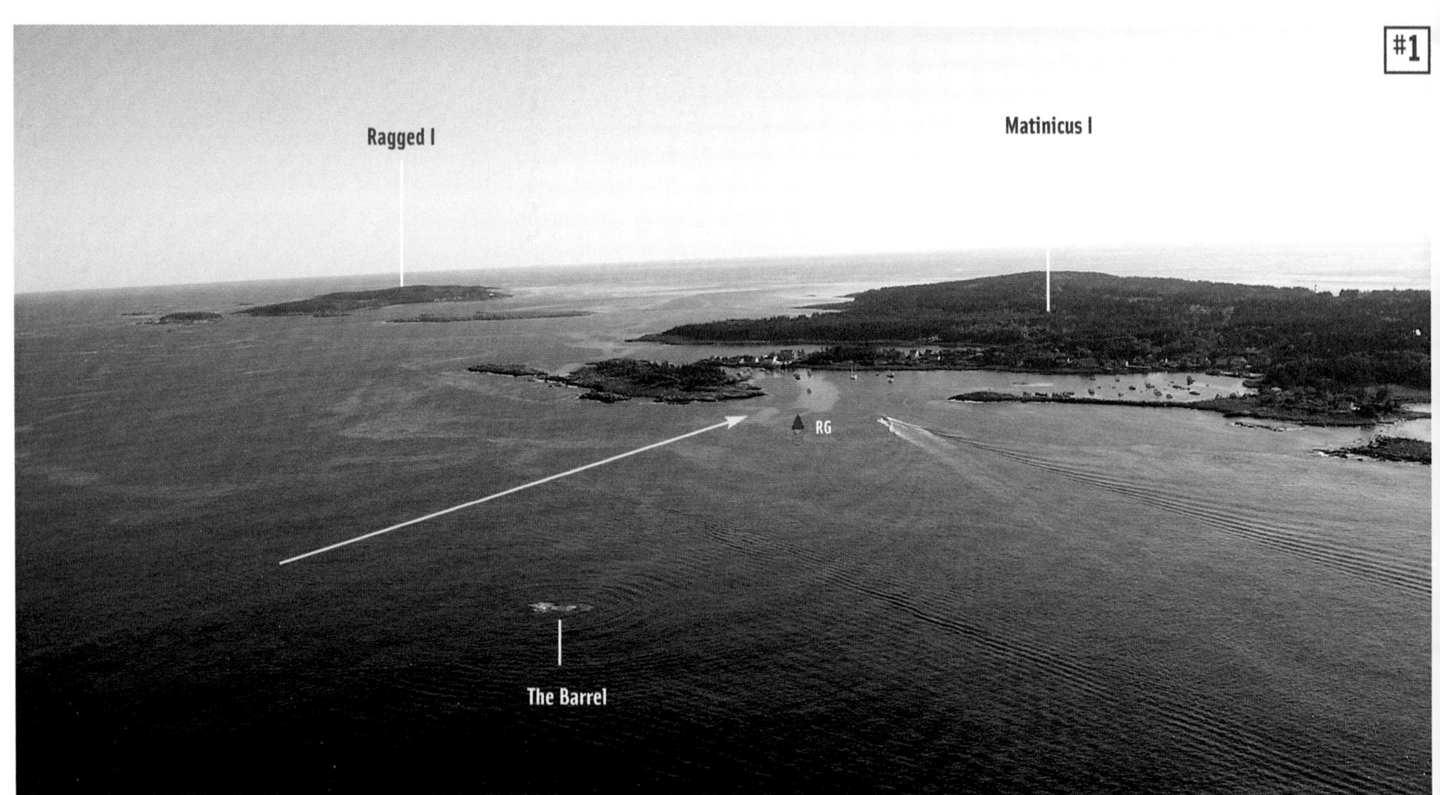

Harbor, leaving West Black Ledge to starboard. But if you are carrying significant draft and it is near the bottom of the tide, it wouldn't take a very large swell to help your keel find the 10-foot spot along the way. Therefore, it is safer to pass between West Black Ledge and East Black Ledge, and then turn west and steer for the red-and-green bell at the mouth of the harbor.

If coming from the west, enter Matinicus Roads well north of red nun "6" so as to stay clear of the 7-foot spot extending from Ragged Island. Pass between Ten Pound Island and The Hogshead and then turn north. As above, it is possible to pass west of West Black Ledge, but transiting between East and West Black Ledges is cleaner, if a little longer.

Once inside the harbor you'll find a working waterfront with few surplus services.

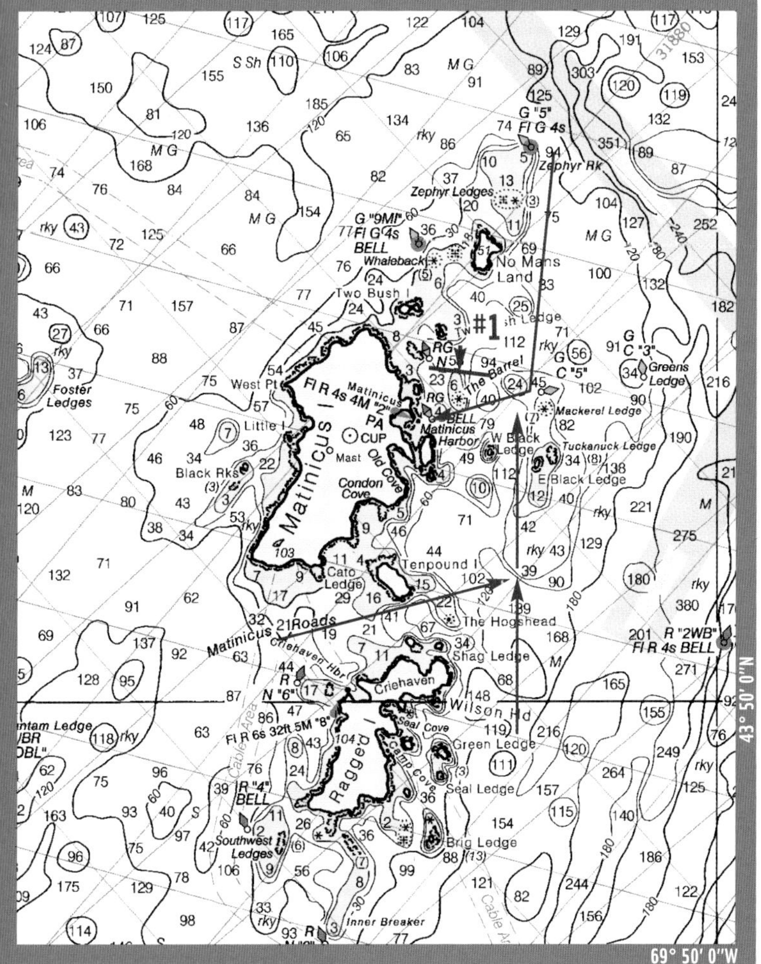

13302
21st ed., Nov. 01
NAD 83
Soundings in feet
1:80,000

■ RAGGED ISLAND ■

RAGGED Island and its settlement Criehaven are testimony to the enduring values of Maine island living—independence and self-reliance. Its residents are more distant from the mainland than any other island community along the coast of Maine. The main harbor of Criehaven is on the northwest side of the island. The harbor, though straightforward to enter, is generally incompatible to visiting boats; its heavily cabled rock bottom affords little room for anchoring. Though a mooring may occasionally be available in summer, a late-spring or early-fall visit to Ragged Island will provide a better chance for an overnight stay. Approach the harbor through Matinicus Roads. Beware of the unmarked shoal that lies between red nun "6" and flashing red "8."

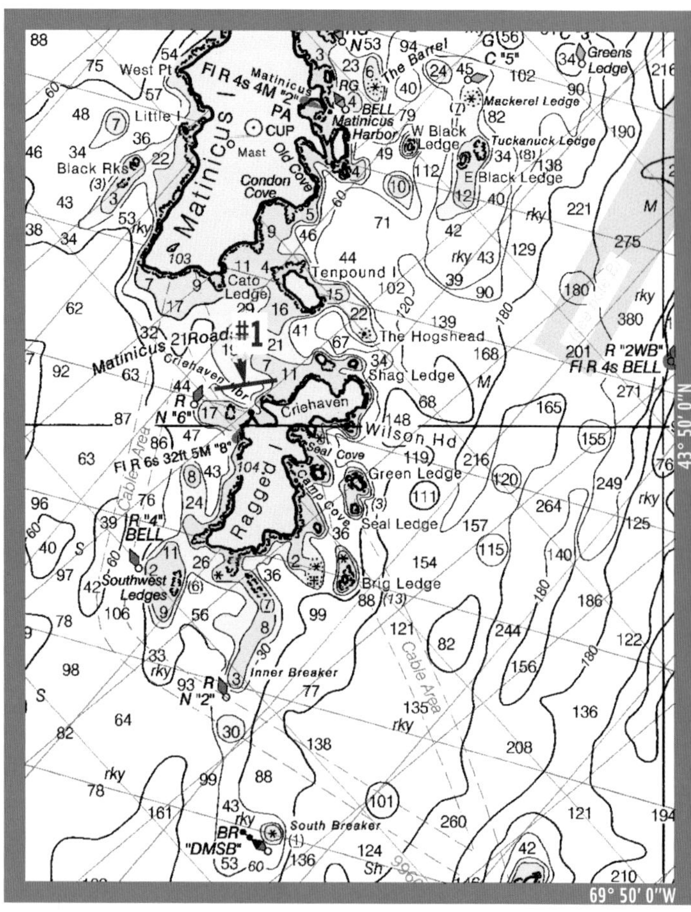

13302
21st ed., Nov. 01
NAD 83
Soundings in feet
1:80,000

#1

■ HURRICANE ISLAND ■

PRIVATELY owned Hurricane Island was once home to a thriving granite carving industry. Nowadays there are no year-round residents, but the Outward Bound School makes use of the island in summer. The eastern side offers the best shelter and landing, but anchoring depths are in short supply. If approaching from the north, skirt inside the unmarked and sometimes submerged ledges off the middle of the eastern side. If you cannot see the ledges, favor the island side; there is good water close to shore. If approaching from th south, come up Hurricane Sound with Greens Island t starboard and the many ledges off Hurricane Island t port. Once you are well past these ledges, turn west an slip down inside them, the same as if coming from th north. Once there, you will find two guest mooring off the Outward Bound docks and limited anchorage i the vicinity. There are several good places to land dinghy near the granite piers.

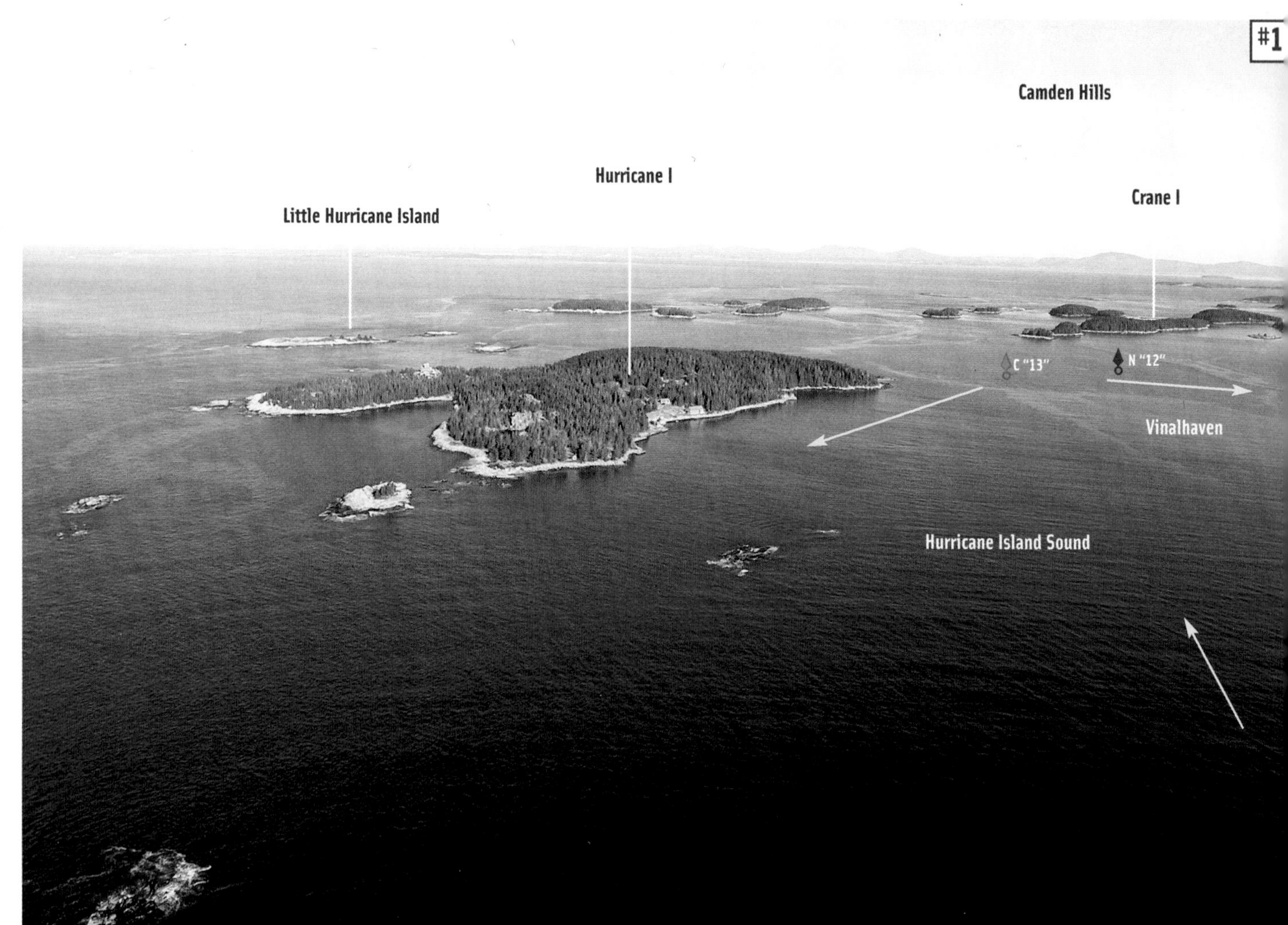

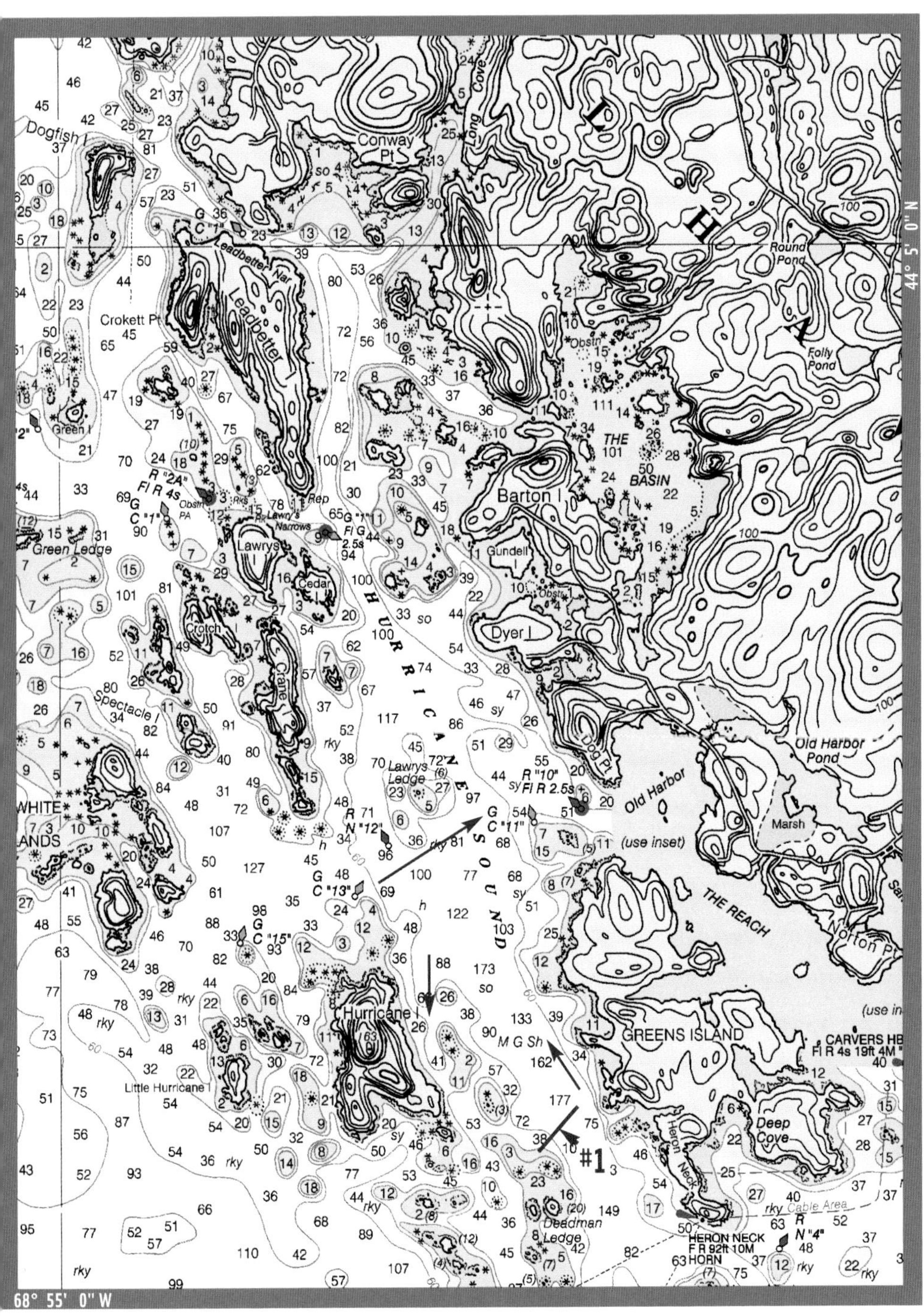

13305
28th ed., May 01
NAD 83
Soundings in feet
1:40,000

■ THE BASIN ■

THE Basin is a tidal saltwater lake on the western side of Vinalhaven. It is entirely protected; its lone navigable entrance is made through a narrow opening that transforms into a reversing falls at various stages of the tide. It is an extraordinary spot but not for the novice, the faint of heart, or for those who resent boat repairs. For best results, make the approach at slack water, high tide. In general, the bigger the boat, the bigger the challenge. The farther from high tide, the bigger the chal lenge (and the more horsepower required).

Whether approaching from the north throug Leadbetter Narrows, or the south through Hurrican Sound, proceed until you're alongside the middle o Leadbetter Island. The chart indicates a number o unnamed islets west of Vinalhaven, and a trough o deep water extending southeast toward Barton Island

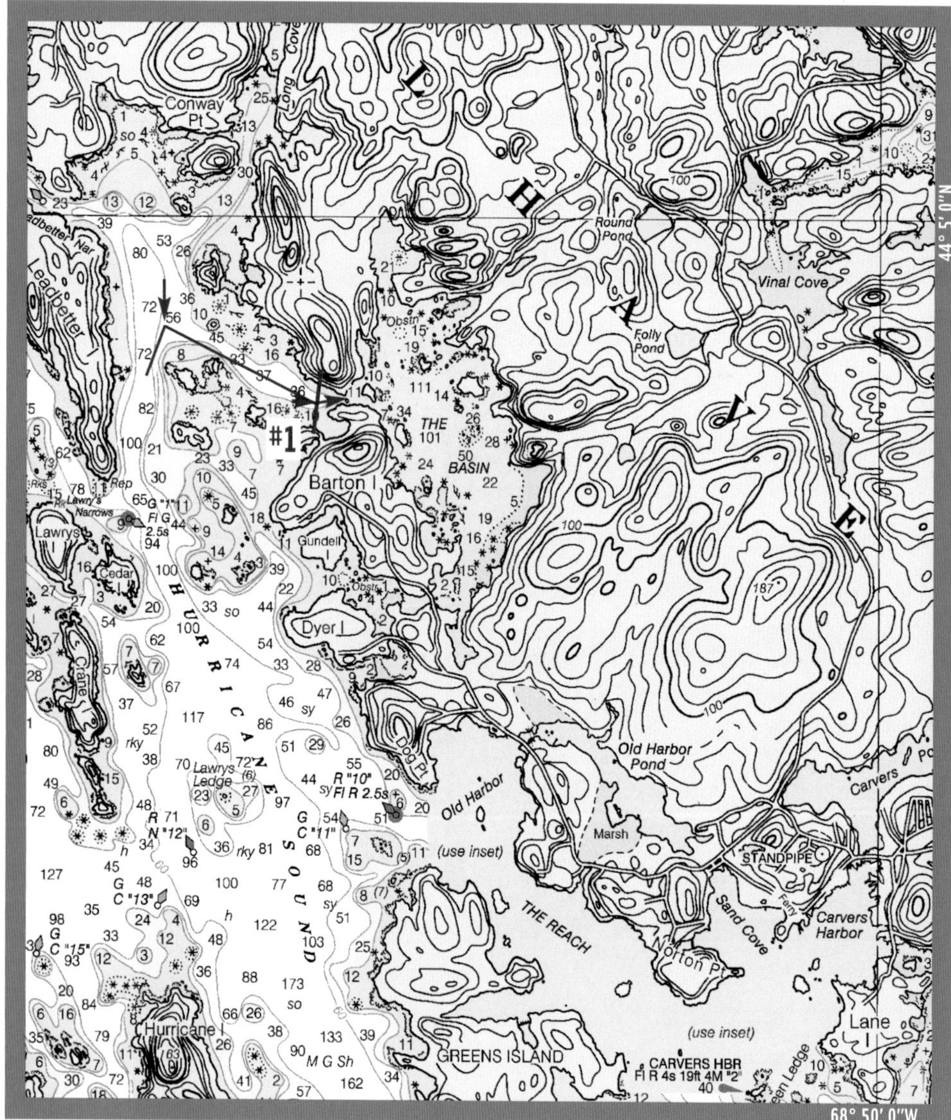

13305
28th ed., May 01
NAD 83
Soundings in feet
1:40,000

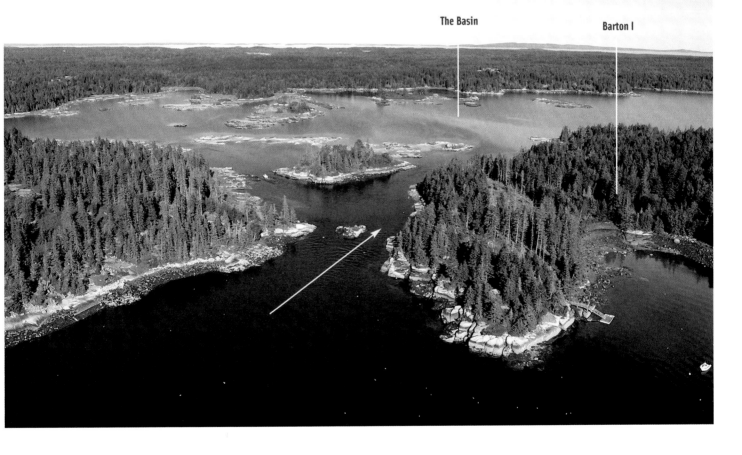

Follow this channel toward Barton Island. As you approach the cliffs to port on Vinalhaven, turn to the east to enter the Basin. A large rock sits directly in the middle of the entrance and is best left to port. Once past the rock, there is a small island ahead that can be left to either port or starboard, though turning south and leaving the island to port appears more welcoming. The Basin is characterized by extreme changes in depth ranging rapidly from 111 feet to zero. The fact that the chartmakers saw fit to omit depth contours suggests their own uncertainties—a good indication that you should be cautious. Reasonable anchoring depths can be found in the southern end of the Basin. This is a wonderful place to explore, and—no matter what happens while transiting the entrance—you'll never forget it.

LONG COVE AT VINALHAVEN

LONG Cove at Vinalhaven is a peaceful and well-protected anchorage. It can be reached from the west by way of Leadbetter Narrows, which is a treat in itself. On a southeasterly heading, leave Leadbetter Island and green can "1" to starboard. Follow the shoreline to starboard until you reach the northeast corner of Leadbetter Island, then swing east for Long Cove. You should be able to see the entrance to Long Cove from here. Steer to pass south of the two unnamed islands immediately south of Conway Point, and then turn toward north to enter the cove. Alternately, if approaching from the south, come up Hurricane Sound, leaving flashing green "1" at Cedar Island to port. When due east of the slot at Leadbetter Narrows turn to starboard to enter the cove. Upon entering, stay to the centerline as you transit this exceedingly skinny cove. Anchor near the 25-foot sounding shown on the chart.

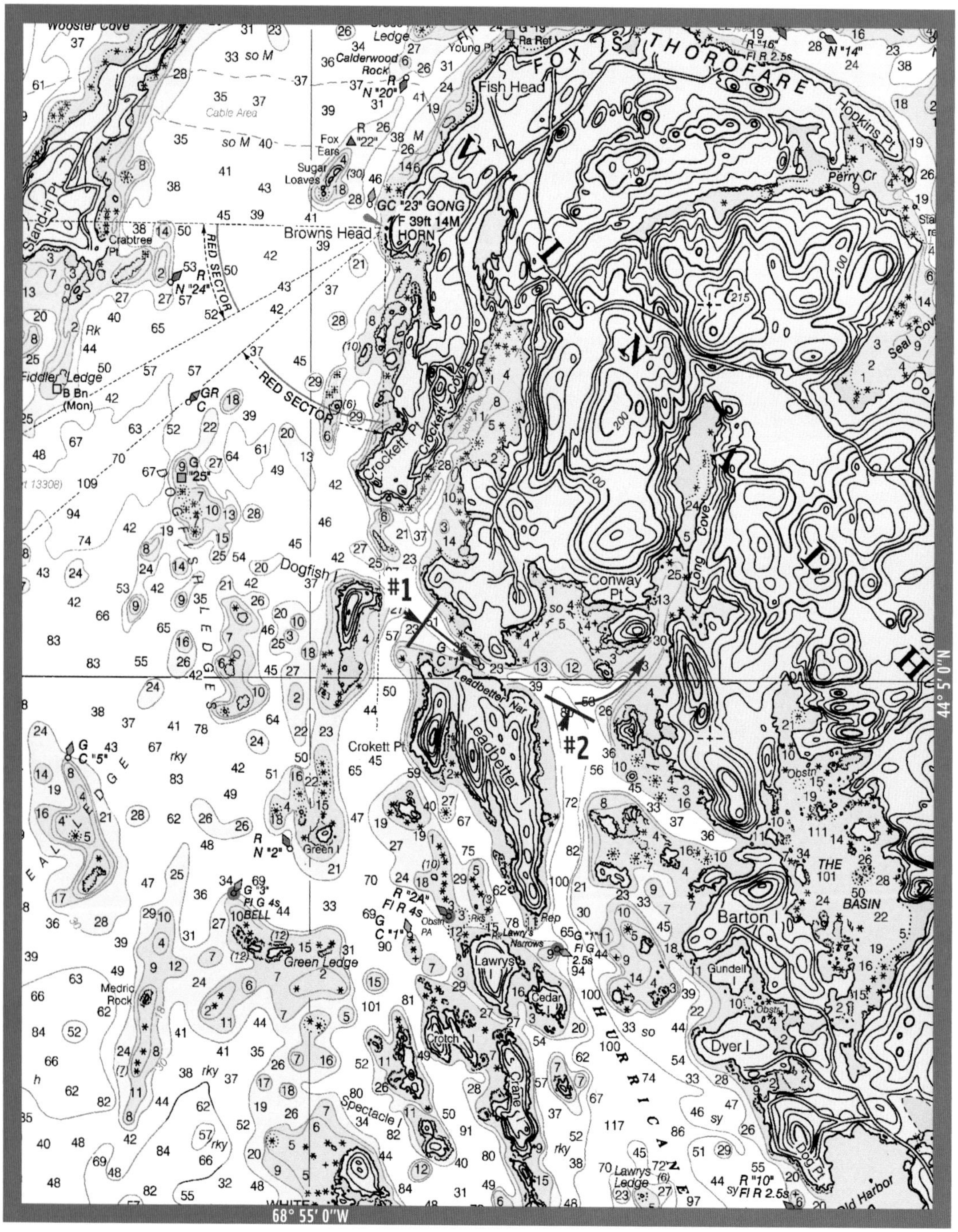

13305
28th ed., May 01
NAD 83
Soundings in feet
1:40,000

#1

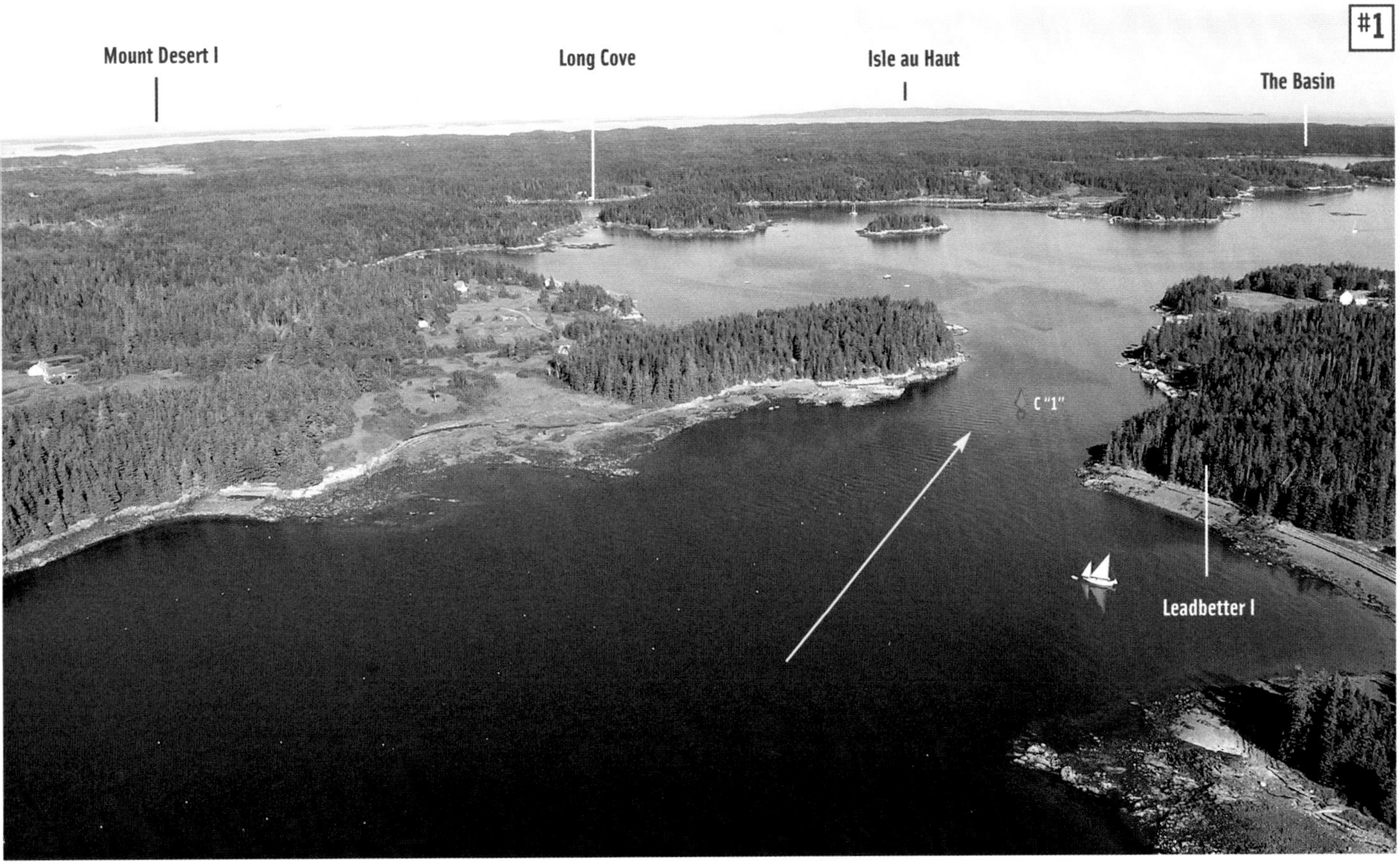

Mount Desert I

Long Cove

Isle au Haut

The Basin

C "1"

Leadbetter I

#2

Long Cove

Conway Point

■ PULPIT HARBOR ■

PULPIT Harbor, located in the middle of North Haven's northwest shore, is one of the most picturesque harbors in all of New England. The entrance is clearly marked by Pulpit Rock, which sits in the middle of the harbor entrance. The approach should be made from the north, as there are hazards seaward of Pulpit Rock. At high tide it may appear possible to pass on either side of Pulpit Rock, but it is absolutely essential to pass east of it, keeping the rock to starboard. Take a southerly heading into the harbor, but then swing east to enter the main anchorage and mooring fields. At the end of the harbor you'll find a town landing and dinghy dock. Numerous services can be obtained within walking distance from Pulpit Harbor. It is a popular destination, so expect company.

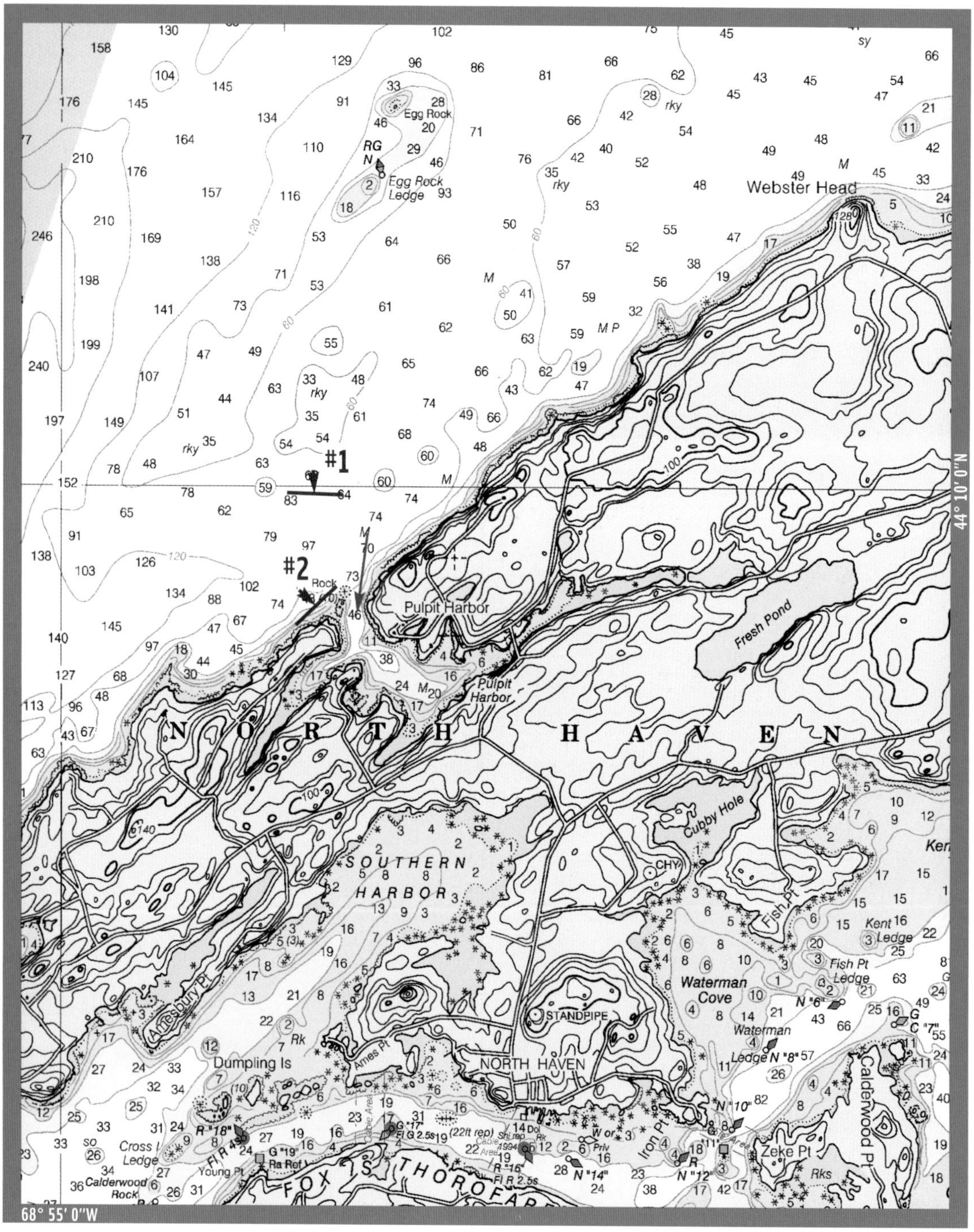

13305
28th ed., May 01
NAD 83
Soundings in feet
1:40,000

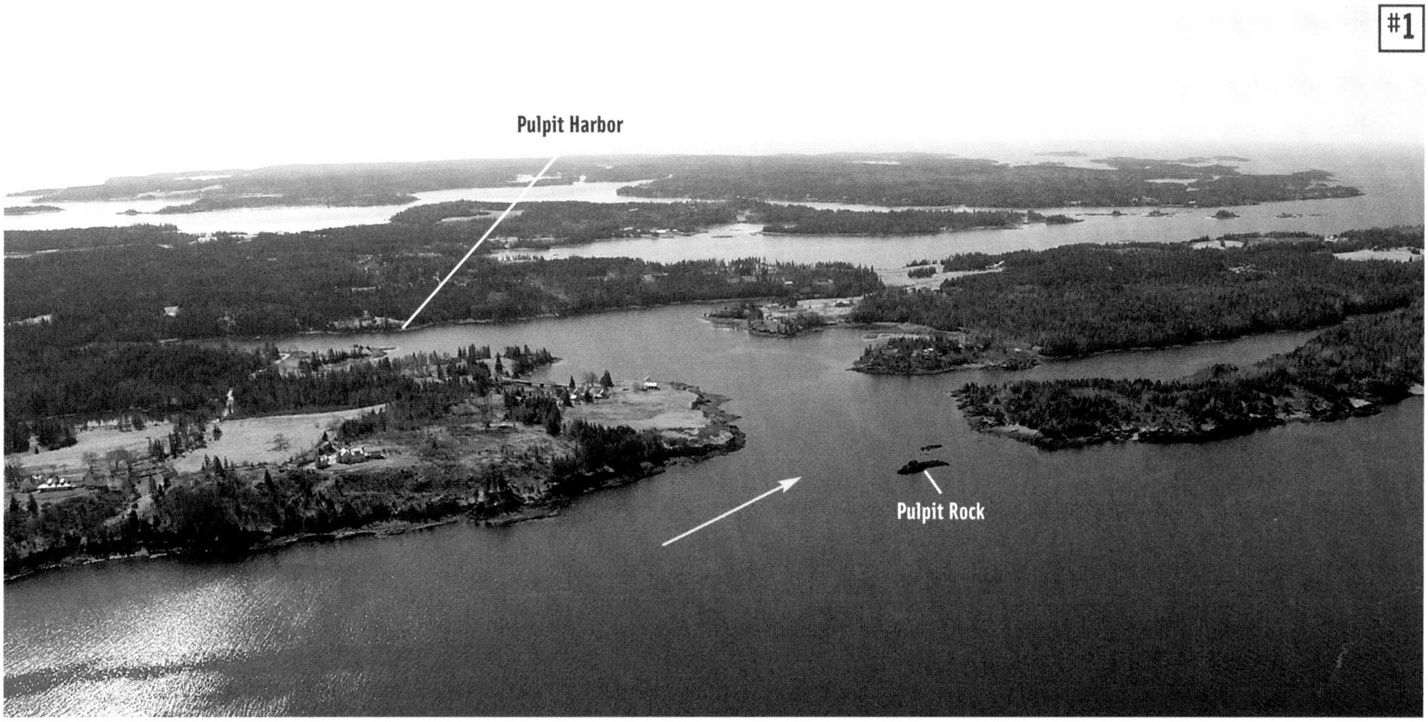

#1

Pulpit Harbor

Pulpit Rock

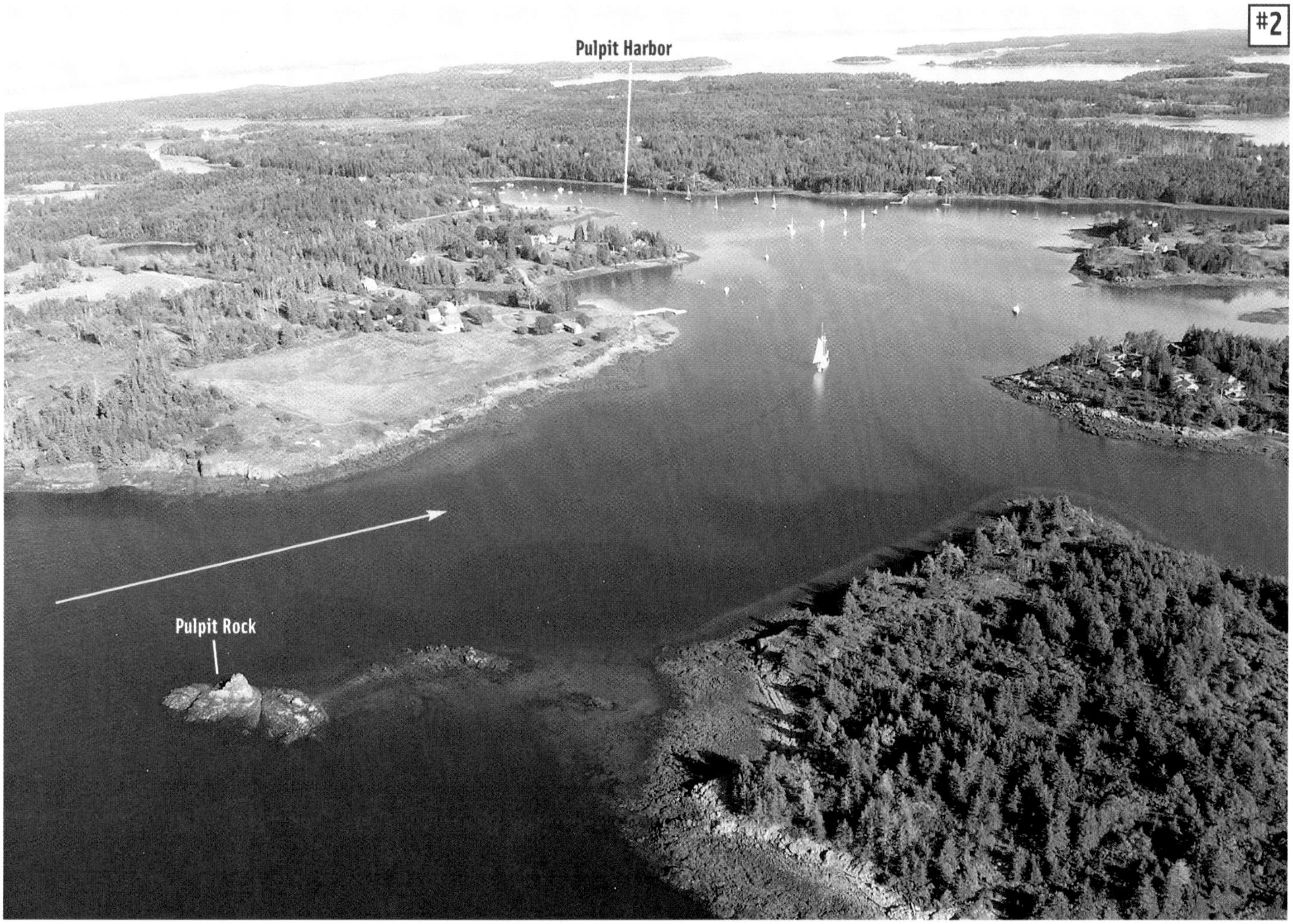

#2

Pulpit Harbor

Pulpit Rock

FOX ISLANDS THOROFARE

THIS watery "highway" separates North Haven from Vinalhaven. If coming from the west, it provides a sheltered shortcut to East Penobscot Bay, Deer Isle, Isle au Haut, and points east. Upon returning, it is an equally useful route back to Midcoast Maine. The passageway is well marked and, with careful attention, can be navigated in all weather. Be mindful of the ferry service that runs to the town of North Haven from Rockland six times a day. There are numerous cable crossings in Fox Islands Thorofare, so choose your anchorage with care. As with the many thoroughfares in coastal Maine, the buoys in Fox Islands Thorofare may appear to be opposite of what you would expect for entering from open water. If you enter Fox Islands Thorofare from the west, red buoys will be to port and green to starboard, defying the maxim "red right returning."

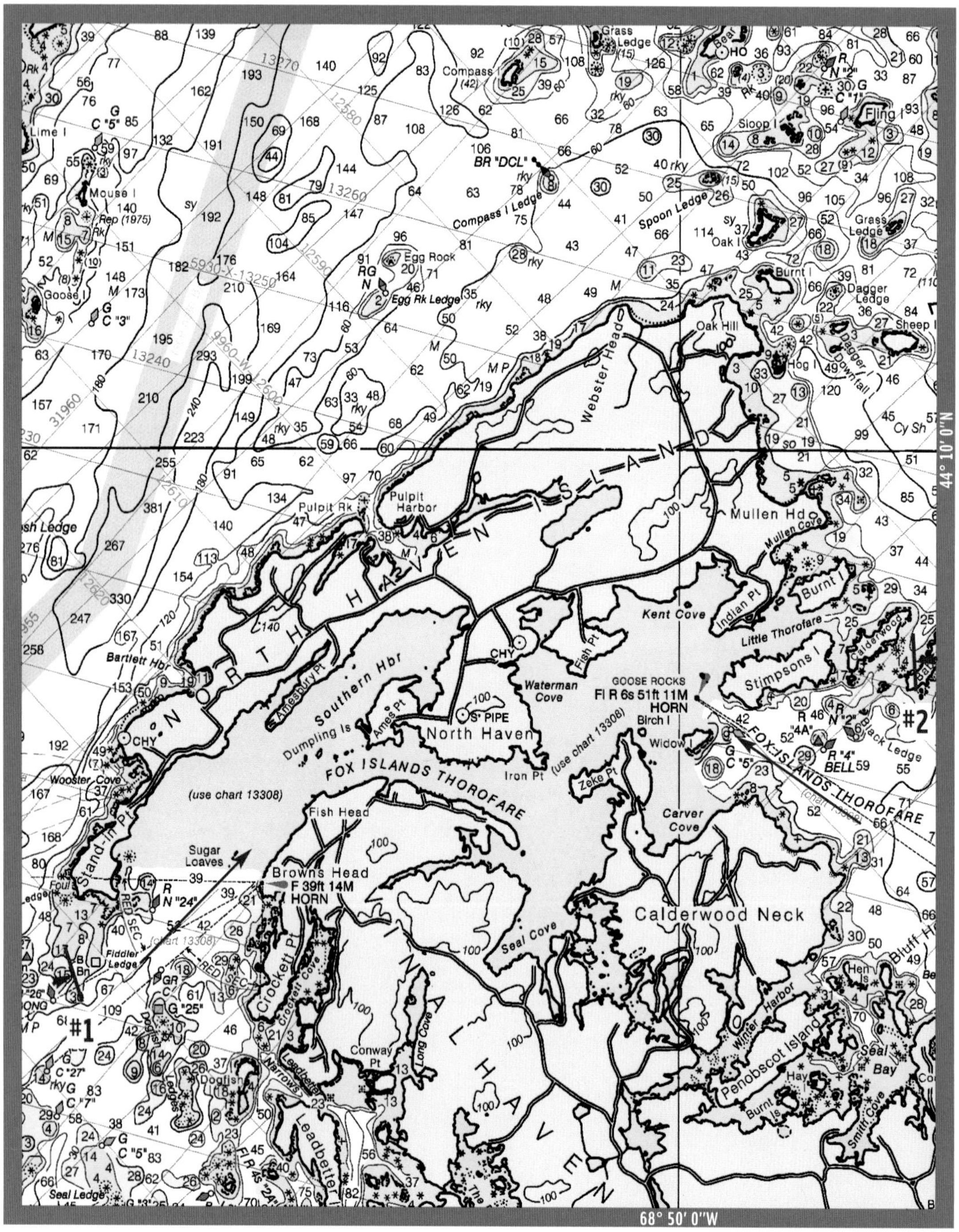

13302
21st ed., Nov. 01
NAD 83
Soundings in feet
1:80,000

#1

Pulpit Harbor
Marsh Cove
North Haven
Stimpsons I
Perry Creek
Calderwood Neck
N "20"
R "22"
G "23"
N "24"
Stand-in Point
Fiddler Ledge

#2

Little Thorofare
Vinalhaven
North Haven
Stimpsons I
C "5"
Widow I
R "4"
R "4A"
Calderwood Neck
N "2"
Calderwood I
Babbidge I

North Haven

Approximately midway through the Fox Islands Thorofare is the town of North Haven on North Haven Island. It's a wonderfully charming spot—complete with its own library, post office, and newly constructed community and arts center. During peak season, there are two restaurants, two gift shops and services for mariners including fuel and marine repairs. Moorings are also available. When entering or leaving the harbor pay careful attention to the ferry. It makes frequent visits to and from the town landing.

13305
28th ed., May 01
NAD 83
Soundings in feet
1:40,000

Stimpsons I
North Haven
Zeke Point
#3
R "16"
G "17"

Perry Creek

Vinalhaven's Perry Creek can be approached by turning south out of Fox Islands Thorofare, just east of the town of North Haven. Keep the islet that is south of Hopkins Point to starboard and enter the creek at the 19-foot mark. Inside you will find a narrow, protected anchorage. The chart indicates numerous cable crossings in the vicinity of Perry Creek and Seal Cove, so place your anchor with care.

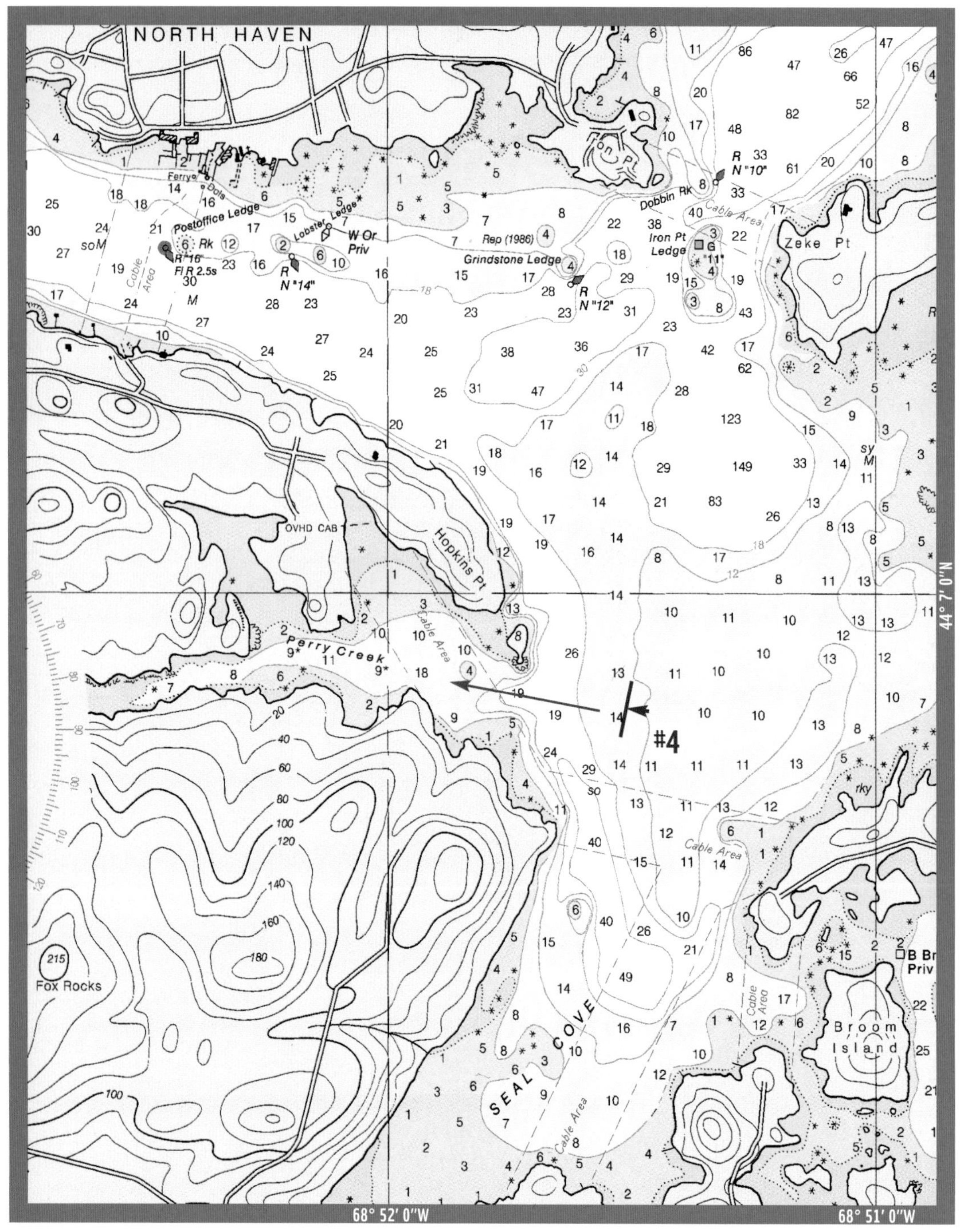

13308
12th ed., April 04
NAD 83
Soundings in feet
1:15,000

#4

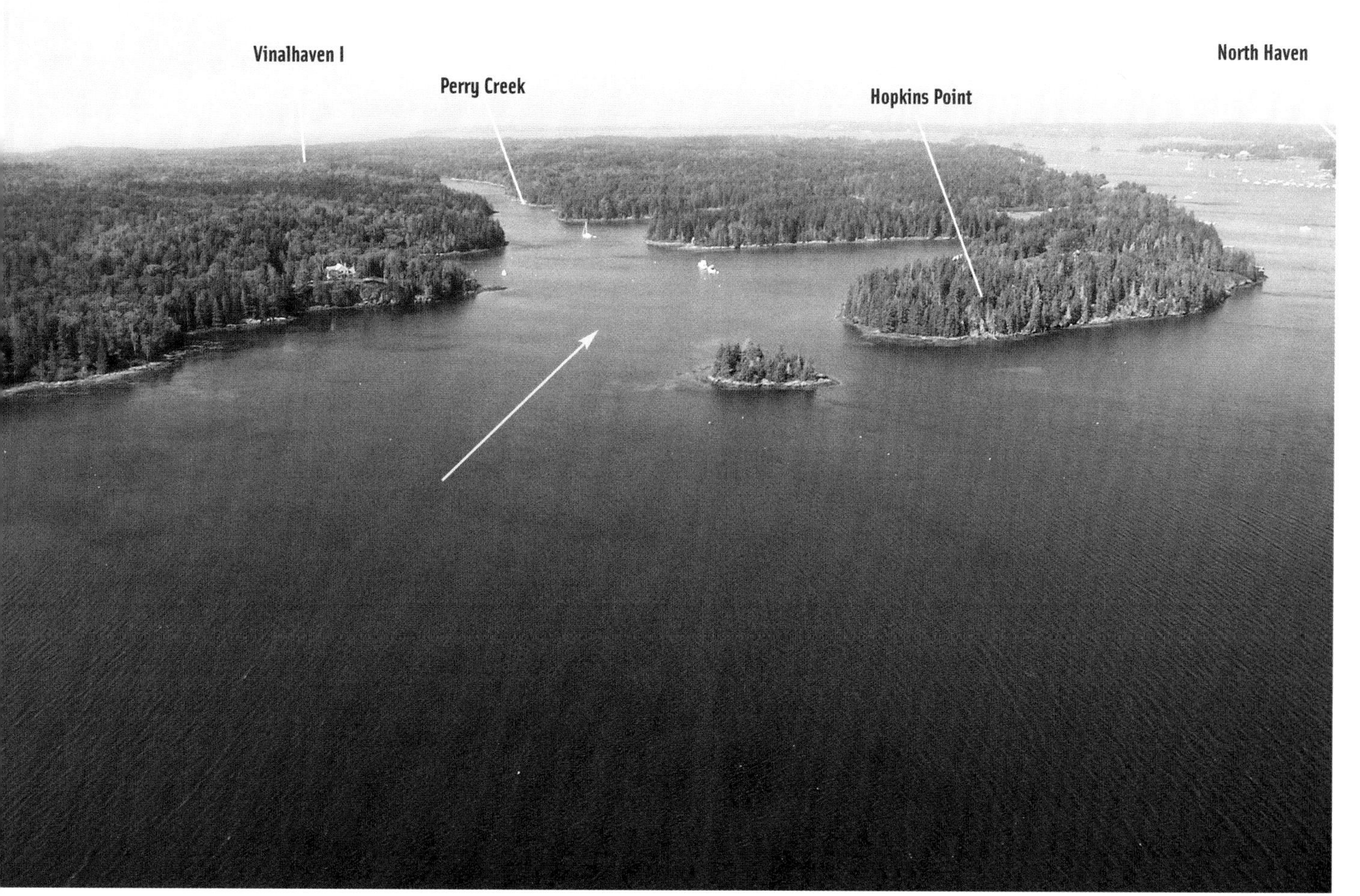

WINTER HARBOR AND SEAL BAY

THE twin anchorages of Winter Harbor and Seal Bay on the east side of Vinalhaven offer good protection and an unparalleled playground for small craft exploration. Enter from sea between Hen Island to port and Calderwood Neck to starboard. Continue on a southwesterly heading and you will enter Winter Harbor. Easy anchorage can be found right up to the rock that precedes the 2-foot mark. Vessels do anchor beyond this point, but getting past the 2-foot spot requires some reconnoitering.

Seal Bay requires careful navigation, as there are numerous unmarked isolated hazards at the entrance and scattered about inside. Arriving at the lower part of the tide will assist in spotting some of these. The approach starts as if you were going into Winter Harbor, keeping both Hen Island and its unnamed little sister island to port. Don't be tempted to make the hard 90-degree turn to the port until the slot between Penobscot Island and Hen Island's sister has opened up and you can see into Seal Bay. This is in the vicinity of the 67-foot sounding. The better water is in the eastern side of the entrance, as there are numerous unmarked shoals on the Penobscot Island side. Proceed southeast into the deep water. Anchorage can be found in a variety of spots along the eastern side of Seal Bay, as well as in the tongue of deep water that extends along the south shores of Davids and Penobscot islands all the way to Burnt Island. Be sure to leave the "turning rock" south of Davids Island to starboard, as there is a sandbar connecting it to the island.

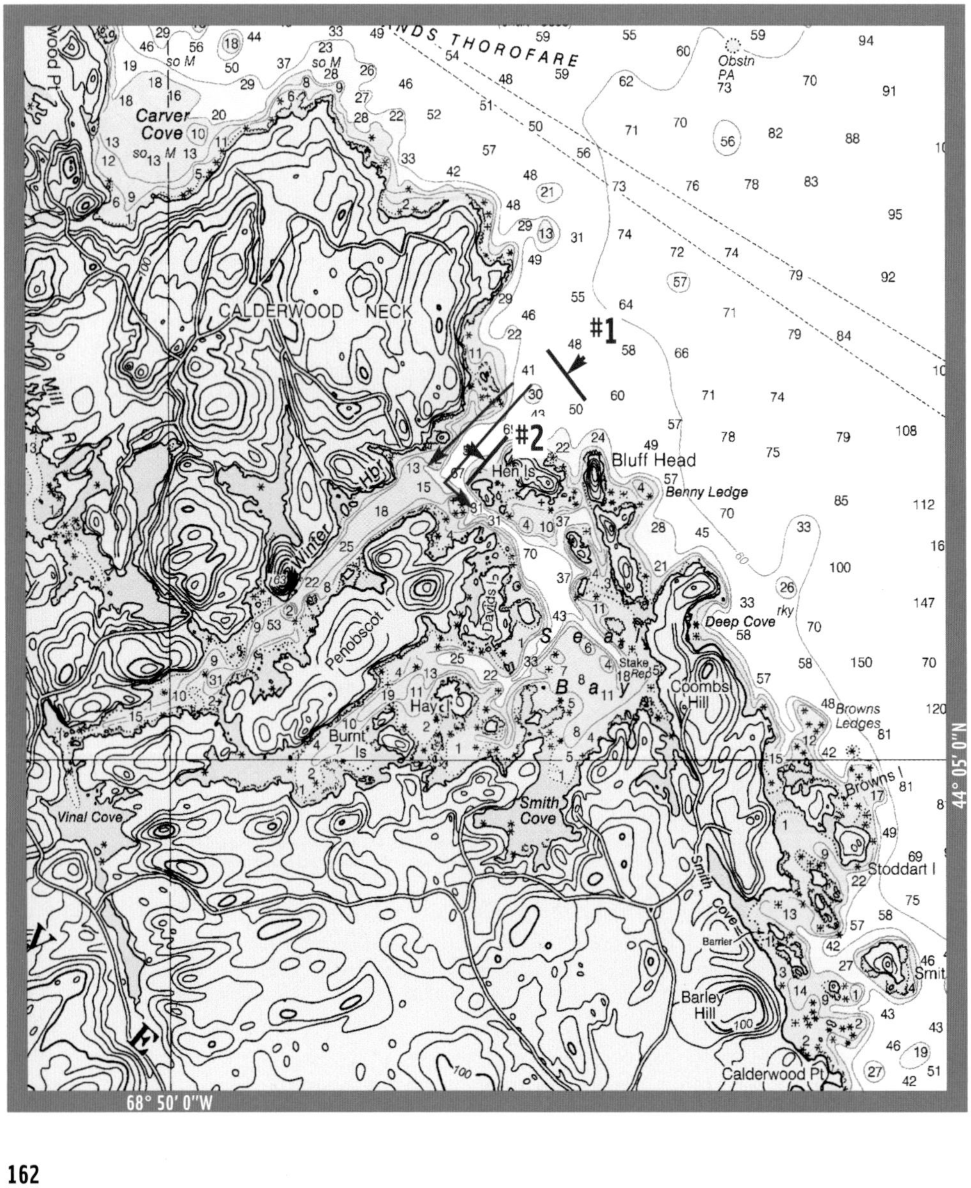

13305
28th ed., May 01
NAD 83
Soundings in feet
1:40,000

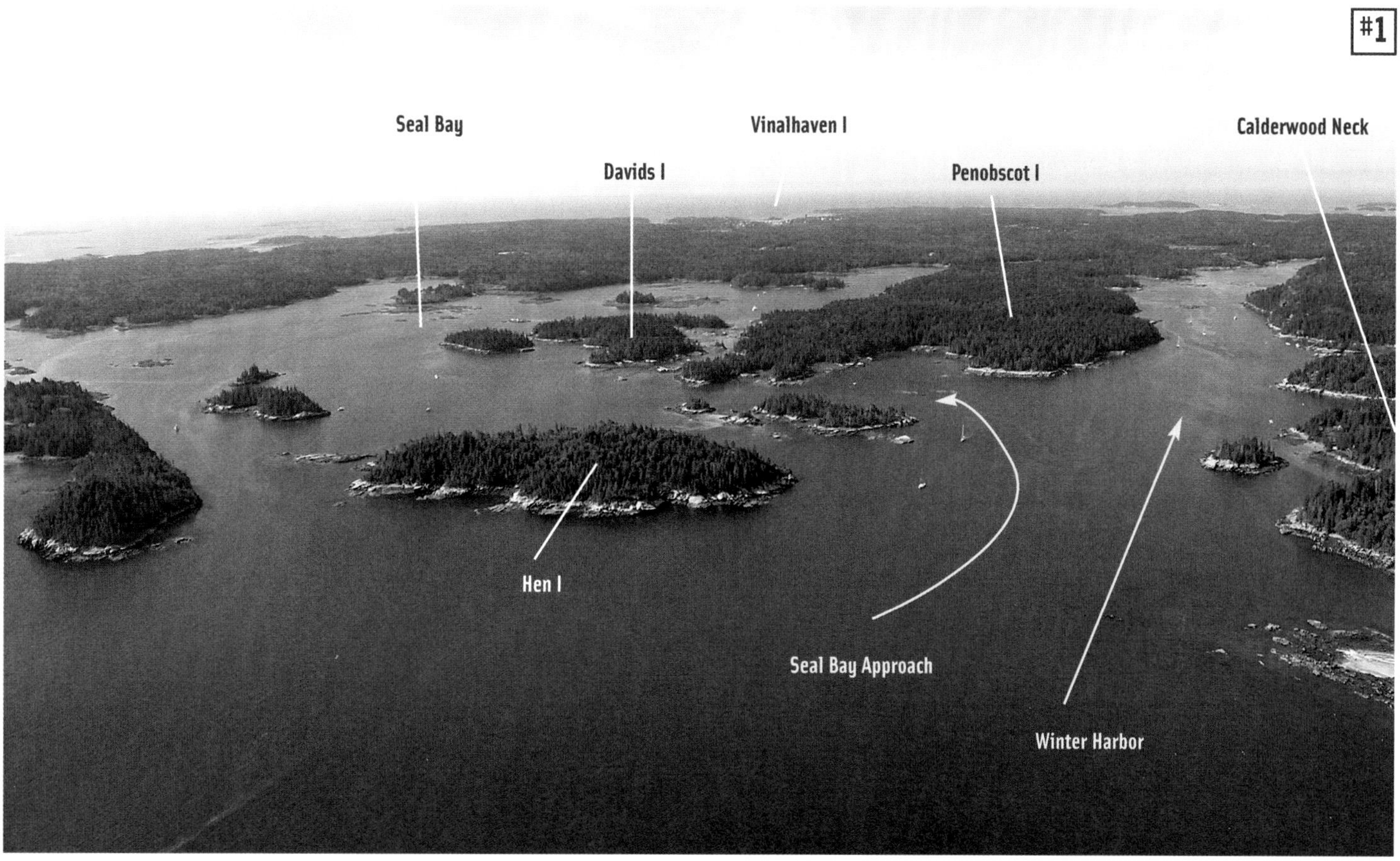

#1

Seal Bay
Vinalhaven I
Calderwood Neck
Davids I
Penobscot I
Hen I
Seal Bay Approach
Winter Harbor

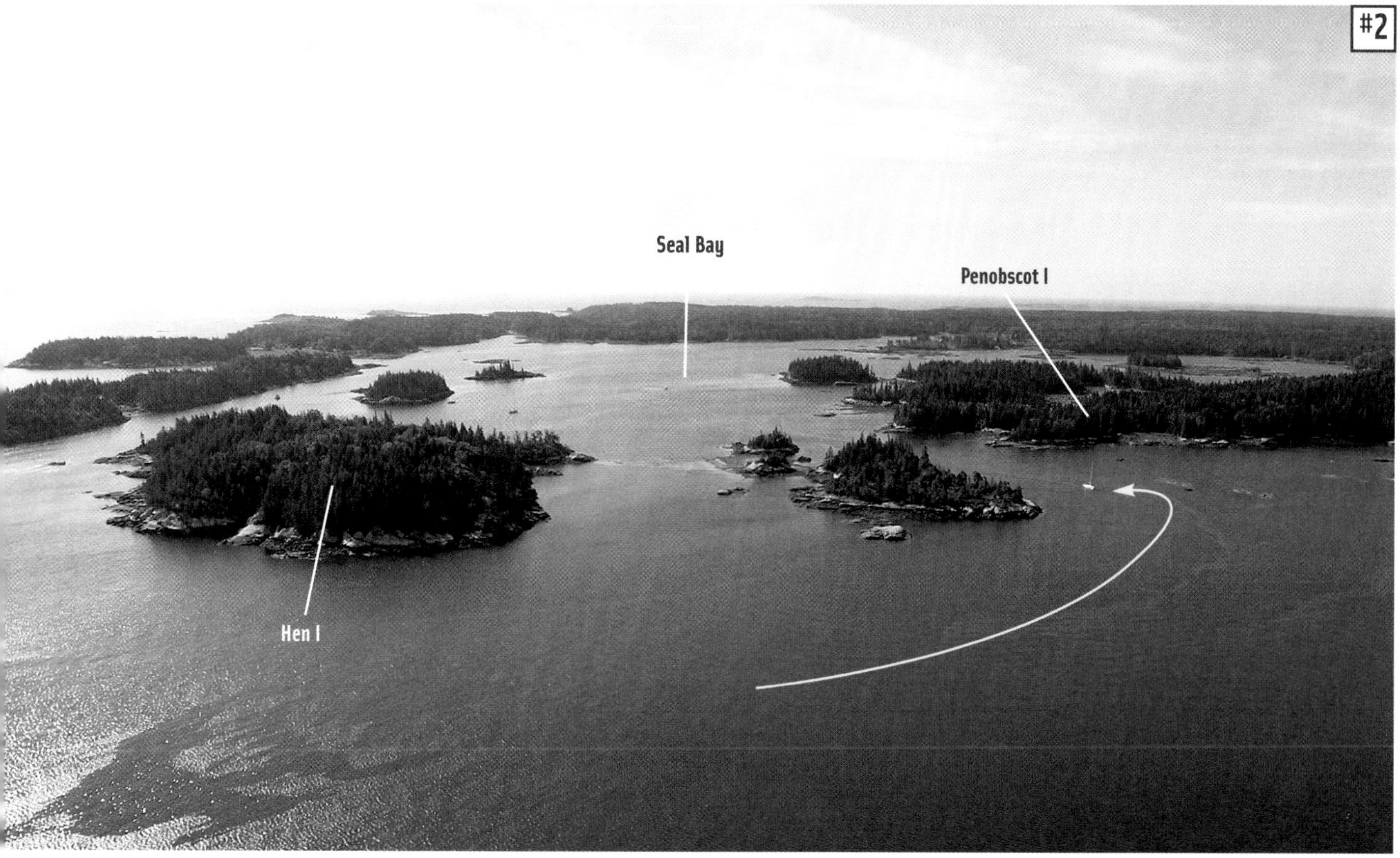

#2

Seal Bay
Penobscot I
Hen I

■ MARSH COVE ■

MARSH Cove, on the northeast corner of North Haven, is easy to enter and provides fair holding ground. The cove is wide open to the southeast, yet it is provided a small measure of protection by Oak Hill and Hog Island.

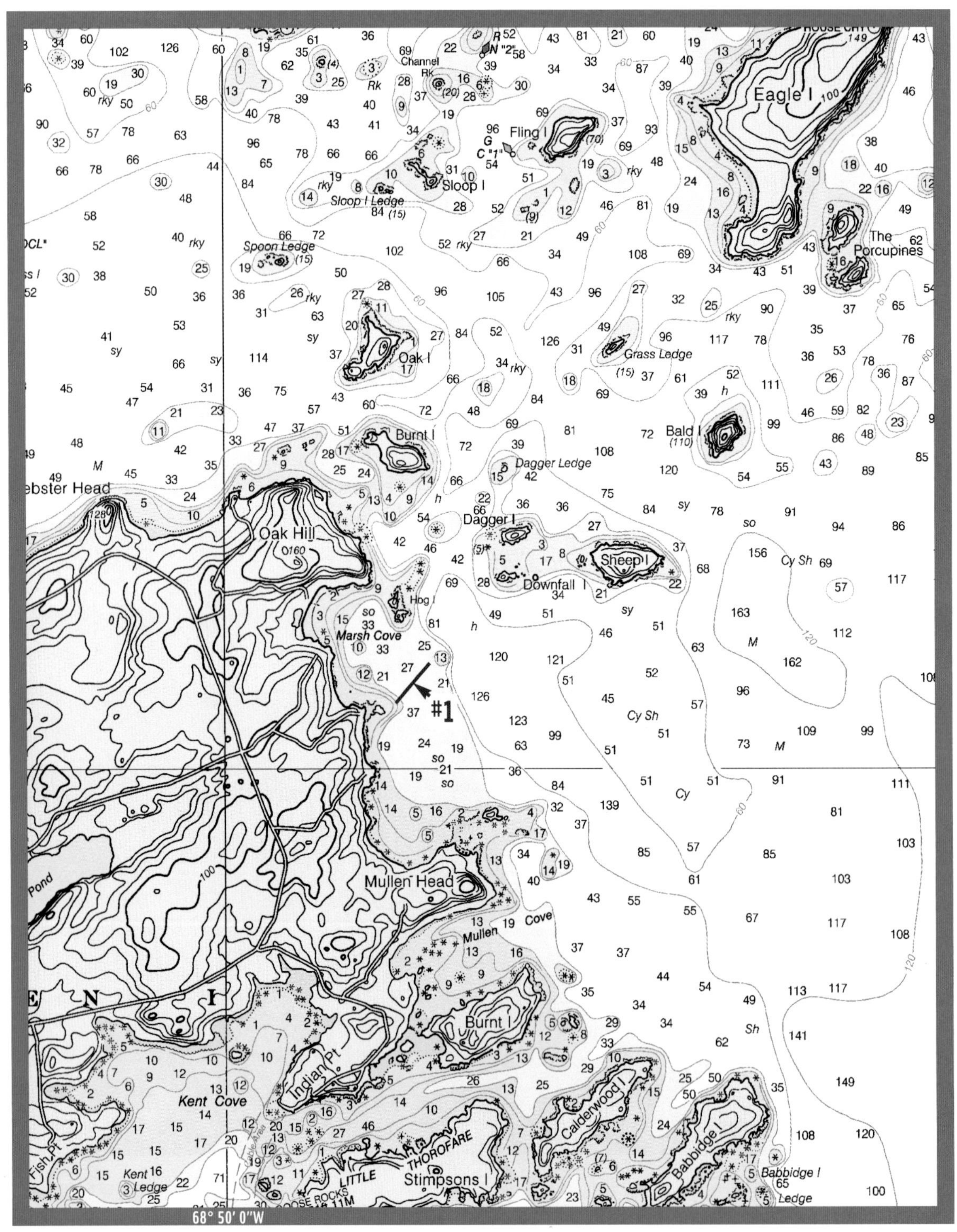

13305
28th ed., May 01
NAD 83
Soundings in feet
1:40,000

#1
Camden Hills
Oak Hill
Marsh Cove
Hog I

■ BURNT COVE ■

AS the picture indicates, the entrance to Burnt Cove is straightforward. Located at the southwest corner of Deer Island next to the town of West Stonington, Burnt Cove offers an easy respite for an overnight stop and leaves the boater well positioned for an early start to points Down East by way of Deer Isle Thorofare. Anchoring conditions are reported to be good, though it is exposed to westerly wind and chop.

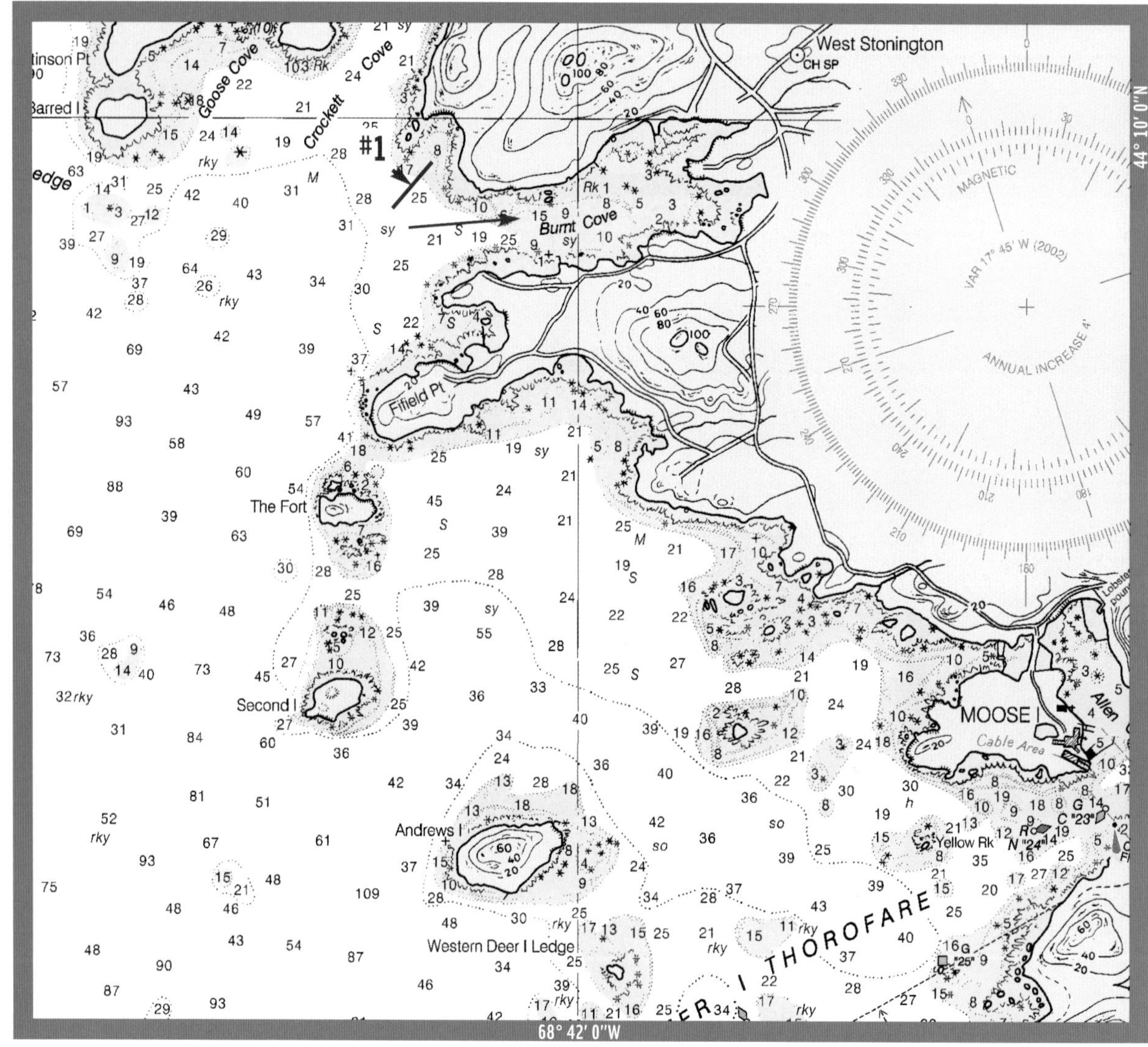

13315
11th ed., Mar. 02
NAD 83
Soundings in feet
1:20,000

#1

■ NORTHWEST HARBOR ■

NORTHWEST Harbor is a large, easily accessed harbor situated on the northwest side of Deer Isle. If coming from the north, it is a straight shot past Pickering Island into the harbor. If coming from south or west you have two options. The simplest is to pass north of the green can "1" off Pressey Cove and Gull Ledge before turning into the harbor. You can also choose the inside route, leaving green can "1" and Gull Ledge to port, and red nun "2" to starboard. There is plenty of water through here but be sure to favor the nun so as not to run afoul of the 3-foot spot off Gull Ledge. A gradual turn to a southeast heading will bring you into the harbor. Northwest Harbor generally has little traffic and good anchoring depths, though it is open to a northwesterly. The village of Deer Isle is at the head of the harbor and can be reached by dinghy, but mind the tide, as the upper reaches of the harbor dry out at low water.

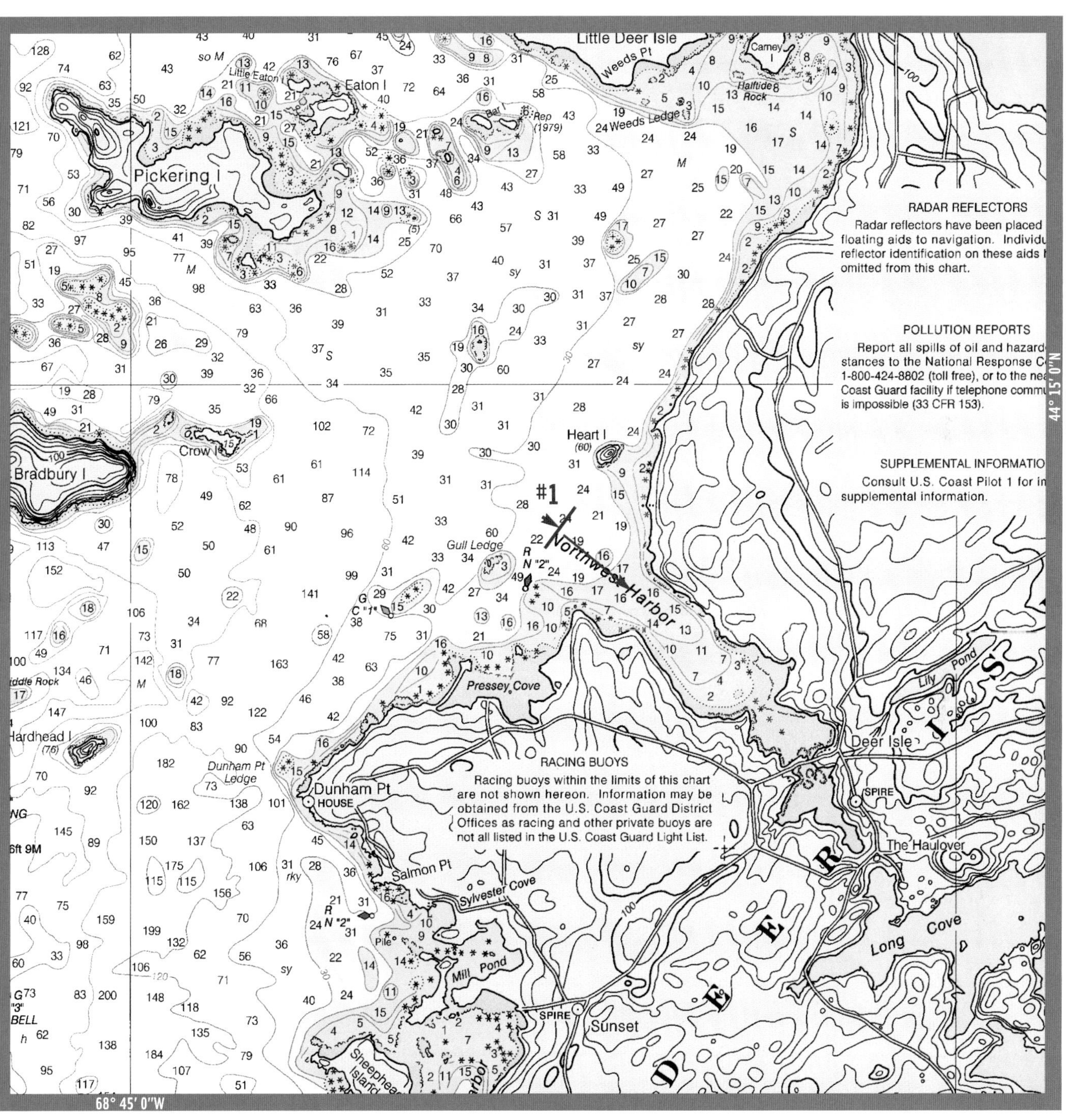

13305
28th ed., May 05
NAD 83
Soundings in feet
1:40,000

■ EGGEMOGGIN REACH ■

EGGEMOGGIN Reach is another major waterway connecting Penobscot Bay to cruising grounds farther east. While transiting these deep and uncluttered waters, you'll encounter the handsome suspension bridge that connects Little Deer Isle to the mainland. The bridge has a clearance of 85 feet. At Eggemoggin Landing—just west of the bridge on the south side of the reach—you'll find a dock providing quick access to the shore and some limited services for the visitor.

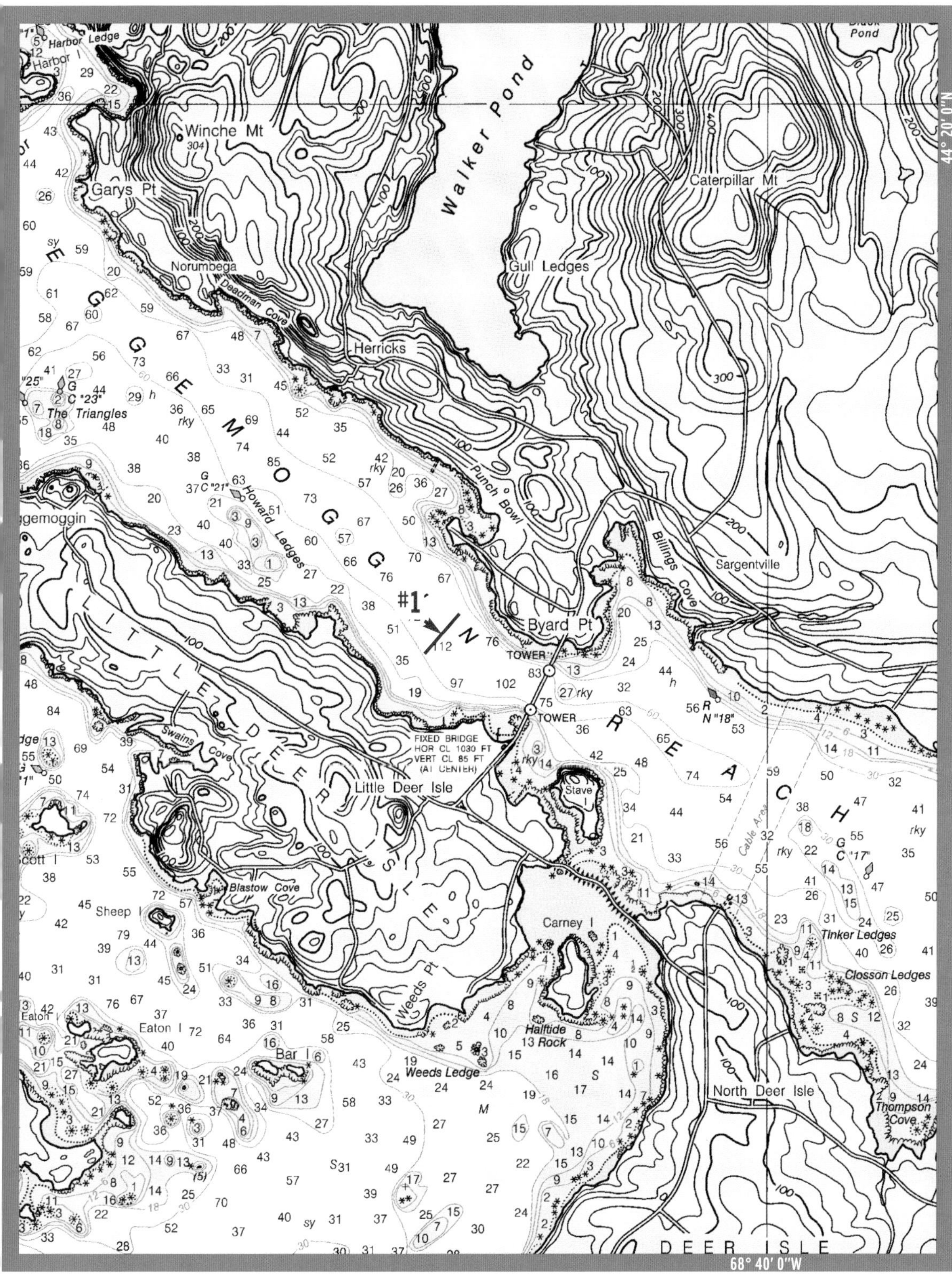

13305
28th ed., May 01
NAD 83
Soundings in feet
1:40,000

■ Horseshoe Cove

Horseshoe Cove is one of several inviting harbors situated at the northwestern end of Eggemoggin Reach. If approaching from the west, pass south of Spectacle Island, keeping it close on your port side. Turn north, passing just east of the larger Spectacle, and steer directly for the mouth of Horseshoe Cove. Keep the small islet on the western side of the harbor mouth to port. If approaching from the south you can follow the same route or, in good visibility, thread between Spectacle Island Ledge and Thrumcap Ledge. It is a fairly straight shot from green can "31" to the mouth of Horseshoe Cove.

If coming from the east, shape a course from flashing red-and-white "EG" to pass north of Thrumcap Island. A weatherworn, privately maintained, red daymark stands on the starboard side of the entrance to Horseshoe Cove. Turn north at the 55-foot sounding and continue for approximately a quarter of a nautical mile. A slight turn to starboard will bring you into the main mooring field running up the center of the cove. The approach to Seal Cove Boatyard at the head of Horseshoe Cove should only be attempted in a dinghy.

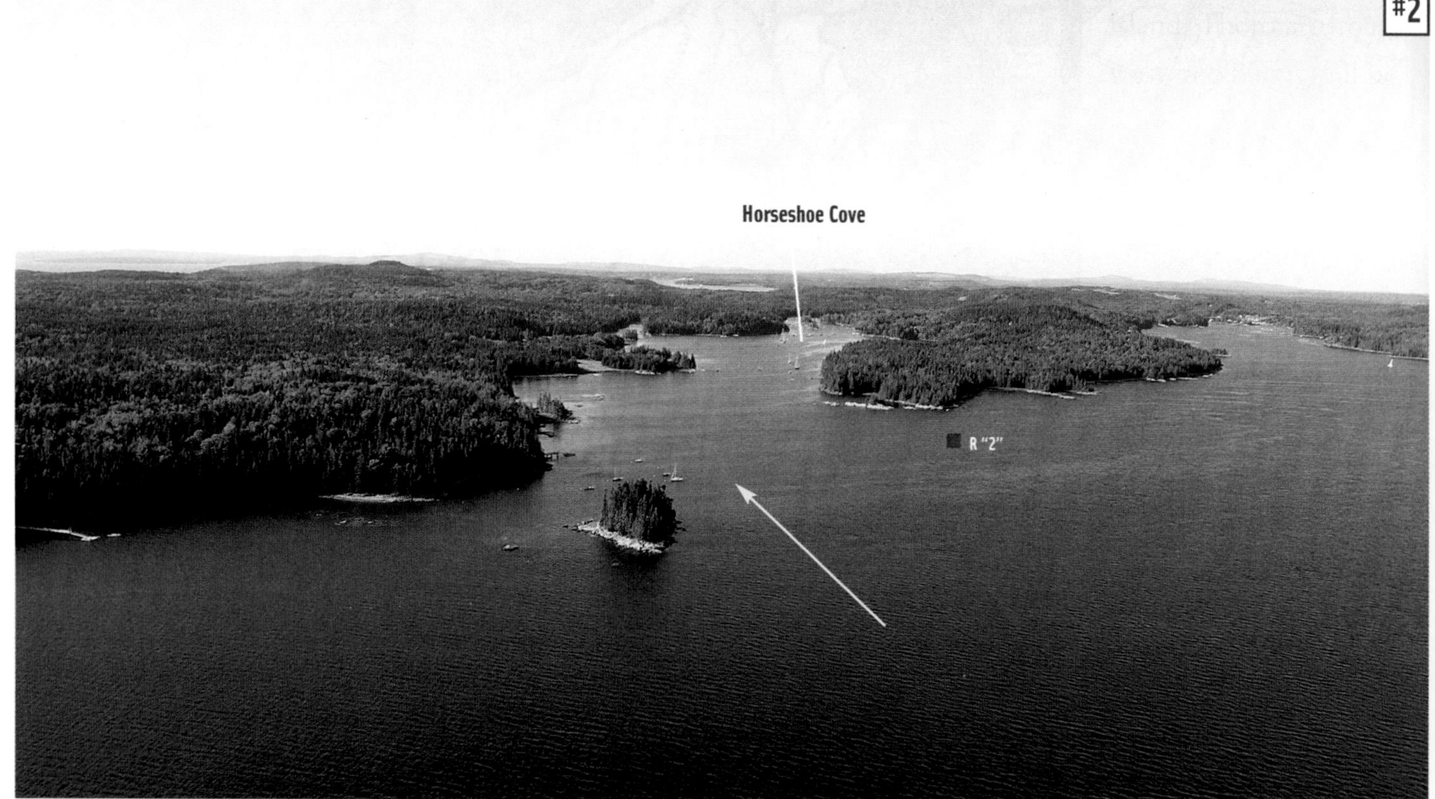

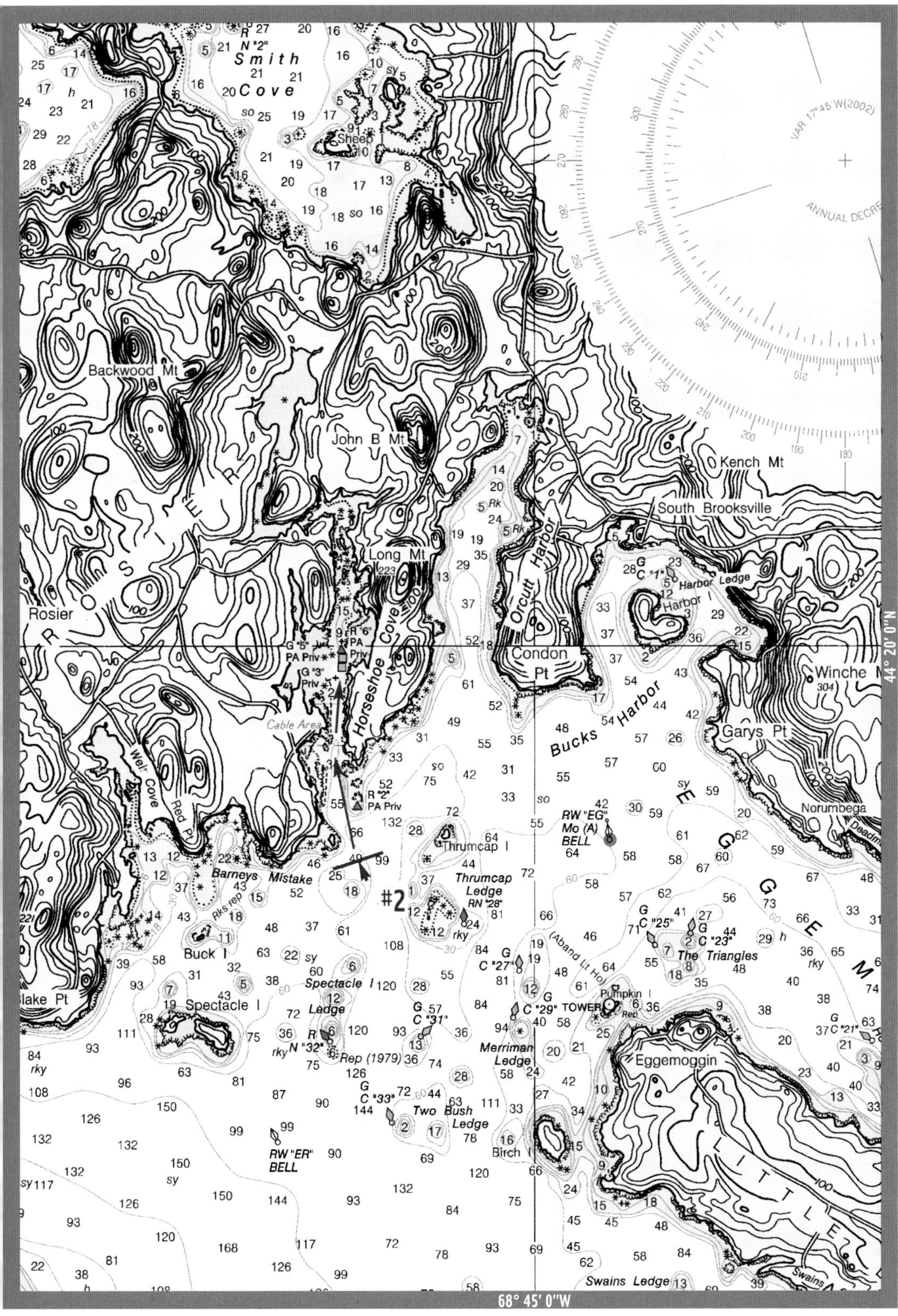

13309
28th ed., Sept. 02
NAD 83
Soundings in feet
1:40,000

Bucks Harbor

Bucks Harbor, at the northwest end of Eggemoggin Reach, offers excellent protection from nearly any direction; however, a thick field of guest moorings limits the space available for anchoring. Not shown on the chart are the tiny red and green lateral buoys that mark the entrances. The harbor can be entered on either side of Harbor Island; the buoys are arranged such that if you enter from the eastern side, near Grays Point, red will be to starboard. Bucks Harbor is a snug but busy place, so it is especially important to mind your wake. Moorings and limited services are available.

13309
28th ed., Sept. 02
NAD 83
Soundings in feet
1:40,000

CASTINE HARBOR

CASTINE, home to the Maine Maritime Academy, is a picturesque little town with a beautiful and busy harbor. The harbor entrance, at the mouth of the Bagaduce River, is marked by the unlit red-and-white "CH" bell west of Nautilus Island. When wind and tide are opposed it can be quite choppy here. Travel upriver, keeping the red daymark on the Hosmer Ledge Monument to starboard. The Maine Maritime Academy training ship can usually be seen alongside the MMA waterfront, which is immediately downriver from the town docks and boat ramp. Castine has many services and rental moorings are available, as much of the harbor is too deep to anchor. If you choose to anchor overnight, Smith Cove offers excellent holding and is considered a first-rate hurricane hole. To enter Smith Cove, make a gradual turn to the southeast once you are abeam of the MMA waterfront; keep Great Island to starboard. Once past Great Island it is important to honor red nun "2" inside Smith Cove, as it marks a large rock. Shoal water extends west from Sheep Island, but there is good water beyond it where the cove opens up again.

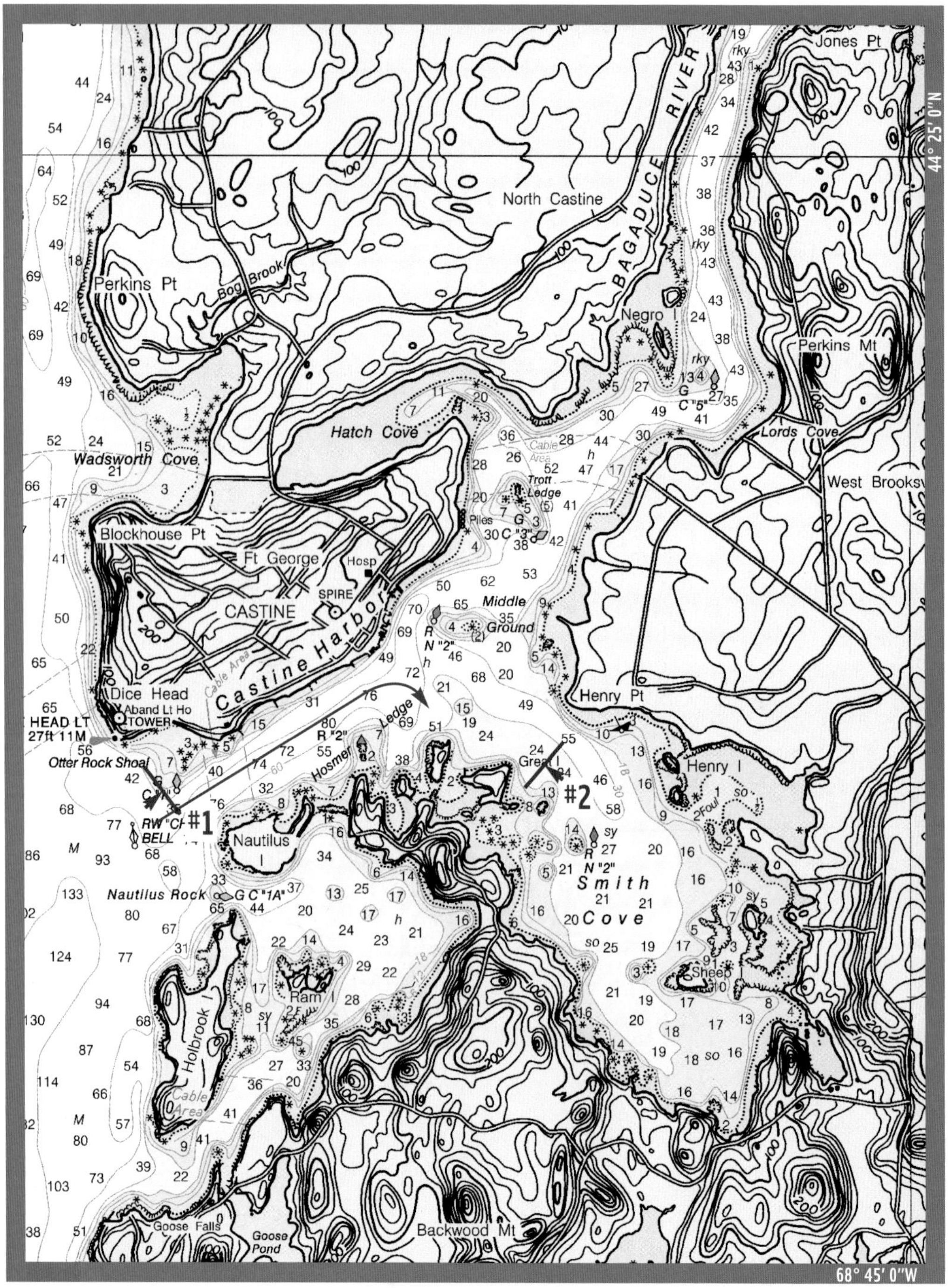

13309
28th ed., Sept. 02
NAD 83
Soundings in feet
1:40,000

Castine

Smith Cove

#1

R "2"

Nautilus I

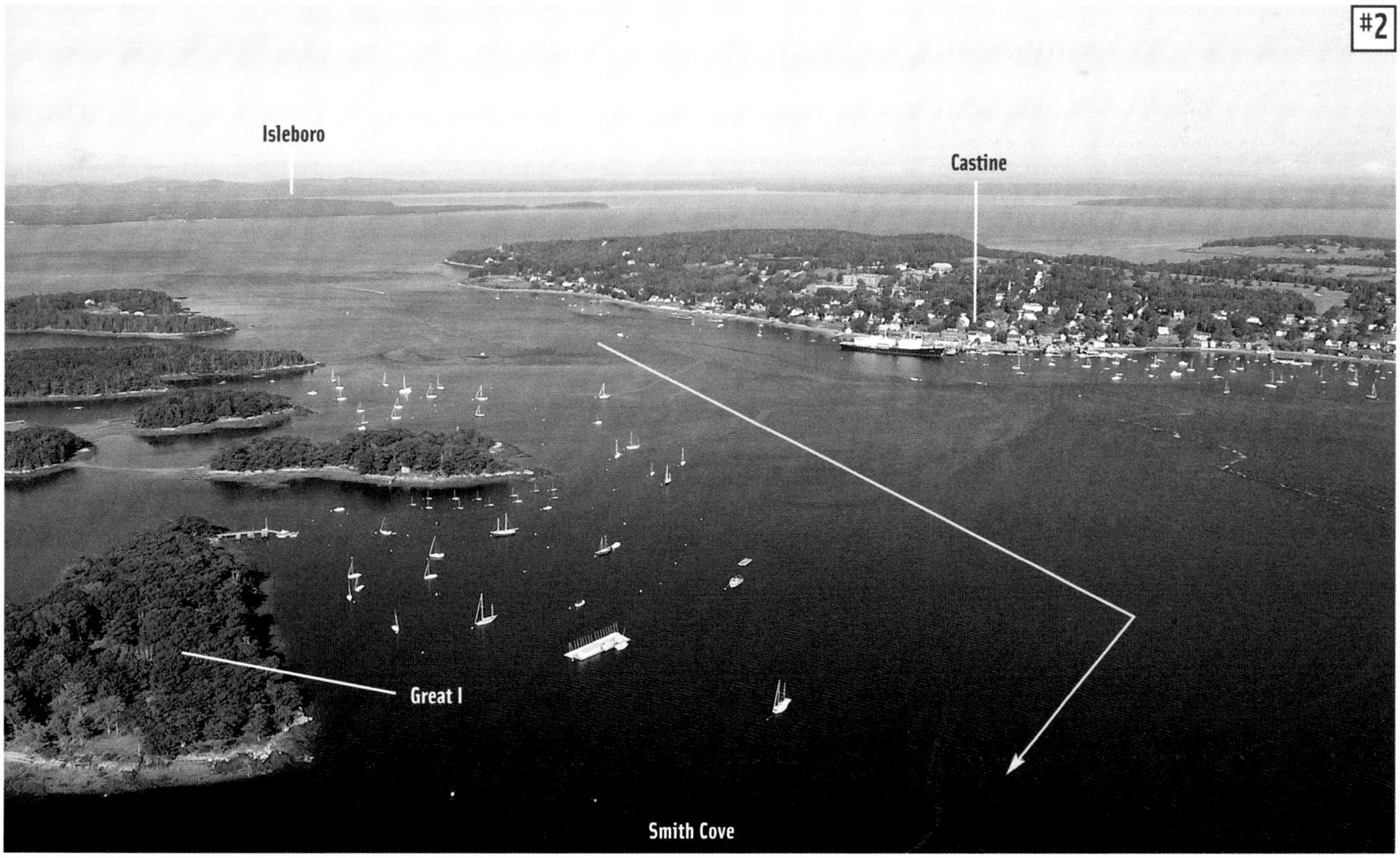

#2

Isleboro

Castine

Great I

Smith Cove

REGION VI

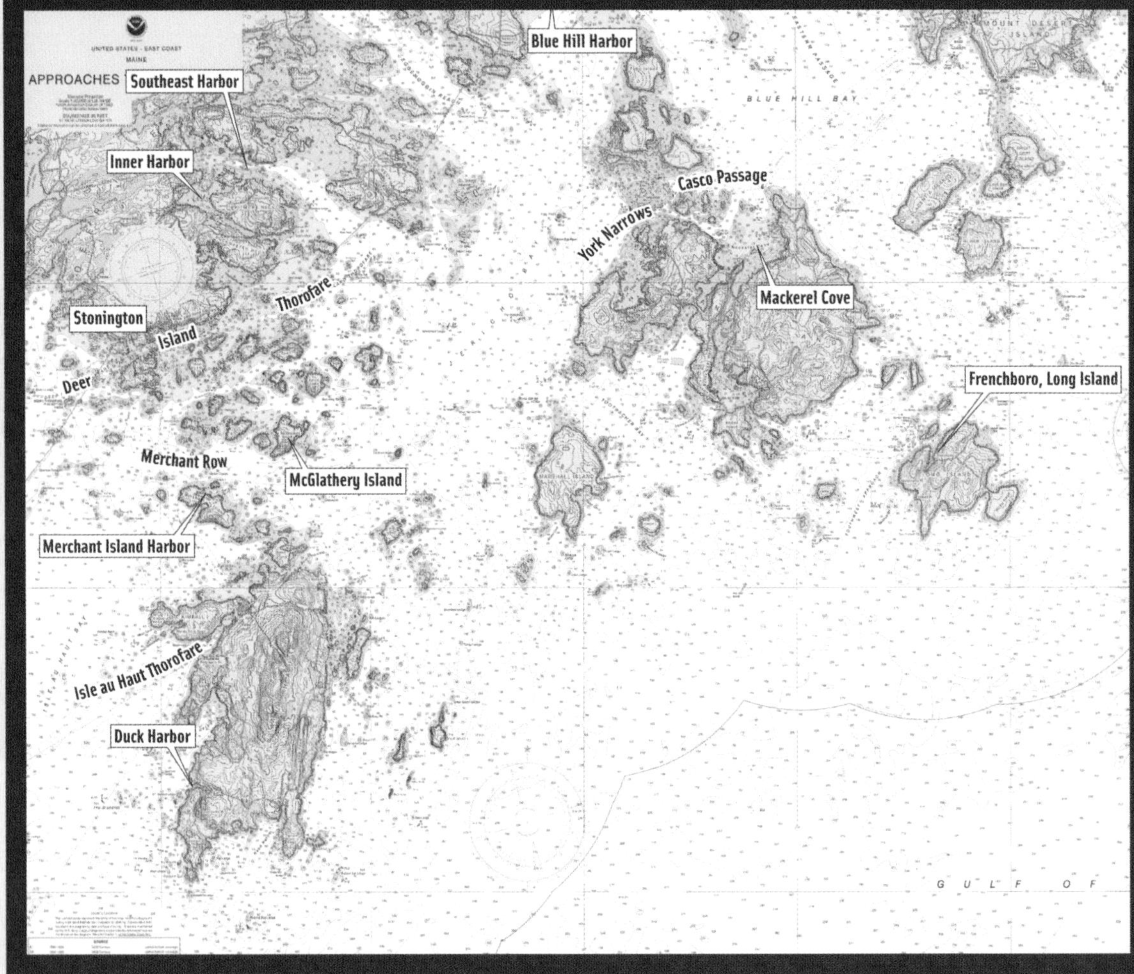

Blue Hill Harbor
APPROACHES
Southeast Harbor
BLUE HILL BAY
Inner Harbor
Casco Passage
York Narrows
Thorofare
Mackerel Cove
Stonington
Island
Deer
Frenchboro, Long Island
Merchant Row
McGlathery Island
Merchant Island Harbor
Isle au Haut Thorofare
Duck Harbor
G U L F O F

BLUE HILL AND JERICHO BAYS
—DUCK HARBOR TO FRENCHBORO—

Deer Island Thorofare looking east toward Stonington (page 186)

From almost any vantage point in this region, the rugged outline of Isle au Haut looms above the nearer vistas, and if it seems to be calling you to visit, you should heed that call. The Isle au Haut Thorofare is a delightful passage back through time to the New England seafront villages of yesteryear, and from there a short hop will take you to fabled Merchant Row, off the fishing village of Stonington, with its pink granite island shores that are suffused with a subtle roseate glow in early morning and late afternoon light. The tides are noticeably bigger here than in southern Maine, the fog more frequent and baffling. But these modest challenges only make the destinations more memorable: Merchant Harbor, close to busy Stonington yet a world apart in solitude; tiny Buckle Harbor on the northwest coast of Swans Island, just off York Narrows; the deep, inviting coves along the eastern shore of Deer Isle; the lobstering community and tight-as-a-drum anchorage of Burnt Coat Harbor; the graceful town of Blue Hill huddled beneath its mountain; and eastward, truly on the "Down East" threshold, Lunt Harbor—Frenchboro, Long Island—one of the crown jewels in Maine's storehouse of cruising treasures. From there the sweeping heights of Mount Desert dominate the horizon to the north, even more dramatically than the Camden Hills dominate West Penobscot Bay.

The sheer beauty of the surroundings is a constant comfort in this region. On a clear, calm night the stars go on forever, and when the fog rolls in or the weather turns foul, bells, gongs, and horns create a nighttime lullaby that reminds us how special this part of the world is.

■ DUCK HARBOR ■

TINY Duck Harbor, on the southwestern shore of Isle au Haut, is a rare treat—among other things, it provides access to this southern outlier of Acadia National Park. The harbor can be approached from the west by passing well north of red nun "4" marking the Brandies, keeping Duck Harbor Ledge to port and Haddock Ledge to starboard. If coming from the north, it is also possible to pass between Moores Harbor Ledge on the port side, and red nun "6" at Rock T. If arrival can be timed for low water, the numerous off-lying rocks will be easier to

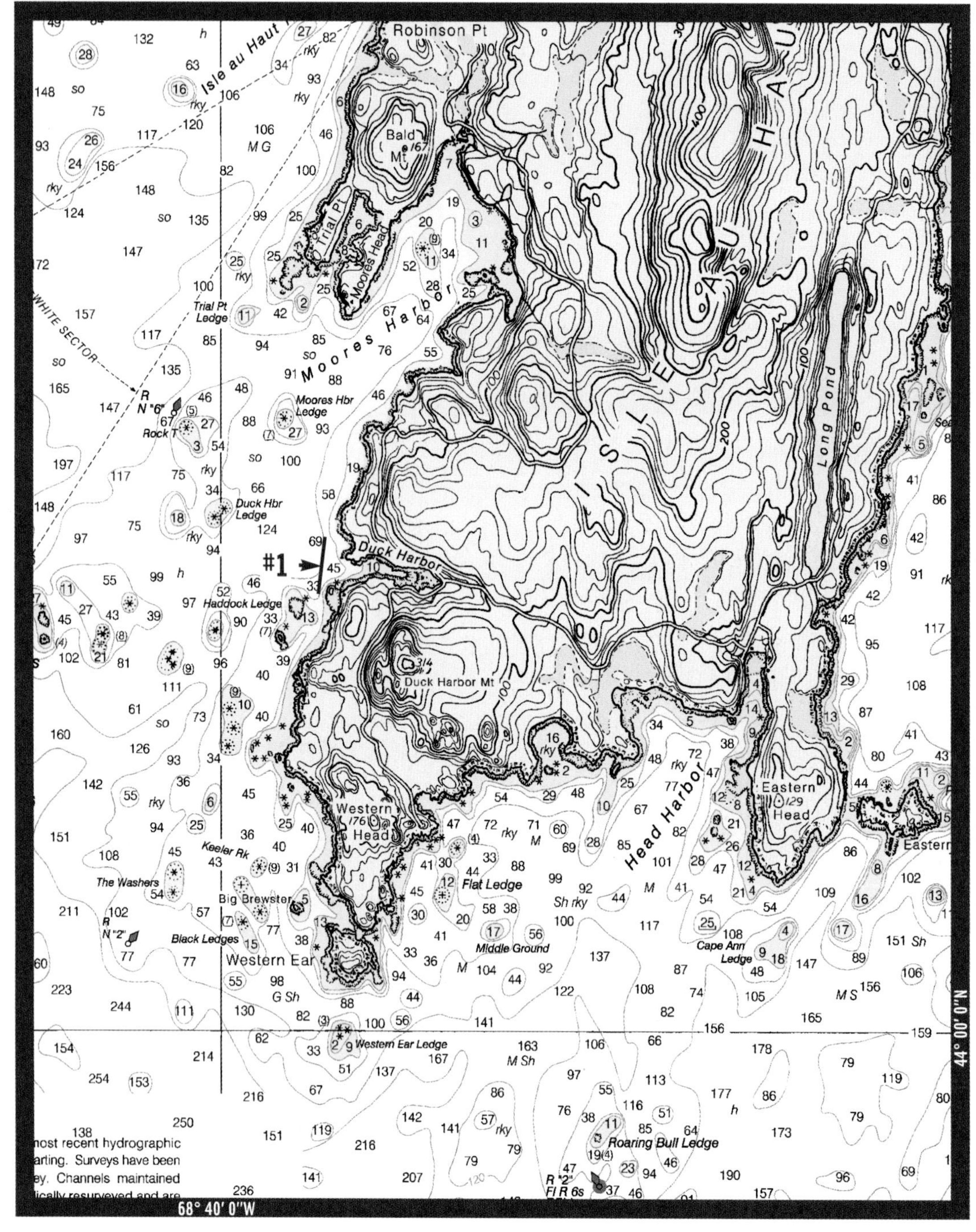

13313
20th ed., July 04
NAD 83
Soundings in feet
1:40,000

spot. Midway down the harbor is a public landing and ferry dock. Anchorage can be found just seaward or just past this, more or less along the centerline of the harbor. Do not block the ferry. Once ashore, a short trail leads from the public landing to the ranger station, which is staffed daily during the summer. Trail maps and other information are available. Duck Harbor is exposed in a westerly, and its upper reaches drain at low tide.

■ ISLE AU HAUT THOROFARE ■

ISLE au Haut Thorofare is a well-marked and easily navigated passageway between Kimball Island and Isle au Haut. Coming from the west, Robinson Point and its 48-foot lighthouse mark the starboard side of the entrance, and green can "1" on Sawyer Ledge marks the port side. Three quarters of the way along, below the spire, is the village of Isle au Haut. There is limited room to anchor in the thoroughfare opposite the village. The eastern end of the thoroughfare is marked by red nun "8" and green can "9." If entering from this direction, keep red to port. An island-owned ferry runs to Stonington from here.

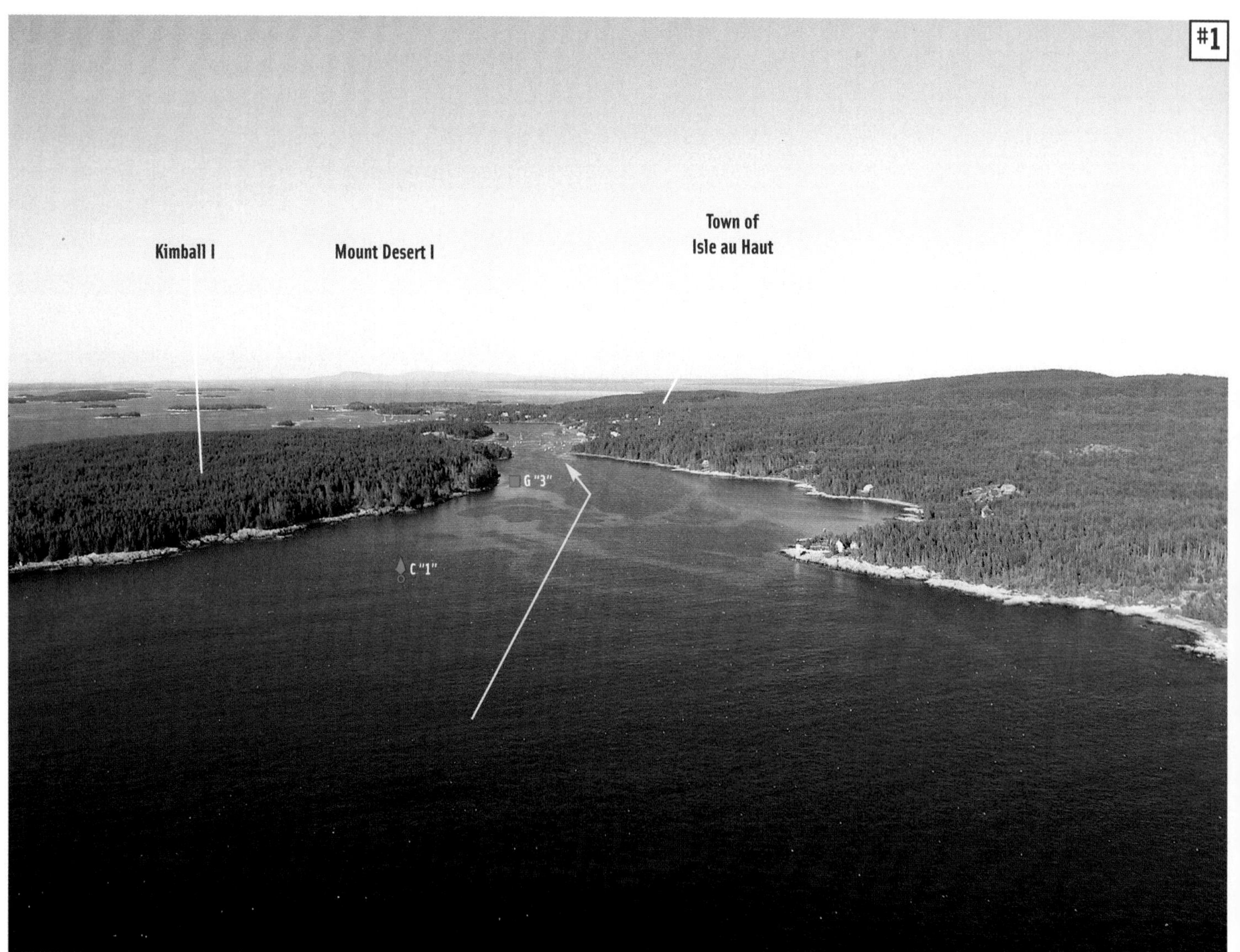

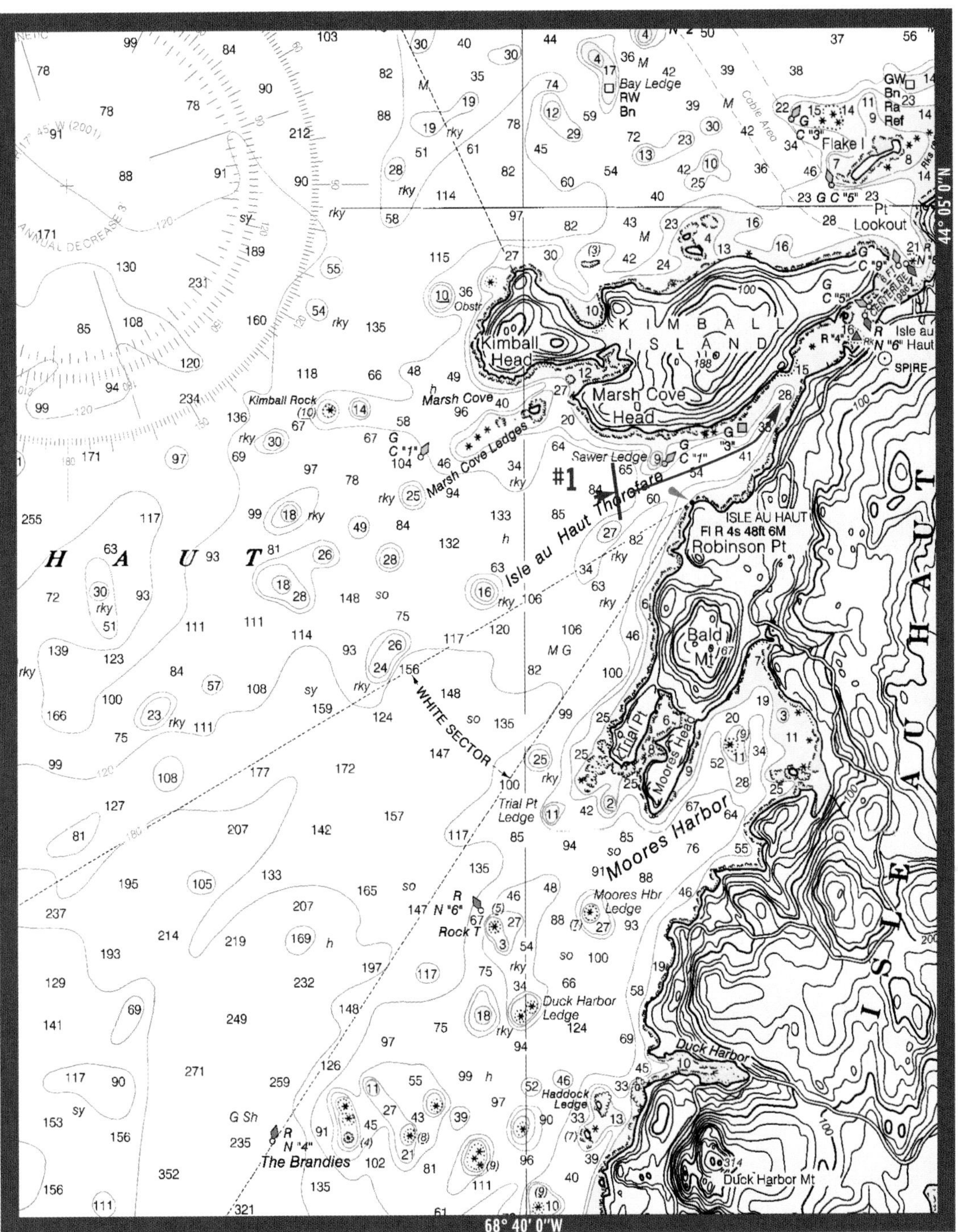

13305
28th ed., May 01
NAD 83
Soundings in feet
1:40,000

■ MERCHANT ROW PASSAGE ■

PERHAPS one of the most interesting waterways on the coast runs through the group of islands known as Merchant Row. This partially protected passageway between Deer Isle and Isle au Haut forms a route leading from East Penobscot Bay to Jericho Bay. Merchant Row can be entered any number of ways, but Scraggy Island, south of Mark Island, marks the western entrance. Whatever route is chosen, all approaches from the west lead to red nun "10" marking a 4-foot spot north of Ewe Island. From this point a series of navigation aids lead the way through Merchant Row until you exit at green can "1" off Colby Pup. When traveling west to east through here, the reds are kept to port, green to starboard.

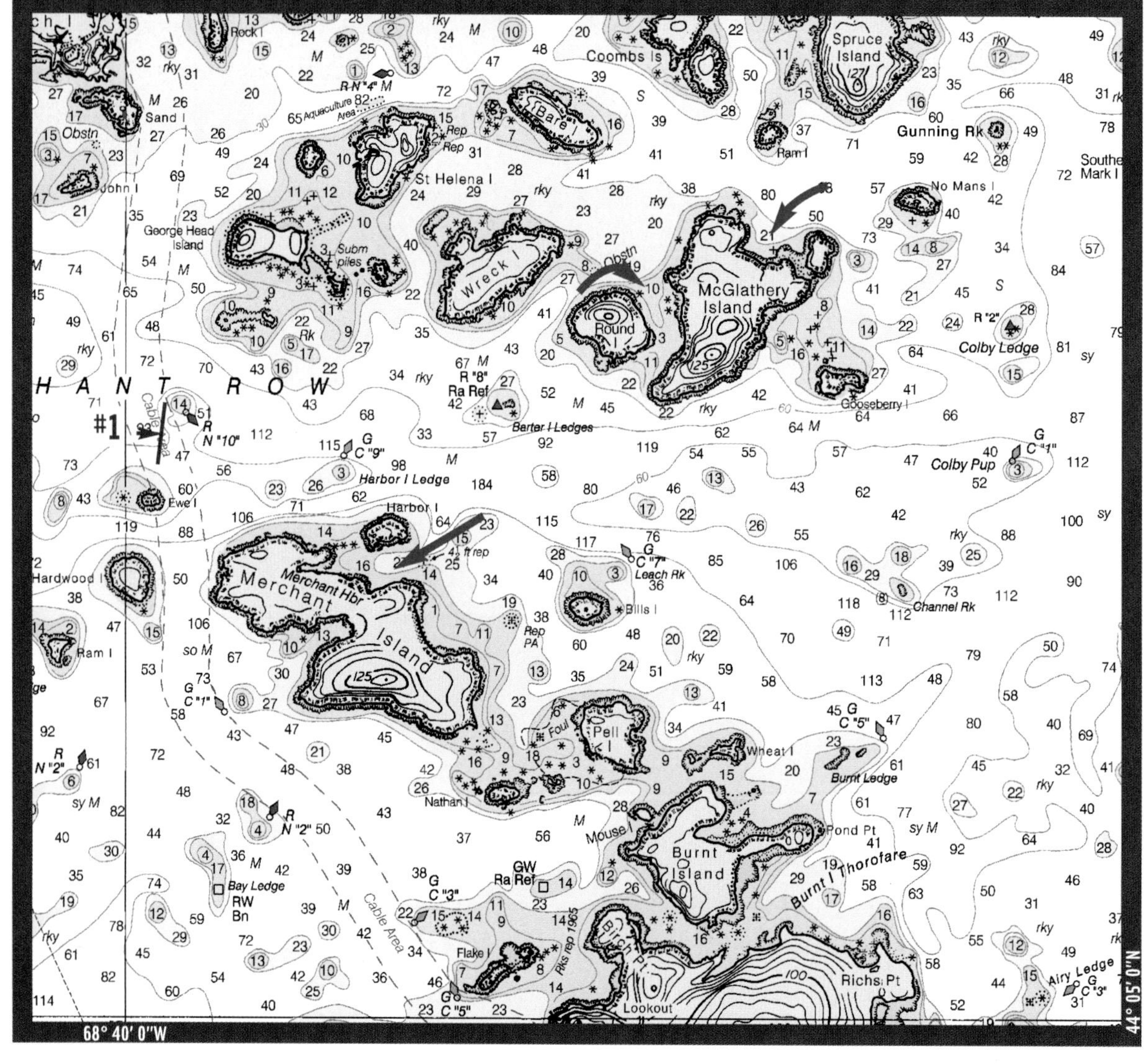

13313
20th ed., July 04
NAD 83
Soundings in feet
1:40,000

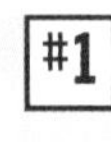

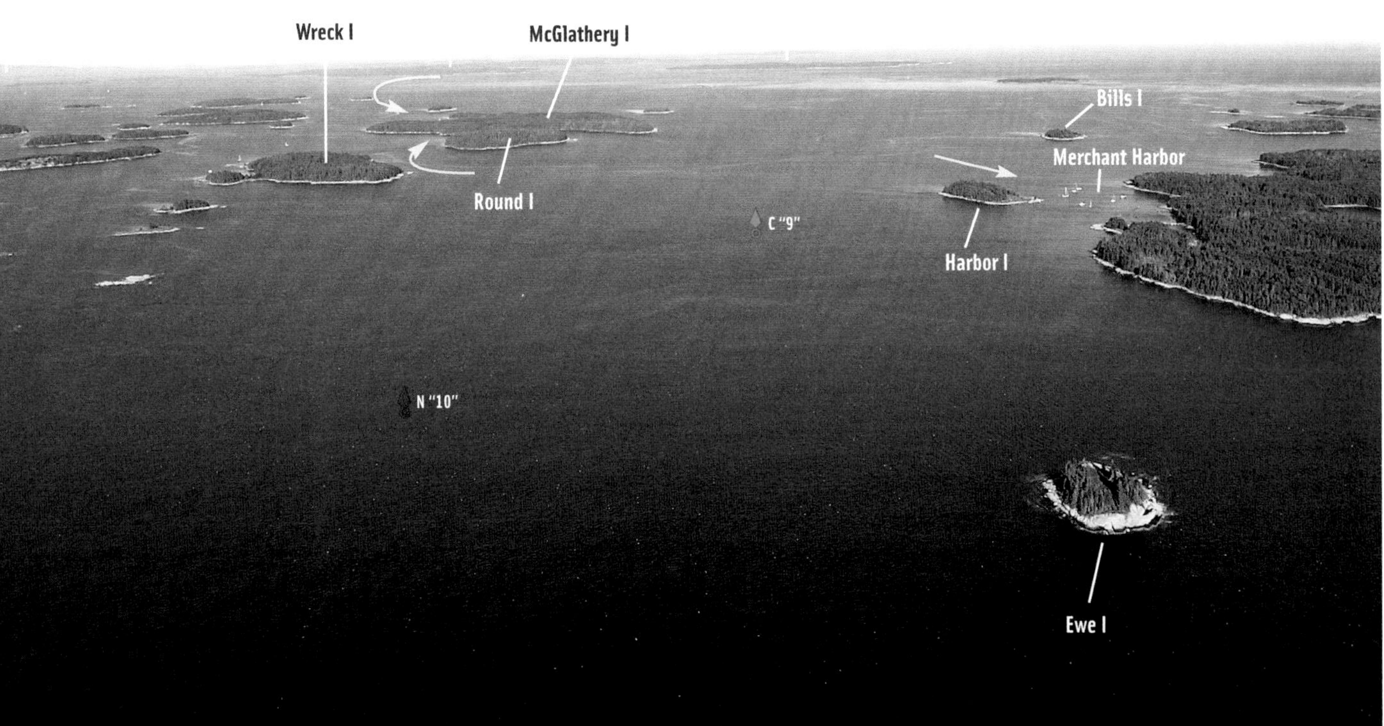

Merchant Island Harbor

Merchant Island Harbor is a neat lunch spot on the way through Merchant Row. From green can "9" off Harbor Island Ledge turn southeast and proceed around to the east side of Harbor Island, then continue your turn to the west to enter Merchant Harbor. Favor the Harbor Island shoreline to avoid the isolated rock reported to be just east of the 27-foot spot.

McGlathery Island

McGlathery Island is considered by many to be the finest stopping point in Merchant Row. The primary anchorage is on the northeast side. The approach is wide open and can be made from several directions. Another anchorage—though exposed to a southwest breeze—can be found between McGlathery and Round Island near the 10-foot sounding on the chart.

■ DEER ISLAND THOROFARE ■

DEER Island Thorofare—running through the islands immediately south of Deer Isle—is another useful east – west passage. It is noticeably tighter than Merchant Row, but more protected and well marked. From the west, Deer Island Thorofare is easily identified by the picturesque lighthouse on Mark Island. Proceed east to green can "27," keeping it to starboard. Continue on to red nun "24" south of Moose Island, leaving it to port.

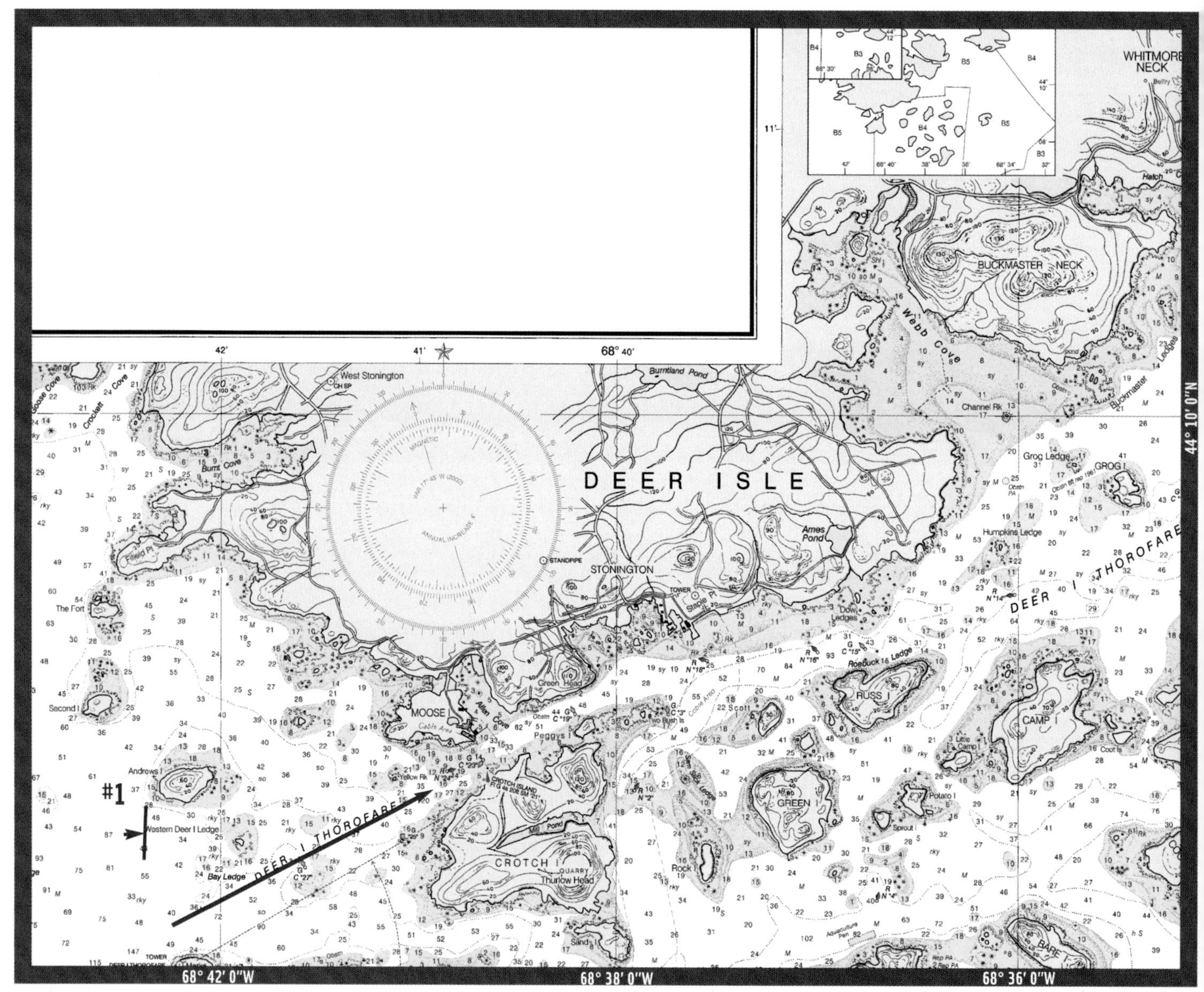

13315
11th ed., March 02
NAD 83
Soundings in feet
1:20,000

Follow the navigation aids past the town of Stonington, keeping red to port and green to starboard. Continue along the south shore of Deer Isle until you exit the thoroughfare at Sheep Island at the eastern end. It is not unusual to see small commercial vessels using the channel.

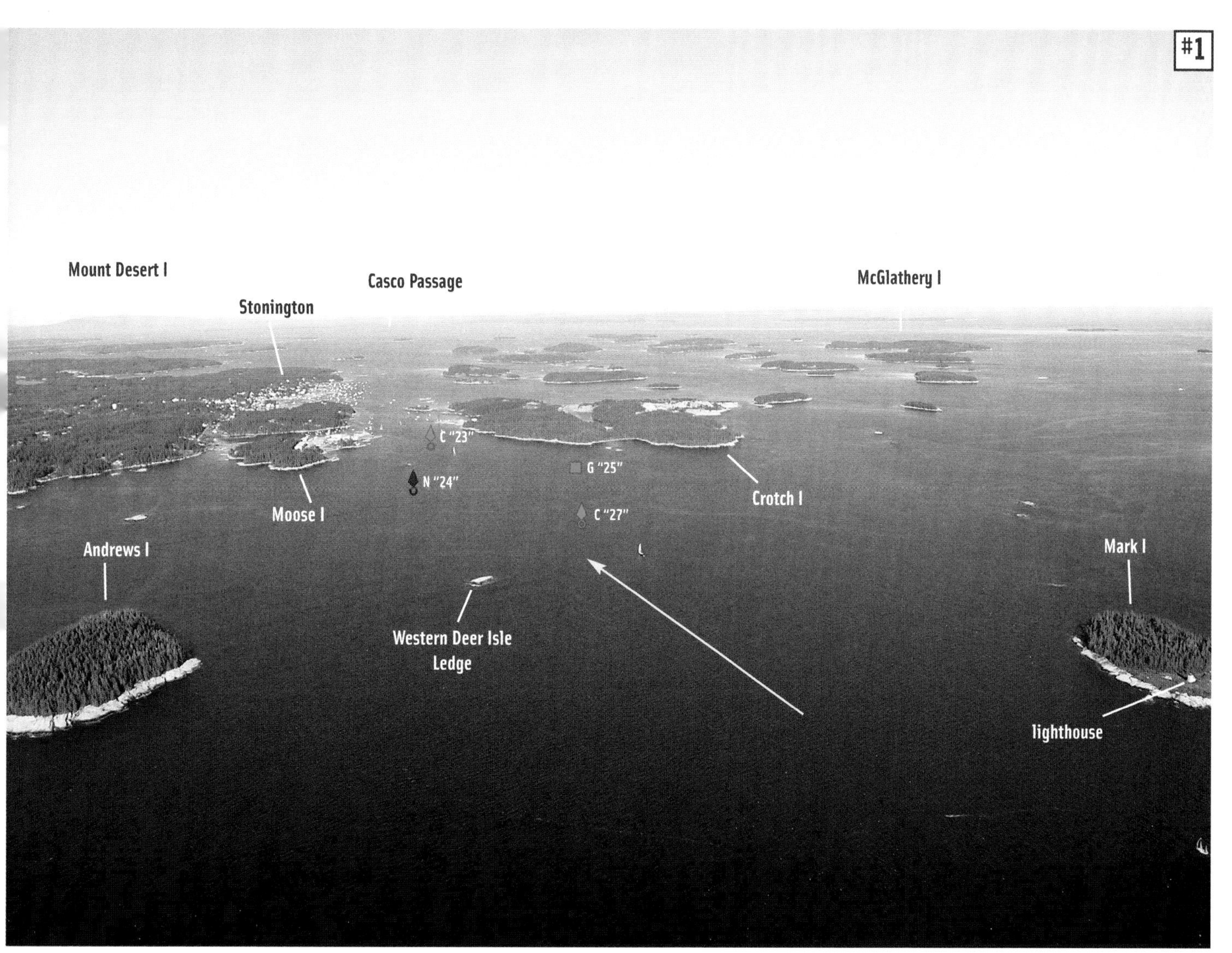

■ STONINGTON

SITUATED near the western end of the Deer Island Thorofare, Stonington is the southernmost town on Deer Isle and its most populous village. This scenic port is home to a colorful mix of artists and commercial fishermen. Ample moorings and anchorages are nearby, and all manner of services are available. Stonington makes a wonderful stopover for those transiting the thoroughfare. Be sure to explore the many gunkholes on the southern side of the thoroughfare toward Merchant Row.

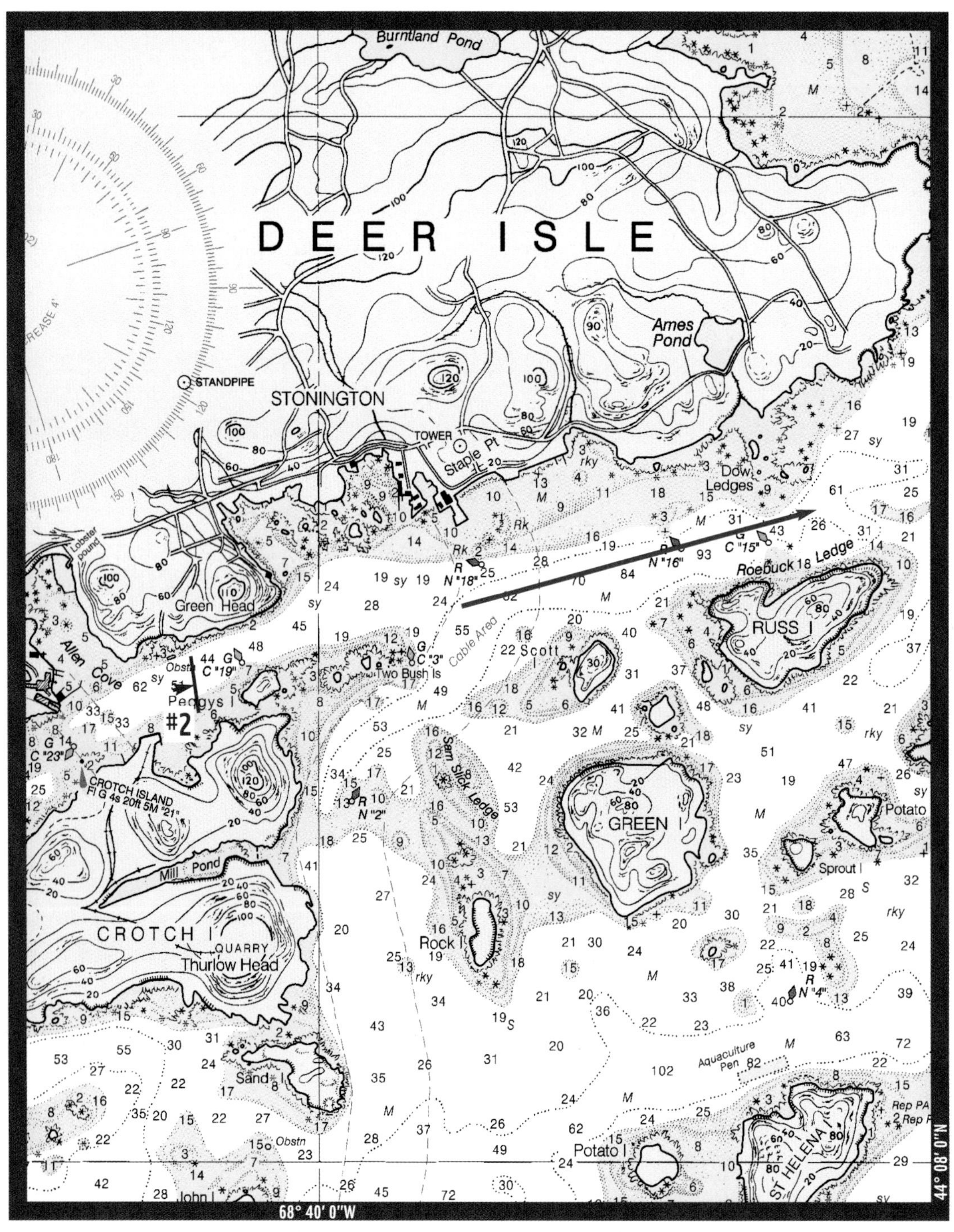

13315
11th ed., March 02
NAD 83
Soundings in feet
1:20,000

#2

■ SOUTHEAST HARBOR AND INNER HARBOR ■

SOUTHEAST and Inner Harbors are two connected anchorages on the southeast coast of Deer Isle. Protected by Whitmore Neck and other surrounding land forms, these waters afford protection from virtually any direction, and fair holding ground to boot. To avoid the rocks cluttering the middle of the harbor mouth, enter by way of the deep water on the far northern edge of the opening. This is a beautiful and secluded spot to spend the night.

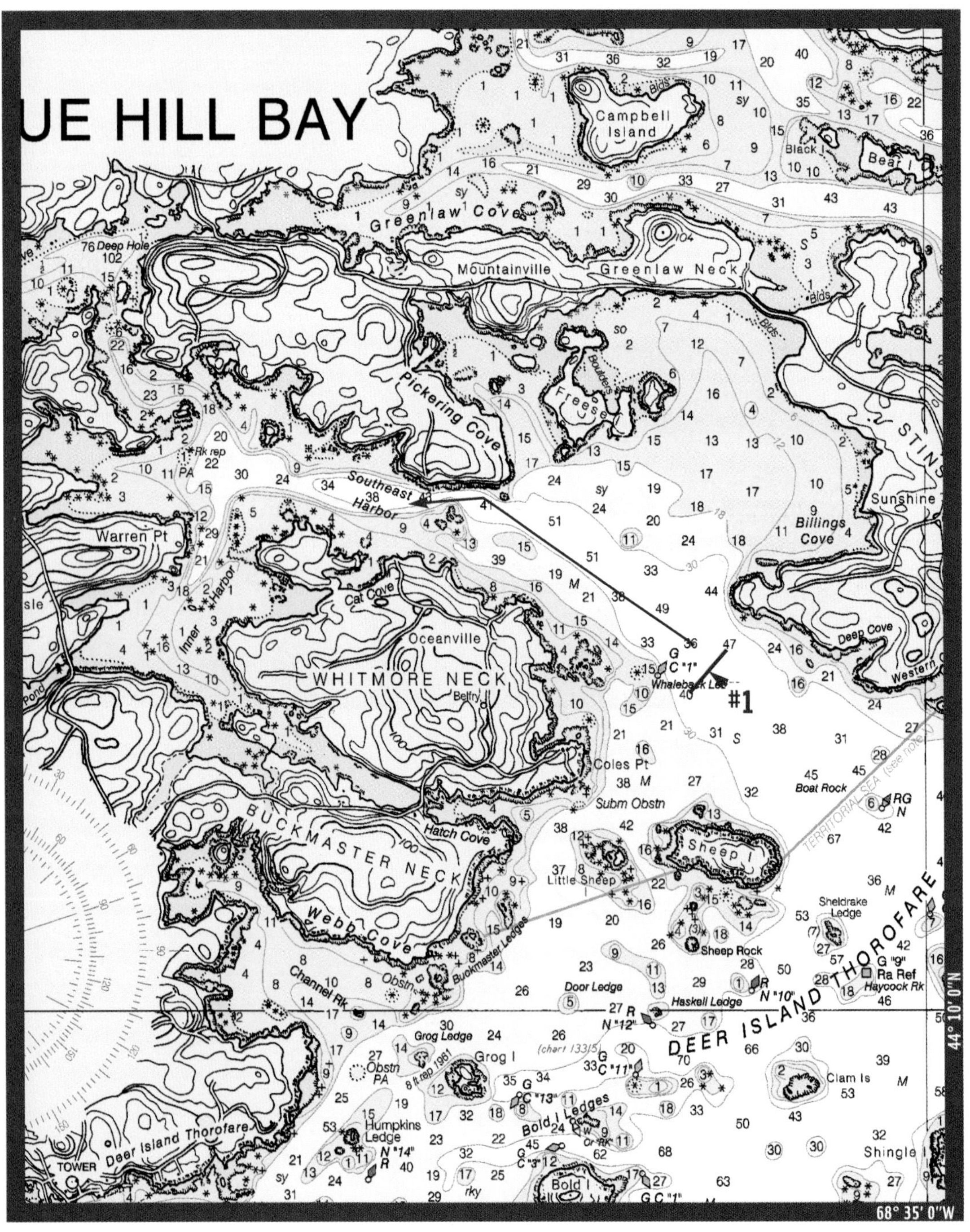

13313
20th ed., July 04
NAD 83
Soundings in feet
1:40,000

#1

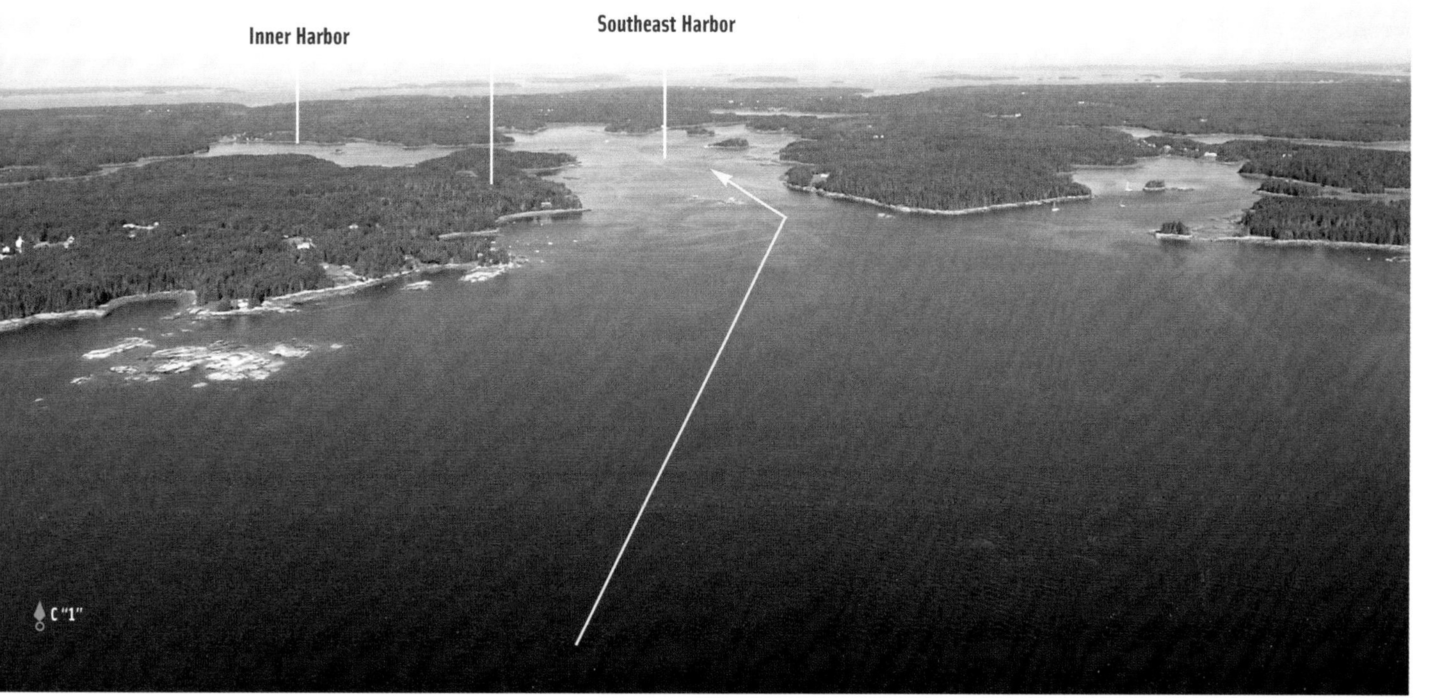

■ BLUE HILL HARBOR ■

BLUE Hill Harbor, located at the head of Blue Hill Bay, is entered through a narrow opening between Sculpin Point and Parker Point. Three green cans mark the port side of the approach. The single red nun "6" to starboard marks the ledges extending from Sculpin Point. The approach involves several large course changes and should be made carefully, honoring all buoys. In season, numerous boats occupy the waters immediately inside the harbor mouth. Anchorage is limited, but guest moorings are available from the Kollegewidgwok Yacht Club located directly north of the entrance on the eastern side of the harbor. It is possible to follow the marked channel farther west, past Triangles and into the inner harbor, though much of the good water is taken by resident moorings. At the far northwest corner of the harbor is a town dock accessible to provisions and services, but it dries out at low tide, as does much of the upper portion of the harbor. Blue Hill Harbor is a busy place in summer, but it's beautiful and well protected. Blue Hill, the promontory from which the town takes its name, is 940 feet high and visible for many miles around.

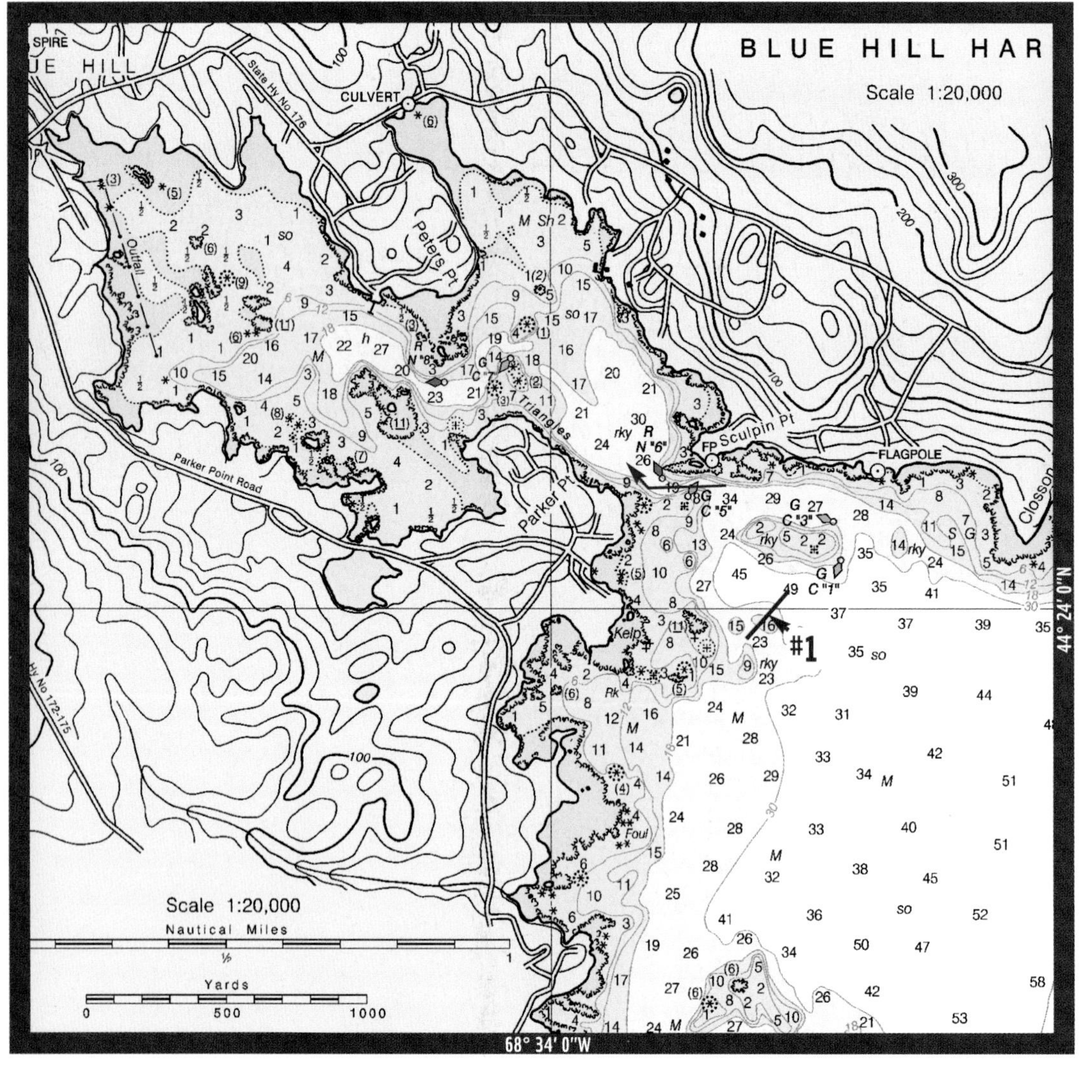

13316
1:20,000

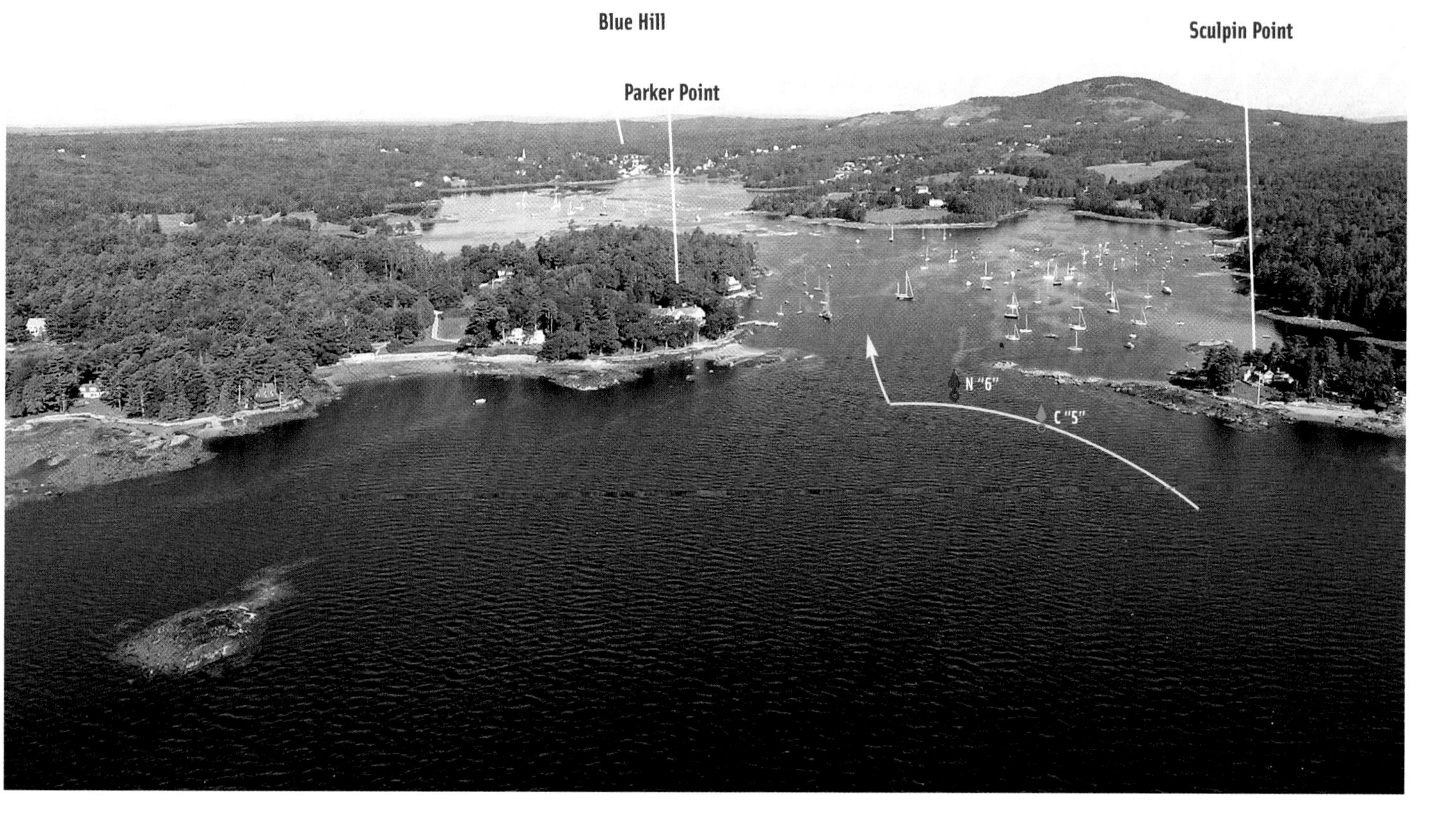
#1
Blue Hill
Parker Point
Sculpin Point
N "6"
C "5"

■ YORK NARROWS AND CASCO PASSAGE ■

YORK Narrows and Casco Passage are just north of Swans Island and connect Jericho Bay to Blue Hill Bay. For the eastbound sailor, they can be accessed either by Eggemoggin Reach or Deer Island Thorofare. Both routes are well marked, but they are narrow and surrounded by hazards. The approach to either one is marked by red daymark "8A" on Egg Rock, and red bell "8" just south of it. From this direction, red will be to port, green to starboard.

York Narrows, the more southerly of the two routes,

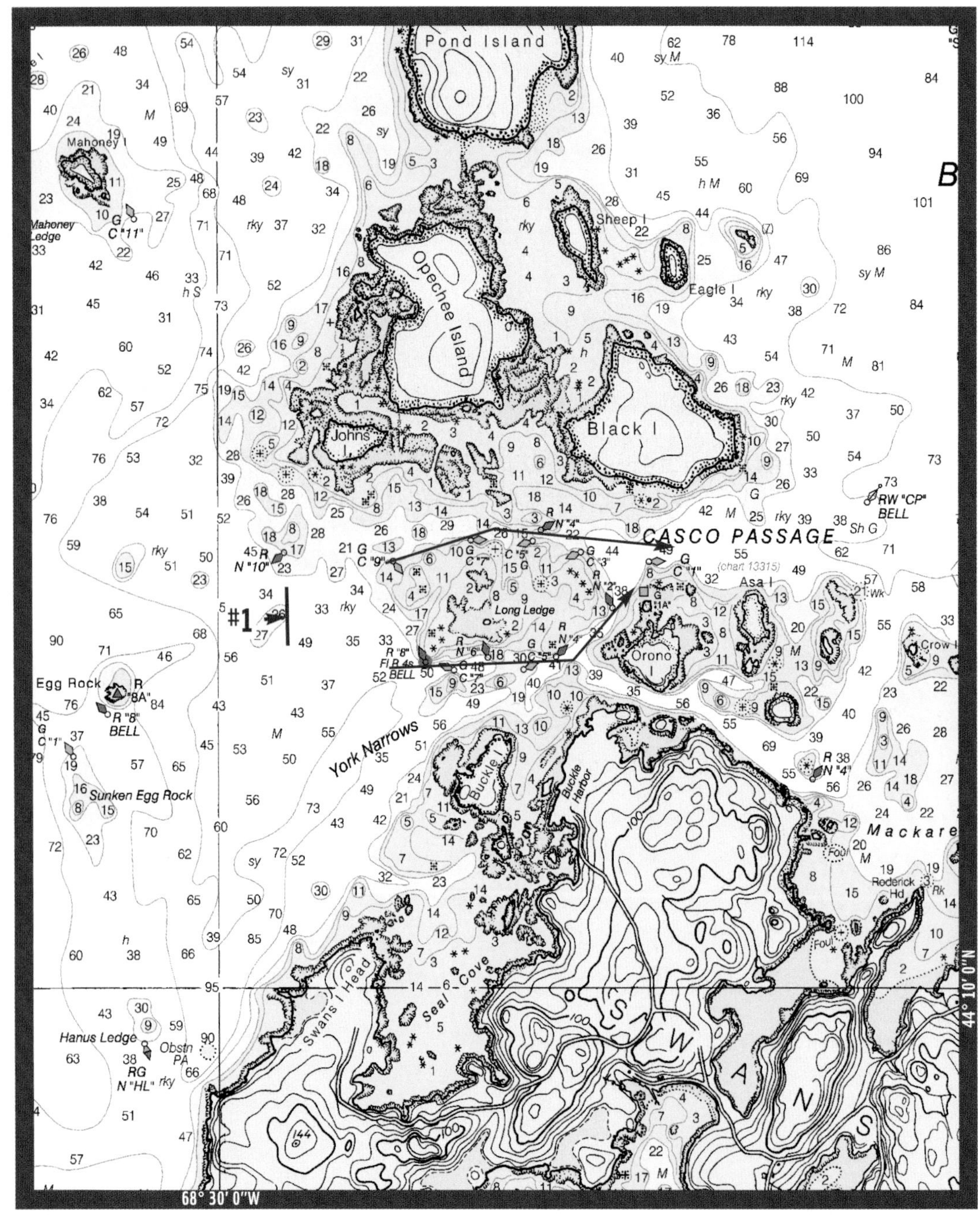

13313
20th ed., July 04
NAD 83
Soundings in feet
1:40,000

is better marked and has deeper water. From flashing red bell "8" north of Buckle Island, sail due east directly toward Orono Island. Upon reaching red nun "4," swing to a more northeasterly heading and follow the buoys toward Black Island. At the green can "1," turn east again for red-and-white "CP" and the open waters of Blue Hill Bay.

Casco Passage starts at the red nun "10." It's a fairly straight shot that starts by steering slightly north of east up to the green can "7," and then turns slightly south of east to the red nun "4" and onward to Blue Hill Bay.

Whichever route you choose, honor all buoys and confirm their numbers as you pass. Periodically check over your stern to determine the effect of the current on your progress. Small commercial vessels occasionally ply these waters.

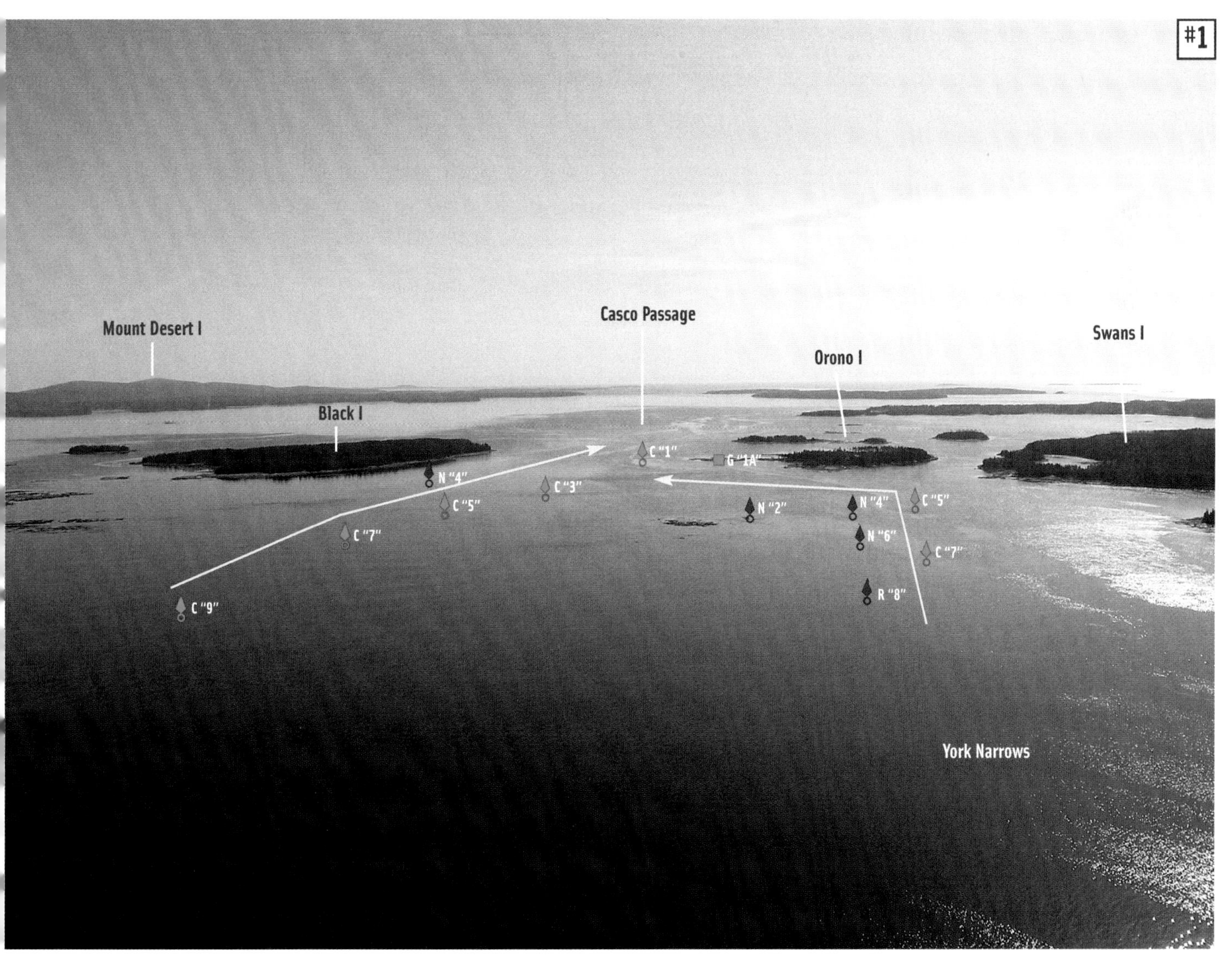

MACKEREL COVE

MACKEREL Cove is a large, open harbor on the north side of Swans Island, just east of Casco Passage. To enter from the north, pass between flashing green gong "1" off North Point and red nun "2" just east of Crow Island. There are numerous places to anchor, but there are also several unmarked dangers, including a large ledge northeast of Roderick Head, so monitor your position carefully inside the cove. It is also possible to enter from the west by way of York Narrows. From the area immediately west of Orono Island, turn southeast out of York Narrows and follow the deepwater passage down to red nun "4" on the western side of the cove. Mackerel Cove is relatively busy in the summer. The ferry from Bass Harbor docks on the eastern side. The anchorage is exposed to the north and the holding ground is not particularly good. Use it as a refuge, but be mindful of its limitations.

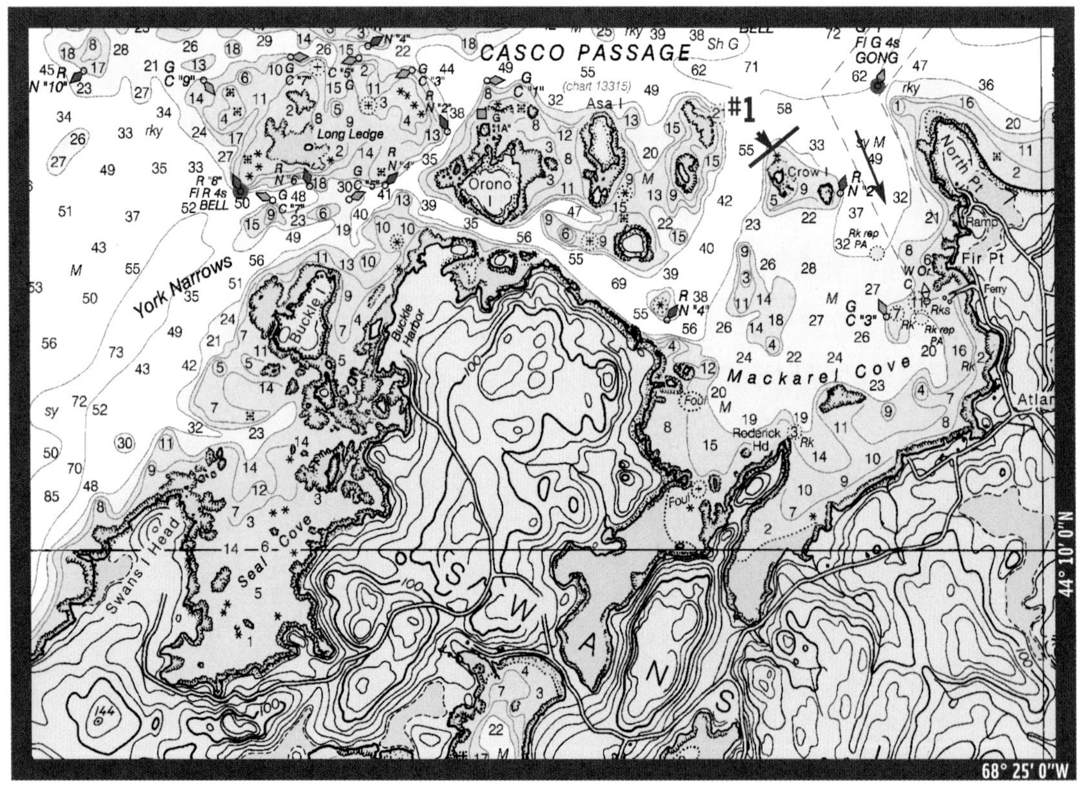

13313
20th ed., July 04
NAD 83
Soundings in feet
1:40,000

#1
Fir Point
C "3"
N "2"
Crow I

■ FRENCHBORO, LONG ISLAND ■

ON the northwest side of Long Island lies the town of Frenchboro and Lunt Harbor—the primary point of access to the island. Primarily a working fishing village, Frenchboro is well worth the visit. Lunt Harbor can be approached from the northeast by passing flashing red-and-white gong "LI" off Northeast Ledge and then slipping between Harbor Island and Long Island. The approach can be made from the west by keeping green bell "1" to port and then steering northeast toward the harbor entrance. Anchorage can be found directly between Harbor and Long Islands. Moorings and some services are available in the inner harbor, not far from the Bass Harbor ferry landing.

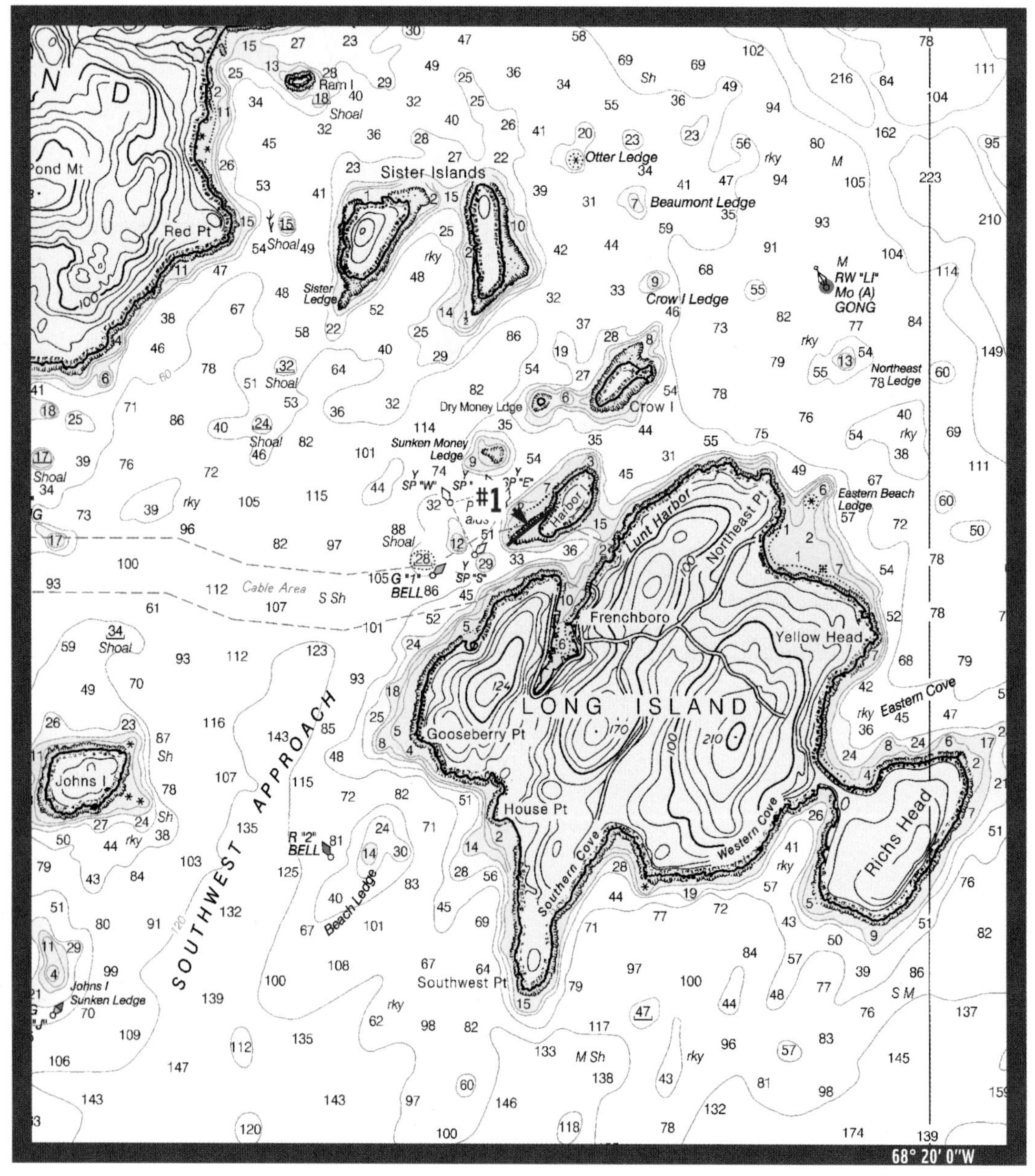

13313
20th ed., July 04
NAD 83
Soundings in feet
1:40,000

#1

REGION VII

ELLSWORTH
Sorrento Harbor
Bar Harbor
Winter Harbor
Mount Desert Island
MOUNT DESERT ISLAND
Somes Harbor
Northeast Harbor
Southwest Harbor
Seal Harbor
BAR HARBOR
FLANDERS BAY
EASTERN BAY
ACADIA NATIONAL PARK
SOMES SOUND

MOUNT DESERT ISLAND AND FRENCHMAN BAY
—SOUTHWEST HARBOR TO WINTER HARBOR—

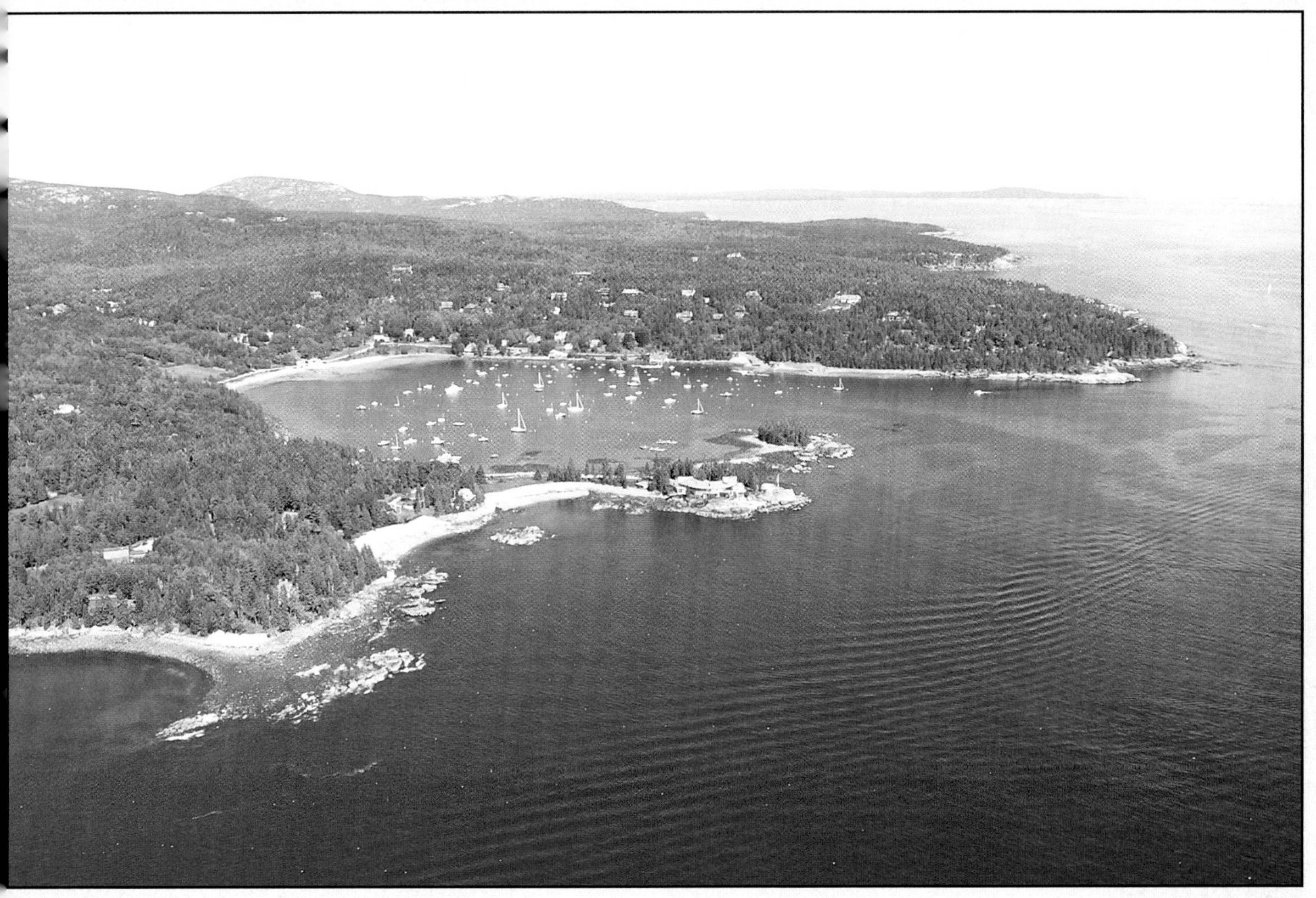

Looking east toward Mount Desert Island's Seal Harbor (page 210)

The upthrust rock bastions of Mount Desert brood above these waters in stony silence. Sheer cliffs endure the constant attack of restless surf at their base and unrelenting winter storms on their heights. To look on this landscape is to read a story spanning eons of time.

Within these waters are some of the most beautiful shorelines in the world. Somes Sound, the only fiord in the continental United States, runs due north, deep into Mount Desert's interior, offering breathtaking vistas of Acadia National Park. At the end of this dramatic waterway, the elegant town of Somesville lies an easy stroll from one of the most serene harbors in Maine, Somes Harbor.

This region offers the full spectrum of harbors, from quiet, tucked-away Pretty Marsh and Sorrento to the cruiser's haven of Southwest Harbor, the tourist mecca of Bar Harbor, the fishing fleets of Bass Harbor and Islesford, and the historic sailing community and summer colony of Northeast Harbor. The waters are equally varied, the cozy security of the Eastern Way yielding within miles to the wide-open expanses in the approaches to Frenchman Bay.

▪ MOUNT DESERT APPROACH ▪

THE approach to Mount Desert's protected waters is from green gong buoy "1" on the southernmost edge of Western Way—the channel between Mount Desert Island and Great Cranberry Island. A series of red nuns in the passage lead to a number of cruising options for the mariner; among these choices are Southwest Harbor to the west, Somes Sound to the northwest, Northeast Harbor to the north, and the passages of Eastern Way and Gilley Thorofare to the east.

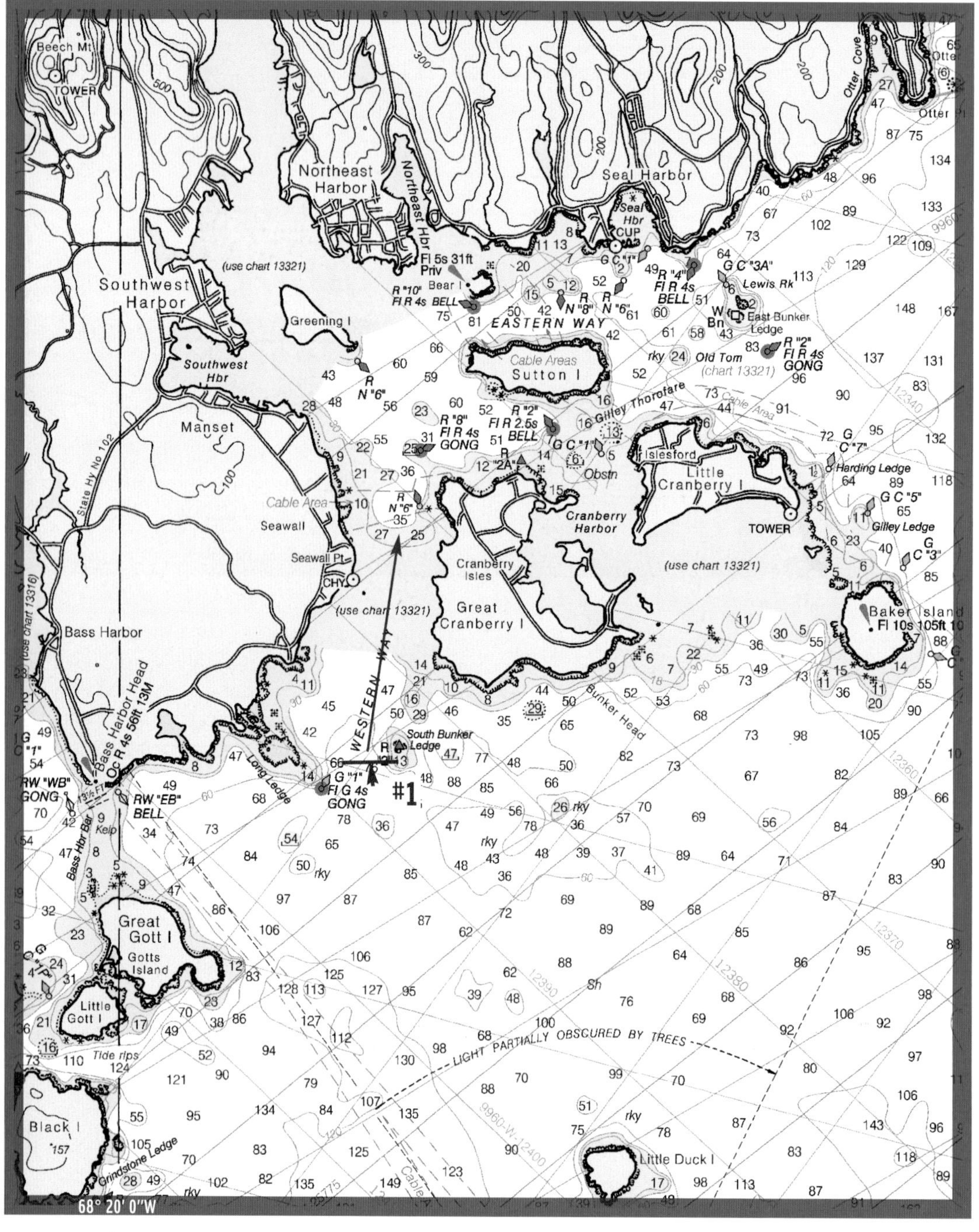

13312
21st ed., Jan. 03
NAD 83
Soundings in feet
1:80,000

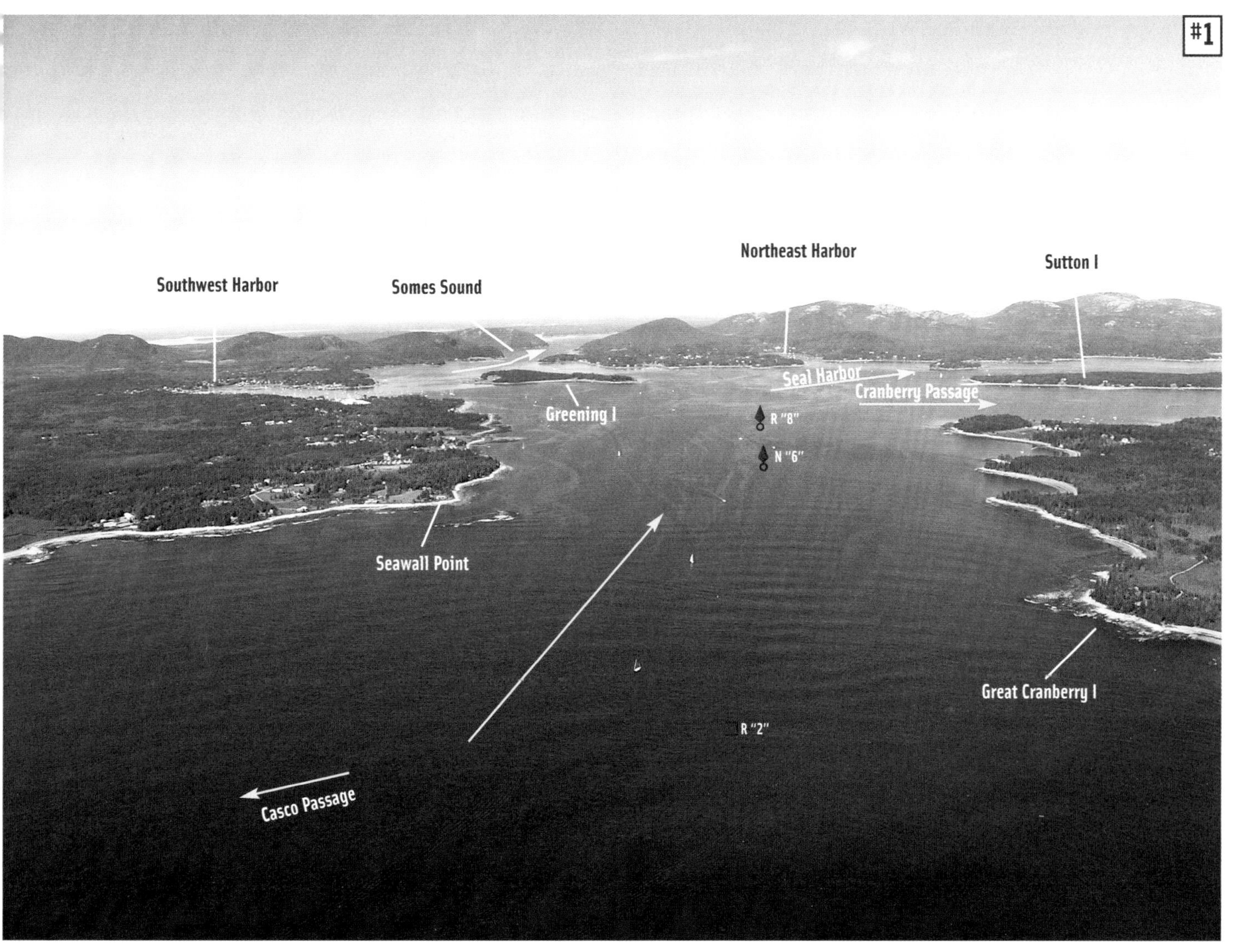
#1
Northeast Harbor
Sutton I
Southwest Harbor
Somes Sound
Seal Harbor
Cranberry Passage
Greening I
R "8"
N "6"
Seawall Point
Great Cranberry I
R "2"
Casco Passage

■ SOUTHWEST HARBOR ■

FROM the northern end of Western Way—marked by red gong "8"—continue on a northerly heading to red nun "6" off the eastern tip of Greening Island. From here, steer westerly toward the center of Southwest Harbor. Once abeam of Clark Point, you'll see world-renowned Hinckley Yacht Service to port, with its mooring field and docks at Manset. Southwest Harbor has every service the mariner needs including moorings, launch service, and plenty of restaurants and entertainment; it's worthy of full exploration.

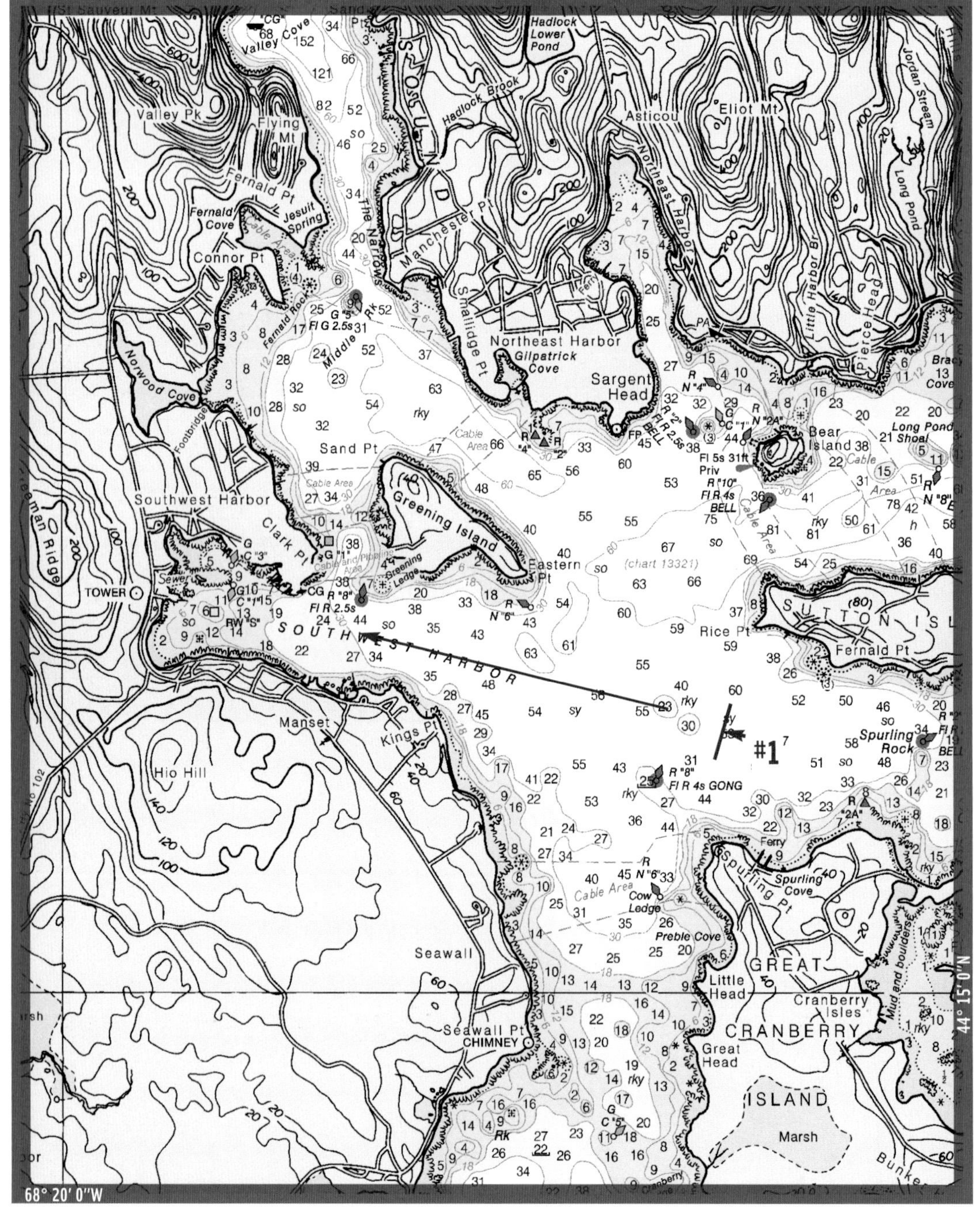

13318
18th ed., Aug. 02
NAD 83
Soundings in feet
1:40,000

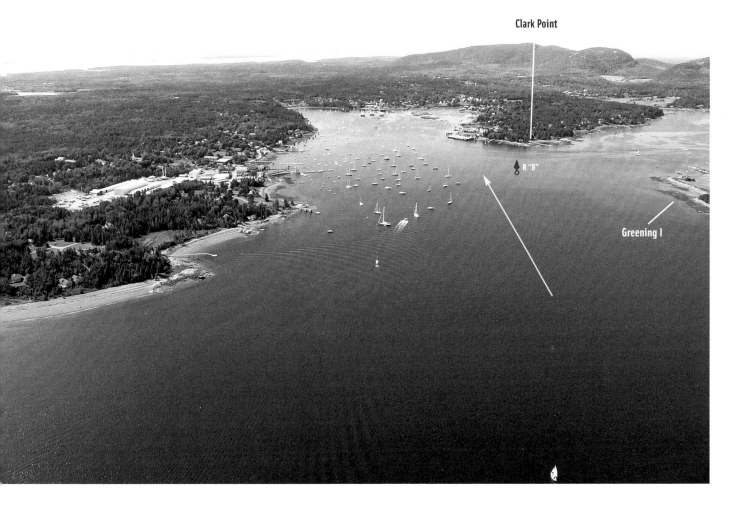

Clark Point

R "8"

Greening I

■ SOMES HARBOR ■

ONE of the true delights of the Maine coast is Somes Sound, and Somes Harbor, at the head of the sound, makes an excellent destination. Approached from the north side of Greening Island, the entrance to Somes Sound is marked by the lighted green buoy "5" east of Connor Point. From the buoy, proceed due north up this majestic fiord until you reach red nun "6" south of Myrtle Ledge, which marks the entrance to Somes Harbor and the town of Somesville. Navigate in mid-channel between green can "7" on your port side and Bar Island and Squantum Point to starboard. Moorings are sometimes available in the harbor, as well as temporary space at the town dock. A night spent in this harbor can be one of the most enjoyable in all of Maine.

13318
18th ed., Aug. 02
NAD 83
Soundings in feet
1:40,000

#1

Somesville
Bar I
C "7"
N "6"

■ NORTHEAST HARBOR ■

TO most Down East mariners, Northeast Harbor needs no introduction. One of the classic Maine coast destinations, Northeast Harbor is also one of the most visited. The approach is straightforward starting at red bell "2" located between Bear Island and Sargent Head. From the buoy, proceed north into the harbor. Two thirds of the way in, you'll see moorings and slip space for transient boaters. Ashore, you will find plentiful facilities and amenities.

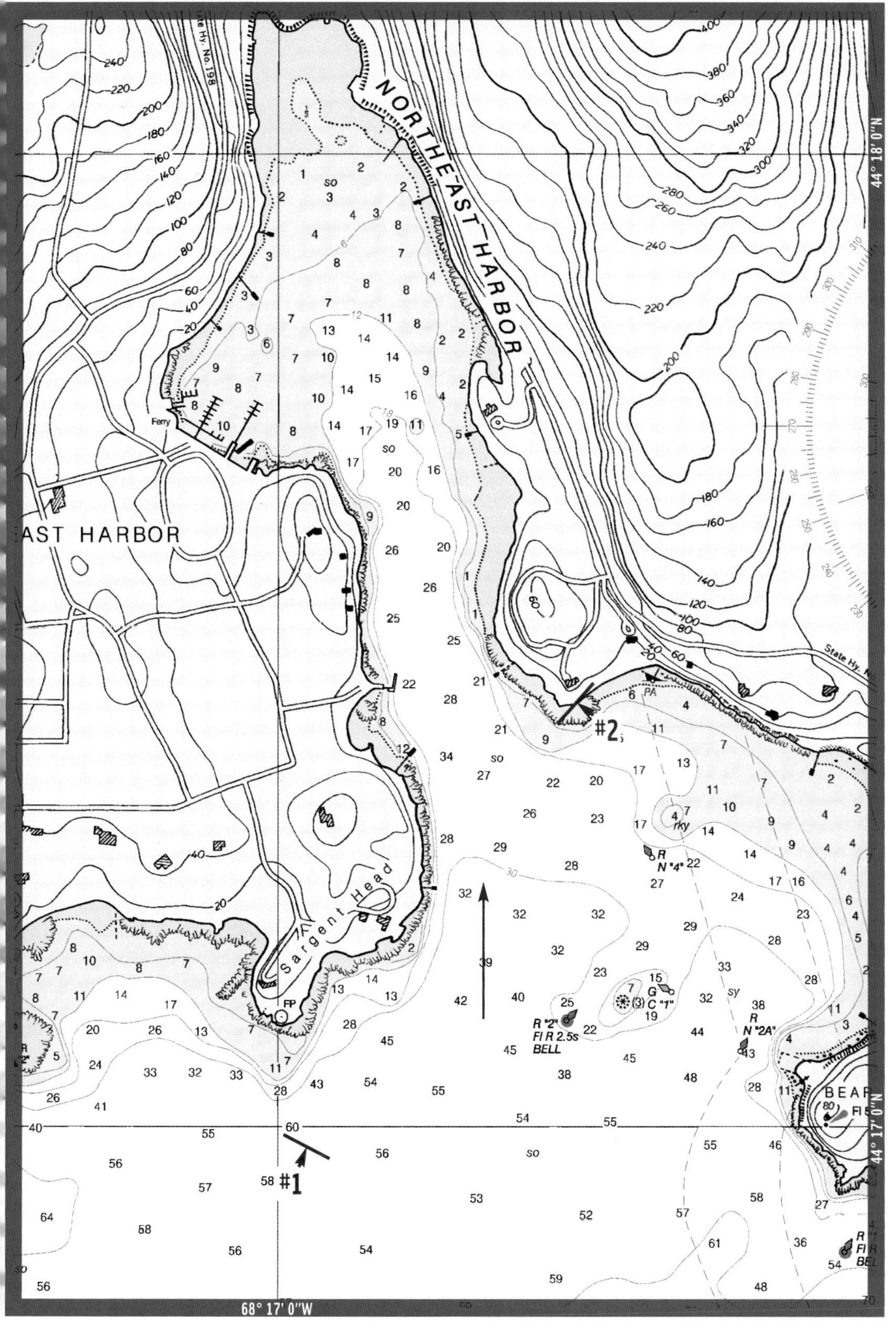

13321
9th ed., March 03
NAD 83
Soundings in feet
1:10,000

■ SEAL HARBOR ■

LOCATED at the eastern end of Eastern Way, Seal Harbor can be a nice lunch break for visitors. The entrance is marked by red nun "6" south of Crowninshield Point and Bowden Ledge. From here, steer northeast to green can "1." Keeping the can to port, favor the East Point side of the cove and head north into the harbor. The harbor is often exposed to ocean swell; overnight stays are rarely comfortable.

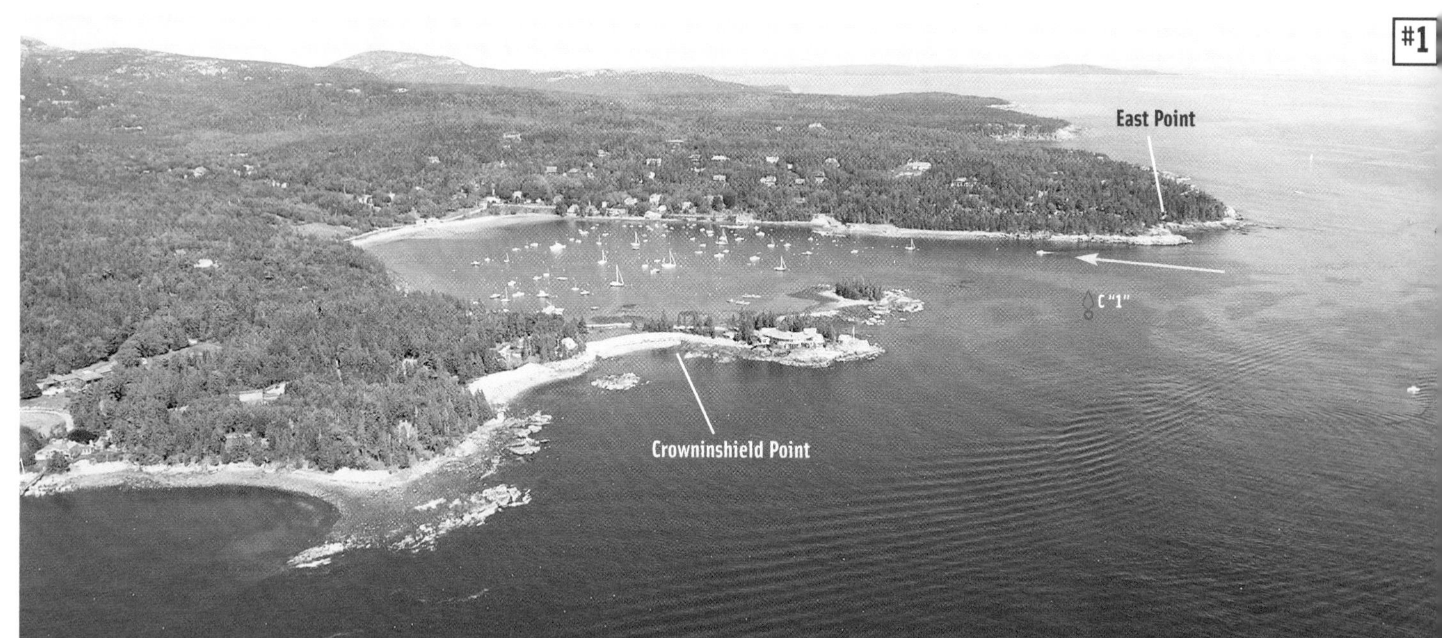

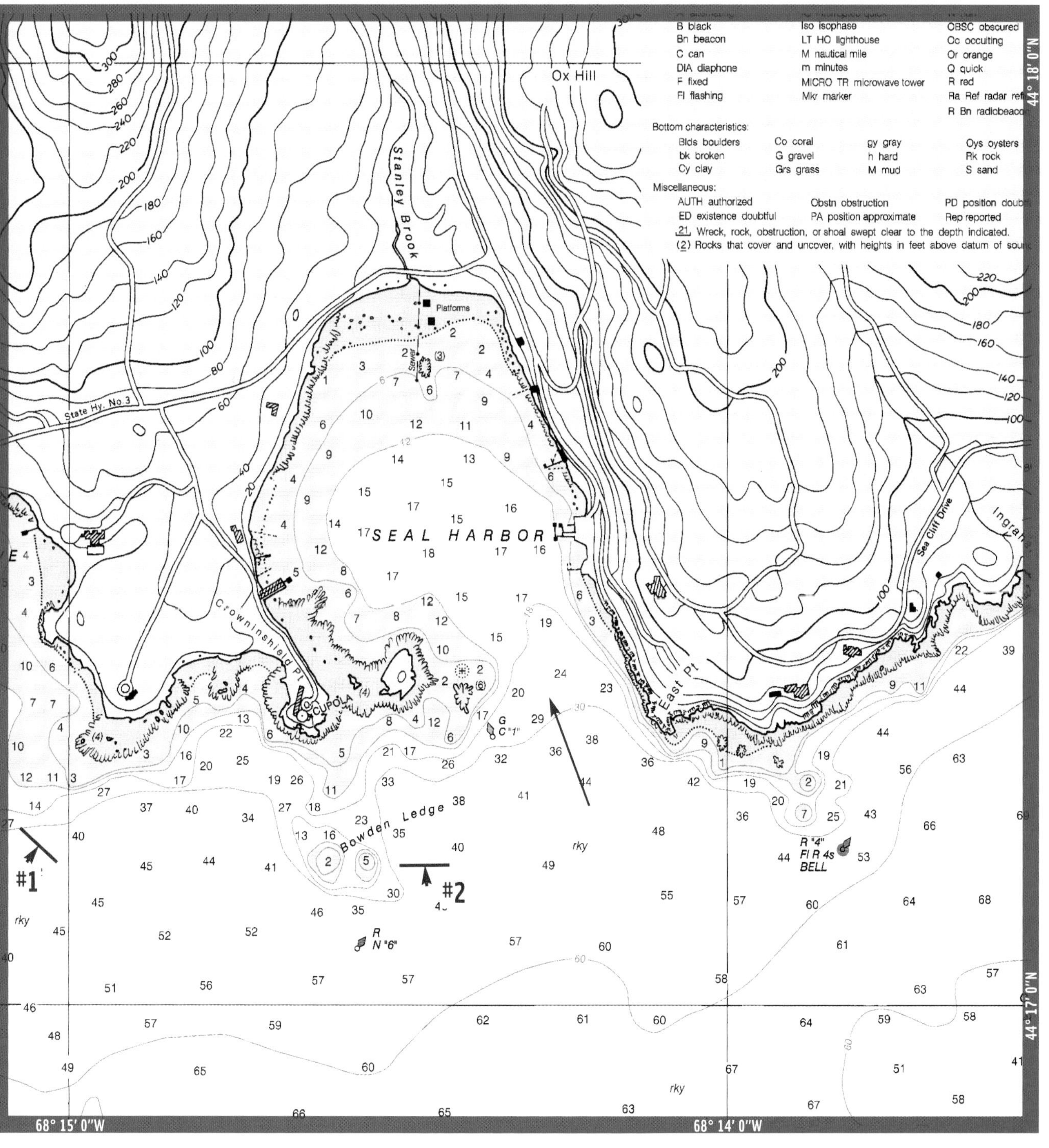
B black
Bn beacon
C can
DIA diaphone
F fixed
Fl flashing
Iso isophase
LT HO lighthouse
M nautical mile
m minutes
MICRO TR microwave tower
Mkr marker
OBSC obscured
Oc occulting
Or orange
Q quick
R red
Bottom characteristics:
Blds boulders
bk broken
Cy clay
Co coral
G gravel
Grs grass
gy gray
h hard
M mud
Oys oysters
Rk rock
S sand
Miscellaneous:
AUTH authorized
ED existence doubtful
Obstn obstruction
PA position approximate
Rep reported
21 Wreck, rock, obstruction, or shoal swept clear to the depth indicated.
(2) Rocks that cover and uncover, with heights in feet above datum of
Ox Hill
Stanley Brook
Platforms
State Hy. No.3
SEAL HARBOR
Crowninshield Pt
CUPOLA
East Pt
Sea Cliff Drive
Bowden Ledge
G C "1"
R "4" Fl R 4s BELL
R N "6"
rky
#1
#2
44° 18′ 0″N
44° 17′ 0″N
68° 15′ 0″W
68° 14′ 0″W

13321
9th ed., March 03
NAD 83
Soundings in feet
1:10,000

■ BAR HARBOR ■

THE entrance to Bar Harbor is between Mount Desert Island and the end of a long breakwater extending from Bald Porcupine Island. Though the breakwater is submerged during most high tides, a navigation light tower at the southwest end of the breakwater marks the channel into the harbor. Keep the light on the breakwater to starboard and the wide-open, easily accessed harbor is straight ahead. This very busy tourist center is loaded with numerous hotels, restaurants, shops, and services. Use of a mooring is recommended as currents, depths, and traffic make anchoring difficult. Note that you cannot pass between Mount Desert Island and Bar Island to the north of town.

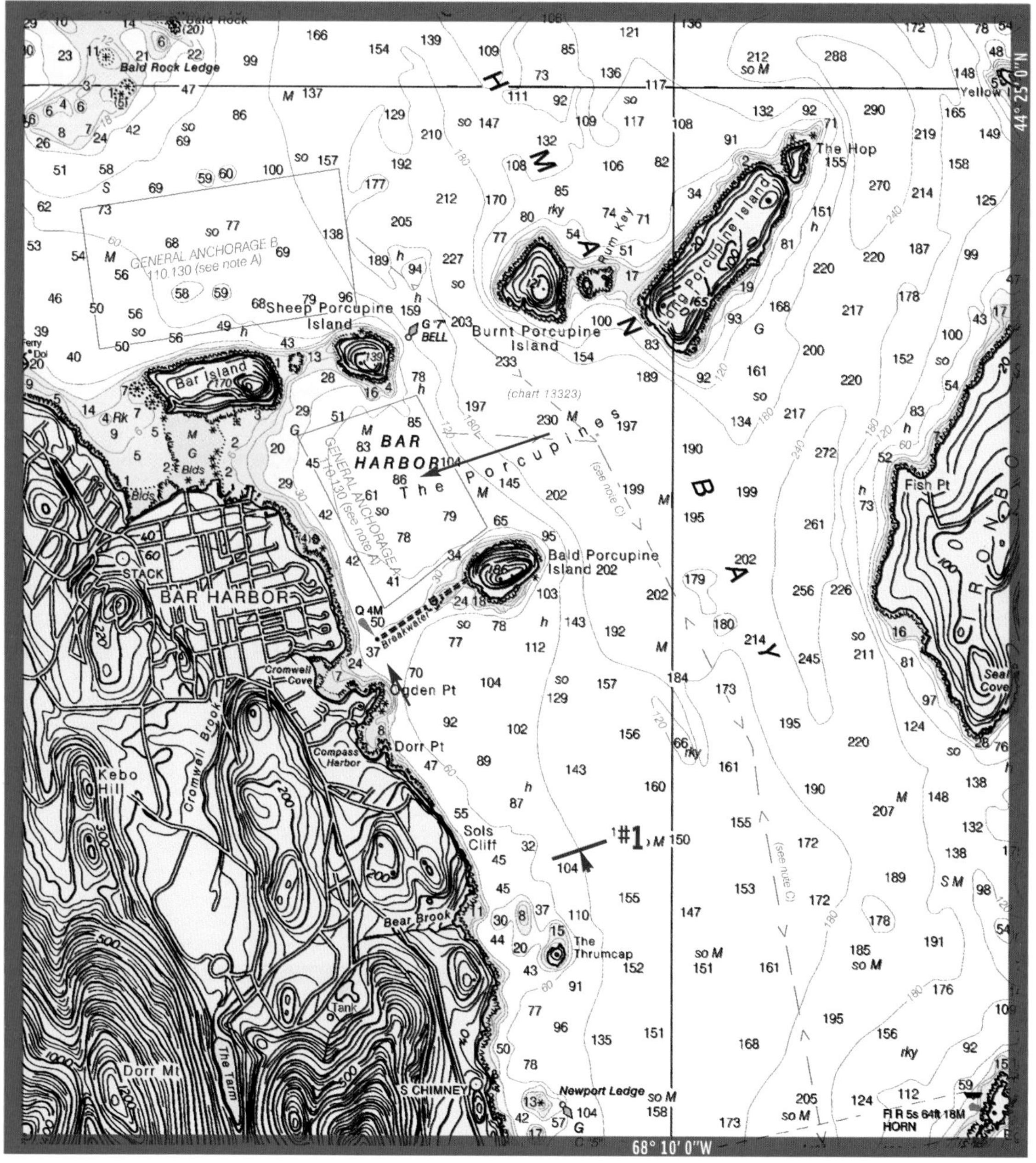

13318
18th ed., Aug. 02
NAD 83
Soundings in feet
1:40,000

#1

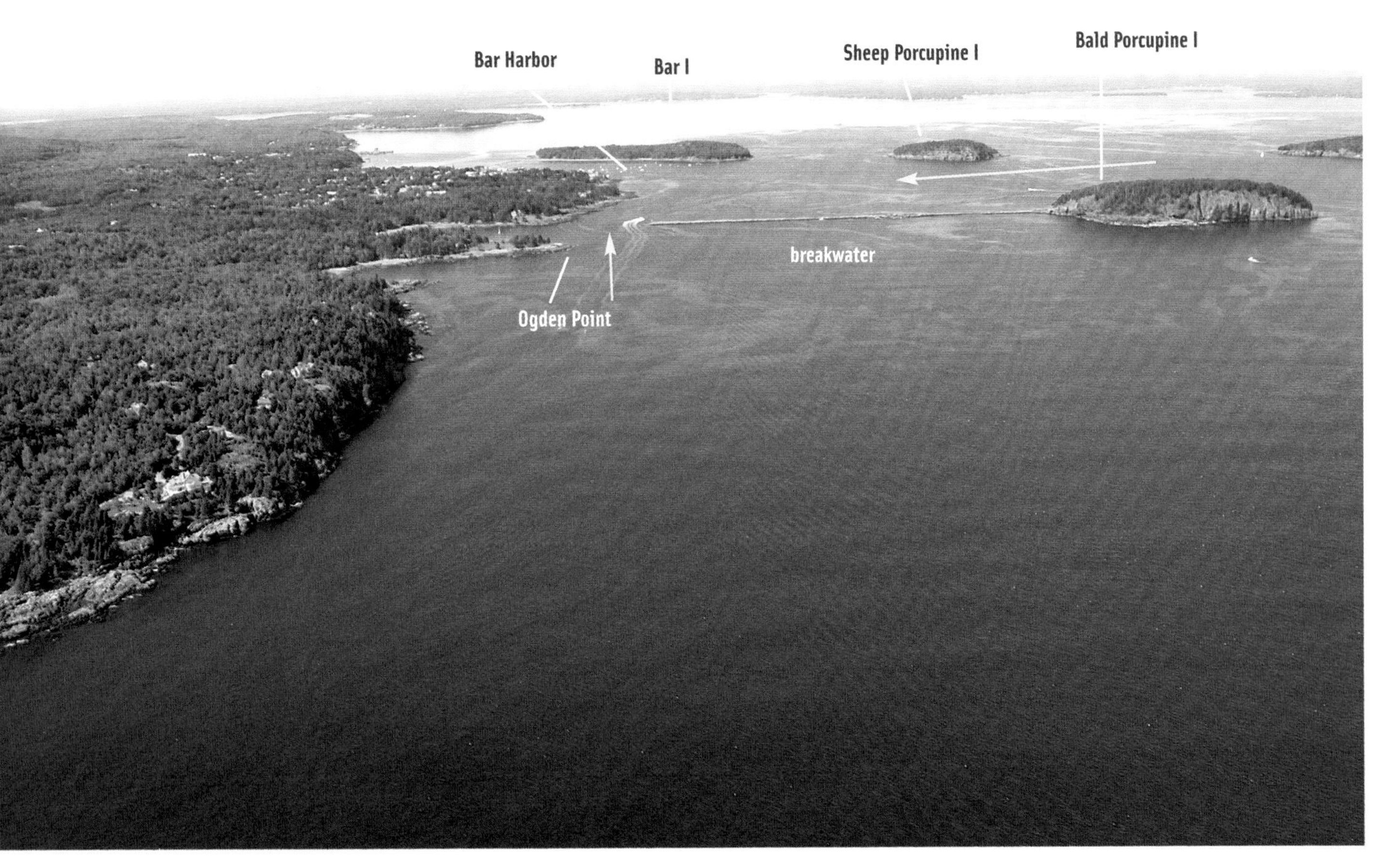
Bar Harbor
Bar I
Sheep Porcupine I
Bald Porcupine I
breakwater
Ogden Point

■ SORRENTO HARBOR ■

AT the northern end of Frenchman Bay lies Sorrento Harbor. The entrance is north of red-and-white bell buoy "SH." From the buoy, proceed between Dram Island to the port and Preble Island to starboard. Once past this narrow entrance, turn to starboard to Sorrento Harbor and the town wharf.

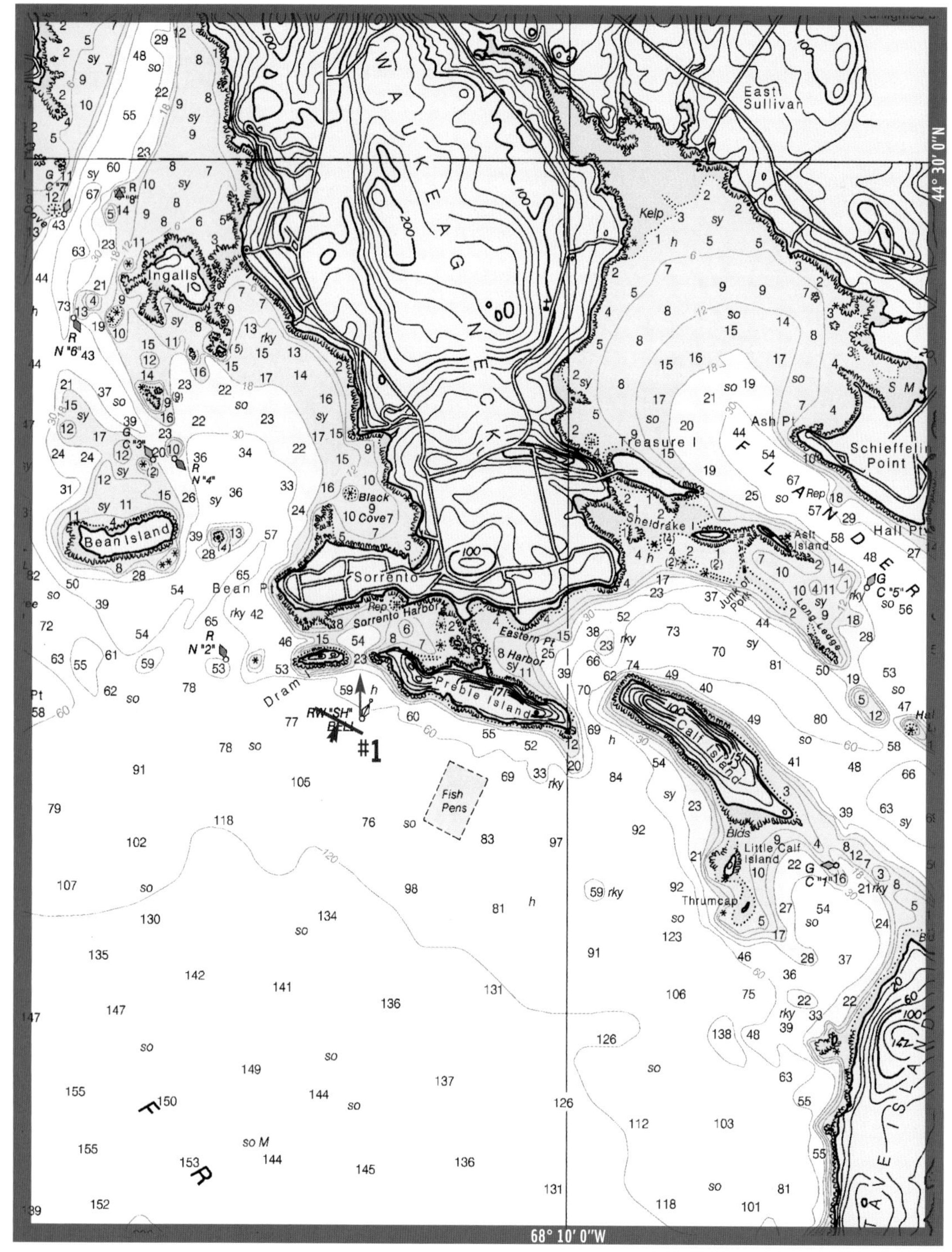

13318
18th ed., Aug. 02
NAD 83
Soundings in feet
1:40,000

#1

Black Cove
Sorrento Harbor
Eastern Point Harbor
Preble I
Dram I

■ WINTER HARBOR ■

WINTER Harbor is on the east side of Frenchman Bay, between Schoodic Peninsula and Grindstone Neck. Although it is wide open to all southerlies, Inner Winter Harbor provides good protection. The entrance is from the green-and-red gong buoy "MI," which is south of the abandoned lighthouse on Mark Island. Proceeding north from the buoy, find the green can "3" south of Guptill Point. Leave it to port and head northwest into the inner harbor where a spare mooring is the best option. Sand Cove and Henry Cove also contain moorings but are exposed to swell.

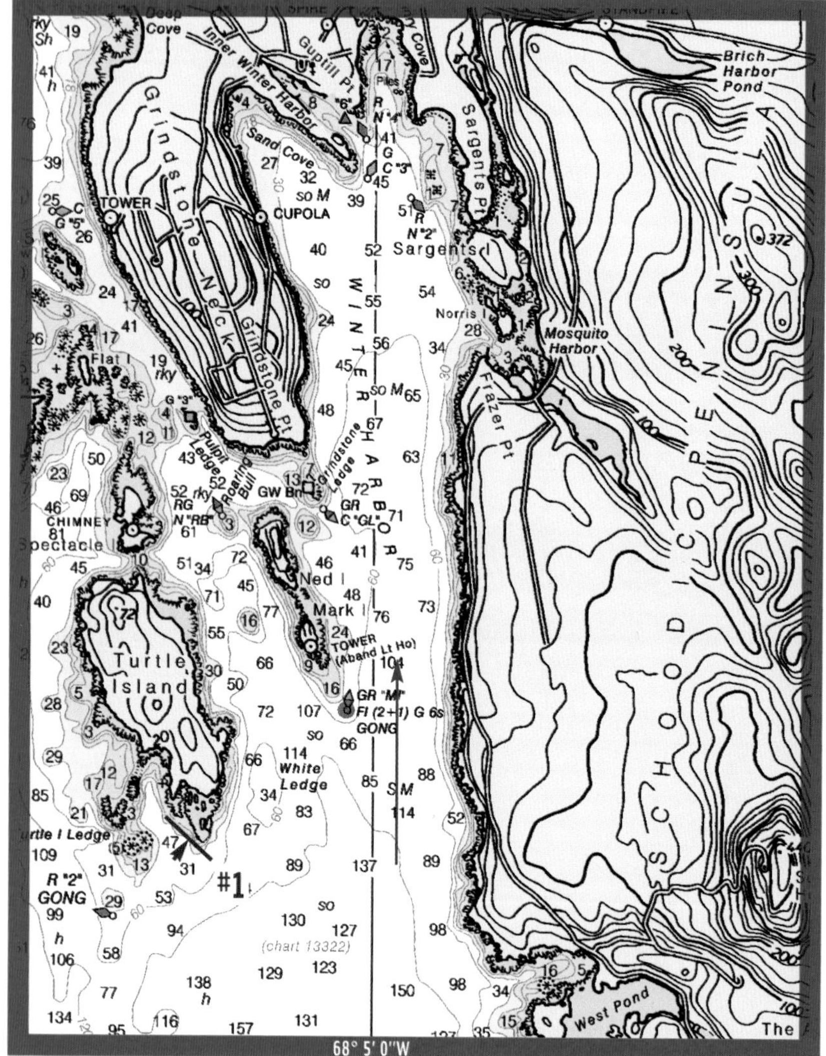

13318
18th ed., Aug. 02
NAD 83
Soundings in feet
1:40,000

#1

Grindstone Neck
Winter Harbor
Lighthouse
(abandoned)
GR "MI"
Turtle I

REGION VIII

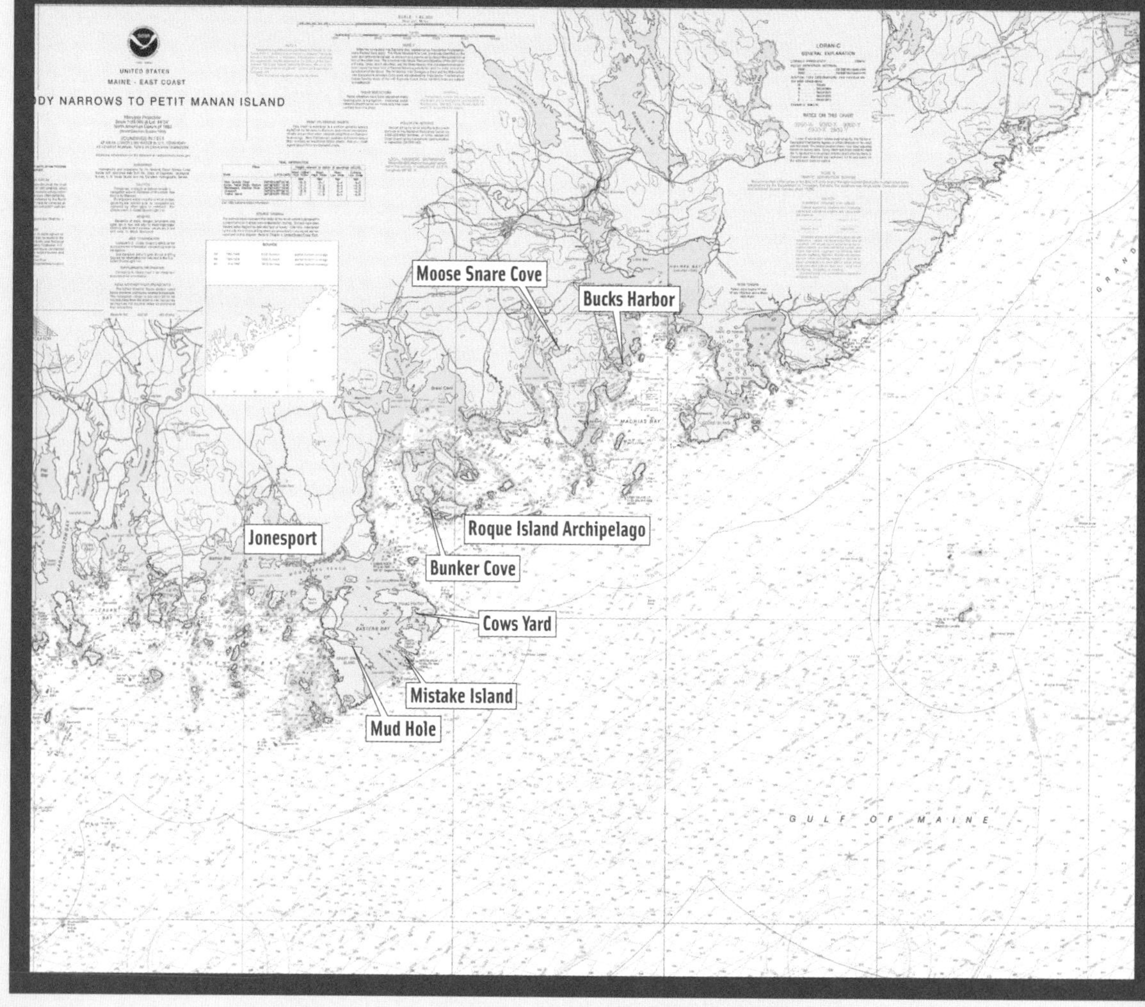

DY NARROWS TO PETIT MANAN ISLAND
UNITED STATES
MAINE - EAST COAST
Moose Snare Cove
Bucks Harbor
Roque Island Archipelago
Jonesport
Bunker Cove
Cows Yard
Mistake Island
Mud Hole
GULF OF MAINE

DOWN EAST
—MUD HOLE TO BUCKS HARBOR—

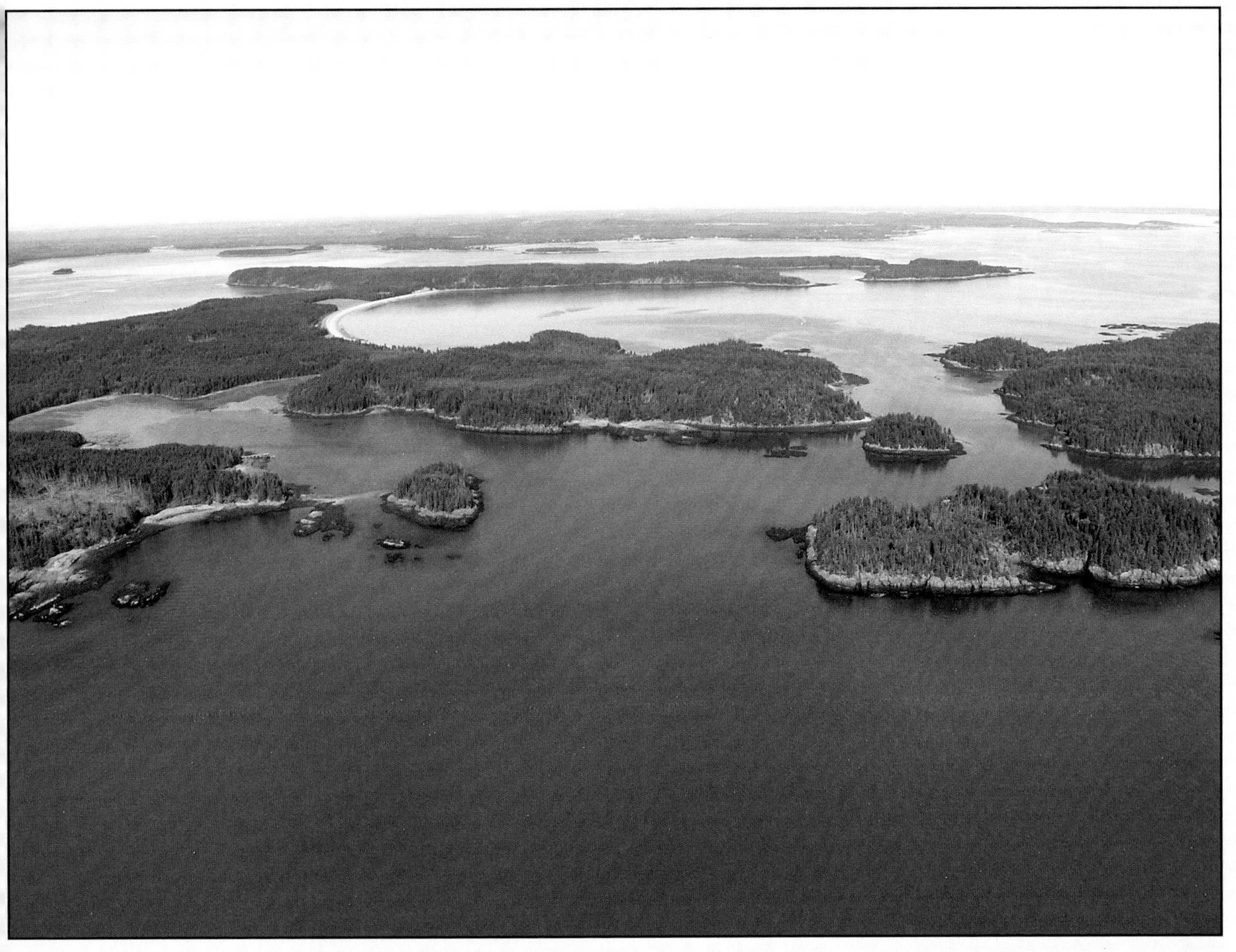

Looking east at the Roque Island Thorofare (page 228)

Beyond Mount Desert Island lie the waters that local sailors think of when someone says "Down East." Here the tides are bigger; the moorings, facilities, provisions, and even navigation aids scarcer; and the passages across open waters longer and more challenging. And then there's the fog, which is not just more frequent east of Mount Desert but somehow thicker too—thick enough to make your clothing drip; thick enough, some say, to cut with a knife.

So why cruise here?

Because tucked inshore of those coastwise open-water passages are islands, bays, and deep inlets you won't regret visiting. Because you might have an anchorage to yourself or share it with just a few other boats. Because you owe it to yourself to visit the fabled mile-long white-sand beach, sheltered passages, and millpond anchorages of the Roque Island archipelago. And because these waters—spectacular in beauty, remote beyond description—will inscribe indelible pictures in your memories.

■ MUD HOLE AND APPROACH ■

HAVING visited Mud Hole many times, I can attest to its spectacular beauty and the equally spectacular challenge of entry. Located on the east side of Great Wass Island and with few navigation aids to inform the mariner, this harbor should be approached with the utmost care. For starters, low-tide depths at the entrance are roughly two feet; you'll have to enter sometime between half tide and high tide. Approach Mud Hole Channel from offshore by first finding Moose Peak Lighthouse on the southeast end of Mistake Island. The channel is located between the east side of Great Wass Island and the west side of the island chain skirting Mistake Island, Water Island, Knight Island, and Green Island. Favor the east side of the channel on a northwesterly heading to Mud Hole Point. Swing wide around the point and head westerly along the southern shore of the cove's entrance. Stay south of the half-tide ledge at the center of the cove and proceed cautiously into Mud Hole, anchoring where soundings are appropriate for your boat. Remember that the average tide in this area is 12 to 13 feet.

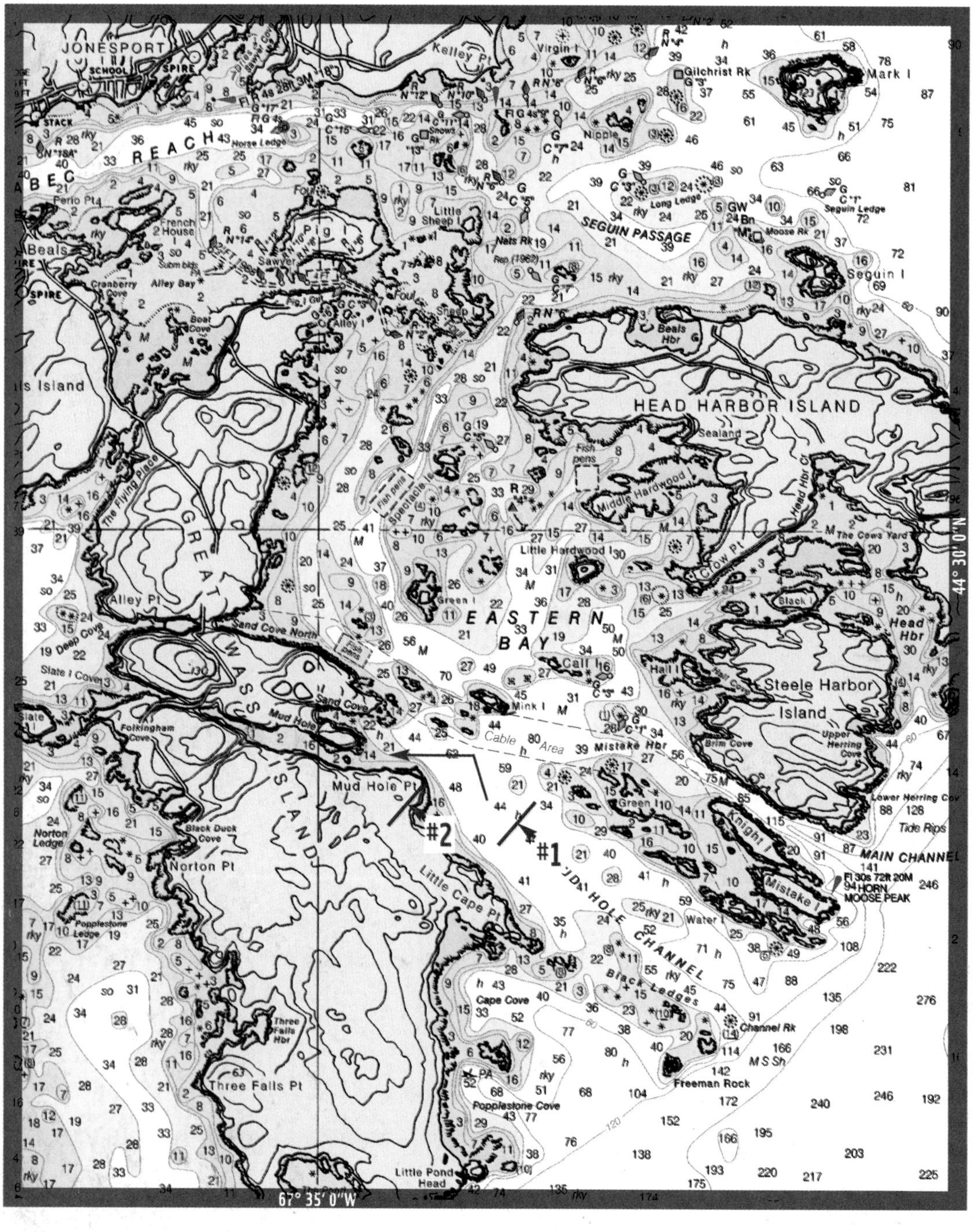

13326
13th ed., April 04
NAD 83
Soundings in feet
1:40,000

#1

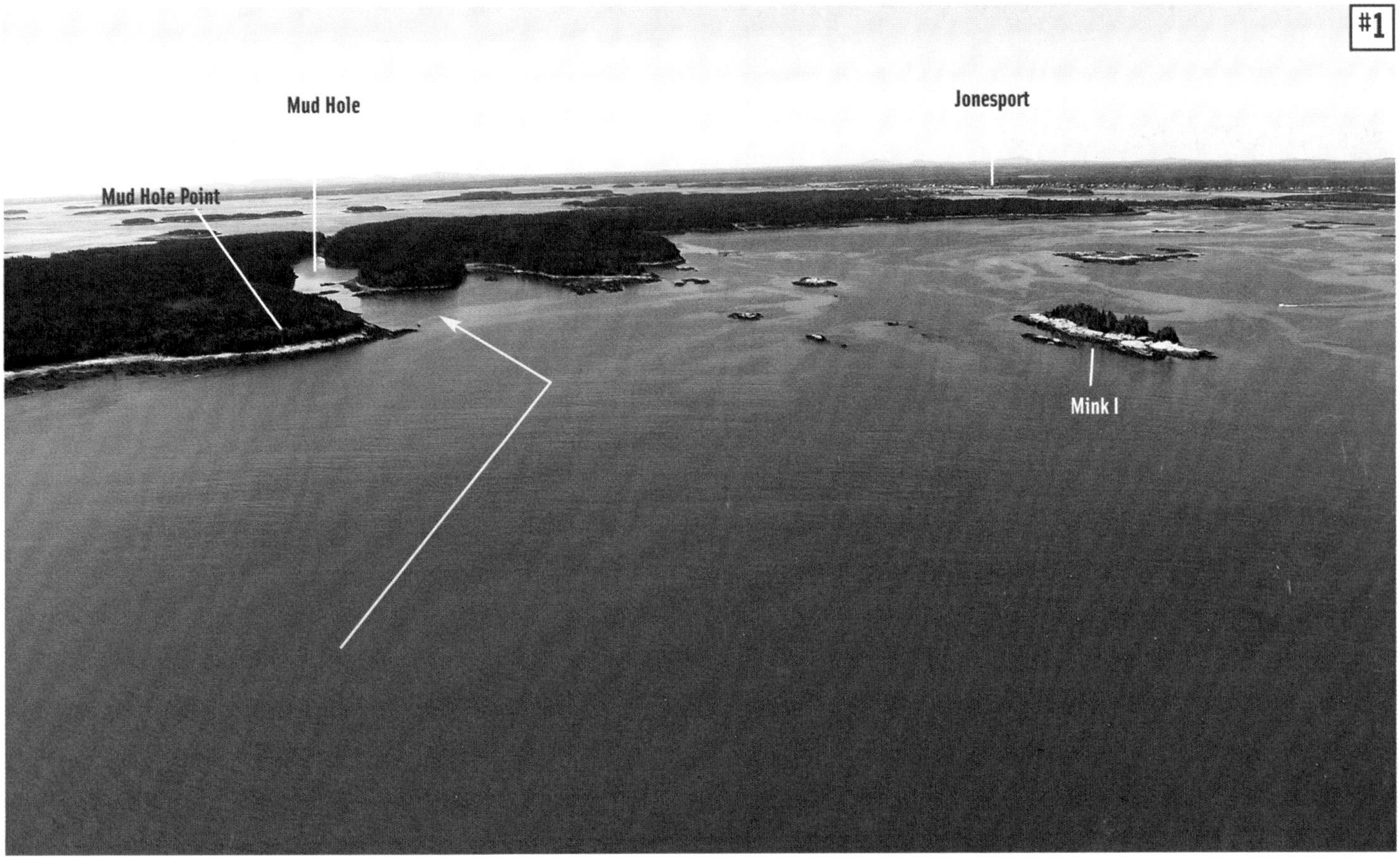

Mud Hole

Jonesport

Mud Hole Point

Mink I

#2

Mud Hole

Jonesport

■ MISTAKE ISLAND ■

ANOTHER well-known harbor is Mistake Island Harbor, located between Knight Island, Mistake Island, Water Island, and its associated ledges. Entrance to the harbor is via Main Channel Way north of Moose Peak Lighthouse. A northwest heading will keep you in the deep water of the channel. Proceed along the northeast side of Knight Island, with Steele Harbor Island on your starboard side. Once beyond Knight, swing 180 degrees around the island's northwest end and enter the harbor, being careful to avoid ledges on the southwest side of Knight.

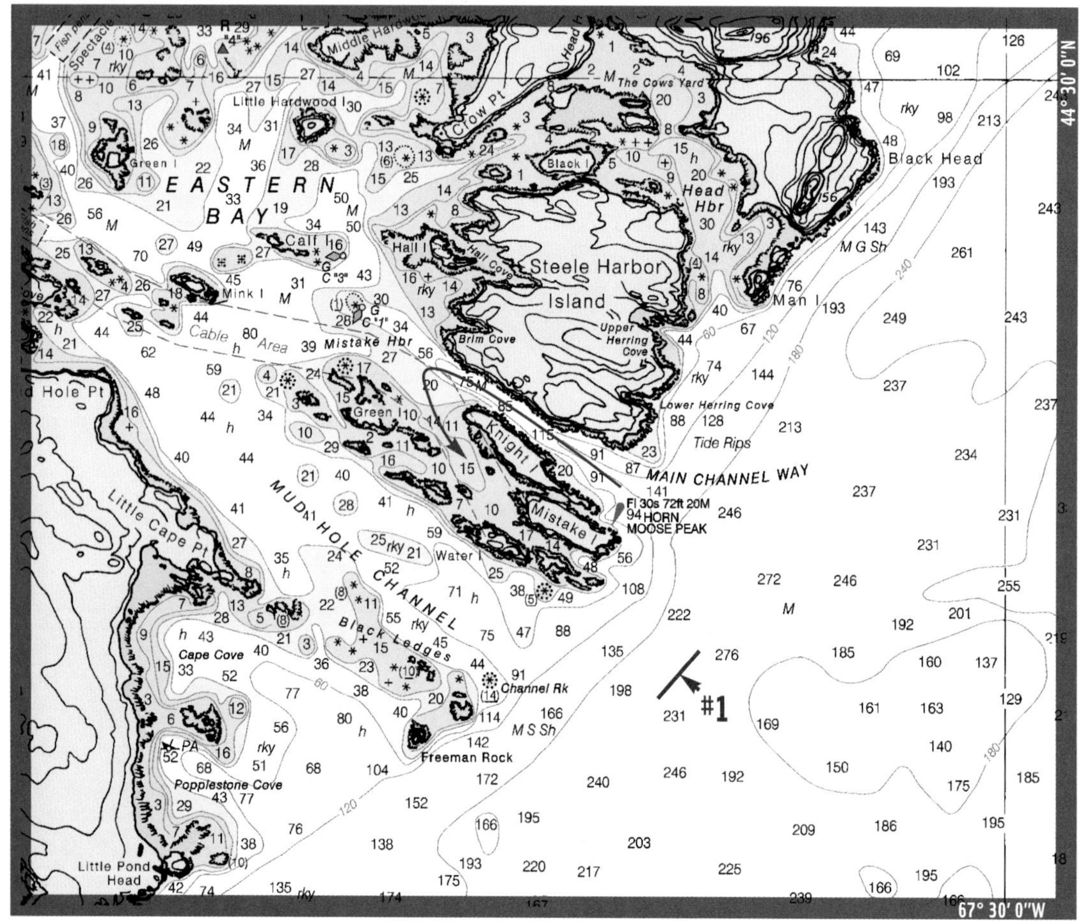

13326
13th ed., April 04
NAD 83
Soundings in feet
1:40,000

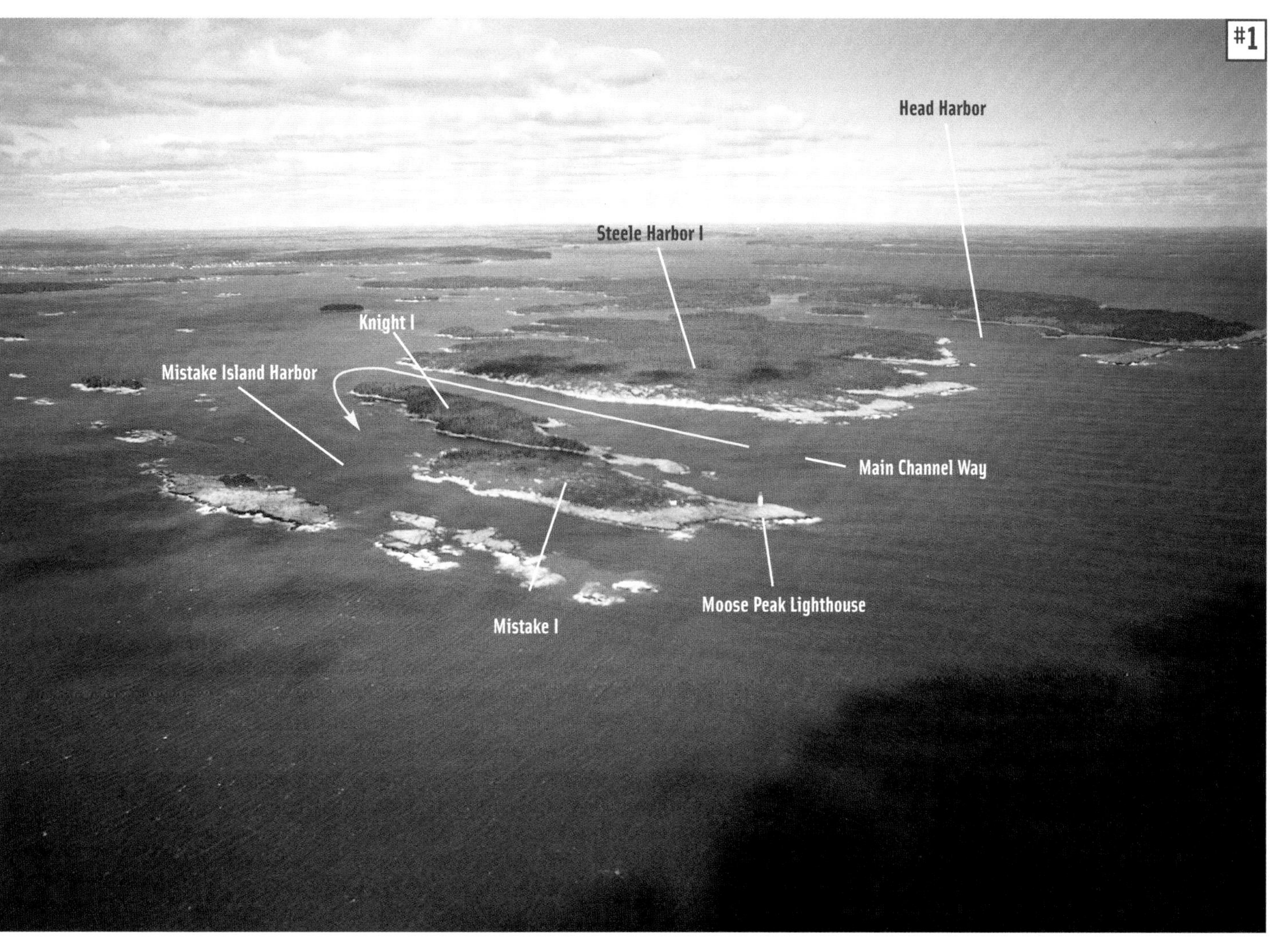
#1
Head Harbor
Steele Harbor I
Knight I
Mistake Island Harbor
Main Channel Way
Moose Peak Lighthouse
Mistake I

■ THE COWS YARD ■

OFFERING superb protection and beauty, The Cows Yard is located at the northern end of Head Harbor between Head Harbor Island and Steele Harbor Island. From Moose Peak Lighthouse, proceed northeasterly along the southern shore of Steele Harbor Island. Enter Head Harbor and turn to a northerly heading. Head Harbor is relatively straightforward and you can proceed due north to the exposed ledges that mark the southern protection for The Cows Yard. Proceed northerly beyond the ledges, and anchor in depths that account for the 12-foot tidal range.

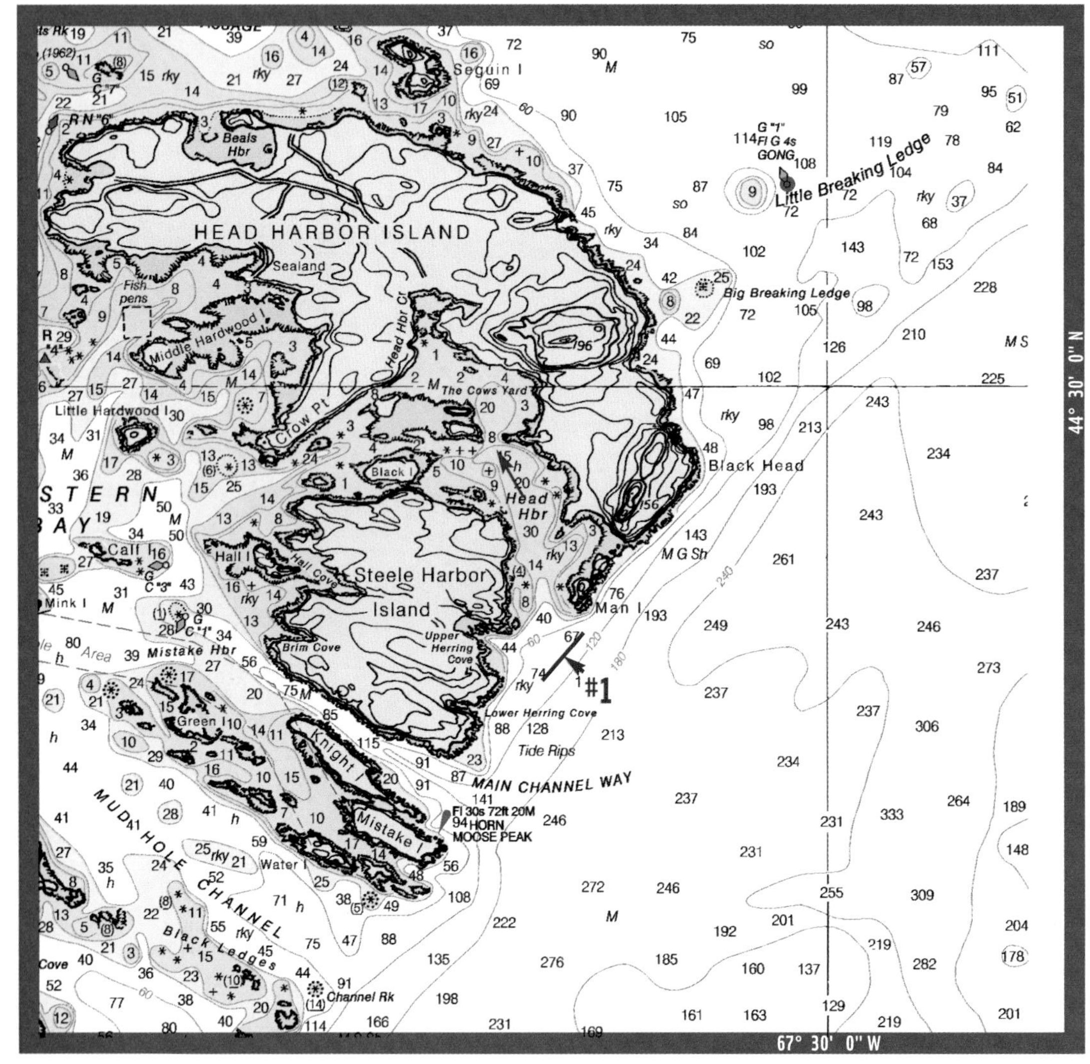

13326
13th ed., April 04
NAD 83
Soundings in feet
1:40,000

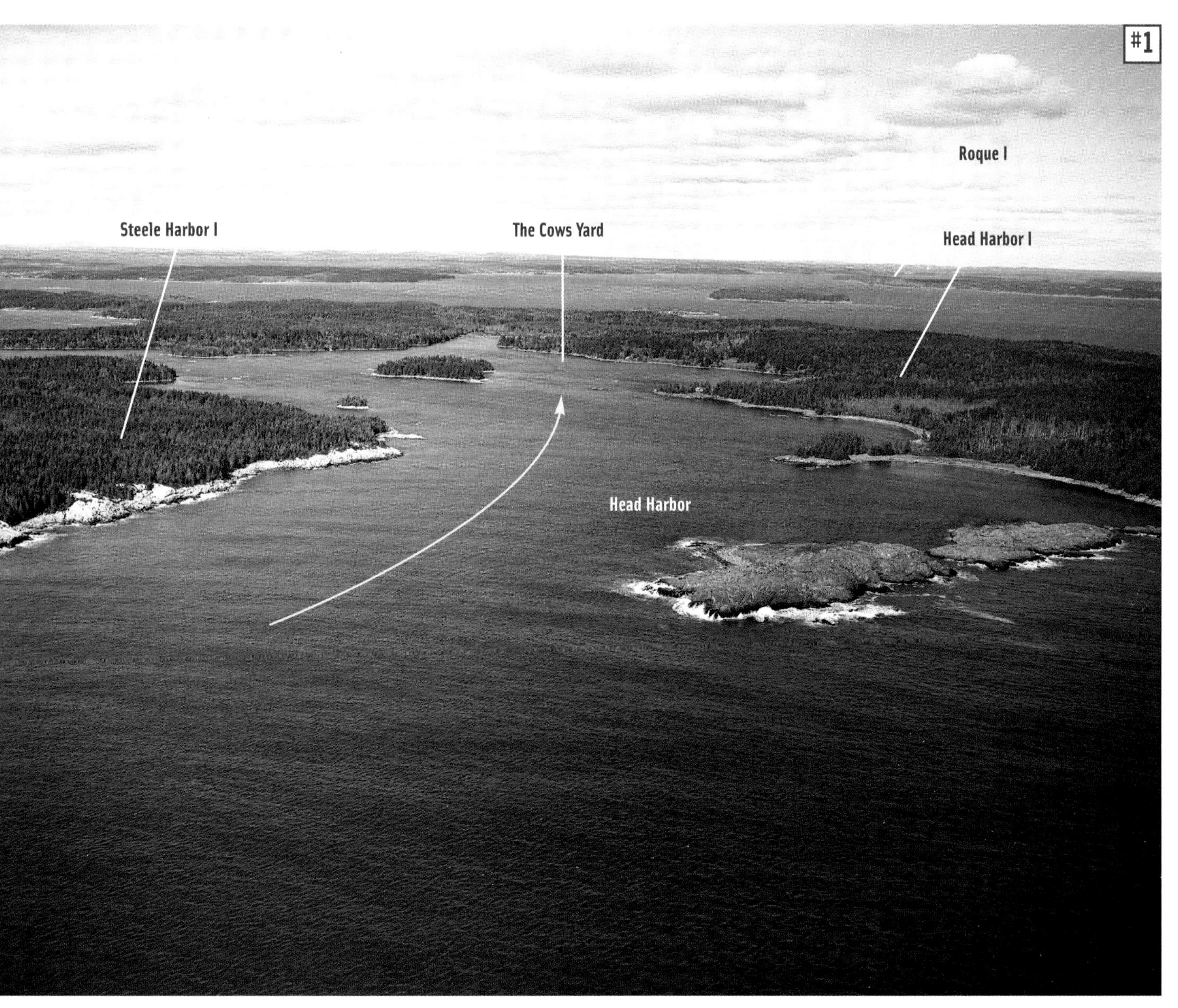
#1
Roque I
Steele Harbor I
The Cows Yard
Head Harbor I
Head Harbor

■ JONESPORT ■

LOCATED midway along Moosabec Reach, the small town of Jonesport is an outpost worth visiting. Moosabec Reach runs east to west and can be entered from the west through Western Bay and from the east via Chandler Bay. From the west, stay in the channel between Hardwood Island to the west, and Pomp and Norton Islands to the east. First, find the red daymark "2" on Pomp Island Ledge off the southwest end of Norton Island. Then proceed a bit east of north to the green daymark "3" on the western side of Pomp Island. Then head for red nun "4," keeping it on your starboard side and turning slightly east. Moosabec Reach and Jonesport will then be readily apparent. Jonesport is halfway down the reach on your port side and has most of the supplies you may need. An anchorage with rental moorings is in Sawyer Cove on the north shore about a mile beyond the bridge that spans Moosabec Reach. Be warned: Clearance under the bridge is only 39 feet.

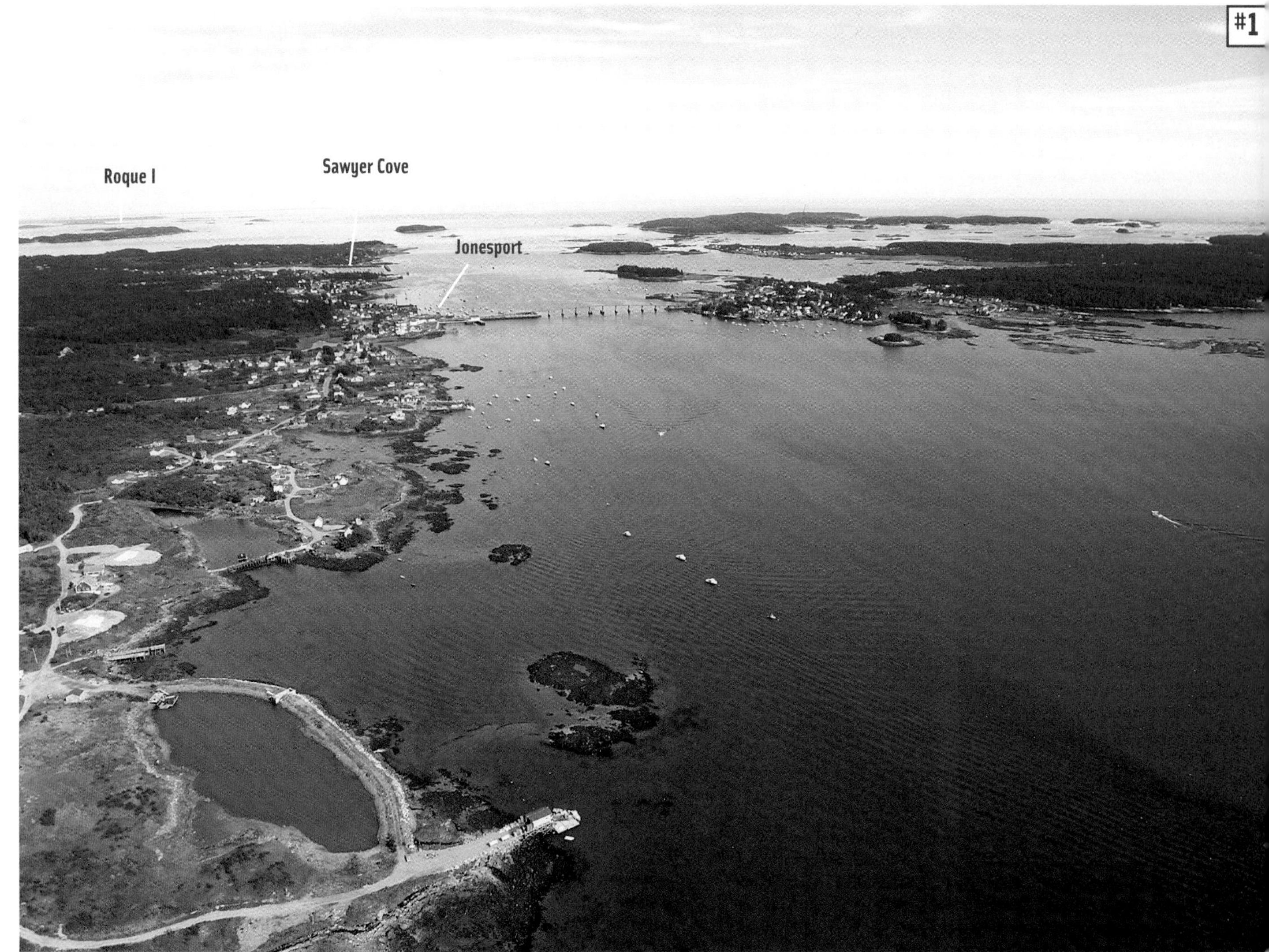

13326
13th ed., April 04
NAD 83
Soundings in feet
1:40,000

■ ROQUE ISLAND THOROFARE/ARCHIPELAGO ■

BY far the most beautiful beach in all of Maine is Roque Island's Great Beach. There are two principal passageways into Roque Island Harbor and its Great Beach. Depending on visibility and weather conditions, the approach can be made from Chandler Bay through The Thorofare—a passageway that weaves between Roque Island, Little Spruce Island, and Great Spruce Island. There are no navigation aids in The Thorofare, so it's important to approach with caution. A more conventional passage into the harbor—though less picturesque—is the approach between Halifax and Anguilla islands to the south of the Roque Island archipelago. A northwest heading between those two islands will bring you to Great Beach at the head of Roque Island Harbor. Owners of the beach discourage landing along the southwestern shores.

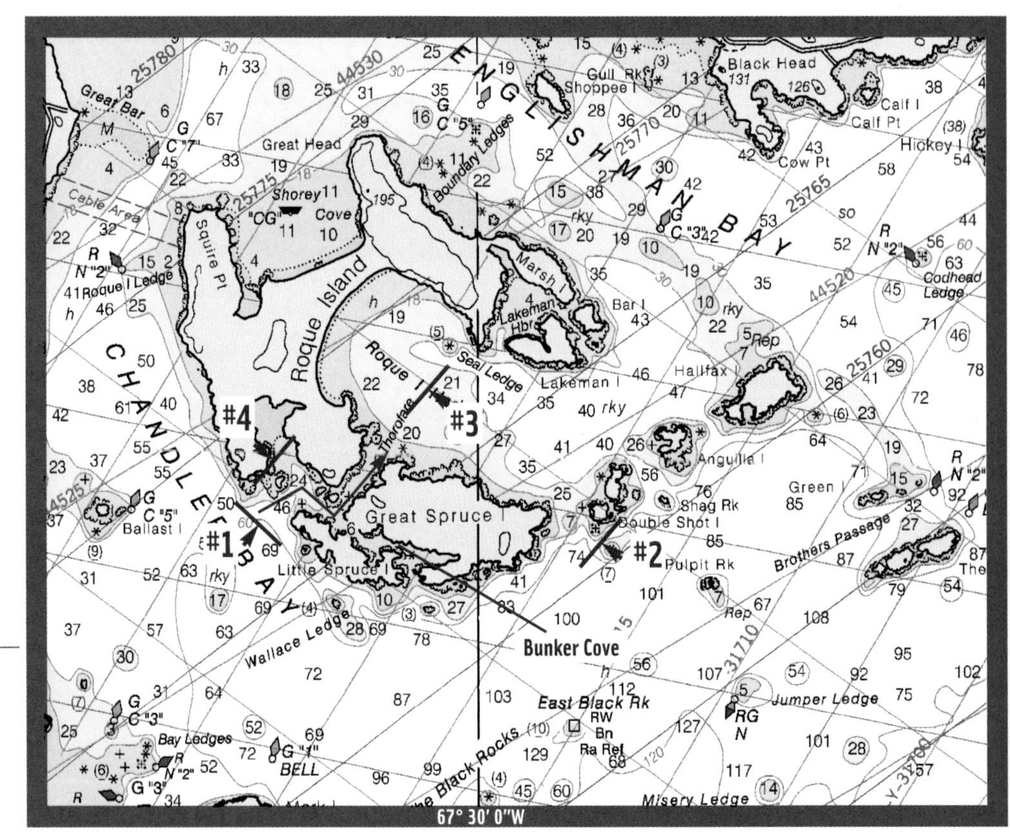

13325
13th ed., April 04
NAD 83
Soundings in feet
1:80,000

#1

Roque I
Great Beach
Lakeman I
Great Spruce I
Bunker Cove
Little Spruce I

#2

Roque Island Harbor
The Thorofare
Bunker Cove
Great Spruce I

#3

Shorey Cove
Great Beach

Bunker Cove

Just past the northwest tip of Little Spruce Island and to the west of Great Spruce Island lies the protected waters of Bunker Cove. Be mindful that this harbor is very small; it should be avoided if you see another boat already at anchor.

#4

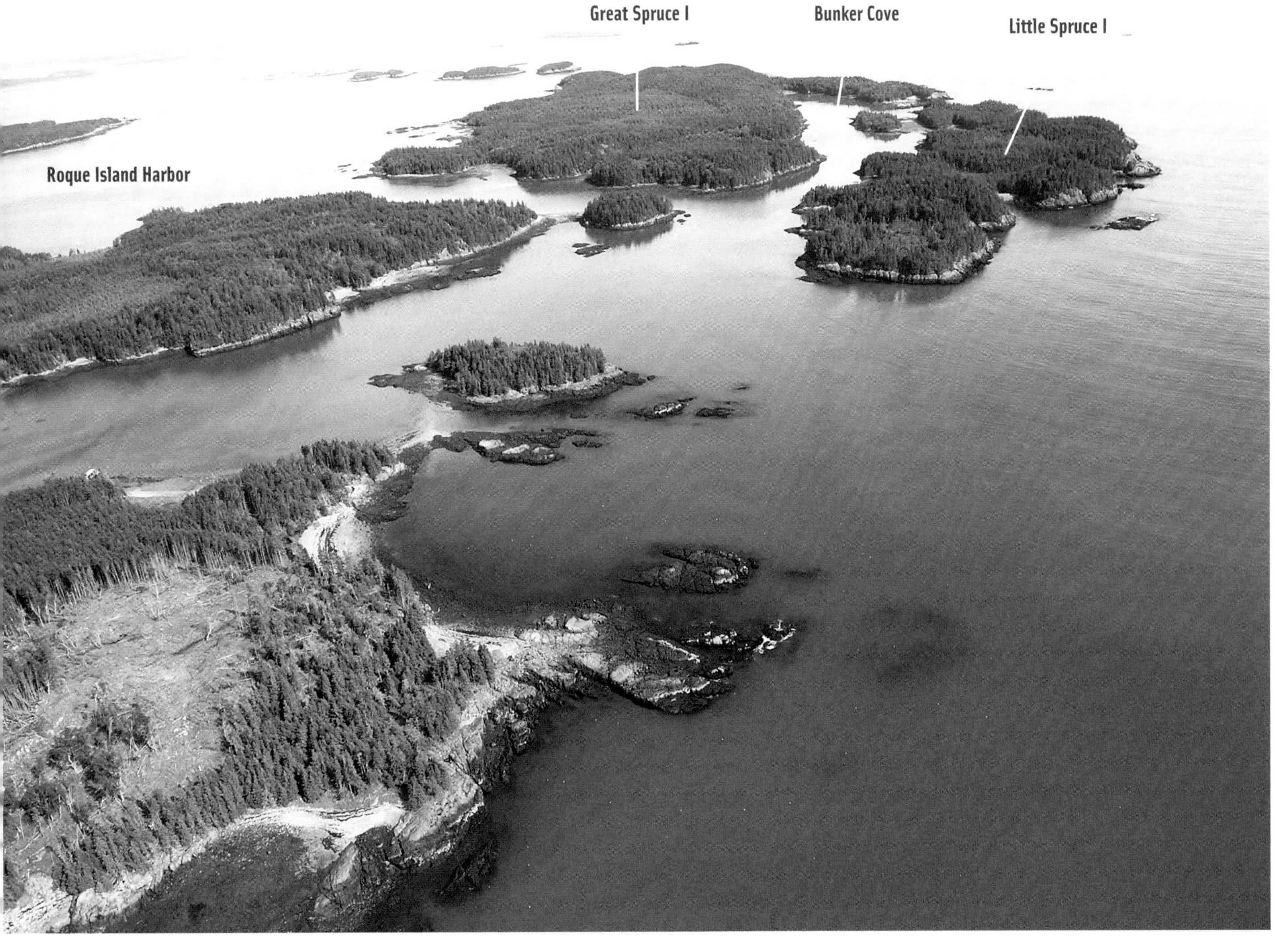

■ MOOSE SNARE COVE ■

FOUR nautical miles east of Roque Island Harbor is Little Kennebec Bay—the entryway to Moose Snare Cove. Although there are no navigation aids to guide you, Hickey Island off Point of Main indicates the southern edge of Little Kennebec Bay. From the island, proceed north to the narrows between Sea Wall Point and Gray's Beach. Farther on, keep Yoho Head on your starboard side and begin the narrow passage up the Collins Branch into Moose Snare Cove, which lies north of Hog Island. This cove provides great protection, wonderful seclusion, and sheer beauty. When anchoring, be careful to account for a 13-foot average tidal range in this cove.

#1

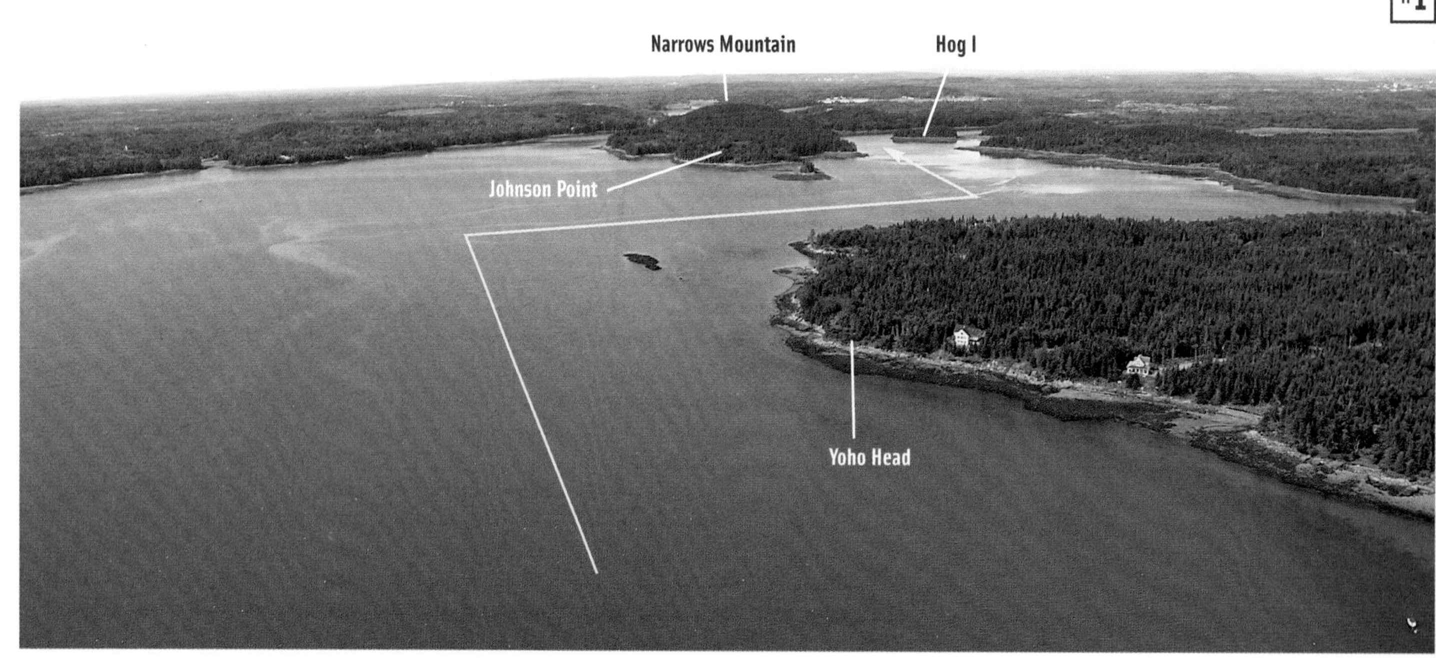

#2

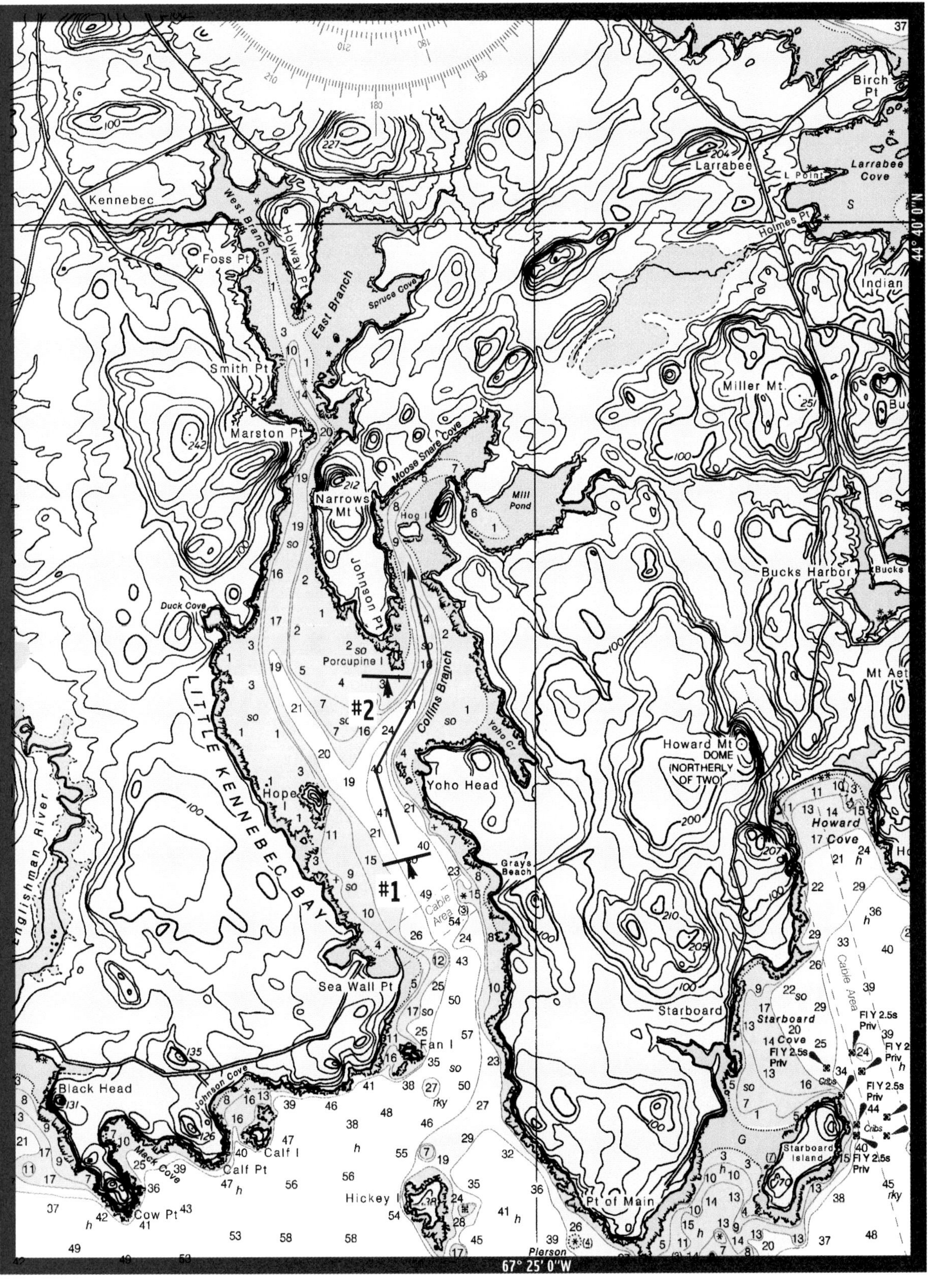

13326
13th ed., April 04
NAD 83
Soundings in feet
1:40,000

BUCKS HARBOR

MIDWAY up the west shore of Machias Bay is Bucks Harbor—a well-protected and pleasant stopping point with decent anchorage. Enter the harbor between Bar Island and Bucks Head.

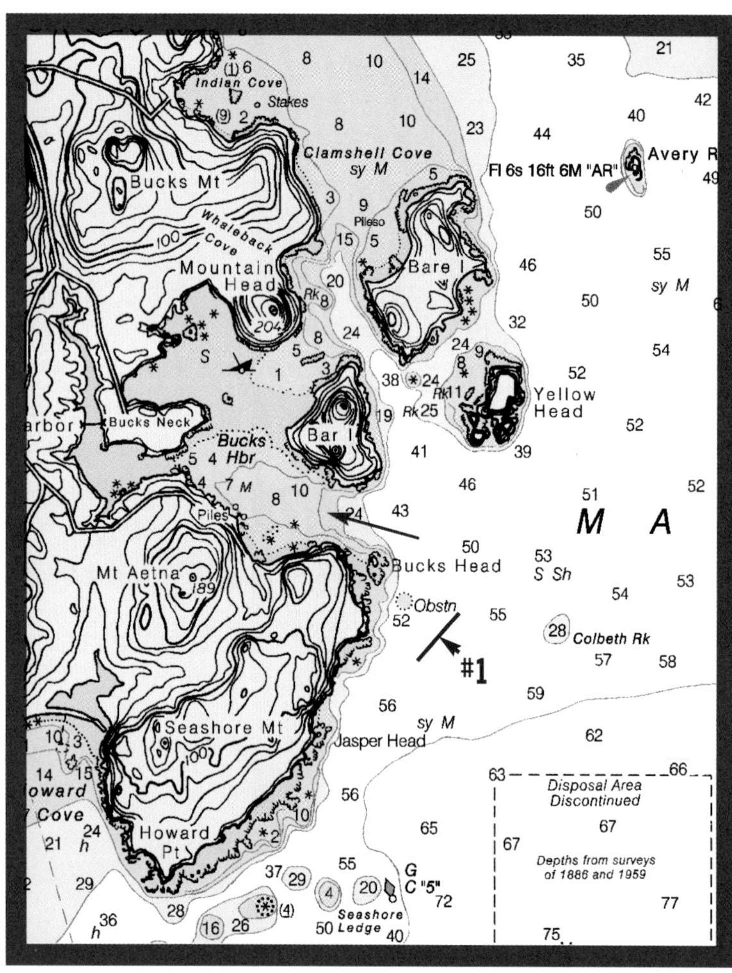

13326
13th ed., April 04
NAD 83
Soundings in feet
1:40,000

#1

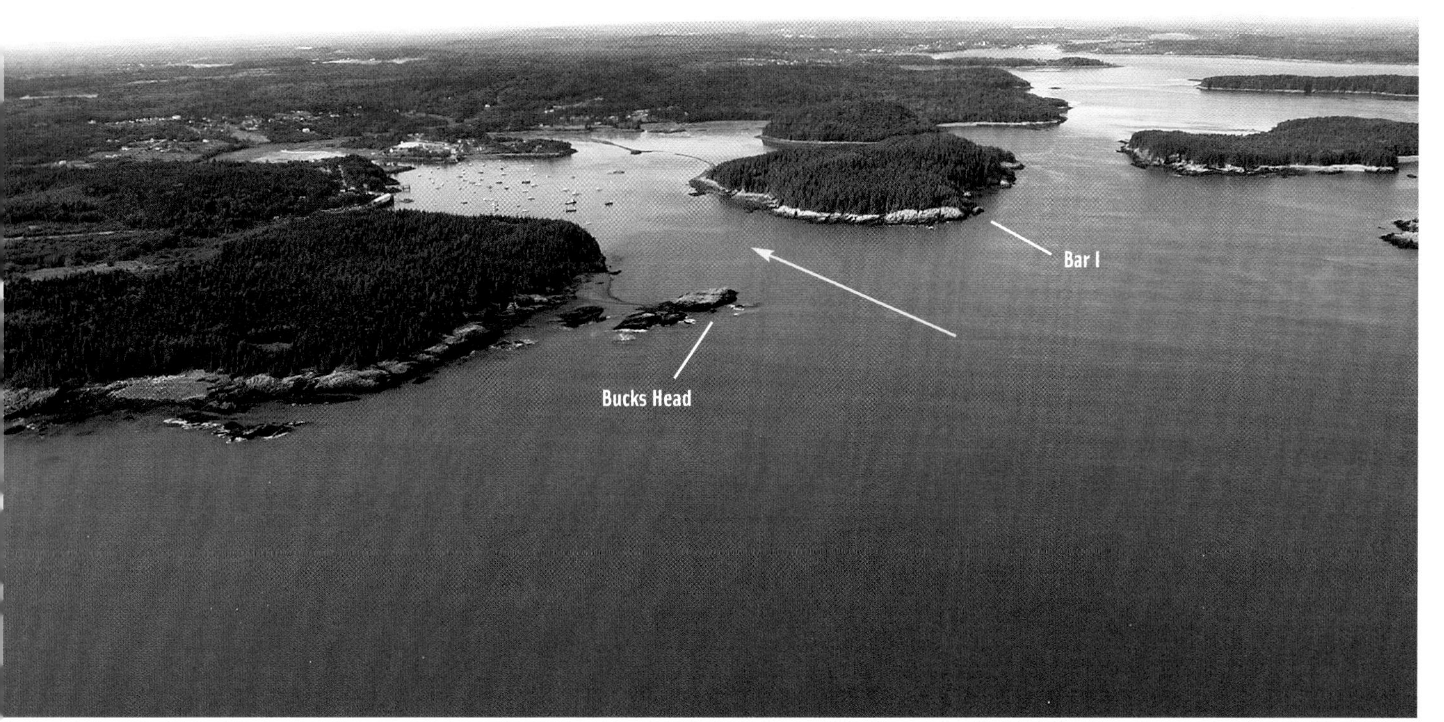

INDEX